Crucible of Hell

Also by Saul David

NON-FICTION

After Dunkirk: Churchill's Sacrifice of the Highland Division: France 1940

Mutiny at Salerno, 1943: An Injustice Exposed

The Homicidal Earl: The Life of Lord Cardigan

Military Blunders

Prince of Pleasure: The Prince of Wales and the Making of the Regency

The Indian Mutiny: 1857

Zulu: The Heroism and Tragedy of the Zulu War of 1879

Victoria's Wars: The Rise of Empire

All the King's Men: The British Soldier in the Era of Sword and Musket

100 Days to Victory: How the Great War Was Fought and Won 1914–1918

Operation Thunderbolt: Flight 139 and the Raid on Entebbe Airport, the Most Audacious Hostage Rescue Mission in History

The Force: The Legendary Special Ops Unit and WWII's Mission Impossible

FICTION

Zulu Hart

Hart of Empire

The Prince and the Whitechapel Murders

SAUL DAVID

Crucible of Hell

The Heroism and Tragedy of Okinawa, 1945

hachette BOOKS
New York

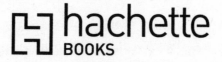

Hachette Books
Hachette Book Group
1290 Avenue of the Americas
New York, NY 10104
HachetteBooks.com
Twitter.com/HachetteBooks
Instagram.com/HachetteBooks

First published in Great Britain in 2020 by William Collins, an imprint of HarperCollins*Publishers*
First US Edition: April 2020

Published by Hachette Books, an imprint of Perseus Books, LLC, a subsidiary of Hachette Book Group, Inc. The Hachette Books name and logo is a trademark of the Hachette Book Group.

Library of Congress Cataloging-in-Publication Data has been applied for.
ISBNs: 978-0-316-53467-3 (hardcover), 978-0-316-53465-9 (e-book)

Printed in the United States of America

LSC-C

10 9 8 7 6 5 4 3 2 1

For Matt

Contents

List of Illustrations

The body of Ernie Pyle, lying in a roadside ditch on Ie Shima. *(Department of Defense)*

Lieutenant General Mitsuru Ushijima commanding the Japanese Thirty-Second Army on Okinawa.

Ushijima and staff plot the battle. *(Japanese Cabinet Intelligence Bureau)*

A Japanese light tank with two of its dead crewmen in the foreground. *(USMCA)*

Marines follow two M4 Sherman tanks into action. *(USMCA)*

American troops use a flamethrower to flush out Japanese snipers on a beach. *(USMCA)*

US Marines assaulting a former Japanese barracks at Shuri in late May 1945. *(Department of Defense)*

Soldier firing a .30 caliber Browning automatic rifle (BAR) on May 2, 1945. *(USMCA)*

A rifleman looks for a target, while his officer talks into his battery-operated walkie-talkie. *(USMCA)*

Standing atop the Maeda escarpment ("Hacksaw Ridge"), PFC Desmond Doss, a Seventh Day Adventist from Lynchburg, West Virginia. *(Department of Defense)*

Colonel Francis Fenton kneels beside the body of his son PFC Mike Fenton, a 19-year-old scout/sniper in 1/5th Marines who was killed in the fierce fighting for the Awacha Pocket on May 7, 1945. *(Department of Defense)*

Ensign Kiyoshi Ogawa, the pilot of one of two kamikaze planes that struck the aircraft carrier USS *Bunker Hill* on May 11, 1945.

Smoke and flames pour from the USS *Bunker Hill* after the kamikaze attacks. *(Department of Defense)*

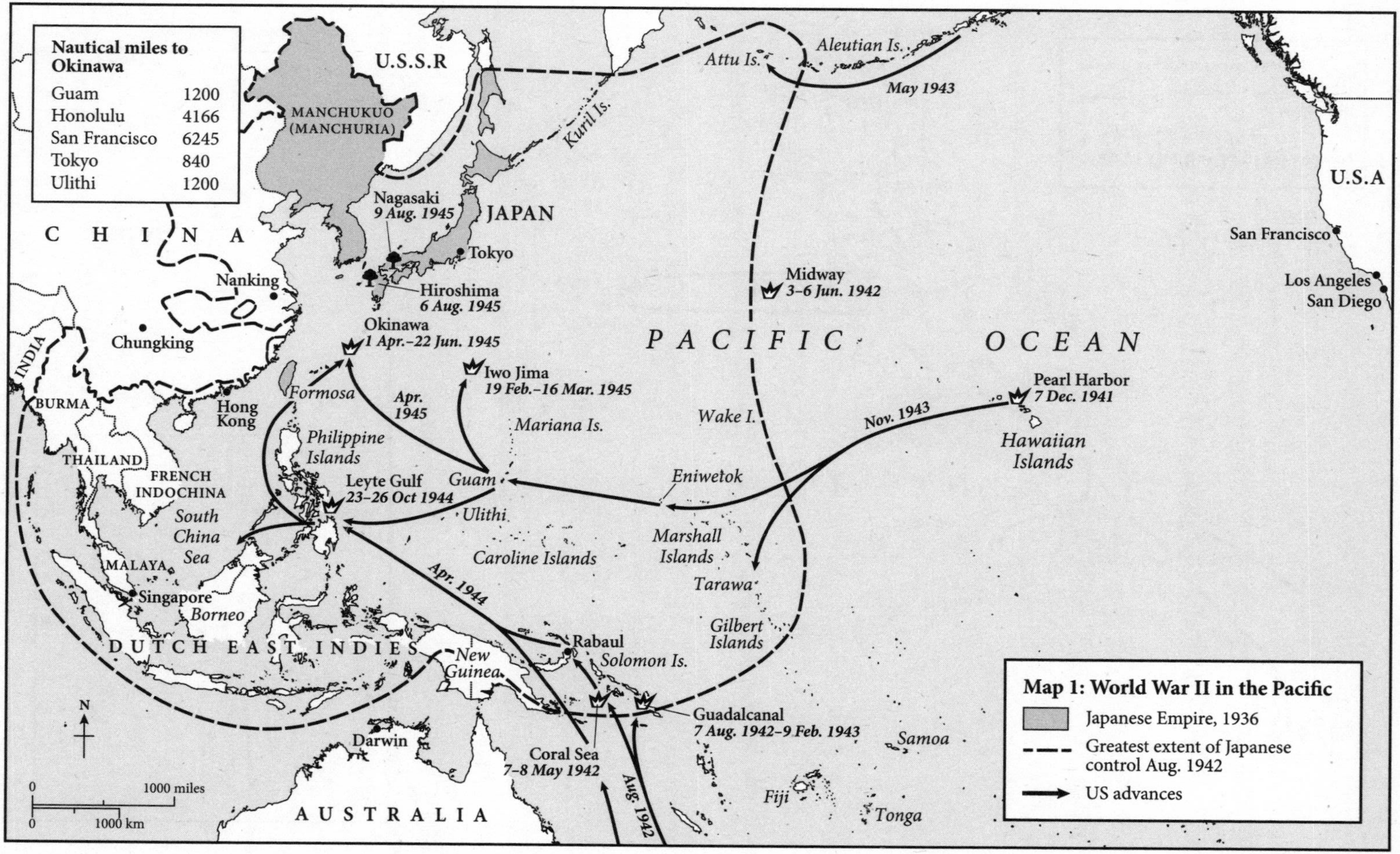
Nautical miles to Okinawa
Guam 1200
Honolulu 4166
San Francisco 6245
Tokyo 840
Ulithi 1200
U.S.S.R
MANCHUKUO (MANCHURIA)
C H I N A
JAPAN
Nagasaki 9 Aug. 1945
Tokyo
Hiroshima 6 Aug. 1945
Nanking
Chungking
INDIA
BURMA
Hong Kong
THAILAND
FRENCH INDOCHINA
South China Sea
MALAYA
Singapore
Borneo
DUTCH EAST INDIES
New Guinea
Darwin
AUSTRALIA
Okinawa 1 Apr.–22 Jun. 1945
Iwo Jima 19 Feb.–16 Mar. 1945
Formosa
Apr. 1945
Philippine Islands
Leyte Gulf 23–26 Oct 1944
Mariana Is.
Guam
Ulithi
Caroline Islands
Apr. 1944
Rabaul
Solomon Is.
Coral Sea 7–8 May 1942
Guadalcanal 7 Aug. 1942–9 Feb. 1943
Aug. 1942
Kuril Is.
Attu Is.
Aleutian Is.
May 1943
Midway 3–6 Jun. 1942
PACIFIC OCEAN
Wake I.
Eniwetok
Marshall Islands
Tarawa
Gilbert Islands
Nov. 1943
Pearl Harbor 7 Dec. 1941
Hawaiian Islands
Samoa
Fiji
Tonga
U.S.A
San Francisco
Los Angeles
San Diego
N
0 1000 miles
0 1000 km
Map 1: World War II in the Pacific
Japanese Empire, 1936
Greatest extent of Japanese control Aug. 1942
US advances

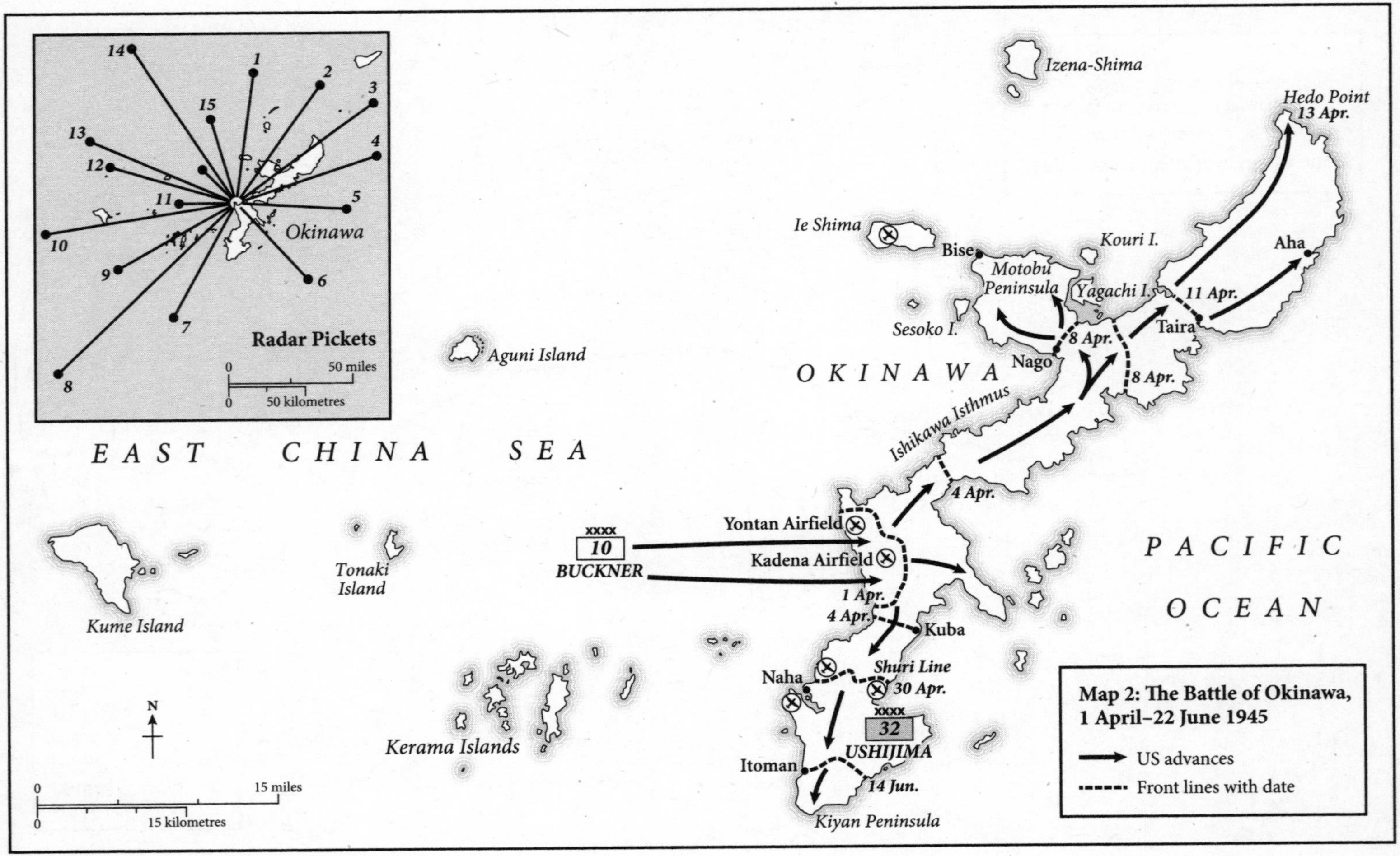
Map 2: The Battle of Okinawa,
1 April–22 June 1945
US advances
Front lines with date
Radar Pickets
1
2
3
4
5
6
7
8
9
10
11
12
13
14
15
Okinawa
0
50 miles
0
50 kilometres
EAST CHINA SEA
PACIFIC OCEAN
OKINAWA
Izena-Shima
Hedo Point
13 Apr.
Aha
11 Apr.
Taira
Kouri I.
Yagachi I.
Ie Shima
Bise
Motobu Peninsula
Sesoko I.
8 Apr.
Nago
8 Apr.
Aguni Island
Ishikawa Isthmus
4 Apr.
Yontan Airfield
Kadena Airfield
XXXX
10
BUCKNER
1 Apr.
4 Apr.
Kuba
Shuri Line
30 Apr.
Naha
XXXX
32
USHIJIMA
Itoman
14 Jun.
Kiyan Peninsula
Kume Island
Tonaki Island
Kerama Islands
N
0
15 miles
0
15 kilometres

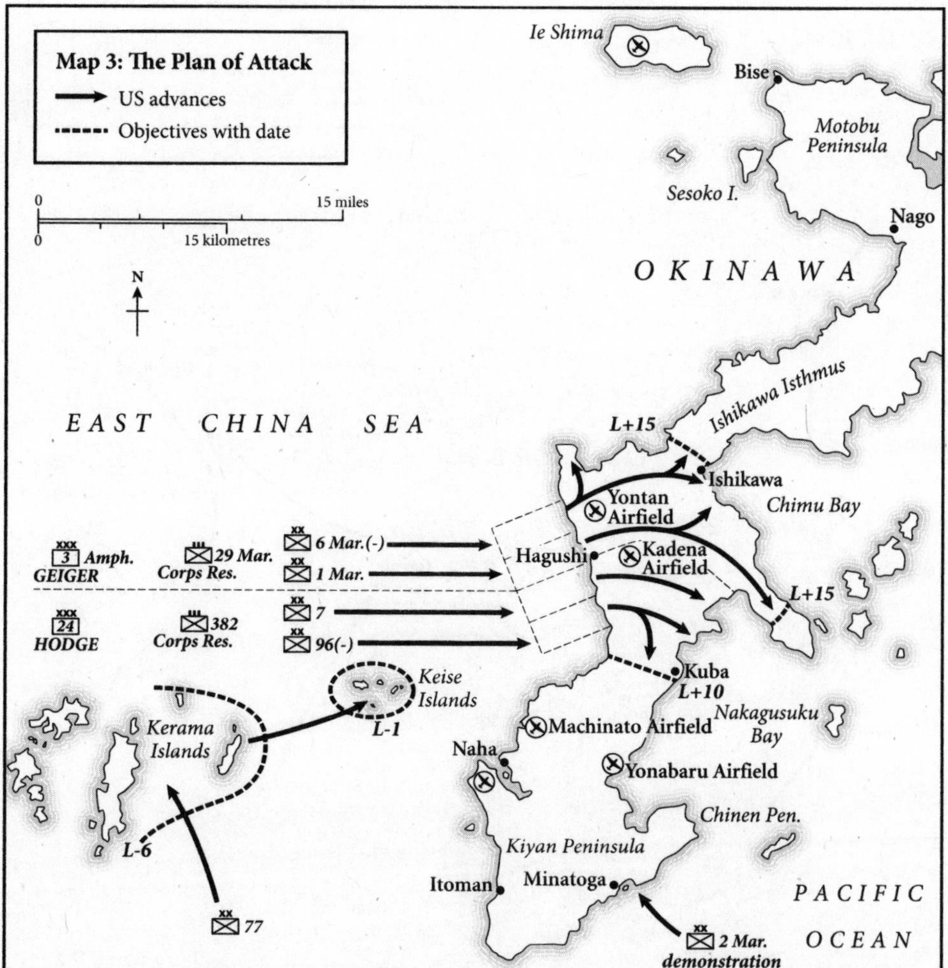

Map 3: The Plan of Attack
US advances
Objectives with date
0
15 miles
0
15 kilometres
N
Ie Shima
Bise
Motobu
Peninsula
Sesoko I.
Nago
OKINAWA
EAST CHINA SEA
Ishikawa Isthmus
L+15
Ishikawa
Chimu Bay
Yontan
Airfield
Kadena
Airfield
Hagushi
L+15
3 Amph.
GEIGER
29 Mar.
Corps Res.
6 Mar.(-)
1 Mar.
24
HODGE
382
Corps Res.
7
96(-)
Kuba
L+10
Keise
Islands
L-1
Kerama
Islands
Machinato Airfield
Nakagusuku
Bay
Naha
Yonabaru Airfield
Chinen Pen.
L-6
Kiyan Peninsula
Itoman
Minatoga
PACIFIC
OCEAN
77
2 Mar.
demonstration

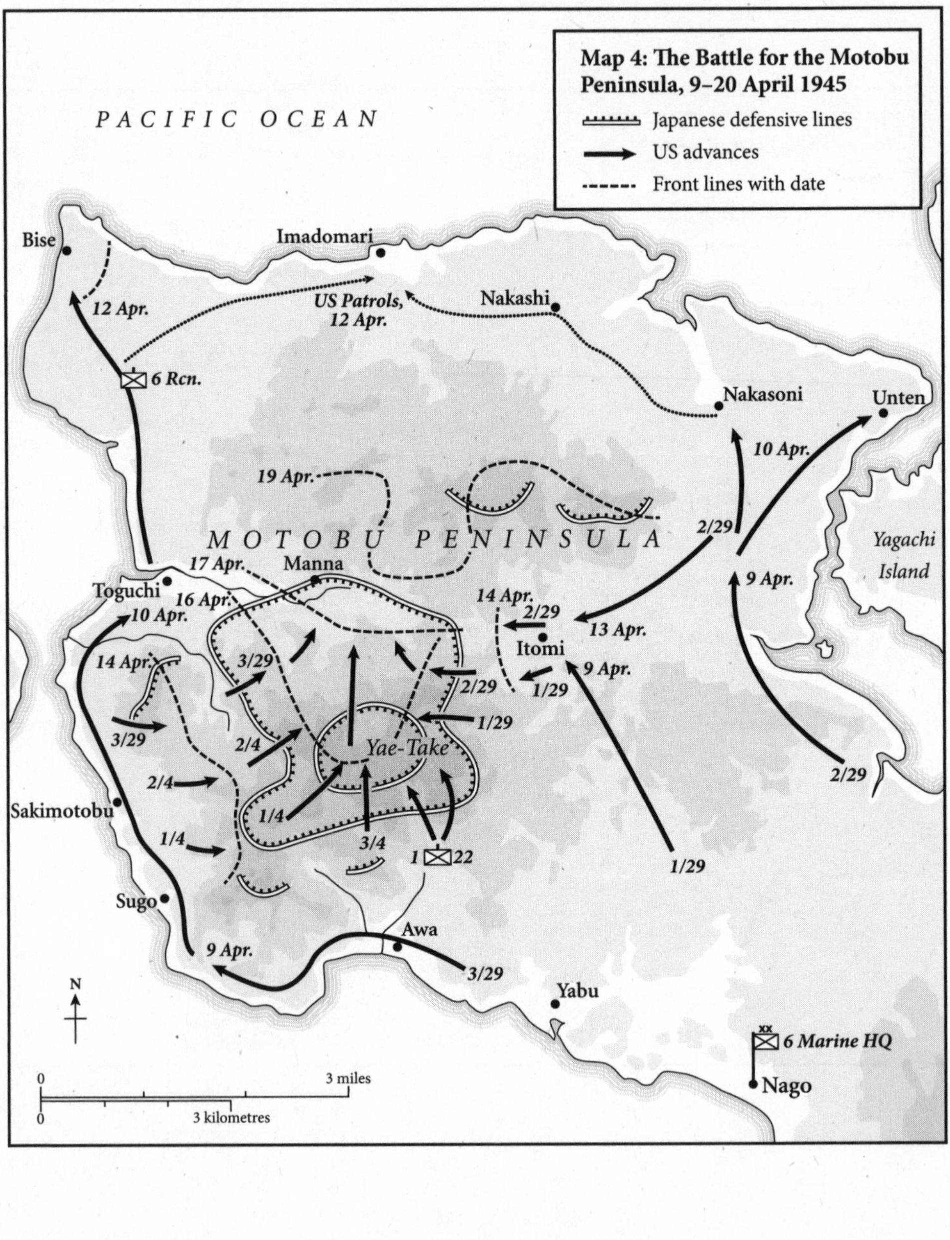

Map 4: The Battle for the Motobu Peninsula, 9–20 April 1945
Japanese defensive lines
US advances
Front lines with date
PACIFIC OCEAN
Bise
Imadomari
Nakashi
US Patrols, 12 Apr.
12 Apr.
6 Rcn.
Nakasoni
Unten
10 Apr.
19 Apr.
MOTOBU PENINSULA
2/29
Yagachi Island
9 Apr.
17 Apr.
Manna
Toguchi
16 Apr.
10 Apr.
14 Apr.
2/29
13 Apr.
Itomi
14 Apr.
3/29
2/29
9 Apr.
1/29
1/29
3/29
2/4
Yae-Take
2/4
Sakimotobu
1/4
1/4
3/4
1 22
1/29
2/29
Sugo
Awa
9 Apr.
3/29
Yabu
N
6 Marine HQ
Nago
0
3 miles
0
3 kilometres

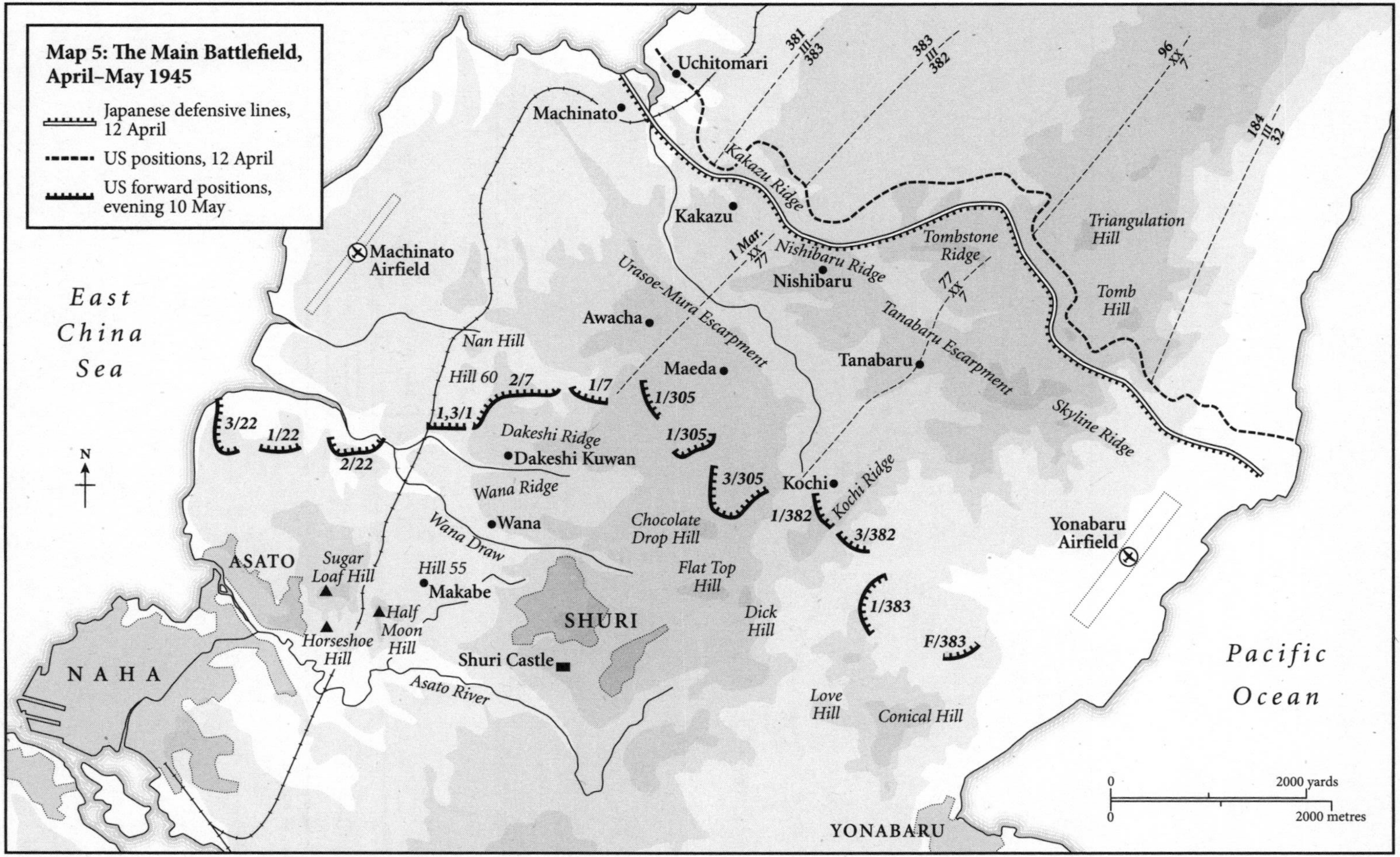
Map 5: The Main Battlefield, April–May 1945
Japanese defensive lines, 12 April
US positions, 12 April
US forward positions, evening 10 May
East China Sea
Pacific Ocean
N
Uchitomari
Machinato
Machinato Airfield
Kakazu Ridge
Kakazu
Nishibaru Ridge
Nishibaru
Tombstone Ridge
Triangulation Hill
Tomb Hill
Urasoe-Mura Escarpment
Tanabaru Escarpment
Tanabaru
Skyline Ridge
Awacha
Maeda
Nan Hill
Hill 60
2/7
1/7
1,3/1
1/305
1/305
3/305
3/22
1/22
2/22
Dakeshi Ridge
Dakeshi Kuwan
Wana Ridge
Wana
Wana Draw
Kochi
Kochi Ridge
1/382
3/382
1/383
F/383
Chocolate Drop Hill
Flat Top Hill
Dick Hill
Love Hill
Conical Hill
Yonabaru Airfield
ASATO
Sugar Loaf Hill
Horseshoe Hill
Half Moon Hill
Hill 55
Makabe
SHURI
Shuri Castle
Asato River
NAHA
YONABARU
381 III 383
383 III 382
96 XX 7
184 III 32
1 Mar. XX 77
77 XX 7
0
2000 yards
0
2000 metres

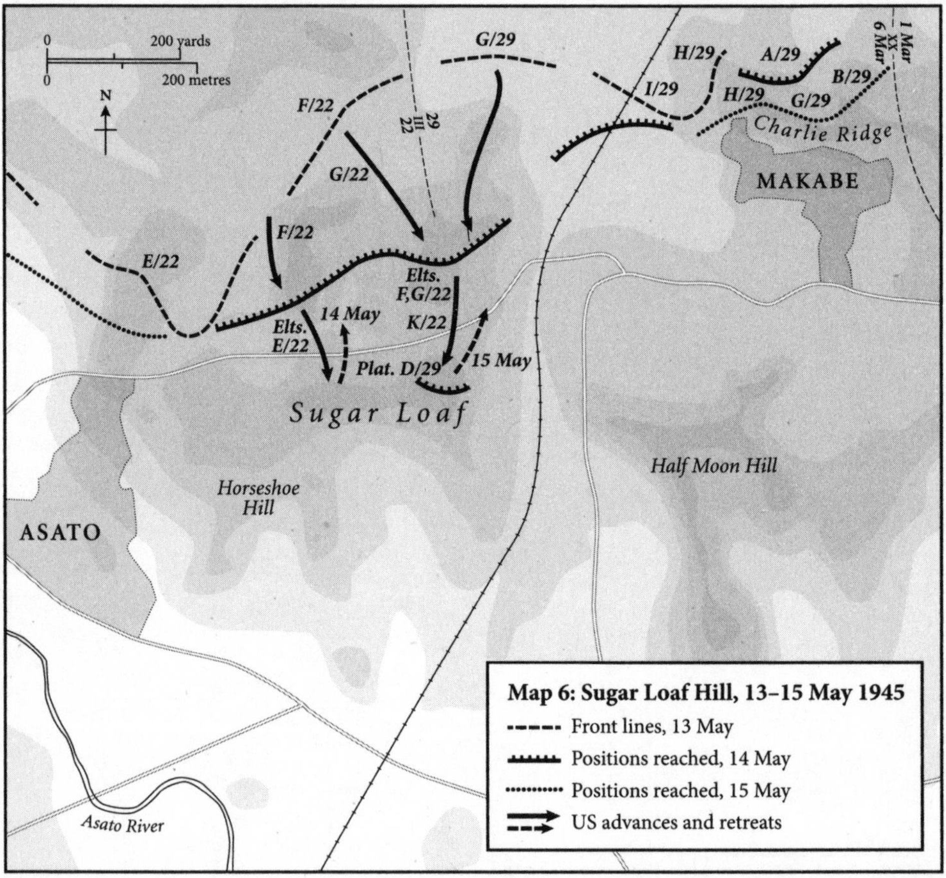
0
200 yards
0
200 metres
N
G/29
H/29
A/29
I/29
B/29
H/29
G/29
Charlie Ridge
F/22
29
III
22
G/22
MAKABE
F/22
E/22
Elts.
F,G/22
14 May
K/22
Elts.
E/22
Plat. D/29
15 May
Sugar Loaf
Half Moon Hill
Horseshoe
Hill
ASATO
Asato River
1 Mar
XX
6 Mar
Map 6: Sugar Loaf Hill, 13–15 May 1945
Front lines, 13 May
Positions reached, 14 May
Positions reached, 15 May
US advances and retreats

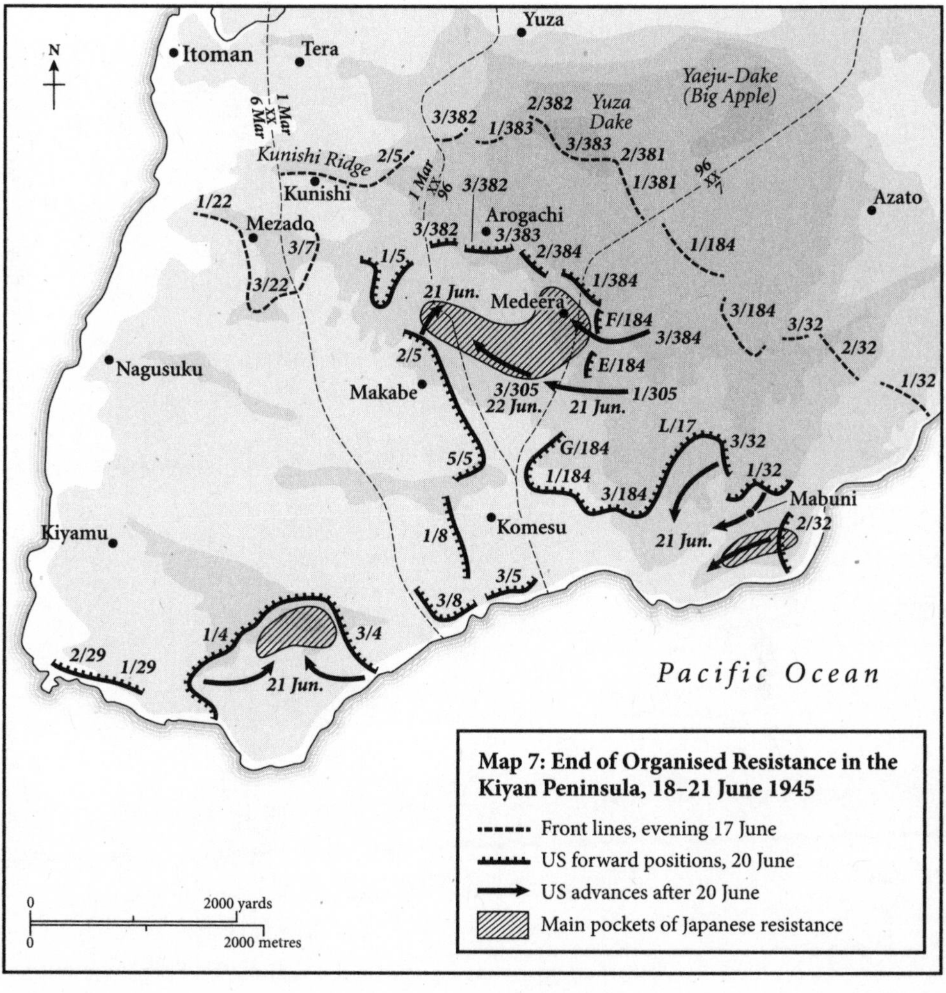

Map 7: End of Organised Resistance in the Kiyan Peninsula, 18–21 June 1945

Front lines, evening 17 June

US forward positions, 20 June

US advances after 20 June

Main pockets of Japanese resistance

Crucible of Hell

Prologue: Love Day

The USS *Eldorado* slowed as it approached the west coast of Okinawa in the pre-dawn darkness. "Ahead," noted a U.S. Marine Corps colonel, "could be seen the muzzle flashes of naval guns, arcing trajectories of red-hot projectiles, the glow of fires on a distant blur of shoreline. Above the hum of our ship's circulating blowers could be faintly heard the roll and reverberation of man-made thunder as our supporting battleships, cruisers, destroyers and rocket gunboats increased the tempo of their shore bombardment."[1]

Designed as a floating command post, the *Eldorado* was packed with advanced communications equipment that left space for only two five-inch anti-aircraft guns. Yet she contained a highly valuable human cargo: Vice Admiral Richmond K. ("Kelly") Turner, USN, the straight-talking 60-year-old commander of the huge amphibious armada of 1,300 ships and 183,000 combat troops that was converging on Okinawa, the most southerly of Japan's forty-seven prefectures; and ground-force commander Lieutenant General Simon Bolivar Buckner Jr., 58, the snowy-haired son of the famous Confederate general. It was April 1, 1945, or Love Day,* the code name for the assault, and an auspicious date for Buckner as it was, he noted in his diary, "Easter Sunday, my father's birthday and the day of my first battle." He added: "I hope I shall be able to look back upon it with the same degree of enthusiasm with which I anticipate it."[2]

Eager for the fray, Buckner had risen from his cramped quarters at 4:30 a.m. and, after a quick breakfast of "hot cakes," joined Admiral

* The day of landing was designated "Love Day" to avoid confusion with Iwo Jima's "Dog Day."

Turner on the bridge where at 5:30 a.m. precisely they observed through binoculars the opening of the pre-landing bombardment of the target beaches at Hagushi, a third of the way up the seventy-mile-long island, by the fire support force of ten battleships, nine cruisers, twenty-three destroyers, and 177 gunboats. Over the next three hours these vessels fired 44,825 rounds of five-inch or larger shells, 33,000 rockets and 22,500 mortar shells, "the heaviest concentration of naval gunfire ever to support a landing of troops."[3]

Shortly before 6:00 a.m., as the gunfire continued, the day dawned bright and clear, with excellent visibility of up to ten miles and only a few scattered patches of mist. A moderate breeze rippled the calm sea, and there was no surf on the target beaches. The weather, as anticipated, was perfect for an invasion. "The golden sunrise," wrote a delighted Buckner, "was not for Japan."[4]

At 7:45 a.m. the bombardment lifted long enough for carrier planes to strafe the beaches with bombs and napalm. "Smoke and dust rose up from the shore, thousands of feet high," recorded the celebrated war correspondent Ernie Pyle as he watched the spectacle from the command ship of the 5th Marines, "until finally the land was completely veiled. Bombs and strafing machine guns and roaring engines mingled with the crash of naval bombardment and seemed to drown out all existence. The ghastly concussion set up vibrations in the air—a sort of flutter—which pained and pounded the ears as though with invisible drumsticks. During all this time the waves of assault craft were forming up behind us."[5]

At 8:20 a.m.—ten minutes before H-hour—pennants were hauled down from the control craft and the first wave of amphibious tanks, covering an almost unbroken eight-mile line, began to move toward the shore, a distance of 4,000 yards, at a speed of four knots. They were preceded by gunboats firing enough rockets, mortars and 40 mm guns to saturate each prearranged hundred-yard target square for up to 1,000 yards inland with at least twenty-five rounds. "The crescendo of the bombardment," noted Buckner on the *Eldorado*, "culminating in the rocket discharge was a magnificent spectacle."[6]

Following a minute behind the tanks was the first wave of assault troops in amphibian tracked vehicles (or "amtracs"), likened by Ernie Pyle to "big trucks" on "tractor treads, built cup-like" that propel them through water and the "moment it touches bottom it crawls along like a tractor." More followed at ten-minute intervals, with Wave 6 scheduled to leave before Wave 1 hit the beach. Pyle watched them go with a "miserable and awful weight" on his heart. "There's nothing whatever romantic," he reported, "in knowing that an hour from now you might be dead."[7]

The advanced elements of four infantry divisions—a total of 12,000 men—were now heading for the shore, fearful of what awaited them. The most experienced was the 1st Marine Division which, in August 1942, had become the first U.S. infantry formation to see action when it invaded Japanese-held Guadalcanal in the Solomon Islands. That bloody campaign had lasted five long months before Japanese resistance was finally broken by the Marines. In 1944 they saw more tough fighting at Cape Gloucester and Peleliu, particularly the latter where the fanatical Japanese defense had cost the division almost 6,500 casualties.[8]

The 'Canal veterans had since rotated home, replaced by 8,000 raw recruits. But many of the rest remembered the storm of fire that had met them on the beaches of Peleliu and, quite understandably, feared a repeat. Among them was 29-year-old First Lieutenant Bill Looney, a graduate in economics from Chicago's Roman Catholic Loyola University who had fought and only narrowly survived the last two campaigns as a platoon commander with Charlie Company, 1/5th Marines. Now second in command as the company XO (or executive officer), he and his men had departed their base camp in the Russell Islands a fortnight earlier, aboard a flat-bottomed "landing ship, tank" (LST) that had bunks for 217 men, expecting their target to be the island of Formosa. But after a six-day stop at Ulithi atoll in the Western Caroline Islands—where they were met by the "awesome, frightening" sight of a "totally gutted" and "listing" aircraft carrier, the USS *Franklin*, which had been bombed by a single Japanese aircraft on March 19*—they finally learned the truth en route to Okinawa.

* Despite being hit by two 550-pound bombs, which caused catastrophic damage and killed and wounded almost half its crew of 2,600 men, the 872-foot Essex-class carrier was towed back to Brooklyn Navy Yard, via Ulithi and the Panama Canal, where she was repaired.

Earlier that morning, after a "great breakfast" of steak and eggs, they had watched a battleship shoot down a Japanese kamikaze* plane after "every other ship in the harbor" had tried and failed. It was as though the battleship had waited "to see if the amateurs could handle it." The excitement over, Looney and his men were ordered into the amtracs that were crammed into the LST's hold where the stench of gasoline and the noise of the engines was almost overpowering. Finally the bow doors opened and, one by one, the amtracs splashed into the water as "Good luck Marines" sounded on the ship's loudspeaker. Looney was half expecting his amtrac to "go directly under," but it stayed afloat and moved slowly toward land.

It was, he remembered, "a nervous and quiet group" crammed into his amtrac, "all with the same questions and anxieties going through their minds: are they waiting for us at the shore? How will we get up those sand dunes? Will it be as bad as Peleliu? Will I make it again?"[9]

Similar thoughts were occurring to Corporal Jim Johnston, a high-school valedictorian who in 1942 had quit the University of Nebraska–Lincoln to join the Marines because he thought it was "the honorable thing to do." Though only 22, Johnston was acting commander of a section of machine-gunners in Easy Company, 2/5th Marines, and felt keenly the weight of responsibility on his shoulders to get his men through the campaign safely. "Everyone who had been in front of me in my unit was dead or gone," he noted. "There was no one to lean on for help. Wherever I looked, someone was looking back at me."

Their briefing on what to expect had left Johnston extremely pessimistic. Protecting most of the shoreline his company was assaulting was a high sea wall, save for a gap of forty yards with flat land beyond that was covered by machine gun-emplacements. "This is our objective," he wrote. "We must try to secure the flat ground so the tanks and supplies can be landed there. All the defenses the enemy can muster—

* Literally "divine wind," a form of suicide attack in which the pilot used his plane as a flying bomb. The first successful attack was in October 1942 when a crippled Japanese torpedo bomber deliberately flew into the destroyer USS *Smith*, killing twenty-eight and wounding twenty-three. But it was not until autumn 1944 that the Imperial Japanese Navy's Special Attack Corps was formed in the Philippines. During the Okinawa campaign, kamikaze would launch more than 2,000 sorties.

artillery, mortars, and machine guns—will concentrate their fire on that strategic forty yards. How in the world can a man live through such a place?" So brutally frank had his officers been that everyone expected Easy Company "to be literally destroyed."[10]

Up ahead the gunboats turned aside as they reached the shallow coral reef that fringes Okinawa's western beaches, allowing the amphibious tanks and tracked vehicles to pass through them and proceed unescorted over the reef, the tanks firing their 75 mm howitzers at any pillboxes and strongpoints they could identify. As the tanks neared the shore, the naval bombardment lifted to targets further inland, "obscuring the ridges with smoke, blinding the Jap observation posts," while scores of carrier planes swooped low over the landing beaches to saturate them with machine-gun fire.

The amphibious tanks landed first, followed soon after by the tracked vehicles. As they covered the last few yards to the shore, Johnston remembered the sight of dead Marines in the water and on the beach at Peleliu, and "wondered what we would look like to the waves that would come behind us."[11] To Looney, however, the absence of "hostile fire" and "no burning amtracs" was "a very good sign." Carrying long collapsible ladders to scale the steep sand dunes, they piled out of the amtrac and headed for the dunes. "Still no action," he recorded. "It is a walk-on. How great."[12]

Johnston approached a pillbox on Yellow 1 Beach, anticipating "the impact of bullets ripping into my body," but there was "no fire." The pillbox was empty. So he and his men moved inland and, within an hour, the beachhead "was several hundred yards deep and growing by the minute." They felt "jubilant, absolutely overjoyed," as if they "had been granted a pardon from the death sentence." But for many it was "only a reprieve."[13]

Ernie Pyle was still on the 5th Marines' command ship when word came back by radio that "waves 1 and 2 were ashore without much opposition and there were no mines on beaches." Peering through binoculars, he could see "tanks moving across the fields and the men of the second wave walking inland, standing upright." There was the odd splash in the water near the beach from desultory small-arms and mortar fire, but no sign of "any real fire coming from the shore." It was indicative rather than definitive, yet he felt the weight of dread begin to lift. "I found myself talking more easily with the sailors," he wrote, "and somehow the feeling gradually took hold that we were to be spared."[14]

From the deck of the *Eldorado* it was "difficult to see exactly what was happening on the beaches," noted the Marine colonel, "but to our amazement there appeared to be little resistance; our troops reported back that they were crossing the thin strips of coral sand 'standing up.' For reasons of their own the Japanese had elected not to defend the beaches." He added: "Wave after wave of our landing craft hit the beaches, unloaded, and pulled away to their mother ship for subsequent loads. Our troops, Army and Marine, were carried forward by sheer momentum to the high ground of the ventral ridge of the island, where they paused to consolidate and reassess the situation. Behind them the tremendous build-up and congestion on the beaches continued, unhampered by enemy action. It had not been this easy on Peleliu or Iwo Jima."[15]

Perhaps the only U.S. serviceman to feel "somewhat concerned about the lack of opposition on Okinawa" that morning was Lieutenant General Buckner. His Marine deputy chief of staff, Brigadier General Oliver P. Smith, put this down to Buckner's bad experience at Kiska in the Aleutians in August 1943 "when Army troops had landed and to their embarrassment…found no Japanese." Buckner, according to Smith, "did not want to be involved in another Kiska."[16]

Certainly Buckner was eager to fight, a pugnacity heightened by his lack of combat experience and the fact that in the months leading up to the campaign, he had been fed a steady diet of Japanese horror stories that included photographs of U.S. soldiers who had been "butchered and eaten by Japs."[17] Intelligence reports had estimated at least 65,000 Japanese defenders on Okinawa. So where were they? "Opposition was light," Buckner wrote to his wife that evening, "the Japs evidently expected us to land elsewhere in the island…I consider the day highly successful. We have nearly 60,000 troops ashore and will land more tomorrow."[18]

Buckner was convinced that the simultaneous feinted landing by the 2nd Marine Division on the southeast coast of Okinawa had fooled the Japanese into concentrating their troops in the wrong place. That was far from the case. Coolly watching the landings through binoculars from an observation platform in Shuri Castle, twelve miles to the south, stood the Japanese commander, Lieutenant General Mitsuru Ushijima, and his senior officers. "Tall and heavy-set" with "ruddy cheeks and a benign countenance," the 57-year-old Ushijima had replaced the ailing General Watanabe as commander of the Thirty-Second Army on Okinawa the previous August. He had some field experience as a brigade and divisional commander in China and Burma; but since 1941 had occupied administrative posts in Japan, first as commandant of the army's Non-commissioned Officers Academy, and then the more prestigious Imperial Japanese Army Academy. Perhaps not surprisingly, he was less hands-on than the fire-eating Watanabe, preferring to leave "all operational details to his subordinates," while still taking overall responsibility. "In this respect," noted a subordinate, "he was faithful to long-standing Japanese military tradition, going back to the great Takamori Saigo, one of the leaders of the Meiji Restoration of 1868."[19]

The "short, stout officer" standing nearest to Ushijima on the viewing platform, "legs set defiantly apart," was his right-hand man and chief of staff, Major General Isamu Chō, an ultranationalist who had been active in the 1930s in the "young officers" military clique that was pushing for Japan's territorial expansion. Implicated in the massacre of at least 200,000 Chinese civilians and prisoners of war at Nanjing in the winter of 1937–8, and briefly arrested for his part in a *coup d'état* against the civilian government, the 50-year-old Chō was a ruthless and aggressive military strategist who thought attack the best form of defense. If it had been his decision, the Japanese troops on Okinawa would have fought the invading Americans on the beaches. Instead, Ushijima took the advice of his talented operations chief, Colonel Hiromichi Yahara, 42, who was convinced the only way to defend Okinawa, given the inevitable imbalance in troop numbers and firepower, was to leave the beaches uncontested and instead concentrate Japanese strength in the south of the island.[20]

The plans recently put forward by Imperial General Headquarters (IGHQ) in Tokyo decreed that the battle for Okinawa would be won on the sea and in the air, and that the troops on the island would merely be needed "to mop up enemy remnants after they landed." Yahara knew this was nonsense and planned accordingly. Born to a modest family of farmers in the sparsely populated south-west of Honshu Island, the bespectacled Yahara had used brains and determination to advance his army career, passing out first from the War College. He had served as a regimental officer, worked undercover in South East Asia and, more recently, taught at the Imperial Japanese Army Academy in Tokyo under Ushijima. But it was his two years as an exchange officer in the United States, including six months with the 8th Infantry, that would serve him best on Okinawa as they gave him an insight into the American military mind.[21]

Arriving in March 1944, Yahara considered Okinawa an obvious future target for U.S. forces as they advanced closer to Japan's home islands, 400 miles to the north, and argued for a significant troop build-up. "I felt it was crucial," he recalled, "that we select those islands where we could expect the enemy to attack, place decisive troop strength there, and make adequate combat preparations while we still had the chance." He eventually got his way, and various formations were rushed to Okinawa until, by the late summer of 1944, the garrison had swelled to 105,000 men, backed by a further 20,000 half-trained Okinawan "Boeitai" (Home Guard).[22]

At this point, Yahara's strategy was to "move in the direction of any enemy landings, launch an offensive, and destroy the enemy near the coast." But when IGHQ decided in November 1944 to move the Thirty-Second Army's best formation, the 25,000-strong 9th Division, to the Philippines, via Formosa, Yahara changed tack. Now with, he believed, too few troops to prevent a major landing, he concentrated the vast bulk of his forces in the southern third of the island, "behind several heavily fortified lines north of army headquarters at Shuri Castle." Well protected in tunnels and caves, they could withstand any amount of enemy bombs and gunfire. Or as Yahara put it: "Against steel, the product of American industry, we would pit our earthen fortifications, the product of the sweat of our troops and the Okinawan people."[23]

The change was controversial as it ran counter to the Imperial Japanese Army's operational doctrine of seeking out a "decisive battle" rather than a "war of attrition." But Ushijima gave his approval, and for the next five months soldiers and civilians toiled night and day to prepare a defensive system across the narrow waist of southern Okinawa where, forward of Ushijima's HQ on Mount Shuri, "several jagged lines of ridges and rocky escarpments" were turned into "formidable nests of interlocking pillboxes and firing positions." All were "connected by a network of caves and passageways inside the hills" that allowed the defenders to move safely to the point of attack.[24]

With their defensive preparations complete, Ushijima and his officers were "full of confidence" as they watched the "enemy's frantic deployment" on the Hagushi beaches on April 1. Some joked; a few lit cigarettes. All were "tense with the warrior's inner excitement at the thrill of preparing to cross swords with a mighty enemy."

Yahara marveled at the sheer scale of the enemy bombardment as "smoke and debris from the explosions" rose into sky. The enemy planes looked to him like "hundreds of oversized beans" as they emerged from the smoke to carry out their bombing operations. Then, finally, American soldiers emerged "from the thousand-odd landing craft, thrusting onto the shore." He wrote later: "It is as if the sea itself were advancing with a great roar."

He chuckled as he tried to put himself into the minds of the enemy commander and his staff. "Advancing with such ease," wrote Yahara, "they must be thinking gleefully that they have passed through a breach in the Japanese defenses. They will be wrong... It is amusing to watch the American army so desperately intent in its attack on an almost undefended coast, like a blind man who has lost his cane, groping on hands and knees to cross a ditch."

Yet, at the same time, Yahara felt "a gnawing sense of unease." The IGHQ plan was for the air force to play the lead role in "warding off the enemy attack." It had been "publicly stated that the best opportunity to destroy the enemy would be while he was still in his ships, before the troops had a chance to land." For the last week, Japanese aircraft had attacked the "enemy fleet under cover of darkness, by moonlight and at dawn." So why now, asked Yahara, "with enemy landing craft swarming around the [Hagushi] beaches, do they not overcome all obstacles, take advantage of this once-in-a-lifetime chance, and make an all-out concerted attack?"[25]

In fact, according to the diary of Vice Admiral Matome Ugaki, the man tasked with the air defense of Okinawa, a full-scale attack on the approaching U.S. 5th Fleet was ordered on March 31. But only a few kamikaze got through the American anti-aircraft and fighter screen the following day. One flew into the superstructure of the battleship USS *West Virginia* and its bomb penetrated to the second deck. Fortunately it was a dud, or the casualties of four dead and twenty-three wounded would have been much heavier. Other kamikaze struck a transport, USS *Hinsdale*, and two LSTs carrying men of the 2nd Marine Division as they feigned a landing off the southeast coast of Okinawa.[26]

Second Lieutenant Otha L. Grisham, 21, from San Marcos, Texas, was eating breakfast in the officers' wardroom of LST *724* when he heard the sound of a plane and the ship's anti-aircraft gunners opening fire. Told to "stay put" and "not get in the way," he continued with his meal. "Suddenly," recalled Grisham, "the ship absorbed a rattling crash, but there was no explosion. It was at midship on the port side, and we rushed to the outside passageway. There sat part of a Jap airplane engine, complete with body parts from the pilot. Our ship's gunners had shot him down before he could do serious damage to his target."

The other two vessels were not so lucky. Looking back, Grisham could see LST *884* and the USS *Hinsdale* burning. As both vessels contained men from the same two Marine units on LST *724*, Grisham and his colleagues "lobbied for slowing (or stopping) to assist our buddies." But the ship's captain refused, and they watched helplessly as survivors jumped overboard to avoid the flames. Their rescue would take many hours and, in total, more lives were lost in these attacks—forty-one—than in the landings proper. "Who said it was 'safer,'" commented Grisham, "to be in Reserve?"[27]

The amphibious operation to capture Okinawa—code-named Iceberg—was the largest of the Pacific War and the greatest air–land–sea battle in history. Admittedly fewer troops (60,000) were landed on L-Day than had, for example, been put ashore on D-Day in Sicily in 1943 (180,000) and Normandy in 1944 (100,000).[28] But the overall scale of Iceberg was arguably greater than both because of the number of naval assets involved, and the distances they had to cover. "This is," wrote one awestruck participant,

> the largest open-seas armada in history. Seven divisions and the whole Pacific Fleet. 1,457 ships and half a million men. Think about this. All those ships and men have to arrive together at the right time and place thousands of miles from the USA. *Remarkable logistics*. The seven divisions all come from different

> places and all are on ships. An awesome sight. Then there were the warships: [aircraft] carriers, battleships, cruisers and lots of destroyers. There were also some forty submarines that had been in the operation and had transported the underwater personnel who had worked on the barriers [at the beaches]. I am sure the public did not realize the size of the Okinawa operation. In some ways it was bigger than D-Day.[29]

Either way it was an astonishing logistical feat. For the assault echelon alone, more than 183,000 troops and 747,000 tons of cargo were loaded onto 430 assault transports and landing ships at eleven different ports, from Seattle to Leyte in the Philippines. The closest Pacific base to Okinawa was at Ulithi, five days' sailing at ten knots. Yet the bulk of the resupply would come from the West Coast of the United States, a distance of 6,250 nautical miles, or twenty-six days' sailing.[30]

Most of the 540,000 Allied servicemen—navy, air and army—who fought in the campaign were American. They included the naval personnel of Admiral Raymond A. Spruance's U.S. 5th Fleet, the most powerful in history with more than twenty fast aircraft carriers, ten battleships and 1,200 aircraft. Yet a small but significant portion of the 5th Fleet's sea and air assets were British and Commonwealth in the form of Task Force 57—otherwise known as the British Pacific Fleet—which comprised two battleships, four fleet carriers, five cruisers (one from New Zealand), eleven destroyers (two from Australia) and 220 aircraft. It was the Royal Navy's most formidable strike force of the war.[31]

The campaign would last for eighty-three blood-soaked days as the fighting plumbed depths of savagery that was as bad as anything perpetrated by the Germans and Russians on the Eastern Front. It is a brutal, heartrending story—made a little more bearable by the many instances of extraordinary heroism and self-sacrifice on both sides—and one best told from multiple perspectives: from the cramped cockpit of a kamikaze plane, the claustrophobic gun turret of a warship under attack, and a half-submerged foxhole amidst the squalor and battle detritus on Sugar Loaf Hill. The narrative shifts from the lofty perch of generals and presidents, to the more humble experience of ordinary servicemen, their families and the Okinawan civilians who were caught so tragically between the warring parties. But first we must go back to the beginning: to July 26, 1944, when the U.S. president met his senior Pacific commanders in Pearl Harbor, Hawaii, to decide on the best strategy to defeat Japan.

1

"Where's Douglas?"

The heavy cruiser USS *Baltimore* was greeted by an immense crowd of cheering Hawaiians as it docked at Pearl Harbor at 3:00 p.m. on Wednesday July 26, 1944. It was carrying President Franklin D. Roosevelt who, despite a recent illness and the start of what would be his third successful reelection campaign, had come to the headquarters of the U.S. Navy's Pacific Fleet with just a handful of close advisers to discuss future strategy.[1]

The first man to greet the wheelchair-bound president* was Admiral Chester W. Nimitz, 59, the Texan-born commander of U.S. forces in the Pacific Ocean Area whose quiet but determined leadership had avenged early American setbacks with a string of victories at sea and on land. Striding up the gangplank at the head of a group of senior officers, Nimitz shook Roosevelt warmly by the hand. The president's response: "Where's Douglas?"

He was referring to 64-year-old General Douglas MacArthur, the colorful and opinionated Supreme Allied Commander in the Southwest Pacific Area (SWPA) who had been controversially awarded the Congressional Medal of Honor—the U.S. military's highest award for valor—"for conspicuous leadership" during the failed campaign to defend the Philippines from Japanese attack in early 1942. Some had even accused MacArthur of abandoning his command by leaving the island fortress of Corregidor in Manila Bay before it fell in May with the loss of 11,000 U.S. and Filipino troops. In truth, Roosevelt had ordered MacArthur to leave and, ever since, the general had worked

* In 1921, at the age of 39, Roosevelt contracted polio, lost the use of both legs and had been partially confined to a wheelchair ever since. In public he used leg braces to give the appearance of mobility.

tirelessly to redeem his reputation. Having secured Australia, he went on the offensive, capturing vast swathes of territory in New Guinea and the Admiralty Islands. His aim in coming to Hawaii was to convince the president that the Philippines—a country he had vowed to liberate—should be the next major objective.

Arriving by plane, MacArthur realized he was late and urged the police motorcyclists escorting his open-topped car to get him to the docks as quickly as possible. They arrived, sirens screaming, as the presidential party was disembarking. "Hello, Doug," said Roosevelt. "What are you doing with that leather jacket on? It's darn hot today."

"Well," MacArthur replied, "I've just landed from Australia. It's pretty cold there."[2]

In the strategy sessions that followed in a big room filled with maps of the Pacific, Nimitz spoke first. His plan—initiated by his boss Admiral Ernest J. King, the commander-in-chief, U.S. Fleet and a member of the Joint Chiefs of Staff—was to bypass the Philippines by launching the next major offensive against Formosa and then the Japanese home islands. Indeed this option was also the preference of the other Joint Chiefs—generals of the army George C. Marshall (U.S. Army) and Henry H. ("Hap") Arnold (U.S. Army Air Force)—who both felt it offered the quickest route to defeat Japan. Nimitz, as it happened, was not convinced the plan would work, and preferred to take the Western Caroline Islands first, before invading the central Philippines and Iwo Jima. But loyal to a fault, he argued for his superior's plan as if it were his own.

MacArthur responded with a masterly presentation, delivered without notes, arguing that the main Philippine island of Luzon was more important than Formosa because with it went control of the South China Sea and Japan's sea communications to its southern possessions. Whereas bypassing Luzon would expose U.S. forces on Formosa and elsewhere to devastating attacks from Japanese bombers stationed there. Nimitz agreed with this point and, when questioned by Roosevelt, said he could support either operation. So a compromise was agreed: the Philippines would be recovered with the forces available in the western Pacific and Formosa could wait. MacArthur was delighted. The president, he wrote, had remained "entirely neutral" while Nimitz had shown a "fine sense of fair play."[3]

During his trip the president was invited to lunch at Nimitz's official residence at Makalapa Hill. But as the house, in the opinion of the secret service, was not up to scratch, a U.S. Naval Construction Battalion of 500 "Seabees" was sent to repaint it, refurbish the bathrooms and even build a new road behind the house so that Roosevelt could be moved from the car to his wheelchair in private. None of the many generals and flag officers also in attendance—one counted 136 stars on the collars of the guests—were any the wiser as they sat down to martini cocktails and a main course of *mahimahi*, a delicious local fish.[4]

Given the seat of honor on Roosevelt's right was Lieutenant General Simon B. Buckner, recently appointed commander of the U.S. Tenth Army, the formation slated to carry out the invasion of Formosa. The president, noted Buckner in his diary, "talked cheerfully & made everyone feel relaxed & at home." He also "looked well but his hand shook a little when he raised his cocktail glass."[5] MacArthur, already back in Australia, was far more pessimistic about the president's health. "He is just a shell of the man I knew," he told his wife Jean. "In six months he will be in his grave."[6]

The practical effect of Roosevelt's visit to Pearl Harbor was to leave the army and navy pursuing joint but separate strategies: MacArthur would continue his advance up through the Philippines and the Dutch East Indies; while Nimitz edged closer to Formosa via the central Pacific, the first step being the capture of Peleliu in the Palau Islands which was finally secured in late November 1944 by the 1st Marine Division and, latterly, the army's 81st Division, after a vicious two-month campaign that was made immeasurably harder by the formidable Japanese defensive system of caves and underground tunnels.*

By then, much had changed. From September 11 to 16, 1944, Roosevelt, British prime minister Winston Churchill and their combined chiefs of staff met at Quebec for the Octagon Conference where they agreed, among other things, that Britain would become a full partner in the war against Japan after the defeat of Germany. Churchill's preference was for an advance across the Bay of Bengal

* Only a handful of the 10,700 Japanese defenders laid down their arms; the rest fought to the death. U.S. casualties were 1,800 killed and 7,000 wounded.

and an operation to recover Singapore and the Malay Peninsula, lost in such ignominious circumstances in early 1942. Roosevelt disagreed. The Americans, he said, had been very successful at "island-hopping" in the Pacific, and bypassing strong Japanese garrisons like Singapore which could be mopped up later. But he was prepared to accept Churchill's offer of naval support in the central Pacific, overruling Admiral King's unwillingness to share victory "with an eleventh-hour entry."[7]

Happy with this concession, Churchill and his chiefs of staff let the Americans decide the optimum route of advance in the Pacific. On September 15, with the Octagon Conference still in progress, the Joint Chiefs authorized MacArthur to bring forward his operation to capture the Philippine island of Leyte from December 20 to October 20. But there was still an assumption that Nimitz would launch Operation Causeway—the invasion of Formosa—once the Philippines were secured. That, however, was about to change.

On September 16, sensing an opportunity to ditch the Formosa operation in favor of a move directly north from the Philippines to the Ryukyu and Bonin islands, and from there to Japan, Nimitz asked his senior army commanders for their opinion. Lieutenant General Robert C. Richardson Jr., commanding U.S. Army Forces in the Pacific Ocean Area, was firmly in agreement. Regarding the occupation of Formosa as a costly diversion, he argued instead for a dual advance along the Luzon–Ryukyus and Marianas–Bonins axes. This would allow MacArthur to seize the island of Luzon after Leyte, and provide air and naval bases in the Philippines to block enemy shipping lanes and neutralize Formosa. But only the next step—possession of the Ryukyu chain of islands, extending 700 miles south of the Japanese home islands, and the Bonins further to the east—would enable extensive air operations against the main islands of Kyushu and Honshu. These, in turn, would prepare the ground for amphibious landings.

Richardson was backed up by Lieutenant General Millard F. Harmon, commanding U.S. Army Air Forces, who pointed out that the acquisition of air bases could be achieved with far less cost in men and materiel in the Ryukus than in Formosa. The final nail in Causeway's coffin was provided by Lieutenant General Buckner who pointed out that his Tenth Army lacked the supporting and service troops for such a large-scale operation.[8]

Nimitz repeated these arguments to Admiral King when they met in San Francisco on September 29. The alternative to Causeway, said Nimitz, was to keep pressure on the Japanese by taking, in turn, Luzon, Iwo Jima and Okinawa. Formosa, meanwhile, could be kept in check by a series of air strikes from carriers. Why Iwo Jima? asked King. Because, explained Nimitz, it would allow fighter protection for the huge B-29 bombing raids on the Japanese home islands that were planned for 1945.[9]

Convinced by Nimitz, King proposed to his fellow Joint Chiefs on October 2 that, because of insufficient resources in the Pacific Ocean Area and the unwillingness of the War Department to make additional resources available until after the defeat of Germany, operations against Luzon, Iwo Jima and Okinawa should precede the seizure of Formosa. They concurred and, a day later, Nimitz was ordered by the Joint Chiefs to "occupy one or more positions" in the Ryukyu Islands, beginning on March 1, 1945. The purpose was to establish bases from which to attack "the main islands of Japan and their sea approaches" with air and naval forces; support further operations in regions bordering the East China Sea; and sever air and sea communications between Japan's home islands and its possessions to the south and west. But the first step was to "capture, occupy, defend and develop Okinawa Island."[10]

2

Operation Iceberg

"Directive received deferring our project," noted Lieutenant General Simon Bolivar Buckner Jr. in his diary on October 4, 1944. He added: "Took physical exam. Blood pressure 120/76. Dr. said he could find nothing wrong except danger from Japs."[1]

The forced humor masked Buckner's understandable nervousness about what lay ahead: not only his first test as a field commander, but in a battle of any kind. It may not have helped that he was the son of a famous Confederate general—named after the Venezuelan soldier and statesman Simón Bolívar, then at the height of his fame as the "Liberator" of South America—who, after a shaky start, won laurels at the battles of Perryville and Chickamauga. He became, as it happened, both the first Confederate commander to surrender an army, and also the last. He was 63 when his son Simon Bolivar Jr. was born in Munfordville, Kentucky, in 1886. A year later, standing as a Democrat, Buckner Sr. became the state's thirtieth governor.

Though he later failed as the vice-presidential nominee of the "Gold Democrats" in 1896, the elder Buckner was a hard act to follow. His young son made a start by graduating from the U.S. Army's military academy at West Point in 1908. But thereafter his career was largely uneventful as he completed two tours of the Philippines, saw no combat in the First World War and spent much of the interwar period as a student or instructor at various military schools, including a final spell as commandant of cadets at West Point. In the latter appointment he was remembered as a martinet, a stern disciplinarian who allowed his cadets few luxuries. "Buckner forgets," commented one aspiring officer's parent, "cadets are born not quarried."[2]

Lacking field experience, Buckner clung to U.S. Army doctrine that artillery played the decisive role in combat. Infantry were needed to find and hold the enemy; but only artillery could destroy it. After war came a second time in December 1941, he was eager to put this theory into practice. But by then he was commanding the army's Alaska Defense Command, a relative backwater that saw only limited action. In 1943, for example, when amphibious landings recovered the Aleutian islands of Attu and Kiska from the Japanese, both operations had been navy-led. A frustrated Buckner clashed repeatedly with both the naval commander for the northern Pacific and the civilian authorities in Alaska, the latter objecting to his illegal hunting of walruses.[3]

Salvation came in the summer of 1944 when Buckner was appointed commander of the new U.S. Tenth Army in Hawaii, a joint army–Marines formation that was intended for the invasion of Formosa. Worried about resupply, he was relieved when the objective was switched from Formosa to the smaller Okinawa; but that still required a completely new plan of assault. Fortunately Buckner had an excellent staff to take care of that, led by Brigadier General E. D. Post who had served with him since West Point. Their relationship, noted a colleague, was "very close, almost that of father and son." It helped that Post had a "pleasing personality and a very even temper," and was a man "it would have been hard not to get along with."[4]

Under Post were two deputy chiefs of staff: one for the U.S. Army, Brigadier General Lawrence E. Schick; and one for the U.S. Navy/Marines, Brigadier General Oliver P. Smith. Like Post, Schick had served with Buckner in Alaska, and was one of Buck's boys. Smith was an outsider, joining the Tenth Army's staff on Hawaii only in early November 1944 after combat stints with the 1st Marine Division on Cape Gloucester (as colonel of the 5th Marines) and Peleliu (assistant division commander). The new job was not one he was looking forward to. "It is hard to come back from an operation," he wrote, "and start over again the whole tedious process of training for a new operation. What is needed is new blood."[5]

Smith had grown up in northern California where he attended the University of California, Berkeley, before joining the wartime Marine Corps as a second lieutenant in 1917. He later matriculated from the École supérieure de guerre in France, the first Marine to do so, and returned to teach at the Marine Corps Schools at Quantico, Virginia, where he was known as "the Professor" and an expert in amphibious warfare. Intelligent, easygoing and with valuable combat experience, he was the perfect choice as Buckner's Marine deputy chief of staff. Not least because army–Marine relations were then at a low ebb, following the sacking of Major General Ralph Smith as commander of the U.S. Army's 27th Division by his Marine superior, Lieutenant General Holland M. "Howlin' Mad" Smith—the so-called Smith vs Smith controversy—during the Saipan campaign in July 1944. Already ill disposed to the 27th Division for a perceived lack of aggression in a previous battle, Holland Smith accused its men of failing to attack on time and costing Marine lives. Ralph Smith was relieved of his command and ordered off the island, a humiliation that his senior army colleagues—including U.S. Army Chief of Staff George C. Marshall—found hard to forgive.

The bad blood probably cost the abrasive Holland Smith the command of the Tenth Army. "I found out later," wrote Oliver Smith, "that both Admiral Spruance and Admiral Turner had recommended that General Holland Smith be given the Okinawa job, but they were overruled by Admiral Nimitz."[6] It was handed instead to the untried Buckner who, in a second snub to Holland Smith, was put in charge of the all-army board of inquiry into Ralph Smith's sacking. The board eventually—and predictably—ruled in favor of the dismissed officer, though he would never command troops in action again. "Saw Holland Smith at Adm[iral] Nimitz's conference," noted Buckner in late August 1944, "and he greeted me without much enthusiasm. (He has probably seen my board report to the effect that Ralph Smith's relief from command was not justified.)"[7]

It was into this potentially poisonous atmosphere on Hawaii that Oliver Smith arrived on November 7. Fortunately Admiral Nimitz had helped to clear the air a month earlier by sounding out Buckner on his attitude to the Smith vs Smith controversy. "Finding," wrote Buckner, "that I deplored the whole matter and harbored no inter-service ill feeling," Nimitz "announced that I would command the 'new joint project.'"[8]

Smith's early impressions of his new boss, after they met at army headquarters in Schofield Barracks on November 8, were mostly positive. "He was," noted Smith, "in excellent physical condition: ruddy, heavy-set, but with considerable spring in his step. He had snow-white hair and piercing blue eyes: the eyes were almost hard."

Though he had "surprisingly little troop duty" and "limited" experience in amphibious operations, he did not lack for "character" and Smith had "no reason to feel he would not continue to operate well in a joint undertaking [with the navy]." While Buckner's "methods and judgments were somewhat inflexible," wrote Smith, "you always knew where you stood."

It helped that Smith thought highly of Buckner's right-hand men, Post and Schick, describing the latter—"a small, wiry man, quick of speech and action"—as the "finest staff officer with whom I have ever had the pleasure of serving." But not every aspect of life at Schofield Barracks, sited on a picturesque red-soiled plateau 900 feet above sea level, was to Smith's liking. He particularly resented Buckner's "fetish" for "physical conditioning," and his insistence that *all* his staff officers, many of whom were over fifty, took part. "For the older officers," noted Smith, "the program resulted in broken collarbones, broken arms, sprained ankles and charley horses [cramps in the leg muscles]. Included in the required conditioning were the running of the Combat Course (for which Lieutenant General Buckner held the record), firing all infantry hand and shoulder weapons, soft ball and conditioning hikes." One of the latter was eight and a half miles in length, with a climb and descent of 2,000 feet. Recently back from Peleliu, Smith gave it a miss. "What I needed was food and relaxation."

Yet there were limits to even that, and the vibrant social life at Schofield Barracks was not, in Smith's opinion, "an appropriate one for troops preparing for combat." He added: "It is true there were no families present, but there were dances every Wednesday and Saturday evening which were not stag affairs; there were plenty of WACs [Women's Army Corps], nurses and Red Cross workers. There were dinner parties, beach parties and cocktail parties. At some... the women wore evening gowns. You had the feeling you were half in the war and half out of it."[9]

Buckner's diary backs up Smith's concern. Hardly a day goes by without him mentioning his attendance at a dinner party or dance, usually in the company of an attractive young woman. One name keeps cropping up: "Missy" Keleher, the wife of a naval officer on duty in the Pacific. A typical entry (for November 21) reads: "Took Missy Keleher...to dinner at Chinese restaurant. Missy wangled a photo of myself and asked me to autograph it with an appropriate message. I did. 'To Missy with misgivings.'"

On another occasion, not long before he departed Hawaii for the theater of war, Buckner took Missy to a dinner and dance at the Wheeler Field Officers' Club, and then for a nightcap at a fellow officer's quarters. It was 2:00 a.m. by the time he got home. "Moral: Don't take girls to parties who live too far away if you want any sleep." Undoubtedly flattered by Missy's attention, Buckner's behavior toward her might have been, as far as we know, entirely honorable. But the number of evenings he spent in her and other women's company—often for tête-à-tête dinners—would surely not have gone down well with Adele Buckner, his wife of almost thirty years, and the mother of their three children, if she had known.[10]

When not carousing, Buckner and his staff were busy planning for Operation Iceberg, the assault on Okinawa. Their first priority was to gather all the geographical, meteorological and demographic information they could find on the island and its people from captured documents and prisoners of war, former residents and old Japanese publications. The bulk of their data came from aerial photographs which, taken by planes 1,200 miles from their bases, were frustratingly small-scale or incomplete. Yet the basic facts they revealed were not in dispute. Okinawa is the largest island in the Ryukyus, a chain that stretches almost 800 miles in a long arc from Kyushu to Formosa, and forms a boundary between the East China Sea and the Pacific. Of these 140 islands, only thirty were inhabited in 1945. The climate is subtropical, with temperatures ranging from 60 degrees Fahrenheit to 85 degrees, heavy rainfall, high humidity and violent typhoons between May and November.

Situated roughly in the center of the Ryukyus, Okinawa is seventy miles long and from two to eighteen miles wide, running north to south, and covering a distance of 485 square miles. Composed of porous coral rock, it is fringed with reefs, close to shore and rarely more than a mile wide on the western side, but much wider on the eastern side, where the coast is more sheltered.

When Commodore Perry's black ships first sailed into Naha Port on the west of the island in 1853, Okinawa was a semi-independent country that paid tribute to both China and Japan. Ryukyuan kings had ruled the surrounding islands from their capital at Shuri Castle, to the east of Naha, since the early fifteenth century. But after the entire Ryukyu archipelago was annexed by Japan in 1879, and the monarchy abolished, the Okinawan people became fully integrated into the Japanese governmental, economic and cultural structure. With a similar racial heritage to the Japanese, and resembling them in looks and physique, the Okinawan stock and culture have also been heavily influenced by the Chinese. In 1945 they spoke Luchan, not Japanese, and their predominant religion was an animistic cult that worshipped fire and the hearth, and venerated ancestors.

Most of the 435,000 inhabitants were poor—subsisting on small-scale agriculture and fishing—and much of the useable land in the bottom third of the island was cut into small fields and planted with sugar cane, sweet potatoes, rice and soy beans. This was because northern Okinawa, the two-thirds of the island above the Ishikawa Isthmus, is rugged and mountainous, with a central spine of 1,000 feet or more running the length of the region. Descending from both sides of this ridge are terraces dissected by ravines and watercourses, and ending at the coast in steep cliffs. A similar terrain is found on the Motobu Peninsula, jutting out to the west, where two mountain tracts are separated by a central valley. Covering the whole of this northern area in 1945 were pine forests and dense undergrowth, with only a few poor roads clinging to the western coast.

South of Ishikawa, on the other hand, is a more benign landscape of rolling hills, ravines and escarpments. It contained three-quarters of the population, four airfields and the large towns of Naha, Shuri, Itoman and Yonabaru. Generally aligned east to west, the hills provided a series of natural lines of defense. There were more roads in the south, but mostly country lanes unsuitable for motorized traffic. Drainage was poor, and heavy rains would quickly turn the deep, claylike mud into a quagmire.

The obvious place for a landing was the 9,000-yard stretch of the western coastline, a little south of Ishikawa, known as the Hagushi beaches. Divided by the Bishi River, the beaches ranged from a hundred to 900 yards in length and from ten to forty-five yards in width at low tide. Composed of coral sand, they mostly had at least one exit road and were flanked by a low coastal plain which was dominated by rolling hills. The plain was also the site of two of the island's four main airfields: Yontan, north of the Bishi, and Kadena to the south.

American estimates of enemy troop strength on Okinawa grew slightly from 48,600 in October 1944 to 65,000 in March 1945. They correctly identified the main infantry formations—the 24th and 62nd Divisions, and the 44th Independent Mixed Brigade—as well as a regiment of tanks and large numbers of heavy artillery pieces and anti-tank guns. These forces were grouped, according to aerial photos, in at least three main areas of defense: Naha, the Hagushi beaches and the Yonabaru–Nakagusuku Bay area on the lower east coast. It was assumed, in the event of the landings being successful, that the main line of enemy resistance would be across the narrow waist of land south of Hagushi.[11]

Operation Iceberg's initial landing plan—known as Plan Fox—was to disembark troops at Hagushi on the west coast where, as Oliver Smith explained, "a very limited advance would put in our hands the Yontan and Kadena airfields." The plan included the capture of the island of Keise Shima, just off the west coast of Okinawa, prior to Love Day to allow the citing of heavy artillery to support the main landings. Eight infantry divisions* were assigned to the operation: the XXIV Corps of the U.S. Army (7th, 27th and 96th Divisions); the III Amphibious Corps of the U.S. Marine Corps (1st, 2nd and 6th Marine Divisions); and two extra U.S. Army divisions, the 77th and 81st, in floating reserve. When support units were added, this brought the landing-force strength up to 183,000. Buckner wanted an additional 70,000 service troops. He was refused on the grounds that the troops were not available and, even if they had been, both the shipping and beach capacity were inadequate.[12]

On November 1, 1944, Plan Fox and an "alternate plan" to land on the southeast coast of Okinawa were presented to Vice Admiral Kelly Turner, commanding the amphibious task force and Buckner's immediate superior. Described by one colleague as "pig-headed and

* Both army and Marine divisions were based on a triangular structure of three infantry regiments, nine battalions (three per regiment), twenty-seven companies (three per battalion), eighty-one platoons (three per company) and 243 squads (three per platoon). They also included support units of artillery, engineers, armor, pioneers and service troops. Marine divisions numbered around 26,000 men; army divisions about 2,000 men fewer.

determined," Turner was a talented naval officer but not easy to get along with. Born in Portland, Oregon, in 1885, the son of a rancher and sometime printer, he had graduated fifth from the U.S. Naval Academy class of 1908. His varied postings since then included battleships in the First World War, naval aviation in the 1920s and the War Plans Division from 1940 to December 1941, where, as director, he said it was "probable" Japan's next act of aggression would lead to war with the United States (the statement was appropriated by President Roosevelt who substituted "possible" for "probable"). Turner then blotted his copybook by failing to pass on to Admiral Kimmel, the naval commander at Pearl Harbor, intercepted Japanese communications that pointed strongly to an imminent attack on the Pacific Fleet's base at Pearl Harbor. Kimmel later claimed that had he known, he would have maintained a much higher level of alert and the fleet would not have been taken by surprise* on December 7, 1941.[13]

Since then, Turner had led a string of successful amphibious assaults in the Pacific, including Guadalcanal, the Russell Islands, Tarawa and Makin, the Marshall Islands, Tinian, Guam and Saipan, and was Nimitz's first choice to do the same for Okinawa. A ferocious worker who would not suffer fools gladly, Turner was known to chew out his subordinates. Which is why, when Buckner's staff told him on November 1, 1944, they had no confidence in the alternative plan, and were presenting it only because they thought there should be one, he loudly disagreed. From the navy's perspective the alternative was preferable because the approach was through open sea, whereas Plan Fox meant sailing through the Kerama Islands just west of Okinawa. Even with these islands in our hands, said Turner, the navigational aspects of the approach would be more difficult, and the weather conditions harder to predict. He therefore requested a reconsideration of the east coast landing and a possible feint at Hagushi. Despite Turner's request, wrote Oliver Smith, "the Plan Fox Estimate was distributed to all hands on November 5th."[14]

* The aerial attack by carrier-borne Japanese planes sank four U.S. Navy battleships and badly damaged another three; fortunately the U.S. Pacific Fleet's aircraft carriers were not at Pearl Harbor and escaped. A day later, shortly before America declared war on Japan, President Roosevelt condemned the unprovoked attack in Congress as "a day that will live in infamy."

Love Day was delayed twice during the next month: from March 1 to March 15, and then to April 1, the final date. This was partly down to weather concerns, and partly the availability of shipping. Admiral Turner, meanwhile, came round to Plan Fox after he requested an in-depth study that described the Hagushi beaches as the "best" in Southern Okinawa "for the purpose." His proviso was that, in addition to Keise Shima, the Kerama Islands were also seized seven or eight days prior to Love Day "to provide a much needed protected anchorage where supporting ships could be refueled and rearmed and thus assure uninterrupted support of the landing."[15] This, of course, meant the allocation of part of an infantry division, the 77th, to take the Keramas, a diversion of resources that Buckner opposed, but could do nothing about. Turner "scattered too much," he noted in his diary. "I prefer greater concentration on the main objective."[16]

For the assault phase of the operation, Buckner would be known as Commanding General, Expeditionary Troops, or CTF 56. His immediate superior was Vice Admiral Turner, commanding Joint Expeditionary Force 51, who in turn reported to Admiral Raymond A. Spruance, commanding the U.S. 5th Fleet (CTF 50), the victor of two of the most significant naval battles of the war, Midway and the Philippine Sea, whose calmness in moments of crisis had earned him the nickname "Electric Brain." A small, trim man of simple tastes—he liked classical music and hot chocolate in the morning—Spruance was surprisingly modest, putting his success down "largely to the fact that I am a good judge of men. I am lazy, and have never done things myself that I could get someone to do for me."[17]

With the chain of command settled, and his assault plans well in hand, Buckner saw in the New Year of 1945 in characteristic fashion by accompanying a young woman to a party given by her aunt, an artist who lived in a house on the valley road "built over a pool with a 10-ft waterfall." The quality of the paintings on display was, according to Buckner, mixed: "Many good and some bad."[18]

His deputy Oliver Smith had more serious concerns. First, how not to alienate Buckner over the issue of who would present the Legion of Merit that Smith had been awarded for outstanding service at Peleliu. As the award had been forwarded via the Tenth Army, Buckner would normally have done the presentation. But Smith thought it more appropriate to receive it from General

Holland Smith, Buckner's hated rival, because he had signed the citation. Luckily Brigadier General Schick agreed with Smith, and the medal was duly awarded by the Marine general at the Fleet Marine Force HQ on January 1.[19]

It was also around now that Smith became aware of a seemingly minor decision of Buckner's that would have, in time, the gravest consequences: his plan for all Tenth Army general officers to wear a metal star on their combat helmets. Smith heard about it from Major Frank Hubbard, Buckner's recently appointed aide, who came to take his order. "I told him," wrote Smith, "that in the type of warfare encountered in the Pacific, it had been found advisable for generals to hide their identity if they valued their skins...There were always hidden Japanese snipers to fire on persons carrying field glasses or other equipment identifying them as officers."

According to Smith, a "compromise was finally reached by which the helmet was untouched, but small white stars were painted on the liner; this on the theory that the helmet without the liner would be worn only in the rear areas." That may have been true for Buckner's subordinates; but the general himself would insist on going through the campaign wearing a liner-less helmet with three distinctive metal stars.[20]

3

"Everybody go home!"

October 10, 1944, was "a beautiful day with soft rays of sunshine," remembered 13-year-old Yoshiko Sakumoto. "I never dreamed that such a bucolic town as Naha would be raided from the air without warning." She was on her way to school with her brother, and had just reached Tomari Bridge, when she saw about twenty people, including several Japanese soldiers, looking toward Naha Port. They were watching three or four low-flying planes approach the port and drop some black objects. "With booming explosions," wrote Yoshiko, "black smoke and flames soared high into the sky. Then gasoline tanks at Naha Port blew up one after the other."

Thinking it must be an air-raid exercise, some of the bystanders seemed confused. "It's unthinkable," said one, "to practice with real bombs." But the soldiers knew the truth. "Everybody go home!" they yelled. Yoshiko did as she was told, pulling her brother along with her.

Born in a modest house in Naha's port area of Tomari, the daughter of a shipbuilder and a maker of panama hats, Yoshiko Sakumoto had experienced a typical Okinawan childhood: celebrating the many festivals with sweet dumplings, playing with bouncy rubber balls decorated with painted flowers, and having her hands tattooed at the age of eight, as local custom decreed. But by then she had experienced the grief of losing two siblings: a younger sister to encephalitis, and a brother who drowned in the sea.

The gloom was lifted five years later by the birth of another brother, Kōkichi, making three children in all. "I was 11," wrote Yoshiko, "and my younger brother, Kōzen, was 6. With the youngest boy, Kōkichi, we three grew rapidly and stayed healthy." Their diet included rice, sweet potatoes, fresh fish, vegetables, seaweed, and, for special occasions, fish cakes, meat and eggs. "Our eating habits were simple, but everybody had enough to eat...Neighbors were thoughtful, warm, generous and forgiving. The island was small, but the islanders' hearts were many times bigger."

Even before the war began, Japanese culture was making inroads into Okinawan life. Expected to speak Japanese at school, children were forced to wear punishment placards if they slipped into local dialect. Yoshiko's mother and neighbors tried to hold back the tide by wearing traditional Ryukyuan kimonos and conversing in Okinawan. But her children could not help being caught up in the excitement of Japan's military victories. On hearing of the Japanese navy's surprise attack on Pearl Harbor, Yoshiko felt "very proud" and "admired the brave Japanese soldiers." Until that point, she noted, "Japan had never experienced defeat and we had a feeling of superiority...People were intoxicated as if at a festival." By the start of 1942 she was "burning with patriotism" and pledged she would do her "utmost for the nation."

But as the tide of war turned against Japan in May 1942, with defeat at the naval battle of Midway (the first of many at American hands), and rationing was introduced, her ardor began to cool. By the summer of 1944, with the war creeping ever closer, Okinawan housewives had been herded into "Japanese Imperial Women's Defense Associations," and everyone, bar young children and the elderly, was put to work constructing tunnels and fortifications. As a middle-school student, Yoshiko was sent to build air-raid shelters and artillery emplacements at nearby Oroku and Urasoe. "Soldiers dug with picks," she wrote, "and put the dirt into small baskets. The first girl in a line handed each basket to the next girl, and then to the next." It was backbreaking work, and the girls' soft hands quickly "became as coarse as those of construction workers." When the soldiers signaled a break, they sat under pine trees and "licked small pieces of seaweed and cubed black sugar."[1]

To reduce the size of the population on Okinawa, and therefore its pressure on "precious foodstuffs," civilians were encouraged to evacuate to the home islands. More than 80,000 were moved to Kyushu, mostly in 1944, on "munitions vessels that were otherwise returning to Japan empty." The evacuees included Tsuru Uezato, the 18-year-old daughter of a family who lived near the Sakumotos, and who was like a sister to Yoshiko. Two days before her departure, Tsuru asked

Yoshiko to spend the afternoon with her. As they lay side by side on a futon, talking, Yoshiko thought she saw a figure appear in the doorway, with water dripping from her hair. "I was so scared," she wrote, "I thought I would faint, and I screamed...They looked under the floor and behind the back door, but found no one."

Two days later, on August 21, 1944, Tsuru boarded the *Tsushima Maru* for her new life working in a parachute factory on the mainland. She never arrived. The ship was torpedoed en route by the U.S. Navy submarine *Bowfin* and sank with the loss of more than 1,500 lives. The dead included Tsuru and 765 of the 834 Okinawan schoolchildren on board. One of the survivors, 13-year-old Tsuneko Miyagi, was on deck when three torpedoes struck at 10:00 p.m. on the 22nd and was blown overboard by the explosion. She counted twenty-five people clinging to debris near her. But as the hours passed, many gave up and slipped under the water. She might have done the same had a soldier not slapped her. "Don't sleep," he told her. "If you sleep you die." For four days Tsuneko struggled to survive, fighting off sharks and rescuing a 4-year-old boy she discovered floating beside her. Finally she and the boy were rescued by Japanese patrol boats and taken to the mainland. "I was angry," she said. "Angry. I wanted to kill ten American soldiers for what they did."[2]

Yoshiko felt much the same as she watched American bombs rain down on Naha six weeks later. She arrived home to find her mother emptying the house of furniture and clothes; her father had been sent to the Ryukyuan island of Miyako to build ships, and Yoshiko had "never felt so helpless" in his absence. Gathering up her younger brothers and as many valuables as they could carry, they headed for a nearby cave that had been designated as an evacuation shelter. Once Yoshiko and her brothers were safely inside, their mother returned twice to their house to collect food and even the family shrine.

Soon many of the city's mostly wooden buildings were burning, and the fires were approaching Tomari. Watching awestruck from the mouth of the cave, Yoshiko saw "Higa's Barber Shop near the Tomari Bridge" go up in flames. "After that the fire spread rapidly and the wind blew sparks on to houses along the shore. Once the houses caught fire, they collapsed one by one with a roaring sound. Finally my house started burning. My mother and I watched in tears. All the furniture and other things that had been left inside were lost."

As the fires raged "ever more furiously," Yoshiko could see residents trying to escape along the shoreline. "Long lines of hundreds, maybe thousands, of people were running, but many did not survive... The city of Naha was destroyed easily by just a few enemy planes."[3]

In fact, the dawn attack on Naha and other targets on Okinawa was one of the heaviest delivered by a U.S. carrier task force to that date in the war. It involved 1,356 strikes, in which 652 rockets and twenty-one torpedoes were fired, and 541 tons of bombs were dropped on airfields, harbor facilities, shipping and other strategic targets. The resultant fires destroyed four-fifths of the city. According to an American report, Japanese losses were twenty-three planes shot down and a further eighty-eight destroyed on the ground; and twenty cargo ships, forty-five smaller vessels, four midget submarines, a destroyer escort, a submarine tender, and a mine sweeper were sunk. Japanese sources added a destroyer and another mine sweeper, 5 million machine-gun rounds and 300,000 sacks of unpolished rice. "The enemy," noted a Japanese soldier, "is brazenly planning to destroy every last ship, cut our supply lines and attack us."[4]

The bombing of Naha had two immediate consequences for the island's defenders: the loss of most of the island's stockpile of gasoline, which meant, in turn, the rationing of motorized transport for the movement of men and supplies; and the decision to relocate General Ushijima's command post from Tsukazan to a system of caves beneath Shuri Castle which were enlarged and filled with beds, office equipment and communication systems.

But it was the withdrawal of the veteran 9th Infantry Division—the best on the island—from Okinawa to the Philippines in November 1944 that forced General Mitsuru Ushijima, commanding the Japanese Thirty-Second Army, and his chief of operations Colonel Hiromichi Yahara to review both their defense plans and their operational doctrine. Now, with far fewer reliable combat soldiers, Yahara chose to defend only the strategically critical bottom third of the island. He assigned his force as follows: the 24th Division would guard the extreme south, including the towns of Itoman and Minatoga; the 62nd Division was given the vital central isthmus sector where the main line of defenses would be sited, and which extended from Naha–Yonabaru to Chatan–Toguchi further north; beyond that, defending the Yontan and Kadena airfields, was the

44th Independent Mixed Brigade (IMB). The only significant force in the north of the island was the Kunigami Detachment of two infantry battalions on the Motobu Peninsula.

The plan at this stage was for the enemy "to be contained by a strategic delaying action," and not openly attacked in a "decisive battle." But Yahara also had to take account of pressure from the IGHQ in Tokyo which wanted a vigorous defense of *all* the airfields on Okinawa. The theoretical task of the 44th IMB was to protect the Yontan and Kadena airfields for as long as possible in the event of a major American landing at Hagushi, and to counter-attack if the opportunity arose. In reality, Yahara wanted the 44th merely to harass the invaders before falling back on the lines of the 62nd Division to the south.

The role of the 62nd, meanwhile, was to prepare to fight on a line facing north if the Americans landed at Hagushi, and to join the 24th Division if the landing was near Itoman or Minatoga. It was also expected to repel any landings on the beaches near Machinato airfield, north of Naha. The 24th Division would do likewise: defend its sector on the coast and reinforce the 62nd if the direction of attack was from the north. So the plan was clear: the Americans would be attacked immediately if they landed anywhere on the rugged central isthmus or the southern landmass; but an assault any further north, particularly against the open Hagushi plain, would be largely uncontested. Either way, the Americans would "eventually come up against the Shuri defenses, where the main battle would be fought."[5]

In January 1945, Ushijima sent his chief of staff, the bullish Major General Isamu Chō, for a conference at IGHQ in Tokyo to discuss the overall strategy for Okinawa's defense. Incredibly Japan's military leadership was still clinging to the belief that suicide weapons alone would be enough to deter a successful invasion. According to Chō's civilian secretary Akira Shimada,* his boss was told by senior officers at the conference that "Thirty-Second Army units were not to fire on [American] shipping in the event of an attempted landing on Okinawa" because "kamikaze suicide planes and similar units" would alone destroy "the greater part of [American] naval forces, without

* Not to be confused with his 43-year-old namesake who was governor of the Okinawa Prefecture. Chō's secretary was eight years younger.

forcing shore batteries to give away their positions by premature firing."[6]

Dismissing such talk as wishful thinking, Yahara went on a tour of his units and concluded that they were too thinly spread to repel a concentrated attack. Imperial Japanese Army (IJA) doctrine recommended a defensive front of six miles per division; whereas at Okinawa the Thirty-Second Army's two and a half divisions were spread over thirty-six miles of front, of which twenty-four miles had to be actively defended. So he shortened the division fronts by withdrawing the 44th IMB from the Hagushi plain to share some of the area that had been covered by the 62nd Division; and by transferring the defense of the Oroku Peninsula, south of Naha, from the 24th Division to a 3,000-strong Naval Base Force under Rear Admiral Minoru Ōta. Now the only force guarding the Yontan and Kadena airfields was a weak regiment of Boeitai (Home Guard).[7]

"In the eyes of IGHQ," noted a study of the Japanese view of the battle, "Okinawa was part of a multitheater, technology-intensive strategy in which Thirty-Second Army's specialized role was to defend the Yontan and Kadena airfields. The Thirty-Second Army staff members' perceptions were simpler: Thirty-Second Army was about to be attacked and needed defensible positions to survive. The staff members had no confidence that air forces could interdict the Americans... Even so, the staff's final operational plans amounted to nothing more nor less than denying the enemy the ground, foot by foot."[8]

For a brief moment in late January 1945 it looked as if help was on its way. IGHQ messaged that the 84th Infantry Division would be sent to Okinawa as a replacement for the 9th. But later that day the order was rescinded because IGHQ had had second thoughts about denuding Japan's home islands of troops when they might soon be under attack. To raise spirits, Yahara wrote and disseminated a pamphlet titled "The Road to Certain Victory" in which he argued that defensive fortifications would counteract the Americans' marked advantage in troop numbers and firepower.

Seemingly convinced, soldiers and civilians carried on with great enthusiasm the work of expanding existing caves, and building a network of tunnels and concrete machine-gun posts. Lacking specialized tunneling equipment, they used entrenching tools, picks and shovels to hack into the tough coral rock. Once through the outer crust, however, the soil was a soft red clay, and relatively easy to dig into. With no cement or iron to shore up the tunnels, each unit cut wooden beams from pine forests in the mountainous north, and moved them south in native boats called *sabenis*, often at night to avoid American air raids. By late March, more than sixty miles of underground fortifications and command posts had been constructed, as well as anti-tank minefields and gun emplacements.[9]

Efforts had also been made from January onwards, recalled Chō's secretary Shimada,

> to mobilize virtually the entire civilian manpower of Okinawa for use as Army auxiliaries. Additional Home Guard levies were made, designed to supplement the earlier conscriptions of the fall of 1944. Almost the entire student body of the Middle Schools, the Vocational Schools and the Shuri Normal School was organized into guerilla units, the most prominent of which was the celebrated Blood-and-Iron-for-the-Emperor Duty Unit (Tekketsu Kinno Tai). The students were trained in infiltration tactics by a Capt[ain] Hirose, an expert on guerilla warfare who had been sent to Thirt-Second Army from Imperial HQ for the express purpose of coordinating the activities of infiltration groups and similar irregular forces.[10]

Among the 2,000 Okinawan schoolboys, aged 14 to 18, who were recruited into the Blood and Iron Student Corps was Shigetomo Higa, a fourth-grader from Sikiyama in Shuri who attended the Okinawa First Prefectural Middle School. When Shigetomo joined the school in 1941, it was "quite free and relaxed." But with the arrival of Principal Norio Fujino a year later, the atmosphere became more militarist. In 1944, Shigetomo's five-year program of study was cut short by a year as part of the Emergency Student Mobilization Outline: most classes were canceled and Shigetomo—like his female contemporary Yoshiko Sakumoto—spent most of his time on labor details constructing airfields and gun emplacements.

After the fall of Saipan in the summer of 1944, Shigetomo attended a lecture given by General Watanabe, Ushijima's predecessor as Thirty-Second Army commander. "There is no doubt," declared a tearful Watanabe, thumping the desk before him, "that the enemy will land in Okinawa and, when that happens, every civilian must share the same fate as our soldiers, so I am asking you to be ready to die a glorious death in the name of the emperor." Shigetomo was shocked by both the general's appearance and message. He had always assumed that Japan would win the war. Now, one of the country's senior generals was admitting that defeat was all but inevitable.

In late February 1945, Shigetomo's father was conscripted into the Boeitai, and attached to the 24th Division. A month later, on March 27, 1945, Shigetomo graduated from middle school and was recruited into the Blood and Iron Student Corps in an evening ceremony that was held in the garden of his school dormitory. As American shells exploded in the distance, he and his 253 fellow graduates stood in rows, facing their principal Norio Fujino, his teaching staff and two VIP guests, governor of Okinawa Akira Shimada and a colonel from the 5th Artillery Command.

Suddenly, a shell landed with a resounding "thump" close to where they were standing. The instinct of Shigetomo and his colleagues was to run. They were stopped by the booming voice of Lieutenant Yashushi Shinohara, the officer attached to the school. "Don't move!" yelled Shinohara. "Nobody is to move!"

The result, according to Shigetomo, was "quite amazing." All the officials and students were "trembling" but "nobody moved a muscle, not even the governor." Another two or three shells landed "almost on top of us" before the ceremony was over, "but not a single soul had moved." Finally, Shinohara introduced the artillery colonel and said that, henceforth, the boys would come under his command.

The following day they were issued with patched-up military uniforms—each with a floating chrysanthemum badge* on its breast—and told they were part of the Blood and Iron First Middle School Unit. Shigetomo was assigned to No. 2 Platoon. But their lowly status as privates second class was soon confirmed when regular soldiers called them "little pricks" and slapped them for failing to salute their superiors. "Just a while ago," remembered Shigetomo, "we were all digging shelters together and the next thing they were looking down on us because of our lower rank."

* This insignia for a Blood and Iron Student unit was later removed.

Told to pen farewell letters to their parents, Shigetomo wrote:

> Dear Mother and Father—You have looked after me for sixteen years but now the time has come for me to leave. Even if you hear that I have been killed in the fighting, please do not feel sad. As your only son, I will be sorry to die without repaying the debt I owe you...I am so grateful to you both and thank you from the bottom of my heart for all you have done for me.

Shigetomo chose not to write the sort of propaganda statements that his superiors expected, and that many of his fellow students produced. One told his parents that he wanted "to die a glorious death for my country," and if they heard of his demise they should "smile." But Shigetomo understood why his comrade did it. "We were," he noted, "only sixteen but the militarist education we had received had gone to the depths of our very souls."[11]

4

The Divine Wind

"The late afternoon sun," recalled Captain Rikihei Inoguchi, "was about to sink below the crest line of the mountains to the west of Mabalacat airfield, which formed part of the sprawling Clark Base complex, some fifty miles northwest of Manila. Ground crewmen wearing the work uniform of the Imperial Japanese Navy Air Forces [IJNAF] scurried here and there like ants, hurrying to conceal planes in revetments before dusk and to carry out attack preparations for the following morning."

It was October 19, 1944, and Inoguchi was sitting in the airfield command post, a tattered old tent, talking with the XO (executive officer) of the IJNAF's 201st Air Group, Commander Asaichi Tamai. Inoguchi had come from Manila, where he was senior staff officer of the 1st Air Fleet, to discuss with Tamai the 201st's attack plan for the following day. Two days earlier, a huge U.S. naval force had appeared off Suluan Island, at the mouth of Leyte Gulf, and it was obvious that a large-scale invasion of the Philippines was imminent.* "Yet," noted Inoguchi, "the Japanese air forces in the entire Philippines area had fewer than one hundred planes still in operational condition to throw into the breach. What could we do?"

Friends since their naval academy days, Inoguchi and Tamai "spoke frankly" of the difficulties confronting the Japanese defenders, but were "at a loss to hit upon any plan that might offer a way out of the desperate situation." As they talked, a black limousine drove up to the command post, flying the yellow pennant of a flag officer. A stocky figure got out, accompanied by a single aide. It was Inoguchi's

* After preliminary operations against three small islands in Leyte Gulf, the main landings on Leyte by General MacArthur's forces began on October 20, 1944.

new boss Vice Admiral Takijiro Ōnishi who, just two days earlier, had arrived in Manila from Tokyo to take command of the 1st Air Fleet.

The two officers sprang to their feet and offered Ōnishi a chair. He sat down and, for a few minutes, watched silently as "the airfield crews worked feverishly in the fading daylight." Eventually he turned to the officers and said, "I have come here to discuss with you something of great importance. May we go to your headquarters?"

Ōnishi gave them a lift in his limousine back to the dusty town of Mabalacat where the 201st Air Group's headquarters were located in a cream-colored house with a green trim that "gave a pleasing, homey effect." Inside, however, most of the regular furniture on the ground floor had been replaced with folding canvas cots for the thirty officer fliers who lived in the building. Scattered throughout were their flight gear, towels, washing kits and personal possessions.

After Vice Admiral Ōnishi had taken a phone call, they gathered in a room on the second floor with another staff officer and two squadron leaders. The only notable absentee was the commander of the 201st, Captain Sakae Yamamoto, who had been called to a meeting with Ōnishi in Manila and, unknowingly, the two cars had passed each other en route. Once all six were seated round a small table, Ōnishi began speaking. "As you know," he said in a low voice, "the war situation is grave. The appearance of strong American forces in the Leyte Gulf has been confirmed. The fate of the empire depends upon the outcome of the Sho operation,* which Imperial Headquarters has activated to hurl back the enemy assault on the Philippines. Vice Admiral Kurita's 2nd Fleet, containing our main battle strength, will advance to the Leyte area and annihilate the enemy invasion force. The mission of the 1st Air Fleet is to provide land-based air cover for Admiral Kurita's advance and make sure the enemy air attacks do not prevent him from reaching Leyte Gulf. To do this, we must hit the enemy's carriers and keep them neutralized for at least one week."

* Operation Sho (or "Victory") was a defensive–offensive plan, formulated after the fall of Saipan, that declared the Americans' next major target as the "theater of decisive battle" to which all available forces would be rushed to defeat the enemy. The plan was activated by IGHQ on October 18. (Inoguchi and Nakajima, *The Divine Wind*, p. 6n.)

Inoguchi was at a loss to know how this could be done. Recent American carrier strikes had crippled Japanese air strength in the Philippines, reducing the 201st Air Group's fighter strength to just thirty operational planes. But sensing that Ōnishi had come to Mabalacat for a reason, he waited for him "to provide the answer." When it came, it caught Inoguchi by complete surprise.

"In my opinion," said Ōnishi, "there is only one way of ensuring that our meager strength will be effective to a maximum degree. That is to organize suicide attack units composed of Zero fighters armed with 250-kilogram bombs, with each plane to crash-dive into an enemy carrier." He let the words sink in, before adding: "What do you think?"

It seemed a shocking suggestion, but not one that floored Inoguchi and his comrades. Instead, he recalled, it "struck a spark in each of us." Such "body-crashing" (*tai-atari*) tactics were not unique. They had already been used by navy pilots in air-to-air combat against enemy bombers, and there were, Inoguchi knew, "many fliers in the combat air units who had urged that the same tactics be employed against the carriers." They did not welcome death; but found it easier to contemplate in the dark days of late 1944 when, as Inoguchi put it, the "chance of coming back alive from any sorties against enemy carriers was very slim, regardless of the attack method employed. If one is bound to die, what is more natural than the desire to die effectively, at maximum cost to the enemy?"

The silence that followed Ōnishi's words was, therefore, neither "consternation nor dread," but calm contemplation. Commander Tamai spoke first. "Yoshioka," he asked the staff officer, "just how effective would it be for a plane carrying a 250-kilogram bomb to smash bodily into a carrier's flight deck?"

"The chances of scoring a hit," replied Yoshioka, "would be much greater than by conventional bombing. It would probably take several days to repair the damage to the flight deck."

Nodding, Tamai turned to Ōnishi and said: "As executive officer I cannot decide a matter of such gravity. I must ask our group commander, Captain Sakae Yamamoto."

There was, said Ōnishi, no need. "I have just spoken on the phone with Captain Yamamoto in Manila. His leg was broken in a plane crash and he is in hospital. He said that I should consider your opinions as his own, and that he would leave everything up to you."

After a pause, Tamai asked for a few minutes to consider the matter with one of his squadron commanders. When Ōnishi gave his approval, the pair left for Tamai's room where they discussed the pilots' likely reaction to the news. Soon they returned and Tamai said: "Entrusted by our commander with full responsibility, I share completely the opinions expressed by the admiral. The 201st Air Group will carry out his proposal. May I ask that you leave to us the organization of our crash dive unit?"

Ōnishi nodded his assent, his face bearing "a look of relief coupled with a shadow of sorrow." He then left to get some rest and the momentous meeting was over.

Tamai's task now was to consider which pilots to choose for the mission. Most had only completed half of their combat training when they were posted to the Marianas for active duty. They had, since that time, "fought continuously, and against terrible odds." In early August the survivors had been sent to the southern Philippines and incorporated into the 201st Air Group, down to about a third of its original strength. "They were now steel-fibered veterans and their morale was high," recalled Inoguchi. "Commander Tamai, who had inspired them during their training period and had shared the hardships of uphill battles...was as deeply attached to these men as a father to his children."

After consulting with his squadron commanders, Tamai held a parade of his remaining twenty-three non-commissioned pilots at which he explained Admiral Ōnishi's proposal. "In a frenzy of emotion and joy," wrote Inoguchi, "the arms of every pilot in the assembly went up in a gesture of complete accord."

Tamai and Inoguchi then chose Lieutenant Yukio Seki, a 23-year-old Naval Academy graduate of the "highest character and ability" to lead the new unit. Originally trained on carrier-based bombers, Seki had been with the 201st for only a month. But in that time he had impressed Tamai with his energy and fervent patriotism. Woken and told that he was being considered for the command of a new suicide unit, Seki paused for a full five seconds, eyes closed and head in hands, before replying: "You absolutely must let me do it."

"Thank you," replied Tamai, tears in his eyes. "You're a bachelor aren't you?"

"No, I have a wife, sir."

It was a shame, but not enough to disqualify Seki. All that remained was to choose a title for the new unit. "Since this is a special mission," said Inoguchi, "we should have a special name. How about Shimpū Unit?"*

Tamai thought it was an excellent idea. Shimpū was, he knew, another name for kamikaze (or "divine wind"), the term used to describe the fierce typhoons that had destroyed the Mongol fleet of Kublai Khan in the thirteenth century, thus saving Japan from invasion. "That's good," he replied. "After all, we have to set a kamikaze in motion with it."[1]

Seki, meanwhile, had returned to his quarters to pen farewell letters to Mariko, his wife of five months, and his parents. "I am very sorry," he wrote to her, "that I must 'scatter' [a reference to the scattering of cherry blossoms, or dying in battle] before I could do much for you. I know that as a spouse of a military man, you are prepared to face such a situation."

With his parents, he was more candid. "At this time the nation is at the crossroads of defeat, and the problem can only be resolved by each individual's repayment of the Imperial Benevolence." He would, therefore, "carry out a body-crashing attack on an aircraft carrier." He added: "I am resigned to do this."

As his deadly mission drew closer, however, Seki seemed to have questioned its rationale. "Japan's future is bleak," he told a journalist, "if it is forced to kill one of its best pilots—myself. I am confident that I can deliver a 500-kilogram bomb on the flight deck of an enemy aircraft carrier and come back alive!" There was, he knew, no backing out now. But he wanted to explain that—contrary to what he had told his parents—the real reason he was going on the mission was not "for the emperor or for the empire," but rather for his "beloved wife" and because he was "ordered to." He added: "Should Japan lose the

* The official name for the new suicide unit was Shimpū Tokubetsu Kōgekitai (Divine Wind Special Attack Units), often shortened to Shimpū Tokkōtai. The alternative word "kamikaze" was only used informally in the Japanese press after the Second World War.

war, only the gods know what the enemy would do to my dear wife. A man dies for the lady he loves most. That's glorious."[2]

To many of the Allies, steeped in the Judaeo-Christian tradition of the sanctity of life, the apparent willingness of Japanese servicemen like Seki to carry out suicide attacks was profoundly shocking. But then, as scholars of the kamikaze point out, the word suicide in Japanese does not always have the same "immoral connotation" that it has in English. Two versions—*jiketsu* (self-determination) and *jisai* (self-judgment)—"suggest an honorable or laudable act done in the public interest." There is, moreover, no ethical or religious taboo regarding suicide in Japan's traditional religion of Shintoism. Instead, the Japanese samurai warrior code of "bushido"—heavily influenced by Shintoism, as well as Buddhism and even Confucianism—revered self-sacrifice and fighting to the bitter end for emperor and country. To surrender, on the other hand, was seen as dishonorable, hence the contempt the Japanese felt for prisoners of war. Japanese soldiers believed that when they fell on the field of battle they would become *kami*, or gods, and join the nation's guardian spirits at the Shinto shrine of Yasukuni in Tokyo. Hence the typical farewell from members of the Shimpū Special Attack Corps: "I'll meet you at the Yasukuni Shrine!"[3]

The Shimpū Unit's first mission was on October 25, 1944, during the Battle of Leyte Gulf, when Lieutenant Seki led five Mitsubishi Zeros, each carrying a 250-kilogram bomb, against a cluster of U.S. Navy escort carriers. Two planes were shot down by anti-aircraft fire, but the other three got through, damaging two carriers and sinking a third, the USS *St. Lo*, after fires caused the ship's magazine to explode. It is believed that Seki hit the *St. Lo*. By the end of the following day, further kamikaze attacks had struck a total of seven carriers and forty others ships (sinking five, badly damaging twenty-three and moderately damaging twelve).

On hearing of these first suicide attacks, the 43-year-old Emperor Hirohito, who had ruled Japan since the death of his father in 1926, asked: "Was it necessary to go to this extreme?" But, he added, "They have certainly done a good job."[4]

These early successes caused an immediate expansion of the kamikaze program to include all types of planes—fighters, bombers and even training aircraft, many flown by inexperienced pilots—as well as piloted flying bombs (Ōhkas),* motorboats packed with explosives (Shinyō), and human torpedoes (Kaiten). One of the earliest volunteers for the Kaiten Corps was Naoji Kōzu, a former student at the Tokyo Imperial University who had been conscripted into the Japanese Imperial Navy. Unlike the early members of the Shimpū Unit, he was never told he would be going to a place "from which I'd have absolutely no chance to return." He found out the truth only when he was assigned to Hikari, the Kaiten base in southern Honshu, and saw the craft for himself.

"The body," he recalled, "was painted flat black. It overwhelmed a man. A small sail and a tiny periscope located at its center seemed to disturb the harmony of the whole. The rear third was a Type-93 torpedo. A maintenance officer described it to us dispassionately. 'The total length is fourteen point five meters. Diameter, one meter. The crew is one man. Explosive charge one point six metric tons. Navigation range seventy-eight thousand meters. Maximum speed thirty knots.'"

The details aside, Kōzu had only to look at the position of the pilot, in a tiny cockpit in the center of the Kaiten, to know it was a suicide weapon from which there would be no escape. Overcome with emotion, he could not speak. "I felt," he wrote, "that I myself turned into something no longer human." There was, he discovered, a way out of the corps: by failing to operate the Kaiten properly during test runs. But he never seriously considered that option because it would have meant someone else taking his place. "I couldn't bear the idea of sacrificing someone else by quitting. I knew if I did, I'd regret it for the rest of my life."[5]

By January 1945, the kamikaze (or special attack) units were at the center of IGHQ plans—codenamed Operation Ten-Go—to defeat the next phase of the American advance in the Pacific, probably against Okinawa. "I firmly believed," said Rear Admiral Sadatoshi Tomioka, chief of operations at the Naval General Staff, "that

* The largest Ōhka attack—featuring small single-seated wooden aircraft, laden with almost 4,000 pounds of explosives, and carried to within thirteen miles of the target by a twin-engined bomber—was made against U.S. aircraft carriers on March 21, 1945. All sixteen bombers and their Ōhka missiles were either shot down or lost before they reached their target.

Okinawa alone was the decisive battleground where we would be able to reverse the war situation." The navy's strategy was to deliver such a severe blow to the attacking American forces that it would force them to the negotiating table. But the problem for the IJN—which was expected to do the bulk of the fighting both on the sea and in the air—was that its surface force was down to just a handful of battleships and no aircraft carriers, while its depleted stock of planes and pilots, particularly its special attack units, would need to be replenished before it could carry out a large-scale air operation. That was unlikely to be before May 1945.[6]

But the navy's warnings were ignored and on February 6, 1945, IGHQ issued the Ten-Go Air Operations Agreement for the navy and army to provide 2,000 and 1,350 planes respectively—those numbers to include 740 special-attack planes—to hurl against the advancing U.S. fleet. With the die cast, the IJN stepped up its preparations. "Although the training could not be completed," recalled Commander Yoshimori Terai, the air operations chief on the Naval General Staff, "we intended to carry out the operations forcibly by employing special-attack tactics."[7]

The navy's intention was to slow down the American advance on Okinawa by launching a kamikaze attack against the carriers of the U.S. 5th Fleet in their anchorage at Ulithi atoll in the Caroline Islands, the so-called Operation Tan No. 2, on March 11, 1945. But only two of the twenty-four twin-engine bombers, each carrying 800-kilogram bombs, made it as far as Ulithi: one struck the stern of the aircraft carrier USS *Randolph*, just below the flight deck, killing twenty-seven sailors and wounding 105; the other crashed into a road on the small island of Sorlen, mistaking a signal tower for a ship. As a result of this largely failed mission, noted Commander Terai, the IJN was "forced to face the Okinawa operations unprepared."[8]

5

"More concerned with furlough than fighting"

At 8:10 a.m. on Thursday January 18, 1945, a four-engine Douglas C-54 Skymaster transport plane lifted off from Hickam Field, near Pearl Harbor, and set a course for Tarawa atoll in the Gilbert Islands. The plane had been specially adapted to carry VIPs, and was fitted with upholstered seats, a washroom and a small pantry, complete with "an electric warmer for heating coffee and food." It even had an Air Transport Command officer on board to ensure that the four passengers had everything they needed. They were Lieutenant General Simon B. Buckner Jr., and three members of his staff: Brigadier General Oliver P. Smith, Colonel Louis B. Ely (his G-2, or chief of intelligence), and Major Frank Hubbard (his aide).[1]

Buckner had spent the last few months assembling the troops of his Tenth Army—a total potential force of 375,000, of whom 175,000 were to take part in the assault of Okinawa—on paper; now he wanted to see them in the flesh. So once the final draft of the operation plan had been distributed in mid-January, he was free to "visit the major combat units, observe the condition of the troops, and personally discuss the operation plan with the corps commanders."

After an eleven-hour flight from Pearl Harbor—during which they crossed the date line—Buckner and his party reached Tarawa, the site of a vicious seventy-two-hour battle in November 1943 that had cost the U.S. 2nd Marine Division more than 3,000 casualties; of the 4,800 Japanese and Korean defenders, only 136 surrendered (including just one Japanese officer and sixteen men). The plan was to stay the night in Tarawa before continuing on to Espiritu Santo the following day. But as they had got in early enough, they went on a tour of the island and found "evidences of the bitter battle which took place there, in the form of ruined Japanese bunkers and blockhouses and a scattering of abandoned amphibious tracked vehicles and tanks. And, of course, the cemeteries were still there."[2]

Espiritu Santo in the New Hebrides, the first proper stop on the tour, was reached during the afternoon of Saturday the 20th. They were met by Major General George W. Griner Jr., commanding the 27th Infantry Division, the formation that had performed so poorly on Saipan. Buckner and his staff knew all too well the controversy concerning the 27th Division—particularly the Smith vs Smith imbroglio—and were hopeful that Griner had put matters right. But it did not seem that way when Oliver Smith heard from Griner's artillery chief, Brigadier General Ferrin, that the division "was beaten down and did not know whether or not it wanted to fight." Griner and his senior officers were doing their best to rectify this—to "instill in the men a desire to prove that the division was really a good division"—but the jury was still out.[3]

Next day, during his tour of inspection, Buckner spent time asking individual soldiers who "look well" what they "wanted to do most." He was hoping to hear they were thirsting for combat. But most were more concerned, as Buckner put it in his diary, "with furlough than fighting." The island was very hot and the men seemed to spend their time swimming, fishing and sailing; the only evidence of training that Smith saw was "a rifle range." The net result of the visit was to "lessen" Buckner's confidence in the 27th. "He did not say this," noted Smith, "but I could feel it. I know I was not impressed with this division and this was not simply because it was an Army division. The difference between the 27th and the other Army divisions we saw later was very apparent."[4]

The first point of comparison was during the next stop at New Caledonia, "a very rugged and beautiful island" where the 81st Infantry Division, part of Buckner's floating reserve, was stationed. Smith thought the division's training area—located on rolling hills overlooking the sea—the best he had seen in the Pacific. "I had," he remembered, "served with a part of the 81st Division (321st RCT) on Peleliu, and at that time did not consider the troops to be of the first order, but after seeing the 27th they looked very good."[5]

A couple of days later they arrived in Guadalcanal where Major General Roy S. Geiger, commanding the III Amphibious Corps (or

III Phibcorps), had his headquarters. Born in Florida in 1885—and therefore a year senior to Buckner—Geiger would celebrate his 60th birthday during the visit. Unusually he had earned a law degree before enlisting in the U.S. Marine Corps as a private at the age of 22. During the First World War, by then an officer, Geiger was just the fifth Marine Corps aviator, leading bombing raids for which he was awarded the Navy Cross. The bulk of his service since then—apart from attending courses at the Command and General Staff College, Fort Leavenworth, and the U.S. Army War College—had been in Marine aviation. During the early part of the Guadalcanal campaign, for example, he had led the legendary Cactus Air Force, earning a Gold Star in lieu of a second Navy Cross. In 1943 he commanded I Amphibious Corps at Bougainville, and a year later led III Amphibious Corps in the Guam and Palau islands campaigns. His capable leadership had earned him the equivalent of three Distinguished Service Medals.

Geiger enjoyed, therefore, a deserved reputation as an unflappable commander who could be relied on in a crisis. Buckner certainly had a high opinion of him and, shortly after this tour of inspection, tried to get Nimitz to nominate the Marine general as his successor if he was a casualty. The letter was sent via General Richardson, Buckner's immediate superior, who returned it with a note stating that only the War Department had the authority to make such a decision and that, henceforth, "no member of the Tenth Army staff" would even mention it to Nimitz. Buckner "was considerably put out, but let the matter rest, with the idea of making the designation after landing on Okinawa, over which General Richardson had no control."[6]

Buckner's first inspection was of units of the 6th Marine Division under Major General Lemuel C. Shepherd, who had fought with the 5th Marines at Belleau Wood in 1918, receiving two wounds and three gallantry medals (including the Navy Cross and the French Croix de Guerre). More recently he had served as the 1st Marine Division's assistant commander at Cape Gloucester, and led the 1st Provisional Marine Brigade—the formation out of which the 6th Division grew—at Guam.

For Buckner's visit, Shepherd had provided a guard of honor in full combat equipment: utility clothing, combat packs and helmets with covers. "They looked very well," noted Oliver Smith, "and very businesslike." Buckner then inspected some of the 29th Marines' quarters and watched the 4th Marines demonstrate a firing problem. "It involved," recalled Smith, "the attack of a hill, using all infantry weapons: tanks, mortars, machine guns, flamethrowers, grenades, demolition charges, rifles and carbines. No punches were pulled and no blank ammunition was used. It was a very impressive demonstration of the [regiment's] state of training...The men knew what they were about."[7]

They then moved up the beach to observe the gunners of the 15th Marines (Artillery) firing their 155 mm howitzers directly at the mouth of a cave, a technique developed on Peleliu to soften up defenders of fixed positions before the infantry moved in. Buckner—who had received a traditional training in artillery techniques at Leavenworth and the Army War College—was expecting the Marine gunners to bracket the cave mouth before getting on target. When they instead "crept" rounds toward the cave, he accused them of being "slow in getting on target in direct anti-cave fire." This irritated Smith who felt that Buckner, with no practical experience of either direct or indirect artillery fire, should have held his tongue. "I explained to him the value of direct fire as demonstrated at Peleliu," wrote Smith, "but I do not know whether or not I convinced him."[8]

After lunch they witnessed a rifle platoon from the 29th Marines assault three caves with live ammunition. First they fired machine guns and rifles to cover the approach, then a bazooka and a white phosphorus grenade, and finally a flamethrower followed by a demolition charge. "It was," thought Smith, "a very realistic demonstration and gave the men a very accurate idea of what they would be up against in the actual reduction of cave positions." Buckner and his staff, he believed, "were thoroughly impressed."

That was only partially true, as Buckner's diary entry makes clear. "29th Regiment," he noted, "had sloppy q[uarte]rs & apparently poor discipline but splendid weapon teamwork." The battalion exercise by the 4th Marines, on the other hand, "got out of hand" as tanks and men "exposed themselves instead of using cover."[9]

Next day, Buckner moved on to the veteran 1st Marine Division, commanded by Major General Pedro Del Valle, the son of the former Spanish governor of Puerto Rico, who had become a U.S. citizen only in 1917.* A Marine artilleryman, Del Valle had commanded the 11th Marines at Guadalcanal and the III Phibcorps artillery at Guam, before taking over the 1st Marine Division from Major General William H. Rupertus after Peleliu. Stationed on Pavavu in the Russell Islands, Del Valle regularly brought his rifle regiments—the 1st, 5th and 7th Marines—over to Guadalcanal where there was more room to train. Buckner watched one of them conduct an exercise with artillery and tanks, and again thought the latter were "too much exposed."[10]

The tour continued on to the Philippine island of Leyte, via the island of Biak (off the northern coast of New Guinea), where they were met by the commander of XXIV Corps, Major General John R. Hodge, a former teacher at Mississippi State whose men were still reducing the final pockets of Japanese resistance. As they traveled the island, meeting the commanders and men of the 7th ("Hourglass"), 77th ("Statue of Liberty") and 96th ("Deadeye") Infantry Divisions, Oliver Smith noted the lack of evidence of "bitter fighting." He wrote: "I saw no caves or pillboxes and no pockmarked terrain. There were burned or destroyed villages, but most of the buildings were of wooden construction and were not suitable for a stubborn defense." Of more concern, however, was the state of Hodge's men. "They were excellent divisions," noted Smith. "However they had been in action on Leyte for three months and two...were still engaged in active operations. The divisions were understrength and adequate replacements were not in sight. There was considerable dysentery and skin infection. Living conditions were very bad."[11]

Buckner worried in his diary that the men of XXIV Corps would get "no real rest" before the Okinawa campaign, and had equipment "badly in need of repair." He considered them "good fighters" and had "great confidence in both my corps." But he was relieved when the staff of MacArthur's South-west Pacific Command assured him on January 29 that their first priority "above everything else" was to get XXIV Corps ready for the next campaign.[12]

One of the low points of the tour was when Buckner was shown pictures by Hodge of the remains of U.S. soldiers who had been "butchered and eaten by Japs." Human flesh, said Hodge, had been

* This was the result of the Jones–Shafroth Act of 1917 which gave U.S. citizenship with limited rights to all Puerto Ricans born on the island.

found in Japanese officers' "mess pans." He also had pictures of Filipino men, women and children who had been "machine-gunned to death" in a church. Buckner was disgusted.[13]

On February 1, they flew on to Guam in the Marianas and, the following day, held a conference with Admiral Nimitz in his new headquarters on the slopes of Mount Tenjo. "The XXIV Corps situation was discussed," recorded Buckner, "and it was decided that no present action would be taken in view of the SW Pac[ific Command]'s promises but that the latter would be watched closely...and action taken if any promises were not lived up to. I expressed myself as preferring to enter the campaign on time but not entirely ready rather than postpone D-Day and give the Japs more time to prepare defenses. In other words, time is working for the Japs, therefore hurry."[14]

That afternoon Buckner's party left for the island of Saipan, just half an hour's flying time from Guam, to visit Major General Thomas E. Watson's 2nd Marine Division. En route, Buckner instructed the pilot to fly via Rota which was still held by the Japanese.* As he entered the cockpit to get a better look, however, Buckner was shocked to find the plane "heading for the center of the island at a very low altitude."

"You do realize," said Buckner, "that there are 5,000 Japs on the island armed with anti-aircraft guns?"

"No, sir," responded the white-faced pilot. He changed course, noted Buckner, "just in time."[15]

On February 3, safely on Saipan, Buckner spent the day with the 2nd Marine Division. The highlight was a divisional parade on a "fairly level" piece of ground. Watson had ordered all uniforms, cartridge belts, canteen covers and packs to be "washed and rewashed until they fairly sparked. Rifles were absolutely spotless." The lead unit was Able Company of the 8th Marines. As it reached the first marker on the parade ground, its commander Captain Fred Haley should have called out, "Left flank—march." Instead he shouted "Column left—march," and chaos ensued. Eventually the battalion commander, Lieutenant Colonel Richard Hayward, stepped in,

* The Japanese garrison on Rota—947 soldiers and 1,853 navy personnel—finally surrendered to a detachment of Marines on September 2, 1945.

"halted the entire Parade, shifted gears into reverse and marched the 1st Battalion off the parade ground in the direction whence it had come." After some choice profanities by Hayward, the parade was resumed and, this time, Haley issued the correct command. He was told later by Marines in the makeshift reviewing stand that the "faintest shadow of a smile" had crossed Buckner's features as the drama unfolded. All Haley noticed was that Buckner had "command presence" and was wearing a steel helmet with three stars that glittered in the sunlight.[16]

Haley's faux pas aside, Buckner was impressed. "Spent the whole day with General Watson inspecting the 2nd Mardiv [Marine Division]," he wrote in his diary. "They appear well trained and well disciplined. I was greatly impressed with the quality of his battalion commanders." He told Oliver Smith that he had "never before had the privilege of meeting such an alert group."[17] They finally arrived back at Pearl Harbor at midnight on February 4, having flown 14,000 miles and crisscrossed most of the Pacific, including eighteen battlefields. Overall, Buckner was "well satisfied with the trip." He was now "familiar with the tools with which he was going to work," and any qualms about the quality of the Marine divisions had been dispelled. His chief of operations (or G-3), Brigadier General Walter A. Dumas, would later describe the Marine divisions as "in magnificent condition and splendidly trained." Bucker's chief concern, therefore, was for his army divisions: he worried that the 27th lacked the stomach for the fight, and that Hodge's XXIV Corps would be under-resourced when it was finally released from MacArthur's command. But, with no time to rectify matters, he would simply hope for the best.[18]

6

"I'm going simply because I've got to—and I hate it"

Soon after Lieutenant General Buckner left Guam in early February 1945, an even bigger celebrity reached the island: the Pulitzer Prize-winning war correspondent Ernie Pyle. Accompanied by twelve officers and three enlisted men, Pyle had flown the 3,500 miles from Hawaii, via the Marshall Islands, in the same type of plane as Buckner, a Douglas C-54, but without its VIP modifications. To make it easier to sleep during the final twenty-four-hour leg, therefore, Pyle had taken his blanket and lain down on some mail bags.

His first view of Guam was from the cockpit, courtesy of the pilot. "We came out of the boundless sky and over our island destination," wrote Pyle, "just a little after dawn. The island was green and beautiful—and terribly far from home. That we could have drawn ourselves to it so unerringly out of the vast Pacific spaces seemed incredible. It was a like a blind man walking alone across a field, and putting his finger directly on some previously designated barb of a wire fence. But…they do it all the time."[1]

Pyle had had an extraordinary career. Born in Dana, Indiana, on August 3, 1900, he saw active service as a petty officer in the U.S. Navy at the tail end of the First World War before attending Indiana University where he edited the *Daily Student* newspaper. Keen to work as a journalist, Pyle quit his economics degree to accept a job at a small newspaper in La Porte, Indiana. He soon moved to the tabloid *Washington Daily News* where he met Geraldine "Jerry" Siebolds, a bright and attractive woman a year his senior, and they married in 1925. But Jerry was a troubled soul, suffering from alcoholism and bouts of mental illness, and they divorced in 1942 before remarrying by proxy a year later. By then Pyle had made his name as a roving correspondent for the Scripps Howard newspaper chain, reporting on the lives of ordinary people in rural America in the 1930s, and ordinary soldiers in the Second World War. His daily column about life at the front for GIs—or "dogfaces" as he affectionately called them—was syndicated to more than 300 newspapers.

In covering the North African, Italian and D-Day campaigns, Pyle had preferred the ground's-eye view to generals' press conferences. He became "the author of letters home" that thousands of soldiers could not, or would not, write. He regarded the average American serviceman as a "good boy," doing "an awful job that had to be done."[2] Their stories deserved to be told, and he was the one to do it. One of his most memorable dispatches, written in January 1944, was "The Death of Captain Waskow." In it he described the demise of a company commander in the 36th Division, a native of Belton, Texas, "only in his middle twenties," who "carried in him a sincerity and gentleness that made people want to be guided by him." After Waskow's body had been lowered from a mule to the ground, a succession of soldiers came to pay their respects. One said: "God damn it to hell anyway."

Another: "I sure am sorry, sir."

Then the first man "squatted down," wrote Pyle, "and he reached down and took the dead hand, and he sat there for a full five minutes, holding the dead hand in his own and looking intently at the dead face, and he never uttered a sound all the time he sat there." Finally he put the hand down, got up, "gently straightened the points of the captain's shirt collar," and "sort of rearranged the tattered edges of his uniform around the wound," before getting up and walking "down the road in the moonlight, all alone."[3]

Pyle continued his unique style of reporting from northwest Europe—living with ordinary soldiers and sharing their privations—until he was almost killed when the USAAF mistakenly dropped bombs on U.S. troops near Saint-Lo in Normandy, on July 25, 1944. A total of 111 Allied soldiers were killed and 490 wounded. The dead included Lieutenant General Leslie J. McNair whose body was so badly mutilated he could be identified only by the three silver stars on his collar. Pyle wrote of "a gigantic rattling" as the bombs fell on the small farm he was visiting. He remembered "hitting the ground flat, all spread out like the cartoons of people flattened by steam rollers and then squirmed like an eel to get under one of the heavy wagons in the shed." Suddenly he and an officer stopped crawling, "feeling it was hopeless to move farther" as the "bombs were already crashing around us." He added: "We just lay sprawled, gaping at each other in futile appeal, our faces about a foot apart until it was over."[4]

After the strain and tension of months on the front line, witnessing countless deaths, the bombing was for Pyle the final straw. He spent more than a week prostrate with fever, diarrhea and nervous exhaustion. Once back on his feet, he decided to go home. "I'm leaving for one reason only," he told his readers, "because I have just got to stop. 'I've had it,' as they say in the Army. I've had all I can take for a while...I've been immersed in it too long. My spirit is wobbly and my mind is confused. The hurt has finally become too great."[5]

He was almost certainly suffering from post-traumatic stress disorder (PTSD), and had been for a while. A year earlier, working on a screenplay of Pyle's bestselling collection of columns *Here is Your War*, the playwright Arthur Miller had traveled to New Mexico to interview the journalist who was on a break from the war. He was, wrote Miller, "a tortured man, uncertain of himself and ridden with guilt. Slight of build, with sandy hair thinning to baldness, gentle and self-effacing, he seemed the last man in the world to bring himself willingly into battle."[6]

Pyle returned to the United States in the autumn of 1944 a national hero, admired by servicemen not only for his honest reporting, but for the material difference he had made to many of their lives by campaigning for soldiers' "fight pay" (the equivalent of airmen's "flight pay"). The law passed by Congress in 1944, giving combat infantrymen an extra $10 a month, was dubbed the "Ernie Pyle Bill." Yet within a few short months he was back in a war zone, this time in the Pacific. The question is: why? The answer is complex. He went partly to escape the demands on him in America: from his wife, who had recently tried to commit suicide; from the public, who were clamoring for his attention; and from his professional commitments, including the motion picture that had been adapted from his book, *The Story of GI Joe*.* He had never liked the film's title, he admit-

* The film was premiered in June 1945 and earned its co-star, Robert Mitchum, his only Academy Award nomination for Best Supporting Actor.

ted in February 1945, "but nobody could think of a better one, and I was too lazy to try."[7] But his greatest motivation was guilt: how could he remain safely in the United States when thousands of ordinary Americans were risking their lives on foreign battlefields? Or as he put it to his readers:

> There's nothing nice about the prospect of going back to war again. Anybody who has been in war and wants to go back is a plain damn fool in my book. I'm certainly not going because I've got itchy feet again, or because I can't stand America, or because there is any mystical fascination about war that is drawing me back. I'm going simply because there's a war on and I'm part of it and I've known all the time I was going back. I'm going simply because I've got to—and I hate it.

He had chosen the Pacific because he assumed the war in Europe would be over before he could return. That was not how it turned out. Yet he thought it best to stick with his original plan. "There are," he explained, "a lot of guys in that war, too. They are the same guys who are fighting on the other side, only with different names, that's all. It's not belittling my friends in Europe to desert them and go to the Pacific for a while."[8]

His decision was certainly appreciated by the first servicemen he met on Guam as he settled in to a room of the Bachelor Officer Quarters—cream-colored huts made of corrugated metal, equipped with a clothes closet, washstand, chest of drawers and two beds with double mattresses—that had been hurriedly constructed by the Seabees all over the Pacific. Spotting him through the open window, one Seabee called out: "Say, aren't you Ernie Pyle?"

"Right."

"Whoever thought we'd meet you here? I recognized you from your picture."

The pair started chatting, and other Seabees joined in. It made Pyle's day, and confirmed his decision to come.[9]

Yet, as he knew already, there were considerable challenges for a journalist covering the Pacific War. The first was distance. "I don't mean distance from America so much," he wrote, "for our war in Europe was a long way from home too. I mean distances after you get right on the battlefield. The whole western Pacific is our battlefield, and whereas distances in Europe are at most hundreds of miles, out here they are thousands. And there's nothing in between but water."

Then there was the issue of boredom as the days went by in their "endless sameness." But the hardest adjustment, Pyle felt, was the "different attitude" toward the enemy. In Europe there was a feeling that the Germans, "horrible and deadly as they were, were still people." In the Pacific, he had quickly got the feeling "that the Japanese were looked upon as something subhuman and repulsive; the way some people feel about cockroaches or mice."[10] The reasons for this hatred were not hard to fathom: the unprovoked attack on Pearl Harbor; Japan's despicable treatment of its prisoners of war (more than a quarter of whom died from malnourishment, disease and overwork); and its soldiers' refusal to surrender, in line with the bushido code of honor that was supposed to dictate the samurai warrior's way of life.*

At first, even the humane Pyle felt this repulsion. The sight of a group of Japanese prisoners "wrestling and laughing" had given him "the creeps," he admitted, and he wanted a "mental bath." But after talking to many veterans on Guam, he got over the "creepy feeling that fighting Japs"—or "Japes," a racist combination of "Jap" and "ape" that many American servicemen liked to use—was "like fighting snakes or ghosts." They certainly held different ideas about the war, but they fought with specific tactics which the Americans had come to know. "Our men," wrote Pyle, "were no more afraid of the Japs than they were of the Germans. They were afraid of them as any modern soldier is of his foe, not because they are slippery or ratlike, but simply because they have weapons and fire them like good tough soldiers. And the Japs were human enough to be afraid of us in exactly the same way."[11]

While still in the United States, Ernie Pyle had told his readers that he planned to spend some time with the U.S. Navy—since it was "so dominant" in the Pacific and he had "done very little in the past on

* Even senior commanders were not immune from this dehumanization of the enemy. "You've got to instill in your men," insisted Major General Lem Shepherd, commanding the 6th Marine Division, "the will to kill the enemy to the point… that killing a Jap was like killing a rattlesnake." (Quoted in Lacey, *Stay off the Skyline*, p. 83.)

that part of the service"—before going ashore on the next major operation with the foot soldiers (or, as he put it, "my noble souls, the doughfoots").[12]

In fact, the first unit he lived with was a squadron of the USAAF flying B-29 Superfortresses out of the Marianas. "Their lot," he wrote, "was a tough one" as they "were over water every inch of the way to Japan and every inch of the way back." They had to contend with flak and Japanese fighters over the target, but their main concern was "sweating out" those six or seven hours of ocean beneath them on the way back, often in darkness. If they were shot up or had engine trouble, and were forced to ditch, their chances of being picked up were only one in five. "It's mighty hard," noted Pyle, "to find a couple of little rubber boats in a big, big ocean."

Pyle even went up in a B-29 on a training run and found it a thrilling, if somewhat disconcerting, experience. The plane was so packed with gas tanks and bomb racks that the only way the crew of eleven could move around was along a thirty-foot narrow tunnel, "just big enough to crawl in on your hands and knees." Some crew members slept in it for an hour or so on missions; but others found it too claustrophobic and preferred to stay awake. They wore regular clothes on missions, usually coveralls, because the cabin was pressurized and heated. But as they approached the target they put on flak vests and oxygen masks in case the Plexiglas was shattered and the plane depressurized.

While he was with the squadron, several planes were lost on missions. One should have been, but somehow survived. Hit over the target, it dropped back and was attacked by five Japanese fighters and shot to pieces. It kept flying, though its horizontal stabilizers were gone, and every so often would go into a spiral. Each time the pilot regained control. He finally reached his home base and crashed on the runway, tearing off the plane's wings and breaking its huge fuselage in two. "Yet," wrote an astonished Pyle, "every man came out of it alive, even the wounded ones."[13]

In mid-March, finally making good his earlier promise, Pyle joined the light-aircraft carrier USS *Cabot*, part of Vice Admiral Marc A. Mitscher's Fast Carrier Force (known as Task Force 58) which was heading north to attack the airfields of Kyushu, and thus weaken Japanese air power before the Okinawa invasion. Pyle had deliberately asked to be put on one of the smaller carriers because they received less attention in the press and had fewer people on board. But he was still shocked at her size: 700 feet long, carrying 1,000 people, and with "all the facilities of a small city," including five barbers, three doctors, two dentists, a preacher, laundry, general store, two libraries and movies every night. The ship had been at sea since November 1943 without once returning to port, and the crew could think of nothing but home. Yet they were inordinately proud of their achievements: steaming 149,000 miles, surviving five typhoons (one of which sank three destroyers), shooting down 228 enemy planes and sinking twenty-nine big ships. Having fought in every battle in the Pacific since the start of 1944, the *Cabot* was known as "the Iron Woman."

One particularly close shave was off Luzon in late November 1944 when a kamikaze plane hit the port side of the flight deck, destroying an anti-aircraft gun, and killing and wounding sixty-two. This caused one disgruntled member of crew to exclaim: "Oh, boy, this is great. Now at last they'll have to send us back to America for repairs."

He was promptly felled by a blow from outraged Boilermaker 1st Class Jerry Ryan, from Davenport, Iowa. Pyle got to know Ryan well, describing him as "a tall, well-built, mustached sailor" who always knew right from wrong. He was, wrote Pyle, "what is known in the Navy as 'a good man': skilled in his work, dependable, and very smart. He'd die before he'd curry favor with anybody." One of Ryan's closest friends on board was "a tall, athletic" black cook from the same town called Wesley Cooper. He was the best basketball player on ship and had a scholarship waiting for him at the University of Iowa.

Some of the *Cabot*'s sailors asked Pyle how their service compared to that in Europe. His blunt response was that it was "much better." Most saw the sense of this. "I can stand a lot of monotony," said one, "if I know my chances are pretty good for coming out alive." But others disagreed, saying "I'd trade this for a foxhole any day." Pyle's scornful reaction: "You just have to keep your mouth shut to a remark like that."

The people on board he had infinite respect for, however, were the pilots. "Landing on the deck of a small carrier in a rough sea," wrote Pyle, "is just about like landing on half a block of Main Street while a combination hurricane and earthquake is going on."

Some came in too fast and blew a tire; others "half-sideways, and the cable will jerk them around in a tire-screeching circle." A few come in so high they missed the arresting cables and hit the high wires stretched across the mid-decks called "the barrier," causing them to somersault and even catch fire. Pyle could hardly watch, telling the air officer he needed "heart-failure medicine." The man replied: "I've had to watch 2,000 of them. It'll drive you nuts."

The start of the cruise north seemed "peaceful and routine," with each sub-unit of carriers protected by an array of battleships, cruisers and destroyers. Messages were constantly being transmitted across the fleet by signal flag, light blinker and even planes dropping packages on the flight deck; only radio messages were forbidden, to prevent the Japanese from eavesdropping. There were daily baths, lots of good food (including steaks and ice cream), movies every night and as many cigarettes as a man could smoke. Pyle even had his dirty clothes laundered and pressed by the cabin boy. It was like a hotel.

But gradually the weather got colder and, as it neared mainland Japan, the ship went into battle stations and the captain "never left the bridge, either to eat or to sleep." Everybody was issued with "flash gear" —including a thin gray hood to cover the head and shoulders, a white mask, glass goggles and long gray gloves—to protect against fire; all compartment doors were closed, and aid stations were manned across the ship. Finally on March 18, from a position about ninety miles from the coast of Kyushu, the strike planes were launched from across the fleet. Finding few Japanese aircraft on the ground, they bombed hangars and barracks instead.[14]

The response of Vice Admiral Matome Ugaki, commanding the 5th Air Fleet on Kyushu, was to order a counter-strike of heavy bombers and kamikazes. Fifty were shot down or crashed, though not before some damage had been done to three aircraft carriers: the *Enterprise*, *Intrepid* and *Yorktown*. The following day two more carriers, *Wasp* and *Franklin*, were hit by Japanese bombs that caused fires and over 1,600 casualties. "Listening to the [Japanese] claims of attacks," noted Ugaki in his diary, "it looked like we had inflicted heavy damage on the enemy, but the fact wasn't so. Each time a search was made, I wondered why so many remained if the claimed result of attack was true."[15]

This was certainly the case with the *Cabot*'s carrier group—TF 58.3—which came through the operation unscathed. Pyle's main concern on the 19th was waiting for the strike planes to return from an attack on ships in the Tokyo area. Slowly but surely they did, until just six were absent. It later transpired that the plane piloted by Ensign Robert Buchanan had been hit by flak and forced to ditch in Tokyo's outer bay. The other five, all members of the same flight, had remained in the area to locate a rescue ship. They eventually found one thirty miles away. But as it steamed slowly toward the outer bay, the aerial escort began to run short on fuel and, one by one, its planes were ordered by their leader, Lieutenant John Fecke of Duxbury, Massachusetts, back to the carrier.

As the rescue ship entered the outer bay, its skipper realized the danger he was in—from mines, enemy planes and shore-based guns—and radioed Fecke he could not go any farther.

"It's only two miles more," begged Fecke. "Please try."

"OK, we'll try."

Incredibly he located the pilot, pulled him from the water and got safely away. Only now did Fecke and the other remaining pilot, Lieutenant Bob Murray, return to the *Cabot*. "They had flown six hours on a three-hour mission," wrote Pyle, "but they helped save an American life by doing so."

Fecke and Buchanan had form. The previous autumn, off Formosa, they had helped to save two crippled American cruisers by engaging seventy Japanese planes with a flight of just eight, commanded by Fecke. They shot down twenty-nine, for the loss of just one of their own planes, and drove the rest away. Fecke and Buchanan each downed five planes—making them "aces" after a single engagement—and were awarded the Navy Cross. "So the little Tokyo Bay incident," wrote Pyle, "didn't rattle them."[16]

7

"I was crying as I did it and she was crying too"

From the deck of the USS *Gunston Hall*, Sergeant Robert C. "Bob" Dick of the 763rd Tank Battalion could see "every kind of ship built, or so it seemed, and there looked to be hundreds" stretching all the way to the horizon. "It was," he thought, "both reassuring and at the same time unsettling. A lot of help is always good, but we must be going to where a lot of help would really be a big necessity."[1]

A veteran of eight previous campaigns, the *Gunston Hall* (or LSD-5 as she was also known), a 7,900-ton flat-bottomed dock landing ship, had left Leyte on March 25, 1945, as part of a convoy of ships carrying the 7th and 96th Infantry Divisions toward Okinawa. Also setting off that day were ships carrying the assault groups of the 1st and 6th Marine Divisions from Ulithi, the 2nd Marine Division from Saipan, and the 27th Infantry Division from Espiritu Santo. Lieutenant General Buckner and his staff were due to leave Leyte on Admiral Turner's faster command ship *Eldorado* on the 27th. Ahead of everyone, however, was the 77th Infantry Division. It had departed Leyte on March 19 and was now nearing its target, the Kerama Islands, which needed to be captured before the Okinawa landings.[2]

Like most enlisted men in the gigantic armada, Sergeant Dick only learned where he was headed en route. "We were told," he recalled, "that the island was only about 350 miles from the Japanese mainland, and that the fight ahead was going to be a tough one." Born and brought up in El Monte, southern California, Dick was just seventeen when he joined the 40th Infantry Division of the National Guard in 1938. He was then six feet two inches tall and "a skinny 155 pounds, with brown hair combed in no particular direction or style." Posted to Hawaii in 1942, he transferred to the 763rd Tank Battalion after an ankle injury put paid to his career as an infantrymen. He was assigned as the driver of Tank No. 60—nicknamed *Cutthroats*—a thirteen-ton Stuart M3 with a 37 mm cannon, later upgraded to the much heavier thirty-ton Sherman M4 with a 75 mm cannon and three .30 caliber machine guns. The Sherman also had "state-of-the-art radio equipment" and "an intercom" so that the four-man crew could communicate in battle, and the commander no longer needed to tap Dick with his foot to get him to change direction.

Dick's first and only experience of combat was with Charlie Company of the 763rd, part of the 96th ("Deadeyes") Division, in the Leyte operation in the autumn of 1944. But the rough terrain on Leyte was unsuitable for tanks and Dick saw little action until one terrifying experience when his tank was part of a platoon of four that was ambushed on a narrow road with ditches on either side by Japanese "carrying mines attached to long bamboo poles." Before anyone could react, the lead and rear tanks had their tracks blown off and the two in the middle, including *Cutthroats*, were trapped. Suddenly, recalled Dick, a Japanese officer jumped onto the back of the tank in front, "and as the turret began to traverse in our direction (in order to shoot the Japs off our tank), the officer began hacking away at the machine-gun barrel with his two-handed sword!" On the fourth blow the blade snapped, and the officer was shot by Dick's gunner. "The attack couldn't have lasted more than a few minutes but it seemed an eternity... Several Jap soldiers, still alive, were found in the ditches among the dead, and they were quickly dispatched by our crews."

At the end of the campaign, Dick was asked by his company commander if he wanted to be considered for a field commission. He agreed, and passed the initial assessment. But when told he would be reassigned to infantry, he changed his mind. "We all knew that another battle was shaping up," he wrote, "and the thought of being in the middle of it on foot really turned me off. I had found a niche in the tanks, and didn't want to take any chances of missing combat in one of the monsters." Eighteen of Charlie Company's "monsters" were now in the bowels of *Gunston Hall* as she headed north from Leyte, and acted as useful ballast when a typhoon hit on day three, though the ship still "rolled and plunged like never before." A day later, the skies cleared and the worst was over.[3]

By then, the capture of the Kerama Islands by the 77th Division was almost complete. On the morning of March 26, once the sea had been cleared of mines and the beaches declared free of underwater obstacles, combat teams from the 305th, 306th and 307th Infantry Regiments landed on the islands of Aka, Geruma, Hokaji, Zamami and Yakabi where they met, for the most part, only minor opposition, much of which quickly melted into the interior. More landings took place on the 27th, including that of the 1st and 2nd Battalions of the 306th Infantry on Tokashiki, at six miles long and one mile wide the largest of the group. By the evening of the 29th, all the islands were in American hands, as were 121 prisoners and 300 suicide boats* that were meant to be used against the American fleet. A further 530 Japanese soldiers had been killed, at a relatively minor cost of thirty-one American dead and eighty-one wounded.[4]

Buckner was on the *Eldorado* heading north when he heard the good news. "Word came," he wrote his wife, "that the Kerama Retto had been occupied according to plan with very few casualties... twelve strangled native women were found in one cave."[5] In fact, many more civilians were dead—the victims of Japanese mendacity and their own naivety. What happened on Tokashiki, in particular, is almost beyond belief; but it would be repeated many times on Okinawa itself, forever haunting the men who survived the months-long battle.

An eyewitness to—and an unwilling participant in—the unfolding tragedy was Shigeaki Kinjo, a 16-year-old who lived with his mother and three siblings in a village in the south of Tokashiki. On March 26, when the Americans began their landings on neighboring islands, they and other civilians were ordered "to move to Nishiyama, in the north of the island, where the Japanese soldiers had their camp." They walked after dark in pouring rain, to avoid American shells, and by morning had reached their destination. There they found themselves in a crowd of "about 700 or 800 people" all "packed together tightly"

* Well dispersed throughout the islands, these plywood boats were eighteen feet long and five feet wide, and powered by six-cylinder Chevrolet automobile engines, generating eighty-five horsepower and capable of twenty knots. Each carried two 264-pound depth charges on a rack behind the pilot, to be detonated close to the target ship on a five-second fuse. (Appleman et al., *Okinawa*, p. 60.)

with many women and children crying. Surrounded by Japanese soldiers, they "feared that something bad was about to happen."

Eventually the village head—himself an ex-soldier—told everyone to shout out "Banzai!" ("Long life!") to the emperor three times. "We knew," wrote Kinjo, "that this was what Japanese soldiers did when they were going to die on the battlefield. The village head didn't exactly tell us to commit suicide, but by telling us to shout banzai, we knew what was meant."

To assist the killings, Japanese soldiers began distributing hand grenades with instructions on how to use them. But there were not enough to go round, and Kinjo's family did not get one. When they had all been handed out, "that was taken as a sign and the killing began immediately." After the grenades had been detonated, most people were still alive so men began to use clubs and scythes on their families and each other. It was, remembered Kinjo, "the father's role to kill his own family, but my father had already died." So Kinjo and his older brother took on the grisly task. His memory of how they killed their mother is understandably hazy: "maybe we tried to use rope at first, but in the end we hit her over the head with stones. I was crying as I did it and she was crying too."

They then moved on to their siblings: a girl about to enter the fourth grade of elementary school, and a brother in first grade. "I don't remember exactly how we killed our little brother and sister but it wasn't difficult because they were so small—I think we used a kind of spear. There was wailing and screaming on all sides as people were killing and being killed."

With their siblings dead, they were discussing how they would kill each other when a boy of Kinjo's age ran up and said: "Let's fight the Americans and be killed by them, rather than dying like this."

Kinjo knew they would be shot instantly if they tried to attack the heavily armed Americans. Yet he thought it a better way to die than by each other's hand, as did his brother, so they "left that place of screaming and death" to "find the Americans." Fortunately for them, the first person they came across was a Japanese soldier. "We were shocked," recalled Kinjo, "and wondered why he was still alive when we had been told to kill each other. Why was it that only the locals had to commit suicide when the Japanese soldiers were allowed to survive? We felt betrayed."

Deciding not to kill themselves after all, Kinjo and his brother stayed in the hills and scavenged for food. After a couple of weeks, close to starving, they surrendered to an American soldier and were taken to a prisoner-of-war camp. There they learned that "300 people had perished that day," and 600 overall in two separate mass suicides in the Keramas. Kinjo, who was later so wracked with guilt for what he had done that he turned to Christianity, put the blame squarely on the Japanese. "Part of the reason we had been prepared to kill our own families," he explained, "was because of the nationalistic education we had received. We were taught that the Americans were not human."[6]

The lie was revealed to one group of survivors when soldiers of the 306th Infantry came upon the site of a mass suicide on Tokashiki—probably Kinjo's—in the morning of March 29. According to eyewitnesses, they "found a small valley littered with more than 150 dead and dying Japanese, most of them civilians. Fathers had systematically throttled each member of their families and then disemboweled themselves with knives or hand grenades." Under a blanket lay a father, two small children, and both grandparents, "all strangled by cloth ropes." As American soldiers and medics did what they could, providing food and care for the survivors, an old man who had killed his daughter "wept in remorse."[7]

On March 25, the day before the first troops landed on the Keramas, the softening up of Okinawa itself began with the long-range shelling of the southeast coast by Rear Admiral W. H. P. Blandy's Amphibious Support Force (TF 52). This was to cover the work of minesweepers and frogmen whose job was to clear the approaches to the Hagushi beaches of mines and underwater obstacles. From March 29, the bombardment proper began when the battleships, cruisers, destroyers and gunboats of Rear Admiral M. L. Deyo's Gun & Covering Force (TF 54) "closed the range" and used their heavy guns to "hit their objectives with increasing effectiveness." In the seven days prior to L-Day, naval guns would fire "more than 13,000 large-caliber shells (six-inch to sixteen-inch) in shore bombardment," a total of 5,162 tons of high explosives. This fire was supplemented by numerous strikes from carrier planes—mostly from Vice Admiral Mitscher's Fast Carrier Force (TF 58)—who targeted barracks, gun positions, airfields and midget-submarine bases with rockets, bombs and napalm.[8]

Forced to endure this storm of steel was the bulk of Okinawa's civilian population, still concentrated in the south of the island. Among them was Kikuko Miyagi, 16, a boarder at the prestigious First Okinawa Prefectural Girls' High School in Asato near Naha. She was one of 222 girls, between the ages of 15 and 19, from the High School and the Okinawa Normal School who had recently been inducted into the Himeyuri Student Corps* to work as auxiliary nurses at the Okinawa army field hospital, sited in underground caves near the village of Haebaru, three miles southeast of Naha.[9]

Like their male counterparts—many of whom were recruited into the Blood and Iron Student Corps—Kikuko and her fellow pupils had long been exposed to nationalist propaganda and were fiercely patriotic. They were taught how to use bamboo spears and the Japanese halberd, practiced air-raid defense drills and went on long marches of up to forty miles to improve mental and physical health. From June 1944, as more and more classes were canceled, they helped construct Oroku airfield. Their training as military nurses began in late 1944 and was continued in early 1945. They were also issued with "The Principle of the Battle" orders which stated that each person must destroy ten of the enemy and one tank.[10]

It was around this time that Kikuko went home to say goodbye to her parents. She promised them she would "win the Imperial Order of the Rising Sun, eighth class, and be enshrined at Yasukuni." This infuriated her father, a country schoolteacher. "I didn't bring you up," he shouted, "to the age of 16 to die!"

Kikuko was ashamed of her father's reaction, and "thought he was a traitor to say such a thing." She felt only pride as she left home for the battlefield.[11]

On March 23, she and her schoolmates were woken in their dormitory and addressed by the school principal: "It's time you demonstrated what you've been trained for and served your country. I was ordered by the military to join the headquarters. You will go to

* "Himeyuri" was the nickname given to the two schools which had been established in the Meiji period and were sited next door to each other. "*Hime*" means princess, and "*yuri*" is lily in Japanese.

the army field hospital with your teachers and do your best there for our country."

That night the 222 students set out with eighteen teachers for the Haebaru army field hospital. It comprised three surgical clinics—the 1st, 2nd and 3rd—hidden in caves under a gently sloping hill. The caves were still in the process of being dug out, lined with wooden supports and filled with medical equipment, so the Himeyuri Corps was recruited to help.

While they worked the American bombardment of the island began. It seemed to Kikuko that it was literally raining shells "for five or six days." On March 29, as the shellfire continued, a graduation ceremony was held for the Himeyuri students in their "crude, triangular barracks." They knelt together on the floor, their faces hardly visible in the flickering candlelight, as their principal spoke of their duty to "Work so as not to shame the First Girls' High School." They then sang patriotic songs, including "Give Your Life for the Sake of the Emperor, Wherever You Go," and one penned by Kikuko's 23-year-old music teacher called "A Song of Parting." It was, she noted, "really wonderful" and "not a war song at all." They had memorized it while they were digging the shelters, particularly the verse "We shall meet again." They sang it as they walked back to their cave, "the reverberations of the explosions shaking the ground." Next morning "that triangular building wasn't there any more."[12]

Another Okinawan almost killed by American shells was Yoshiko Sakumoto, the young schoolgirl who had witnessed the bombing of Naha. Now 14, but still too young to be called up for military service, she and her family were part of the exodus to the north of the island in January 1945. They went in a horse-drawn carriage, with Yoshiko and her father pushing a cart filled with their belongings, and found refuge with a family in the village of Seragaki, near Mount Onna, in the center of the island. But her father traveled back to Naha every few weeks to get supplies and check on relatives, and Yoshiko went with him. They were returning from one such trip with two friends, making their way along the prefectural highway south of the Hagushi beaches, when Yoshiko looked out to sea and froze. "The ocean," she recalled, "was crowded with a colossal number of ships that stretched north from the Naha area. They had surrounded our island. We could tell right away they weren't Japanese ships."

They hurried on and were close to Kue, near the town of Chatan, when the ships opened fire on March 29. "Shells flew over our heads," remembered Yoshiko, "making a 'shoo-shoo' sound, and exploded with an enormous thump. At the same time, planes began dropping bombs. I could see the machine guns firing from the planes."

Abandoning the cart, they looked desperately for somewhere to hide. On their right was a sugar-cane field; the beach to their left. Neither provided much cover. They dived under some bushes. But when the explosions got close, showering them with "small rocks and dust," they knew they had to escape to a safer spot. "If we stay here," shouted her father over the tumult, "we'll all be killed. Let's run for the woods."

He was gesturing to a small wooded area about thirty meters away. They set off for it, but more explosions forced them to the ground. "When we finally made it to the woods," wrote Yoshiko, "we looked back and saw huge holes, about the size of eight tatami mats,* blasted open by the bombs." In the wood were some thatched houses and a small concrete shed. Three of them dashed into the shed, leaving Yoshiko's father outside. Seconds later "a huge explosion lifted the shed and shook the ground." Yoshiko could not hear and feared her eardrums had burst. She had wounds on her elbow and her head. As these were being bound, her father appeared, "pointing at a spot just behind the shed" where the shell had exploded. Yoshiko was shocked. A direct hit, she knew, would have killed them instantly.

They decided to head back toward Naha and seek refuge in the tomb of Chatan Moshi on a rocky hill. On they way, they passed the bodies of four Japanese soldiers. "One lay by the sugar-cane field," recalled Yoshiko, "the second on the roadside, and two others near a bridge." It was a chilling reminder of how close they had all come to death.[13]

* A typical tatami mat is six feet by three feet.

8

"Tomorrow is our big day"

"At 10:45 a.m.," wrote Lieutenant General Buckner in his diary on March 27, "our convoy weighed anchor and moved with an air of dignified confidence on its nonstop trip to strike the enemy."

He was heading for Okinawa from Leyte in the Philippines on Admiral Turner's flagship *Eldorado*, the last leg of a 6,000-mile journey that had begun for him and his senior staff on March 5 with a flight from Pearl Harbor to Guam, via Kwajalein Atoll. They boarded the *Eldorado* at Guam on March 7 and reached Leyte five days later. The time since had been spent watching amphibious exercises, going over the plans and waving goodbye to the slower-moving landing ships bound for the Keramas and Okinawa. Now that it was his turn, Buckner felt both nervous and excited. The day before, he had received a warning from Vice Admiral Mitscher that Okinawa was "honeycombed with caves, tunnels and emplacements," and the fight would be "very tough." Buckner preferred to see it as a "great adventure."[1]

He had a cabin to himself, but most of his senior officers were doubled up. Brigadier General Oliver P. Smith, for example, was bunking with Major General F. G. Wallace, the prospective island commander of Okinawa, in a stateroom on the main deck. As one of its portholes was near an exhaust ventilator from the galley, they "got a choice assortment of odors."[2] Colonel Vernon E. Megee, 44, a veteran of Iwo Jima who would command all Marine air-support units on Okinawa, thought himself lucky to be sharing a small stateroom with only three other officers: an army brigadier, a navy commodore, and an air-force colonel. "We were not only integrated but entwined when it came to dressing in that restricted cubbyhole... We all accepted the situation in good spirits and not without humor—it was all part of going to war."

They were part of, wrote Megee, "a most formidable armada" with other ships stretching as far as the horizon. As darkness fell, "not a light showed nor siren or bell sounded. Radio transmitters were silent for the voyage." He imagined the thousands of soldiers and Marines in those darkened hulls, "standing in little silent knots about the decks, or lying wide-eyed in their crowded bunks in stifling troops compartments, thinking the thoughts that men think on the eve of battle."[3]

For the first day or so, the sea conditions were rough as the *Eldorado* changed course to avoid a typhoon. The Tenth Army staff used the time to conduct a command-post exercise by "reenacting the first day of the battle for Iwo Jima with everyone performing his appropriate duties." It took place in the Joint Operations Room where one large table had places for Buckner, his chief and deputy chiefs of staff, and G-2 and G-3. At another sat the naval gunfire officer and artillery officer, while naval officers manned a U-shaped table for the Air Support Control Unit. With no actual messages coming in "over the air," they flashed up those sent and received during Iwo Jima on screens. "The exercise proved," wrote Oliver Smith, "to be very interesting and instructive."[4]

Buckner also found time to finish the third volume of Douglas Southall Freeman's *Lee's Lieutenants: Gettysburg to Appomattox*, a history that featured Buckner's own father. Was he looking for inspiration? For tips? His diary gives no clue, beyond the comment: "A tragic epitaph to a nobly defended cause."[5]

He and his staff were cheered by news that the 77th Division's landings on the Kerama Islands had been conducted "aggressively, effectively, and according to schedule."[6] By March 29, the anchorages in the Keramas had been buoyed, and "ships were able to refuel and rearm without enemy interference." Two days later came word that a battalion of 155 mm guns had been sited on the small island of Keise Shima and were ready to fire.[7]

Also on the 31st, Buckner's chief of intelligence, Colonel Ely, returned from the Keramas with the "latest pictures and reports of the landing beaches." These, said Ely, had been "distributed to every battalion that is to land tomorrow."[8] After months of meticulous planning, Operation Iceberg—the invasion of Okinawa—was ready to be launched. Thirteen hundred naval ships of all sizes were in position: some in the Demonstration Group off the southeast coast of Okinawa; but most off the west coast where the actual landings would take place. "All ships arrived on time," noted Oliver Smith, "and there were no collisions. Gunfire ships, which had been pounding Okinawa for several days, were still pounding away. The combat air patrol from the escort carriers was over the ships of the convoy to guard against Japanese interference."[9]

With the final say, Vice Admiral Turner announced late on the 31st that weather and surf conditions appeared to be suitable for a landing the following morning. H-hour was set for 8:30 a.m. "With members of my staff, I am attending Easter service this evening," Buckner wrote to his wife. "Tomorrow is our big day."[10]

Across the vast fleet, soldiers were ruminating on the task ahead. "My thoughts," wrote 20-year-old Private First Class (PFC) Don Dencker of L Company, 382nd Infantry, "and those of my buddies...were on the coming battle and the dangers to be faced. Would we all come through this one unscathed? The mortar section had been lucky on Leyte. Would our luck hold on Okinawa?"

A tall, skinny kid with prominent ears, Dencker was the only child of a home builder who rarely sat still: having finished a house, he would sell it and move on. Fortunately for his family, he always bought in the same neighborhood of southern Minneapolis where Dencker attended the Roosevelt High School. A good student whose hobby was raising and racing homing pigeons, Dencker had completed three terms of a chemical engineering degree at the University of Minnesota when he was drafted into the army in the summer of 1943. After basic training he was accepted into the Army Specialized Training Program (ASTP) and sent to complete an engineering program at the Illinois Institute of Technology in Chicago with the "implied promise" of Officer Candidate School after graduation. But a manpower crisis caused the program to close in spring 1944, and Dencker was one of 250 former ASTP students assigned to the 96th Infantry Division, a reserve formation that was composed almost entirely of draftees.

On joining Love Company, 3/382nd Infantry, Dencker was asked by the XO what specialty he preferred. "Mortars, sir," he replied, adding that he had got to know the weapon well during basic training.

What he did not say, for obvious reasons, was that he thought that "being with the mortars was a safer place to serve than being in a Rifle Platoon." Assigned to the 3rd Mortar Squad—one of three, making a section, in the 4th Weapons Platoon—he served in Leyte as a lowly ammunition bearer before being promoted to private first class and assistant gunner (with responsibility for preparing and loading the mortar shells).

Dencker had been "somewhat relieved" to learn that the assault troops for the next landing would be from the 381st and 383rd Infantry Regiments, while his 382nd was in reserve. Yet he and the rest of Love Company were loaded aboard the 8,000-ton attack transport ship USS *Banner* (APA 60) on March 13, a fortnight before their departure from Leyte. "Why we all boarded so early I do not know," he wrote, "as the transport and cargo ship group did not depart Leyte Gulf...until March 27th."

Once under way, they were given details about their destination—Okinawa—and lectured on what to expect. "We were told," recalled Dencker, "that the climate on the island was temperate, that the people were of mixed Chinese and Japanese heritage, and that the Ryukyu Islands had been an independent feudal nation before being annexed by Japan." Hazards included the Habu snake, said to be so poisonous that if bitten you had to "take a trench knife and make cross-shaped slits across the fang marks, then quickly suck the venom out." Their indoctrination also included Japanese translations for useful phrases like "Come out," "Hands up" and "Take off your clothes." Dencker only remembered the first one: "*Dete koi*," pronounced "De-tay-ko-ee."

Dencker's ship hit rough weather on March 28, with "strong winds, rain, and large waves" making almost everyone seasick. "The whole below-deck quarters reeked from vomit and body odors," wrote Dencker. "It was best to stay up near the deck hatches where the air was fresher." By the 31st, however, the "weather was clear and the sea calm as we moved steadily toward our objective." That afternoon, Love Company was told about the 77th Division's successful landings on the Kerama Islands. "Everything looks encouraging" was the theme of a message from Dencker's divisional commander, Major General James L. ("Smiling Jim") Bradley. That evening, having attended a Protestant service at which the chaplain gave a "reassuring message," Dencker read the 23rd Psalm ("The Lord is my shepherd") from his pocket New Testament before getting some rest.[11]

Also traveling on an attack transport ship from Leyte was Private Don "Slim" Carlton, a machine-gunner with the 1/184th Infantry. Raised in rural Minnesota, where he "learned to love the outdoors along with hunting and fishing," Carlton was working in an aircraft factory in San Diego, helping to build B-24 Liberator bombers, when the news of the Japanese attack at Pearl Harbor prompted him and two friends to quit their jobs and join the army. Having seen "too many John Wayne movies," he felt he was "missing out on some fun."

After completing his basic training in Fort Fannin, Texas, Carlton was sent as a battle replacement to the 7th Infantry Division on Leyte. He was assigned to the 184th Infantry's Dog Company (Heavy Weapons) where the officer took in his massive build—six feet four inches and 180 pounds—and said: "Wow! Look at the size of this guy. He'll be good at toting a machine gun." So Carlton was assigned to a squad in the Machine-Gun Platoon, equipped with the old water-cooled .30 caliber Browning M1917A1 heavy machine gun, weighing 103 pounds (including the seventy-pound tripod) and firing 600 rounds a minute. His job was to carry the tripod, in addition to all his other gear. Fortunately, most of the heavy fighting on Leyte was over by the time Carlton arrived there, and his contribution was "mopping up" patrols in the mountains and jungles. Okinawa, therefore, would be his first proper campaign.

Having set off from Leyte, he and his fellow soldiers wondered where they were going. "Darned if I know," said one. "According to the sun we are headed roughly north so it's not Australia."

When eventually told their destination was Okinawa, one soldier asked: "Where in the hell is that?"

They were soon enlightened by an officer who told them that the island was 350 miles from Japan and in easy range of enemy aircraft. According to intelligence reports, the Japanese "were well entrenched and willing to fight to the death." Their division, the 7th, would "make the assault landing on 'L' [Love] day, April 1st." Their initial objective on day one was Kadena airfield. "After that," said the officer, "we will cross the island to the eastern shore, then turn south. For the first three days you are to take *no* prisoners."

He did not explain what they should do with any Japanese who did surrender. "I guess," wrote Carlton, "he left that up to each of us."

Later, as he considered the task ahead, Carlton's "thoughts were a mix, worried about facing a determined enemy again, but anxious to be able to come to grips with whatever the future had in store." He was no "gung-ho" warrior, but felt he could do his job. "It was a little quieter in the hold that night," he recalled. "I cleaned and oiled my carbine for the tenth time."[12]

Sergeant William Manchester, commanding the 2/29th Marines' intelligence section, had spent much of the voyage from Ulithi on the attack transport ship USS *George C. Clymer* "absorbed in an endless chess tournament" with one of his men. The others "read, wrote letters home, shot the breeze, told sea stories, played hearts, and sang songs based on awful puns." While not relishing the prospect of combat, he did feel "a kind of serenity, a sense of solidarity" with his men, a disparate group of bright if unconventional ex-college kids from across America he had dubbed the "Raggedy Asses." It was a feeling that did not fit with the "instinctive aloofness" which had been part of his "pre-war character and would return, afterward, like a healing scar."[13]

Born in Attleboro, Massachusetts, the son of a Marine veteran who returned from the First World War with a badly withered arm, Manchester came from one of New England's oldest families with a pedigree dating back to the seventeenth century. Two William Manchesters, for example, had fought under George Washington in the Revolutionary War. Any remaining family money, however, had been squandered by Manchester's grandfather Seabury, a "gambler and drinker." Manchester himself was a sickly child who almost died of pneumonia and spent much of his early childhood indoors. As a result he became an avid reader and a prolific writer, penning his first poems at the age of seven. Though puny for his age, and often picked on because he refused to fight back, Manchester came to admire martial achievement. "The pacifism of the 1930s maddened me," he recalled. "I yearned for valor... Most of the rest of my generation believed in appeasement, at least when it came to war, but I was an out-and-out warmonger, a chauvinist dying for the chance to die."[14]

He was an 18-year-old freshman at the Massachusetts State College in Amherst when his father died in January 1941, partly from war wounds. "It was my first experience of traumatic amnesia..."

I was in deep shock." Just over a year later, in the wake of Pearl Harbor, he enlisted in the Marine Corps. He did his basic training at the infamous Parris Island in South Carolina, "an isle whose reputation was just marginally better than those of Alcatraz and Devil's Island." Yet, incredibly, he "adored" his time there. "Boot camp," he wrote, "is a profound shock to most recruits because the Corps begins its job of building men by destroying the identity they brought with them. Their heads are shaved. They are assigned numbers. The DI [drill instructor] is their god."

Minor infractions drew brutal punishments and woe betide the recruit who failed to use the correct terminology for field boots (boondockers), rumors (scuttlebutt), company commander (skipper), coffee (Joe), battle dress (dungarees), bar (slopchute), latrine (head), information (dope) and neck (stacking swivel). There were three ways of doing things: the right way, the wrong way, and the Marine way. Yet Manchester embraced all this "petty tyranny" because, in the wake of his father's death, he "yearned for stern discipline" and Parris Island gave it to him "in spades." Though physically frail, he had "limitless reserves of energy" and could feel himself "toughening almost hourly." It helped, too, that he was an excellent shot, scoring 317 out of 330 on the rifle range with the M1 Garand and easily earning the highest rating of "Expert" rifleman.

Thanks to his college education and easy adjustment to Marine life, Manchester won a place at the corps' Officer Candidate School (OCS) in Quantico, Virginia. But he did not take to his fellow cadets. "I had known many of them, if distantly, in college," he wrote. "They were upper-middle-class snobs, nakedly ambitious conservative conformists, eager to claw their way to the top. In another ten years their uniforms would be corporate gray-flannel suits." Yet he stayed on and had been measured for his uniform when he came to grief: he had earlier refused to evaluate critically his fellow cadets; now he disobeyed a corporal's chickenshit order to cancel the cadets' final weekend leave to clean their rifles properly (they were already clean). He was court-martialled and thrown off the course just days before graduation.

Posted instead to Camp Lejeune, North Carolina, where new battalions were forming for overseas duty, he took over the intelligence section of the 2nd Battalion, 29th Marines (2/29th). Its main tasks were, wrote Manchester, to "estimate enemy strength on the battalion's front, to identify enemy units by the flashes on the tunics of their dead, to patrol deep behind enemy lines, to advise our junior officers who were having trouble reading maps, and to carry messages to company commanders whose field radios...were out of order." Of the nineteen men in his section, most were "military misfits, college students who had enlisted in a fever of patriotism and been rejected as officer candidates because, for various reasons [they] did not conform to the established concept of how officers should look, speak, and act." They resembled a "slack-wire, baggy-pants act out of a third-rate circus" and were "rarely given liberty, because the skipper was ashamed to let civilians see us wearing the Corps uniform."

Shipped out of San Diego in early August 1944 for Guadalcanal in the Solomons, Manchester's 2/29th became part of the newly activated 6th Marine Division. Of the 29th Regiment's three battalions, only the 1st had previously seen action, in Eniwetok and Guam, whereas many of the soldiers in the division's other two infantry regiments, the 4th and 22nd, had fought on Guadalcanal, New Georgia, Bougainville, Eniwetok, Saipan and Guam.

As the commander of his section, Manchester's main task on the voyage from Ulithi was to brief his men. He did this by spreading a big map of Okinawa in the fantail of the *George C. Clymer* and explaining that their division, the 6th Marine, would assault the five most northerly of the Hagushi beaches.* Further south would land, in turn, the 1st Marines, the 7th and the 96th Divisions. The assault troops' immediate objectives were the Yontan and Kadena airfields. Once they had been seized, the 6th and 1st Marine Divisions would wheel north, while the two army divisions moved south. It seemed to Manchester that the "most ambitious goals," including the mountainous Motobu Peninsula, had been assigned to his division because it was assumed that "the enemy was entrenched in the north."

He then passed on the "usual crap" about the dangers of "malaria, dengue, filariasis, typhus, leprosy, dysentery and jungle rot," and

* The troops landed on twenty-one beaches. From north to south: Green 1 and 2 (22nd Marines); Red 1, 2 and 3 (4th Marines); Blue 1 and 2 (7th Marines); Yellow 1, 2 and 3 (5th Marines); Purple 1 and 2 (17th Infantry); Orange 1 and 2 (32nd Infantry); White 1, 2 and 3 (381st Infantry); Brown 1, 2, 3 and 4 (383rd Infantry).

stressed the need to "watch out for snipers, don't shout names (a Jap would shout the same name again a minute later and drill the poor jerk who stuck his head up), maintain fire discipline when the enemy screams to draw fire and thus spot automatic weapons, and if you face a banzai charge, stay loose: don't fire till you see their buck teeth."

As he prepared for his first taste of combat, Manchester felt intensely close to the "Raggedy Asses," an emotion contrary to all his instincts. "I had been," he wrote, "and after the war I would again be, a man who usually prefers his own company, finding contentment in solitude. But for the present I had taken others into my heart and given of myself to theirs." Only later would he realize how vulnerable that made him, and "how terrible" the price he "might have to pay."[15]

9

"It was quite a show"

"I had a good rest," recalled PFC Don Dencker on the USS *Banner*, "and was awakened by reveille at 4:00 a.m. Love Day had arrived!" After dressing, he and his squad joined "a long chow line to be served a fine breakfast of steak and eggs, bread, fruit cocktail, and coffee." They were then issued their Love Day rations: a D-bar* of "hard, waxy chocolate," a K-ration† and one assault ration—"a form of candy." As dawn broke, they were allowed up on deck to watch the landings. "It was," recalled Dencker, "a beautiful, clear, calm morning with excellent visibility after the haze lifted... What a sight! About a mile from the beaches a line of battleships and cruisers engaged in the softening-up process. Flame and smoke belched from their guns as they fired repeated salvos."

Shortly before 8:00 a.m., he saw "U.S. Navy planes come in waves of horizontal bombers, dive-bombers, and fighters, giving the entire length of beach in front of our four divisions a thorough working over with bombs, rockets and strafing." Then waves of amphibious tanks and amtracs began moving toward the beach, "crawling successfully over the reefs starting about 800 yards from the shore." At 8:30 a.m. the tanks reached the breaches in the sea wall, "and a minute later our troops were scaling the walls" from the amtracs. "With a few minor hitches," wrote Dencker, "the entire landing validated the detailed planning and preparation put into our effort. It was quite a show."[1]

* A high-energy chocolate bar, made by Hershey's, that would not melt.

† First introduced in 1942, the K-ration consisted of three boxed meals of candy, hard biscuits and canned processed meat, totaling 2,830 calories, for a single day's consumption.

Part of that "show" in the 96th Division's sector, following the assault troops of the 383rd Infantry on to Brown Beach 3, were the Sherman tanks of Sergeant Bob Dick's Charlie Company, 763rd Battalion. Dropped off by a landing craft at the coral reef, about half a mile from the shore, the tanks used "deep-water wading stacks" to prevent water getting into the engine while they covered the remaining distance across the coral shelf. Unfortunately the tank running parallel to Dick's *Cutthroats* drove into a shell hole and capsized. "They went into the water upside down," he wrote, "and our reports said that the driver drowned." In fact the whole four-man crew was lost.[2]

Approaching the shore, Dick headed for a large opening in a huge sea wall that appeared to be at least twenty feet thick and twenty feet high. As he drove *Cutthroats* through, he was astonished to see "quite a number of photographers, both still and movie type," milling around on the beach, as well as MPs directing traffic. His mission was to "find and drive up a fairly narrow dirt road for approximately one mile" and then "stop and sit there, in plain sight, and wait." He did exactly that, nervous in the knowledge that *Cutthroats* was to act as bait for a hidden coastal gun. As soon it showed itself, they had been told, the navy would "take it out." Fortunately the only sign of movement was a goat wandering by.

"All of us were in disbelief," recalled Dick, "over the total lack of opposition by the Japanese. We had not heard a single shot fired by them, and the longer they delayed in opposing us, the more our forces would pour ashore. The lack of any enemy seemed almost scary. What's going on, what do they have up their sleeves?" Knowing that his division was due to head south, Dick hoped "that just maybe all the Japs were up north and the Marines could take care of them for us." It was wishful thinking.[3]

Back on the USS *Banner*, meanwhile, Don Dencker heard the welcome news that GIs from the 381st and 383rd Infantry had met "only scattered light opposition and that some units were already one mile inland." With the landings well ahead of schedule, Dencker's L Company was ordered below to prepare for their own disembarkation. Told to leave behind their duffel bags and shelter halves—which would be put ashore later—they put on their light packs, containing a waterproof jungle poncho, spare socks, toilet articles, mess kit, writing paper and envelopes, personal photos, a pocket New Testament, and other minor items like matches. Attached to the back of the pack was an entrenching tool, while each soldier also carried two full canteens of water, plus his specialist arms and ammunition.

In the case of most U.S. infantrymen, that meant the .30 M1 Garand, the first standard-issue semi-automatic military rifle. Weighing nine and a half pounds, the Garand could rapidly fire a clip of eight bullets, one after the other, by repeated pulls on the trigger. Once the last bullet had been fired, the clip would drop out and the bolt lock open, ready to be reloaded. This gave it a much higher rate of fire than the bolt-action Arisaka Type 99 rifle used by the Japanese army. The Garand was a fine weapon: well constructed, durable and easy to operate and maintain. But as Dencker was an assistant gunner—with responsibility for carrying the 60 mm mortar's baseplate—he was armed only with a .45 semi-automatic M1911 pistol, which could fire repeated single shots from a seven-round detachable magazine. Trying it out on a range in Leyte, Dencker had found it almost impossible to hit a target more than twenty-five yards away, and concluded that his sidearm "was strictly a close-in personal protection weapon."

Dencker wore the standard infantry M1 helmet, a one-size-fits-all steel construction with chin strap and a hard inner plastic liner with an adjustable sweatband and cotton webbing for comfort. On a chain around his neck was suspended a pair of stainless steel dog-tags, debossed with his name in reverse order (DENCKER DONALD O), his serial number (37570375), the year or years he was given a tetanus shot (44), blood type (A) and religion (P for Protestant, a detail included for the benefit of those who might need to administer last rites). Finally, to assist with the battlefield control of troops, each man had a unit symbol stenciled onto the back of his fatigue shirt. In the case of Dencker's 3/382nd Infantry, this was the "Queen of Battle" logo, the outline of a naked lady wearing a helmet, and holding a rifle with a bayonet attached in front of her crotch. It was, according to Dencker, the "envy of every other unit."

Shortly before 11:00 a.m., Dencker and the rest of Love Company, heavily burdened with packs, weapons, life belts and gas masks, climbed down the *Banner*'s cargo net and into a line of large landing craft. They then transferred to amtracs for the trip across the reef, reaching White Beach 1 at 11:30 a.m. "So far," noted Dencker, "Love Day for Love Company could not have been more benign."

The beach was a hive of activity as the Corps of Engineers unloaded supplies from "Ducks."* Reaching slightly higher ground, about a hundred yards from the edge of the surf, the men of Love Company dropped their gas masks and life belts before moving quickly inland, in the wake of the 381st Infantry, though the latter were "nowhere to be seen." After an hour they stopped at the junction of two small roads to eat a K-ration lunch and to drink water from their canteens. "It was sunny and mild," remembered Dencker, "with a temperature of about 70 degrees, so we weren't very thirsty. It would have been a perfect Easter Sunday back home."

The only indication they were in a war zone was the "disconcerting sight," on the far side of the road, of the bodies of five U.S. soldiers, covered by ponchos with only their combat boots protruding.[4]

A little further to the north, Private Don "Slim" Carlton of Dog Company, 1/184th Infantry, had been forced to walk through chest-high water to get to Purple Beach 1 after his landing craft grounded on the reef. "Some of the shorter men were having trouble with the depth of water," he wrote. "Lucky for me I was well over six feet tall and was having little difficulty. The heavy machine-gun tripod kept me firmly anchored to the bottom as I churned my way shoreward."

Suddenly the man in front of him went under the water and did not resurface. Had he been shot, wondered Carlton, or just fallen into a hole? Just to be certain, he skirted a few yards to the left, scanning the water for any sign of the man. There was nothing. He continued on and, once on dry land, realized he and a few other Dog Company men were north of the Bishi River in the 1st Marine Division sector, when they should been to the south. As they discussed where to cross back, they saw several Japanese planes target some of the big ships offshore. Instantly the air was filled with tracers and black puffs of smoke as scores of anti-aircraft guns opened fire. "One plane was hit," recalled Carlton, "and exploded with an orange flash," leaving "a trail of black smoke as it spiraled to the sea."

* DUKW, a six-wheel-drive amphibious truck, produced by Sparkman & Stephens and the General Motors Corporation.

Led by a non-com back across the Bishi, they moved inland, passing Kadena airfield which had been their primary objective. What was wrong? Where were the Japs? they wondered. "We had landed almost unopposed much to our surprise," wrote Carlton. "Were we being led into a trap?" They continued on across "small hills covered with scrub trees and bushes." In a cave they found twenty or so bewildered civilians, mostly elderly. Unsure what to do with them, they left one man to guard the cave entrance and continued on up the next hill where they established a perimeter and dug in for the night. Still wet, Carlton put on an extra sweater and wrapped himself in his poncho. Unable to sleep, he listened to the sound of naval shells passing overhead "like a distant freight train."[5]

Having watched the assault troops of the 5th Marines land without incident, the journalist Ernie Pyle followed in the 7th wave with the regimental command group at around 9:30 a.m. "We had all expected to go onto the beach in a hailstorm of tracer bullets, mortar shells throwing sand, and artillery shells whistling into the water near us. And yet we couldn't see a bit of firing ahead. We hoped it was true."

It was. Stepping from the amtrac onto Japanese soil, he heard an incredulous Marine say: "Hell, this is just like one of MacArthur's landings," which were famously unopposed.* It was a beautiful day, "sunshiney and very warm," and Pyle soon stopped to take off one of the two pairs of trousers he was wearing. Like the Marines, he was dressed in a green herringbone combat uniform, known as "corduroy," and wearing a helmet with its distinctive Marine camouflage cover. He also had two water canteens and was carrying, in a pack on his back, three rubber life preservers, two jackets, the extra pair of trousers, assorted knives, first-aid kits, a shovel and a blanket rolled up in a poncho. He was, he wrote, "overladen as usual."

Pyle followed the headquarters group for about a mile and a half inland, stopping every now and then to rest while the others forged ahead. "A lifetime of sin and crime," he commented ruefully, "finally does catch up with you." The land was mainly cultivated, and "rose gradually from the sea in small fields." It was not, he thought, unlike

* After his unopposed landing on the island of Leyte on October 20, 1944, MacArthur announced: "People of the Philippines: I have returned."

his native Indiana in late summer "when things have started to turn dry and brown, except that these fields were much smaller." Edged by ditches and small two-foot wide dykes, they were filled with sugar cane, sweet potatoes and wheat, which the Marines cut with small sickles. Further inland the fields gave way to rougher, hilly country with less cultivation and more trees. "It is," noted Pyle, "really a pretty country."

Not so attractive were the farmhouses destroyed by the bombardment, some reeking of the "sickening odor of death." There were, Pyle knew, "always people who won't leave, no matter what." Those civilians who had survived were either "very old or very young" and all "very, very poor." The women were dressed in traditional Okinawan kimonos, the old men "in skintight pants." All were filthy and seemed "shocked from the bombardment"; one or two spoke scant English but did not make much sense. They were handed over to officials of the Military Government whose job it was to look after the civilian population. "The poor devils," commented one Marine officer. "I'll bet they think this is the end of the world."

That evening, having caught up with the 5th Marines' headquarters group, Pyle dug his foxhole alongside the others, at the foot of a small embankment, and inflated his three life preservers to use as an improvised mattress, a trick he had learned in Europe. The Marines seemed impressed. "Well, I'll be damned," commented one. "Why in the hell couldn't I have thought of that?"

At dusk, three planes flew overhead which Pyle assumed were friendlies. He was wrong. "In a moment," he noted, "all hell cut loose from the beach. Our entire fleet and the guns ashore started throwing stuff into the sky. I'd never seen a thicker batch of ack-ack." It seems as if, said one Marine, there were more bullets than sky. All three planes were shot down.

Lying in his foxhole, Pyle could hear the low voices of officers nearby, directing troops by field telephone and radio. Every now and then the stillness was broken by the boom of a naval gun, a burst of machine-gun fire or a few scattered rifle shots. These sounds were eerily familiar, "unchanged by distance or time from war on the other side of the world." It was a pattern, wrote Pyle, "so embedded in my soul that, coming back to it again, it seemed to me as I lay there that I'd never known anything else."[6]

10

"There's always some poor bastard who doesn't get word"

"We hit with a jolt that tumbled us in a heap," recalled First Lieutenant Chris Donner, "and ground up onto a coral shelf, then onto sand. The stern ramp dropped, and as some of the infantrymen swarmed over the sides, I led the rush out onto the beach."

A forward artillery observer attached to George Company, 2/7th Marines, Donner had come ashore in the first wave of amtracs. But thanks to an error by the amtrac's driver, he and his four-man team were deposited on a beach in the 6th Marine Division's sector, when they should have been 300 yards farther to the south. Anxious to get back to the 1st Marine Division, he led his men obliquely to the right. "We began to run up the hill after the advancing infantry," he recorded, "who were still blazing away at every bush or hole in the fields of vegetables." Helping to carry his team's heavy radio set, he felt "exhilarated that there was as yet no enemy action," and was only "slightly concerned about our confusion in landing."

The 32-year-old Donner was a married Stanford graduate student with one child—a son born three weeks after Pearl Harbor—and could probably have avoided the draft. But he volunteered anyway, determined to do his bit, and had been overseas since the spring of 1943, seeing service with the 9th Defense Battalion of artillery on New Georgia and Guam. By late December 1944, he was just a month short of "stateside liberty" when he was sent as a replacement to How Battery, 3/11th Marines, an artillery outfit in the 1st Marine Division.

Appointed a forward observer—the "roughest" job in the artillery, with responsibility for directing fire for the grunts in the front line—he was given a crash course in "how to operate sets and phones, send messages in code, and arrange barrages of a sort," and went on a week-long exercise with the 7th Marines' George Company to get "an insight into how the infantry really moves," "how fouled up it can become," and "how little one should carry along as personal gear." His own light pack for the landing included a poncho, field glasses, map case and gas mask. He was also carrying an M1 carbine,* and a jungle knife, ammunition and two canteens on his belt. His only luxuries were a seven-foot strip of green baize—"of the type used in covering pool tables"—to wrap himself in at night, and a pint of whiskey.

Moving inland with his team, Donner eventually met up with George Company's HQ, and together they reached the edge of Yontan airfield "and saw a mass of junked Japanese planes at one end of a runway which was not too badly scarred by bombs and shell craters" At the far side of the airfield they met a large patrol of the 4th Marines who "were amazed to find our company here, for they were supposed to be the first unit to take this section."

After a brief stop for lunch, they continued on into the nearby village of Irammiya where they found a "decrepit old man, clad in black robes, his chin trailing a long, scraggly white beard." Many of the village's houses were still standing, though their tile roofs and wooden walls had been riddled with shrapnel. Beyond Irammiya the forward platoon heard voices from a cave in the hillside. When no one responded to calls in Japanese for them to come out, the Marines shot into the cave with Browning automatic rifles (BARs).† Edging inside, they found three corpses—two men and a woman—and only a 3-year-old boy still alive, crying and "covered with his mother's blood." The boy was handed over to Monahan, one of Donner's team, who washed off the gore and carried him on his shoulders.[1]

Landing later that day on the beach that Donner missed—Blue 1—was Second Lieutenant "Jep" Carrell, a platoon leader with King Company, 3/7th Marines. Raised in Philadelphia, Carrell was studying for a degree in physics at Swarthmore College in Pennsylvania when he switched to a V-12 program as a prospective Marine

* The smaller version of the M1 Garand rifle, weighing just five pounds and with a fifteen-round magazine. It was carried by officers and members of weapons teams.

† The M1918 BAR was a .30 caliber light machine gun with a twenty-round magazine that could be fired from the hip or steadied by a bipod.

officer. After boot camp at Parris Island—"really just one big nine-week adventure" for the V-12 candidates, most of whom had "played intercollegiate sports" and "completed at least the junior year of college"—he was put through the eleven-week Special Officer Candidate School (SOCS) at Camp Lejeune that had been set up in late 1944, in the wake of heavy Marine casualties on Saipan, Tinian and Guam, to produce junior officers in a hurry. Carrell and his fellow officer candidates "thought this was a great idea." They might have been "a hair less enthusiastic," he wrote later, if they had "known what we were getting into": fifty percent of their class of 376 candidates would be killed or wounded within six months of graduation.

Posted with three other SOCS friends to King Company of the 3/7th Marines, part of the famed 1st Marine Division (or "Old Breed" as it was known), Carrell chose a rifle platoon. He knew perfectly well "that the survival rate for Machine Gun Platoon and Mortar Platoon Leaders was much better than Rifle Platoon Leaders," yet he chose the latter, "not because of bravado," but because his training had concentrated on that type of work and he "didn't know as much about the other two jobs." He would have no regrets, and became especially close to the forty or so men of his No. 1 Platoon (giving him the call sign King One). "In infantry combat," he wrote later, "every member of a rifle platoon is dependent upon other members…Virtually every man will take serious risk to protect or save a member of his team. This translates into a fierce devotion to his buddies who have gone through the same, dangerous experiences. Having one of them killed or wounded affected me as if I had lost, or nearly lost, a brother."

Part of the reserve battalion for the assault on Okinawa, Carrell got only as far as the southern end of Yontan airfield where he and his men spent the night. "While we were digging in," he recalled, "and about 45 minutes before dark, a small Japanese military plane came in for a landing, south-to-north. I could have thrown a rock underhand, and hit the fuselage."[2]

The plane was a Zero that had just flown from the mainland. Unaware the airfield was in American hands, the pilot taxied up the runway and came to a stop near the control tower. He jumped down from the plane and was approaching a group of soldiers when he realized they were the enemy. Turning to run, he was shot in the back.

"There's always some poor bastard," muttered a Marine, "who doesn't get word."[3]

Love Day was Sergeant William Manchester's 23rd birthday and his chances of becoming 24 were, he reflected, "very slight." He viewed Okinawa as "the last island" before the invasion of mainland Japan, and was certain "the enemy would sacrifice every available man to drive us off it."

When it was time, he and the "Raggedy Asses" climbed down the side of the *George C. Clymer* into a waiting amtrac. "Yellow cordite smoke blew across our bows," he remembered. "Battleship guns were flashing, rockets hitting the shore sound *c-r-r-rack*, like a monstrous lash, and we were, as infantrymen always are at this point in a landing, utterly helpless." Once his wave of amtracs were properly aligned, they headed for the beach, "tossing and churning like steeds in a cavalry charge." Incredibly there were "no splashes of Jap mortar shells, no roars of Jap coastal guns, no grazing Jap machine-gun fire." The enemy was not shooting back, because "there wasn't any enemy there." It was, thought Manchester, "the greatest April Fool's Day joke of all time."

Manchester and the rest of the 2/29th Marines walked inland—passing the northern edge of Yontan airfield—and into the low hills beyond where the Okinawans had built "quaint, concrete, lyre-shaped burial vaults." He felt "jubilant."[4]

Another Marine who landed on the 6th Division's beaches was 20-year-old Private Salvatore Giammanco of Love Company, 3/4th Marines. An Italian immigrant who had settled with his family in Brooklyn, Giammanco volunteered for the elite 2nd Marine Raiders* after the bombing of Pearl Harbor and served with them in Bougainville in late 1943 where he "spent days in water-soaked positions filled with rats, crocodiles and every kind of bug you can think of." When the Marine Raiders were converted into the new 4th Marine Regiment in 1944—the original had been captured on Bataan and Corregidor two years earlier—he fought with the 3rd

* The Marine Raiders were created in 1942 to carry out amphibious operations behind enemy lines. By early 1944 there was no longer a need for such specialized units and the Raider battalions were redesignated the 4th Marine Regiment.

Battalion as a machine-gunner on Guam as part of the 1st Marine Provisional Brigade.

By early 1945, Giammanco had been overseas for more than two years and was due leave. When it was canceled because the next operation was imminent, he was offered the chance to stay with the rear echelon. He refused, saying he could never think of leaving his squad when they were about to go into action. Which is why, having hit the beach three hours earlier, he found himself at the northwest edge of Yontan airfield at 11:30 a.m. on Love Day. "I was," he recalled, "surprised to see our tanks there and everybody messing around, telling Jap jokes."

Out of the corner of his eye, Giammanco saw a single Japanese soldier with a rifle running up a nearby hill, but thought nothing of it. Eventually word came for Love Company to saddle up and move out. They did so in single file: riflemen, machine guns and then mortars. After all the riflemen had passed over a small incline, they were followed by Giammanco's No. 1 Squad of machine-gunners. That was when they heard the first crack of a rifle bullet. Giammanco turned to "Meathead" Bernachet, one of the replacements, and said: "You are now a combat veteran."

He had barely finished speaking when a sniper's bullet hit him in the left side of his chest, narrowly missing his heart, puncturing his lung and exiting through his back. The impact spun him around and, as he fell, his rifle and two boxes of ammunition went flying.

"I'm hit!" he yelled.

His friend Paul "Peu" Ulrich dropped down beside him and used his Ka-Bar knife* to cut away Giammanco's pack, dungaree jacket and skivvy shirt. When Peu saw how close the bullet had come to his heart, he said: "Don't worry, GI. You're going to live. The bullet went right through you."

Given morphine and a little brandy, Giammanco felt furious that someone had shot at him "without my permission." He began to struggle and, to calm him, Peu handed him the rifle the New Yorker had dropped. Peu was dressing his wounds when two more bullets narrowly missed them. "Peu, get down!" shouted Giammanco.

* First issued to Marines in 1942, the Ka-Bar was a utility/fighting knife with a leather non-slip handle and a broad seven-inch carbon steel blade.

A minute after Peu had moved on to rejoin the rest of the squad, two corpsmen arrived with a stretcher. But when one saw the seriousness of his injury, he told the other to get a jeep with a stretcher. "This guy has a hemorrhage interplural. I'll start him with a plasma bottle, but he's going to need whole blood. He's bleeding inside."

Five minutes later, the corpsman returned with a jeep and Giammanco was driven slowly back to a large medical tent. As they took him inside, a young corpsmen said: "Why bring him in, too? He's dying, like this guy lying here." He was gesturing toward another badly injured Marine.

Hearing this, another corpsman got up, grabbed the loudmouth kid and threw him outside, with the words: "Can't you see this guy is still alive, you sonofabitch?"

But as it was obvious that Giammanco needed whole blood to survive, he was taken down to the beach, loaded into a Higgins boat and taken out to a hospital ship where he fell into coma. He was saved by a transfusion.[5]

The news that the landings were unopposed, meanwhile, had prompted Admiral Turner to bring his command ship *Eldorado* closer to the northern beaches. From his station on the ship's searchlight platform, Brigadier General Oliver Smith now had a panoramic view of the coastline. "Coral ledges, pitted with caves, jutted out from the beaches north of the Bisha Gawa [River]. Back of the beaches was flat or gently sloping terrain, culminating in the flat high ground on which the Yontan Field was located. Further back was still higher and more rugged terrain. All beaches were under observation from the higher ground inland."

Smith knew from intelligence reports that the Japanese had at least 400 large-caliber artillery pieces on Okinawa. He could now see with his own eyes that the ground was ideal for defense. "Yet," he wrote, "our troops went in standing up with no greater obstacle than the terrain itself."[6]

By nightfall, the beachhead was 15,000 yards long and, in places, 5,000 yards deep. More than 60,000 men were ashore, including all reserve regiments and 15,000 service troops. In addition, numerous tanks and anti-aircraft units had been landed, as had all the divisional artillery and, by evening, guns were in position to support the forward troops. Kadena airfield, moreover, was serviceable for emergency landings.[7]

Lieutenant General Buckner was elated. "From start to finish," he wrote in his diary, "the landing was a superb piece of teamwork, which we could watch from the fifty-yard line in the command room on the flag deck. We landed practically without opposition and gained more ground than we expected to for three days, including the Yomitan [*sic*] and Kadena airfields. [Major General Archibald V.] Arnold's 7th Div made the furthest gains and got halfway across the island...The Japs have missed their best opportunity on the ground and in the air. When their counter-attack comes we will be holding strong ground."[8]

Admiral Turner was even more optimistic. "I may be crazy," he signaled his boss Admiral Nimitz, "but it looks like the Japs have quit the war."

Knowing full well the fight would be a tough one, Nimitz messaged back: "Delete all after crazy."[9]

11

"The smell of burnt flesh hung about for days"

Private Second Class Masahide Ōta, a 19-year-old from Kume Island, felt a thrill of excitement standing just yards from Lieutenant General Ushijima and his senior officers, notably Major General Chō and Colonel Yahara, as they watched the Americans land on the Hagushi beaches from their viewing platform on the battlements of Shuri Castle. A former pupil of the Okinawa Normal School in Shuri, Ōta had recently been mobilized into the Blood and Iron Corps and assigned, as one of the top twenty-two students, to the elite Chihaya Unit which was attached to the staff intelligence at Thirty-Second Army headquarters. "Whenever information came in," recalled Ōta, "our job was to carry the latest on the battle situation to the civilians and soldiers in the caves."

Convinced by one of his teachers that the huge American fleet they could see arrayed before them had been drawn into a carefully laid trap, he could not wait to play his part in the destruction of the invaders.[1] As the reality of Colonel Yahara's strategy of attrition became clear, however, Ōta's martial ardor would fade. On April 1, the best Japanese troops were kept well away from the Hagushi beaches and the only minor threat the Americans faced on land that day was from the 1st Specially Established Regiment whose job was to protect the Yontan and Kadena airfields. But its men—drawn from the 44th and 56th Air Base Battalions—had had little combat training and, already weakened by the shelling, put up little resistance before withdrawing to the north to join the Kunigami Detachment.[2]

A Japanese soldier posted in an elementary school, two miles from the beaches, described the sea and air bombardment as like "a hundred thunders striking at once." At one point during the morning, he recalled, "a soldier from the small unit assigned to defend the beach came to tell us about the landing, amazing everyone that those men down there had survived the ten days of relentless bombing." He then returned to "guard his position to the death—and, indeed, everyone [Japanese] at the landing site died fighting."[3]

Another watching Japanese soldier was mystified when the American vanguard of "tanks, other vehicles and infantry" reached the beaches untouched. "What a great opportunity!" he thought, "Why didn't our air force come and attack them? Maybe they were waiting for all the transport ships to come and line up for us. But that's just what they did—and still our planes didn't appear. Finally the enemy began landing in a leisurely manner, so to speak, and made our airfields into *their* unsinkable aircraft carriers."[4]

Some Japanese kamikaze planes did reach Okinawa on April 1, damaging the battleship USS *West Virginia* and three troop transports (as we have seen). Others targeted the British Pacific Fleet, operating against airfields 200 miles to the south of Okinawa, while still more suicide missions were being, or had been, launched from the Japanese home islands. On March 29, for example, four submarines had left their base on the island of Kyushu and set a course for Okinawa. They were carrying on their decks a total of twenty Kaiten human torpedoes. The pilot of one was 20-year-old Yutaka Yokota, a graduate of the Naval Flight Training Academy at Yokaren and a "militaristic youth." Inspired by the exploits of the IJN's two-man midget submarine crews at Pearl Harbor,* he volunteered for the Kaiten Special Attack Corps and, on selection, felt a "slight sense of sadness": his life, he knew, "had no more than a year to go." Yet he was not thinking of survival. He knew his death was inevitable and, "rather than getting shot down by some plane," it was "better to die grandly." His life was "dedicated to self-sacrifice, to smashing into the enemy," and his only fear was that his mission would fail to sink an American ship and he would have to "self-detonate."

On the morning of his departure from Hikari, he and fellow Kaiten pilots were given a ceremonial short sword, a tantō, and a headband with the words "Given Seven Lives, I'll Serve the Nation

* Five two-man midget submarines had been lost: nine crew members were killed and one, Kazuo Sakamaki, taken prisoner. His fate was never mentioned by the Japanese press during the war.

with Each of Them." Climbing onto the deck of the *I-47* submarine, he kissed the explosive-laden nose of his Kaiten, and shouted: "In a week it's Okinawa! Nothing less than 30,000 tons! No suicide for any tiny ship!"

During the voyage, the Kaiten pilots joked and played shōgi, go and cards. One ensign, who would later sink an American destroyer, impressed his colleagues with card tricks. But their relaxed demeanor would not survive March 31, two days out, when the *I-47* was discovered by American planes and badly damaged by bombs and depth charges. The Kaitens "looked like they'd been made of celluloid," noted Yokota, "all bent and twisted out of shape. We had to return to Hikari empty-handed."[5]

The following day, as American troops landed on Okinawa, a far bigger suicide operation—code-named Heaven Number One—was authorized by the Combined Fleet HQ. The fateful meeting that resulted in this operation had taken place on March 29 at the Imperial Palace in Tokyo between Emperor Hirohito and Admiral Koshirō Oikawa, the chief of the IJN's general staff. A veteran of the Russo-Japanese War of 1904–5 and former minister of the navy who had opposed the war with America, Oikawa had come to brief the emperor on current operations at Okinawa.

Once seated with his staff around a conference table in a damp bomb shelter, close to the imperial library—all facing sideways in order to avert their gaze from the man they believed to be a demigod—Oikawa told the bespectacled emperor, who looked more like a nervous academic than a belligerent war leader, that kamikaze operations had already begun against the massive U.S. 5th Fleet off Okinawa.

"Then you must leave nothing to be desired," responded Hirohito, "in executing those plans with a hard struggle by all our forces, since they will decide the fate of our empire."

Assuring him that that was the case, Oikawa said that no fewer than 2,000 naval aircraft were available for suicide attacks.

"Is that all?" asked a clearly disappointed Hirohito, his voice even more high-pitched and reedy than usual.

No, said the admiral, adding that an additional 1,350 army aircraft would also be used.

Still not satisfied, the emperor asked: "But where is the navy? Are there no more ships? No surface forces?"

There were, but not many. At the start of the war, the IJN was the third most powerful navy in the world—after the U.S. Navy and the Royal Navy—with twelve battleships, fifteen fleet carriers, forty-three cruisers (heavy and light), 169 destroyers and 195 submarines. But almost all those vessels had since been sunk—most by U.S. Navy carrier planes in the Pacific at Coral Sea, Midway, Philippine Sea (the "Great Marianas Turkey Shoot") and Leyte Gulf—and the IJN's remaining operational surface fleet was just one superbattleship, a light cruiser and eight destroyers. Yet that superbattleship, *Yamato*, was not only the pride of the IJN, she was also recognized as the most powerful warship in the world.

Laid down in 1937 in a dry dock screened by bamboo matting, and named after an ancient Honshu kingdom, the huge 72,000-ton *Yamato* had consumed enough steel to build a 250-mile railroad from Tokyo to Osaka. She boasted nine 18.1-inch guns, capable of firing a 3,220-pound shell more than twenty-seven miles, many smaller cannon, and no fewer than 162 anti-aircraft guns of up to five-inch caliber. Her main armor was sixteen inches thick—even heavier around her gun turrets—and designed to withstand the heaviest enemy shells. She was also a "singularly beautiful ship," according to the naval historian Samuel Eliot Morison, with a long sweeping foredeck, a single funnel angled back at twenty-five degrees, and a streamlined superstructure. Her teak weatherdeck ran for 863 feet from bows to stern—almost the length of three football fields—and she was powered by four turbine engines capable of generating 150,000 horsepower. Her crew of more than 2,750 was served by eighty chefs and enjoyed air conditioning in many compartments. Yet despite her lumbering size, she was capable of a maximum speed of 27.5 knots (more than 30 mph). The latest American *Iowa* class of battleship, by contrast, displaced 57,000 tons fully loaded and was armed with nine sixteen-inch guns, and despite her lighter weight could only travel a few knots faster than *Yamato*.

For all the *Yamato*'s power and grandeur, the war had demonstrated that naval aviation was now the dominant factor in sea battles, and that battleships had been supplanted by aircraft carriers as the key to naval victory. Air power had decided Pearl Harbor and every major naval engagement since, costing the Royal Navy the *Repulse* and *Prince of Wales* off Malaya in December 1941, and the IJN countless surface ships, notably the *Musashi*, sister ship to *Yamato*, which sank after she was hit by nineteen torpedoes and seventeen bombs at Leyte Gulf on October 24, 1944.

When Hirohito asked that fatal question—"Are there no more ships?"—he sealed the fate of *Yamato* and most of her crew. Not because Admiral Oikawa was unaware of the consequences of sending the superbattleship and its small escort against the might of the U.S. 5th Fleet's carrier planes. He knew perfectly well what the outcome would be. But the way the emperor had framed his question, his voice almost dripping contempt, made it impossible for Oikawa and his colleagues at the Combined Fleet HQ not to throw the *Yamato* into the fray.

To do otherwise would have been perceived as defiance and, more than that, a loss of face for the IJN. There were those, too, who felt it was better to lose the *Yamato* on one final glorious mission, than allow it to be sunk at its moorings—an end that, sooner or later, was almost inevitable. "Even if the odds were only ten percent in favor," argued Captain Shigenori Kami, the Combined Fleet's chief of operations, "the effort would be worthwhile. A true samurai doesn't ask whether his efforts pay. He merely seeks the opportunity to sacrifice himself."

On April 1, 1945, Vice Admiral Seiichi Itō, commander of the *Yamato*'s Task Force II, was ordered to "destroy the enemy convoy and task force around Okinawa" in cooperation with the Japanese air forces and army. He knew the task was hopeless, as did his captains, many of whom said they could accomplish more by lone-wolf missions. But Itō was adamant. "A samurai lives," he told them, "so that he is always prepared to die."

This argument of self-sacrifice for its own sake was rejected by Tameichi Hara, captain of the light cruiser *Yahagi*, who told his crew: "Our mission appears suicidal and it is. But I wish to emphasize that suicide is not the objective. The objective is victory...You are not to be slain merely as sacrifices of the nation."[6]

* * *

At 7:25 a.m. that day, the British Pacific Fleet* (or Task Force 57) had just launched its first fighter sweep of the day from its operating area close to the Sakishima Islands, 200 miles south of Okinawa, when the enemy hit back. "The guns suddenly opened up," wrote N. B. Gray, a young steward on duty in the sealed magazine of the aircraft carrier HMS *Indefatigable*, "and we passed the ammo as quickly as we dared, using the starboard hoist, then switching over to the port hoist. This meant that the guns were following on to something big."

The frantic burst of firing was ended by a "dull thud." Unsure what was happening on deck, Gray and his colleagues waited for what seemed an eternity. Eventually the ship's captain, Q. D. Graham, spoke: "I am sorry to say that this morning the Japs presented us with a lovely Easter egg. Although we have been damaged, and have casualties, it hasn't impaired our operational capabilities."[7]

It was typical British understatement for a near-fatal kamikaze attack. The plane was one of five Japanese Zero fighters—or "Zekes," as the Allies called them—that had been detected by radar when they were seventy-five miles from the fleet, closing at 210 knots at an altitude of 8,000 feet. Additional British fighters were launched, and those on combat air patrol were vectored on to the intruders, engaging them at a distance of forty miles and shooting down four. But one got through and, though closely pursued by a British fighter, managed to strafe the carrier HMS *Indomitable*'s flight deck before crashing into the base of the *Indefatigable*'s island, and starting a fire in the deckhead of "B" hangar below the point of impact. Moments earlier, the Zeke had been struck in its port wing by long-range cannon fire from its pursuer, a Seafire,† but the damage had not been enough to bring it down.[8]

Gray at once thought of his fellow stewards with jobs on the flight deck: Thomas, a father of two young girls who had joined at the same time as him, and whose job was to serve the officers on the bridge;

* Commanded by Admiral Sir Bruce Fraser, the BPF was operating as part of Admiral Spruance's U.S. 5th Fleet, but had been allocated a separate group of targets, chiefly airfields in the Sakishima Islands, so that it could operate alone. Its first airfield strikes were carried out on March 26.

† The carrier-borne variant of the famous British Spitfire fighter plane.

Munro, "whose position in action was just abaft the island on a pom pom gun"; and Askew, "a likable fellow and very religious." What had happened to them, he wondered, "in that sudden, sharp attack"?

Eventually, the captain ordered the men to "Fall out," and Gray raced up the iron ladders to the mess deck where he discovered, to his horror, that the table was being used as a temporary surgery. "Men lay all over it," he observed glumly, "in pools of their own blood."

His worst fears were realized. Mortally wounded by the explosion, Thomas had been taken to the main sickbay where he spent his last moments "smiling and puffing a cigarette." Askew "had been up near the bridge when the explosion happened" and "was blown to pieces" with "only his glasses" found. Munro, meanwhile, had just left his gun position to relieve himself when the plane struck nearby. He was "very badly burned," noted Gray in his diary, and "died some time later." Though sickened by what he had witnessed, Gray was philosophical: "It was war, and what we expect of war." Gray's colleagues were among four officers and ten ratings killed in the attack; another fifteen were wounded.[9]

The kamikaze had intended either to sink the *Indefatigable* or put her out of action for a considerable time. He managed neither. "In spite of the direct hit," wrote Vice Admiral Sir Philip Vian, commanding the 1st Aircraft Carrier Squadron (with his flag on HMS *Indomitable*), "the *Indefatigable* was able to operate aircraft again within a few hours."* This was chiefly thanks to her armored flight deck, a feature of the British carriers. With more vulnerable flight decks, wrote Vian, "American carriers similarly struck were invariably forced to return to a fully equipped Navy Yard for repairs." But then the U.S. Navy had many more carriers and could afford to replace those put out of action. They also had the advantage over the British, noted Vian, of "greater speed and endurance, and a more effective anti-aircraft armament."[10]

Delighted by *Indefatigable*'s quick recovery, Vian signaled to her captain: "Well done! I say again, Well done." For Gray, though, these congratulations would not bring back his three friends, or dispel the gruesome "smell of burnt flesh" which "hung about for days."

* An additional consequence of the attack was the loss of the *Indefatigable*'s forward flight deck barrier, giving its planes less room to land. Five Seafires, as a result, were damaged on landing "beyond immediate repair." (Hobbs, *British Pacific Fleet*, p. 139.)

12

"War is indeed hell"

Benefiting from "perfect weather and light resistance," Buckner's men made rapid progress during the next few days. By 2:00 p.m. on the 2nd, the forward patrols of the 7th Infantry Division had reached Nakagusuku Bay on the east coast, cutting the island in half. That evening, however, the 96th Infantry Division faced stiffening opposition as it advanced through hills in and around the village of Momabaru, and was forced to use air strikes, artillery support and tanks to take one ridge line. On April 3, both divisions of the XXIV Corps turned south, with the 7th advancing three miles to a line facing Hill 165, "the coastal extremity of a line of hills that swept south-west" of the village of Kuba, while the 96th also made good ground to the right.

Further north, the 1st Marine Division was hampered more by primitive roads and rough terrain than the enemy, though it did reach the sea at midday on the 3rd and send patrols into the Katchin Peninsula which it found to be unoccupied. The 6th Marine Division, meanwhile, had patrolled the peninsula northwest of the Hagushi beaches and captured the coastal town of Nagahama, killing more than 250 Japanese defenders in two strongpoints in the rugged terrain of Yontan-Zan, where "well-worn trails criss-crossed the wooded hills and ridges, and caves pitted the coral walls and steep defiles."[1]

The scenery "was lovely," recalled Sergeant William Manchester of the 2/29th Marines. "To the left lay the sea; to the right, the hills rose in graceful terraces, each supporting rice paddies. Our path was of orange clay, bordered by stunted bushes and shrubs, cherry trees, and red calla lilies...Even the remains of the bridges, which had been taken out by our bombers, were beautiful."

A sight he found hard to stomach, however, "was the sprawled body of a girl" which he discovered on a beach. She had been murdered, and he suspected a Marine. "The thought that an American could commit such a crime," wrote Manchester, "in fighting a just war raged against everything I believed in, everything my country represented. I was deeply troubled."[2]

Still embedded with the 5th Marines, Ernie Pyle's most pressing concern during his first couple of days on Okinawa was how to prevent swarms of mosquitoes—the "noisiest" and most "persistent" he had ever had to deal with—from eating him alive. He tried dousing his face liberally with insect repellent, and pulling his blanket down over his head at night so that he could hardly breathe, "but it did no good whatsoever." He still woke up on April 2 with his face a swollen mass of lumps and his left eye almost closed. "So, bright and early," he recalled, "I started taking Atabrine for the first time in my life."

Having come ashore with the regimental HQ, Pyle now joined Able Company of 1/5th Marines for the march across the island. Its "skipper" was Captain Julian D. Dusenbury from Claussen, South Carolina, who had joined the Marines in 1942, shortly after graduating from Clemson where he was president of the senior class, master cadet and a member of one of the oldest fraternities. Dusenbury had turned 24 on Love Day and shared his birthday with William Manchester of the 6th Marine Division who, though a year younger, would have regarded him as the sort of "upper-middle-class snob" that he had so resented at Quantico.

Yet Pyle, an acute judge of men, found no trace of inbred arrogance in Dusenbury. Instead he wrote of "a young man with a soft Southern voice," his black hair shaved to a crew cut and his skin "a little yellow from taking Atabrine." More tellingly, he was "easy-going with his men and you could tell they liked him." Perhaps they were grateful for the protective power he seemed to grant them, going through Love Day, which happened to be Dusenbury's birthday, without a single casualty in the company. "That," he told Pyle, "was the happiest birthday present I ever had."

A veteran of Peleliu, Dusenbury had won the Silver Star for repulsing two Japanese tank counter-attacks and then leading his men across 1,400 yards of fire-swept airfield to a point where, though severely wounded by shell fragments, he "continued to direct his troops in driving the Japanese from strongly fortified positions until he was ordered by the battalion commander to return to the rear for treatment." He was clearly an inspirational leader who was determined to keep alive as many of his men as possible.[3]

When Pyle joined Able Company on Okinawa, it was dug in on a hill beyond Yontan airfield. Given the choice of bedding down in Dusenbury's command post—"a big, round Japanese gun emplacement made of sandbags"—or with some of his men, Pyle chose the latter and "roomed" with two NCOs—Corporal Martin Clayton from Dallas and PFC William Gross from Lansing, Michigan—in a "little gypsylike hideout" they had made halfway down the hill. Clayton, nicknamed "Bird Dog," was "tall, thin, and dark, almost Latin-looking," and sported a "puny mustache he'd been trying to grow for weeks." Gross, noted Pyle, was "very quiet, and thoughtful of little things, and both of them looked after me for several days." The pair were delighted to share Pyle's inflatable preservers and blanket, as they had been sleeping "on the ground with no cover, except for their cold, rubberised ponchos," and had "almost frozen to death."

While eating rations and some roasted pig—the donation of another Marine—round a camp fire, Pyle was asked what he thought "about things over here and how it compared with Europe," and also when he expected the war to end. "Of course," he wrote, "I didn't know any of their answers but it made conversation. The boys told jokes, they cussed a lot, they dragged out stories of their past blitzes, and they spoke gravely about war and what would happen to them when they finally got home." When Pyle woke next morning, after another mostly sleepless night, his "right eye was swollen shut, as usual."[4]

On the move, Able Company was the oddest sight. "Some wore green twill caps," wrote Pyle, "some baseball caps, some even wore civilian felt hats they found in Japanese homes. For some reason soldiers the world over like to put on odd local headgear." Men of the mortar platoon had commandeered local horses to help carry their heavy equipment, and Pyle remembered the bizarre sight of one Marine, "dirty and unshaved, leading a sorrel horse with a big bow tie of black and white silk, three feet wide, tied across its chest, and another one tied under its belly, the ends standing out on both sides."

They had just reached their bivouac area when two Marines, hunting for souvenirs, spotted two Japanese soldiers hiding in some brush.

Though well armed with rifles and grenades, the enemy soldiers chose not to fight and were easily taken prisoner. "One Jap was small," wrote Pyle, "about 30 years old. The other was just a boy of 16 or 17, but good-sized and well built. He had the rank of superior private and the other was a corporal. They were Japanese from Japan, and not the Okinawan home guard. They were both trembling all over."

The prisoners were sent back to regimental HQ, but without their weapons which were kept by their captors, one of whom, Corporal Jack Ossege from Silver Grove, Kentucky, was offered $100 for the Arisaka rifle by a 33-year-old NCO called "Pop," but "the answer was no." When the offer was raised to eight quarts of whiskey, he wavered, before asking Pop where he would get such a quantity from. Pop had no idea, so Ossege kept the rifle.[5]

Colonel Vernon E. Megee, commanding the Marine air-support units, went ashore from the *Eldorado* on April 2 and set up his headquarters in a farm between the Yontan and Kadena airfields. He was struck by the plight of the native Okinawans who "had deserted their farms and villages at our approach, and had later to be rounded up and placed temporarily in concentration camps." These refugees were, wrote Megee, "pitiable in the extreme, mostly old men and women and small children." He added:

> When these frightened and starving people found that we meant them no harm their relief and gratitude were touching. They had been told by the Japanese that we meant to kill them, or worse. Day after day they filed down from hiding places in the hills in family groups, old and incredibly bent, and ragged beyond imagination. The very ancient were carried on the backs of their middle-aged sons, the little ones peeped shyly and wide-eyed from grandmother's skirts. As soon as time permitted we resettled them in their villages and farms and did what we could to alleviate their distress. War is indeed hell—not only for the combatants.[6]

Back on the *Eldorado*, Lieutenant General Buckner remained convinced that he had outwitted his opponent. "We got across to the east coast of the island today," he wrote to his wife on April 2, "cutting it in two. Resistance is stiffening somewhat on both flanks but the Jap commander failed to counter-attack this morning... So far the Jap's apparent misconception of our plan, his failure to oppose our landing and his concentration near our pretended landing have made things very easy for us." A day later, he added: "Everything is going well and so far my opposing general has not displayed any noticeable degree of military brilliance. At least, he has not done any of the things that I hoped he would not think of. I hope he keeps this up."

He was aware, however, that the main Japanese defenses were in the south and that "heavy fighting" was about to begin. With that in mind, he admitted to his wife that his "responsibility for so many lives" was "sobering," yet he took solace in the "fine fighting qualities" of his men.[7]

Supplying the 100,000 or so men who had already landed was the responsibility of the service troops, who had set up floodlights on the beaches to facilitate the unloading of landing craft throughout the night. Pontoon causeways were also established, as was a T-pier with a 300-foot single-lane approach and a 30- by 170-foot head, and a U-pier with two 500-foot approaches and a 60- by 170-foot wharf section. They were soon supplanted by six single-lane causeways and a massive L-shaped pier. These measures were so successful that, despite changeable weather, the assault shipping was eighty percent unloaded by April 16, at which time more than 577,000 tons of food, ammunition and other supplies had crossed the Hagushi beaches.

"Thus," noted the campaign history, "in an amazingly short time the beachhead had been won and the supply lines established. By April 4, Tenth Army held a slice of Okinawa fifteen miles long and from three to ten miles wide. The beachhead included two airfields of great potentialities, beaches that could take immense tonnage from the cargo ships, and sufficient space for dumps and installations that were rapidly being built. The months of planning and preparation had borne their first fruit."[8]

Yet the kamikaze aerial attacks continued and on May 2 the attack transport ship USS *Henrico*, carrying the regimental headquarters of the 305th Infantry, recently re-embarked from its successful capture of part of the Kerama Islands, was struck by a single suicide plane at

7:00 p.m. Penetrating the commodore's cabin, the plane plunged through two decks before its bomb exploded. "The Nips must have had a sixth sense when they aimed at that particular ship," commented the regimental history, "for important documents, records and maps relative to future operations were destroyed."

Far worse, however, was the loss of senior officers: the naval dead included the commodore of Transport Division 50, the captain of the *Henrico* and forty-eight of the ship's complement (and a further 120 wounded); the 305th lost its popular commanding officer Colonel Vincent J. Tanzola, his XO, adjutant, operations officer and eighteen other key personnel. Most of the surviving officers of the regimental staff were among the seventy-six wounded and ten missing. The soldiers were devastated. "He was a great guy," said one of Tanzola, who had led the regiment on Guam and Leyte. "One of the best. A lot of times I never thought of him as an officer. He acted like any other soldier."

General Hodge, the commander of the XXIV Corps, had wanted the 77th Infantry Division (including the 305th Infantry) to land on Okinawa and "cover the rear" of his other divisions, the 7th and 96th. But Buckner refused* because the 77th was due to take part in the capture of Ie Shima, an island off the northwest coast of Okinawa, scheduled for later that month. With that in mind, Tanzola was replaced by Lieutenant Colonel Joseph B. Coolidge, the former commander the 1/307th Infantry. Coolidge had done well on Guam, and was seen by General Bruce, the divisional commander, as a safer pair of hands than any of the 305th's existing battalion commanders.[9]

* Instead of the 77th, Buckner ordered the 27th Infantry Division to set off from Ulithi and land on the east coast of Okinawa around April 10.

13

"I could see him floating by, face upward"

Late on April 3, Major General Isamu Chō called a staff conference in the Thirty-Second Army's underground HQ at Shuri Castle to discuss a possible counter-attack. Despite his earlier support for Colonel Yahara's plan to fight a defensive battle of attrition, he was under pressure from his superiors in the 10th Area Army on Taiwan and Imperial GHQ in Tokyo to recapture the Yontan and Kadena airfields, and feared the harm that would be done to General Ushijima's reputation if no attempt was made.

Addressing the senior staff, he said that the American position was still in "flux" and that to "annihilate the enemy" it was necessary to counter-attack immediately, "relying on night infiltration and close combat," a method of fighting that would favor the IJA. He then canvassed his staff officers one by one to see if they agreed. Most were junior to Chō in both rank and age, "being only majors and lieutenant colonels and eight to twenty years younger." Taking their cue from Chō, and acknowledging that his suggestion "represented rock-solid IJA doctrine," the younger officers enthusiastically gave their backing. The most emphatic approval came from Major Naomichi Jin, the aviation staff officer, who was "eager to retake the airfields because of their importance to IGHQ's larger air and sea strategy."

When it was Colonel Yahara's turn to speak, he angrily denounced the proposal, saying the young staff officers had agreed to it as if it "were just a five-minute problem on an academy exam." They knew "nothing of the terrain," he added, "or other particular factors affecting the attack, even though this data was critical and actually had been gathered by Chō's subordinates." They were, as a result, making plans on the hoof and "abandoning the policy of attrition warfare that had been carefully developed since the preceding autumn." Moreover, if they thought they would find the Americans unprepared, that was a "complete fantasy." He added:

> The Americans are already established on the beachhead, projecting orderly assault lines north and south, and will be still better organized after the three days it will take us to prepare a large-scale attack. Moving in the open under American guns would be suicidal and wreck the Thirty-Second Army in a few days, which would be especially sad given the long toil preparing the elaborate tunnel positions. Besides all this, the radioed order from Tenth Area Army for attack is not completely explicit, and leaves local commanders some latitude to disregard it if doing so is in the army's interest on account of local circumstances.

When Yahara had finished, Chō rose to his feet and insisted that the consensus still favored attack. They would break for thirty minutes, he added, and reconvene in Lieutenant General Ushijima's office in full uniform and battle ribbons where he would request "an attack by the main body of the army on the Yontan and Kadena airfields." True to form, Ushijima endorsed the "decision" taken by his staff and a "general attack was now the army's intention." To that end, an "attack plan in six paragraphs was drafted."[1]

Horrified by this turn of events, which in his view was about to throw away the cream of the Thirty-Second Army, not to mention "the past eight months of his own labors," Yahara tried to bring the division and brigade commanders round to his way of thinking when they were briefed on the attack orders on April 4. They included lieutenant generals Tatsumi Amamiya and Takeo Fujioka of the 24th and 62nd Infantry Divisions respectively, and Major General Shigeji Suzuki of the 44th Independent Mixed Brigade.

Not a War College graduate, Fujioka owed his promotion to field commands and was, in Yahara's opinion, "quiet and conservative," the "embodiment of the samurai type." Like Ushijima, he relied heavily on his chief of staff. Suzuki was slightly resentful of Fujioka, having graduated above him at the Military Academy, and was a competent if unspectacular officer who was handicapped by the lack of experienced staff officers. The best of the bunch was Amamiya. "Hard-working and competent," noted Yahara, "he was regarded as an excellent leader." He shared Fujioka's conservative outlook, but was "more inclined to exert his personal authority."[2]

One of the three was persuaded by Yahara to voice his opposition to Chō's plan. It was almost certainly Amamiya. But his words had little effect and the orders "remained in force." The attack was scheduled for April 6. With two days to go, an air unit reported to Ushijima's HQ that it had spotted a large naval force of three aircraft carriers and fifty transports and cargo vessels ninety miles south of Naha. Yahara at once showed the message to Chō, arguing that an American landing at Machinato airfield, north of Naha and just south of the existing forward defensive line, at the same moment as the Japanese attack would be "catastrophic." Forced to agree, Chō canceled the April 6 offensive. Yahara had won the first battle of wills with his immediate boss: but there would be many more.[3]

While Japanese commanders debated the merits of a counter-attack, the casualties from the fighting were already trickling into the underground wards of the Haebaru army field hospital where 16-year-old Kikuko Miyagi was among the auxiliary nurses who helped to treat them. The first time one of Kikuko's friends saw a casualty with his toes missing she sank to her knees and almost fainted. "You idiot!" screamed one of the medics. "You think you can act like that on the battlefield?"

Every day the auxiliary nurses were shouted at: "Fools! Idiots! Dummies!" They were, Kikuko admitted, "so naive and unrealistic." They had expected to be placed somewhere far to the rear, where they would "raise the red cross and then wrap men with bandages, rub on medicine, and give them the shots as we had been trained." They imagined they would use tender voices to tell the wounded, "Don't give up, please."

The reality was very different. "In no time at all," recalled Kikuko, "wounded soldiers were being carried into the caves in large numbers. They petrified us. Some didn't have faces, some didn't have limbs. Young men in their twenties and thirties screaming like babies."[4]

The Japanese land offensive might have been postponed, but separate strikes did take place on April 6 by air and sea. The air mission—the first of ten massed raids that made up the Ten-Go suicide campaign—

involved no fewer than 230 navy and 125 army air force kamikazes, escorted by an additional 344 planes from both services. Thanks to messages intercepted from the Japanese Combined Fleet HQ, Admiral Nimitz knew in advance that a major air operation from airfields on Kyushu and Formosa was planned for April 6. So the day before he warned all units to prepare for an attack whose main target would be convoys, but with strikes on the main carrier force also possible.[5]

The ships most vulnerable to this first mass attack were those on distant radar picket duty, tasked with intercepting incoming aircraft, either with their own guns or by alerting the combat air patrol (CAP). There were nineteen radar picket stations (RPS) ringing the island, each manned by a specially equipped destroyer with fighter director teams and radar equipment, and at least two supporting gunboats. Arguably the most vulnerable was RPS 1, sited due north of Okinawa on the flight path from Kyushu. On April 6, the destroyer USS *Bush* was patrolling RPS 1 with a single gunboat, the *LCS(L) 64*. A second gunboat had just returned to the transport area.

The first aircraft were spotted on the *Bush*'s radar at 2:45 a.m. She opened fire with all her anti-aircraft guns and hit one. The destroyer at the neighboring RPS 2—USS *Colhoun*—also reported attacks by multiple planes, but none got through. The CAP coverage of the stations by carrier-borne fighters began at 7:00 a.m., and soon after a twin-engined Japanese navy night fighter (known to the Americans as an "Irving") was shot down close to the *Colhoun*.

At noon, four Marine Vought F4U Corsair fighters* from the carrier *Bennington* (part of Vice Admiral Mitscher's TF 58 Fast Carrier Force) were on patrol when they sighted various enemy planes. They forced one to ditch, and another was chased by Major Hermon Hanson Jr., the flight leader, who "climbed on his tail" and "opened fire." Unfortunately G-forces caused Hanson's guns to jam and, moments later, he was just yards from the enemy plane. Yanking bank on his joystick, he cleared the tail and fuselage with barely

* With its retractable inverted gull wings, 2,000 horsepower Pratt & Whitney Double Wasp radial engine (giving it a top speed of more than 400 mph), and six .50 caliber wing-mounted machine guns, the F4U Corsair was one of the most formidable fighters of the Second World War.

twelve inches to spare. "I could see the rivets on the plane," recalled Hanson. "There were two yellow stripes on the wings, where patches had evidently been placed. I saw the pilot clearly. Lashed beneath the plane was a big bomb. It was suspended by a makeshift arrangement of wires and ropes."

No sooner had Hanson overshot than one of his colleagues took up the chase, opening fire at 800 yards. He had closed to within twenty-five feet when the plane finally caught fire, rolled over and crashed into the sea.

At 2:30 p.m. the *Bush*'s radar picked up another incoming flight of planes. She shot down two; another two were brought down by the CAP. But the attacks kept coming. At 3:13 p.m. *Bush*'s lookouts spotted a single-engined navy torpedo bomber (known as a "Jill") dead ahead and closing fast. It was part of a group of fifteen that had taken off that morning from Kushira Naval Air Base on Kyushu. The destroyer opened up with all available anti-aircraft guns, but the plane kept coming and crashed amidships on the starboard side, its bomb exploding in the forward engine room. Water flooded in and within minutes the ship was listing ten degrees to port. With emergency power failing, and some guns inoperable, the stricken *Bush* radioed for immediate assistance.

The *Colhoun* rushed to her aid, as did fourteen Grumman F6F Hellcat fighters* from the carrier *Belleau Wood*. Over the next ninety minutes the Hellcats encountered an estimated sixty to seventy enemy planes in small groups. Most were kamikazes with inexperienced pilots who took no evasive action when attacked. Of the forty-six shot down by Hellcats, Ensign C. C. Foster accounted for seven. Two more got five apiece. It was, commented one, "Turkey Shoot Number Two."

But the kamikazes kept coming and at 4:30 p.m., as the *Colhoun* arrived on the scene, the CAP had retired to refuel and at least ten Japanese planes were circling overhead, waiting for their chance to attack. Some were shot down by Wildcats arriving from the carrier *Anzio*. But when they also left, the two destroyers were alone. On the *Colhoun* was a Marine pilot, First Lieutenant Junie Lohan, who had

* Powered by the same engine as the Corsair, the Hellcat shot down a total of 5,223 enemy aircraft, more than any other Allied naval aircraft.

been plucked from the sea the previous day. "Out of the clouds," recorded Lohan, "came…a Zeke, diving straight at our port side. Everyone started running but I was too fascinated to move." He added:

> I stood by the rail on the main deck forward of amidships watching him come in. It was a horrible sound. The Zeke hit near me, wrecking the forward fire room. Many men were wounded and hurt…I looked for Doc Casey and began to help him with the wounded. We carried the worse cases into the wardroom… We were moving the wounded to a safer place when the Jap came in from the starboard side. The bomb burst hit the fire room—killed all but two men. The scenes were horrible.

Already hit by two kamikazes, the *Colhoun* was then targeted by a third which "got through the AA fire and hit the port side of the bridge." It was, noted Lohan, "hell again—even worse. The Jap pilot was blown overboard by the blast. I could see him floating by, face upward. He looked not a day older than 14."

The *Bush* also suffered multiple kamikaze strikes and, after valiant attempts to save her, the captain ordered his surviving crew to abandon ship in a heavy swell at 6:30 p.m. Minutes later she sank, the first ship lost on picket duty. A total of seven officers and eighty-seven men were killed; of the 240 survivors, many were so exhausted and badly wounded they could not save themselves. "We picked up more dead than alive," remembered a gunboat officer who helped in the rescue. Next morning, when the sun came up, he "looked out over the horizon and it was just filled with people in their jackets," dead in the water. It was a "terrible sight."

Some of the corpses were from the *Colhoun* which was finally abandoned at 8:15 p.m. when her captain ordered his remaining 227 crew to transfer to the gunboat *LCS(L) 84* (and later to the destroyer *Cassin Young*). The survivors included Marine pilot Junie Lohan, rescued for the second time in two days. "I don't think I'll ever forget the sight of the other ship as we came upon them," he recalled. "It was wonderful. A lot cried, too."[6]

Most of the kamikaze attacks were against the ships manning the outlying radar picket stations, but one lone plane got as far as the fleet anchorage off the west coast of Okinawa where it selected the command ship *Eldorado* as its target. "He was hit in the final stage of his dive," wrote Colonel Vernon Megee, watching the drama beside Admiral Turner on the bridge, "by a shell from one of our own five-inch guns, which knocked off a wheel from his fixed landing gear, causing him to veer off course slightly and splash barely astern our ship. He was so close that we could clearly see the goggled head of the pilot. Fortunately for us the bomb he carried did not explode." During the whole nerve-jangling drama, Turner "seemed to be enjoying himself immensely, alternating admonition and cheers for the defending gun crews as if he were a spectator at a ball game." Megee, by contrast, "was too scared to cheer and too proud to duck below decks."[7]

A total of twenty-six American ships were sunk or badly damaged by this huge kamikaze raid, which continued on into the 7th. The early reports received by Vice Admiral Ugaki, commanding the 5th Air Fleet, were encouraging. "Judging from the enemy telephones in hurried confusion," he noted in his diary on the 6th, "and requests for help it was almost certain that we destroyed four carriers." The sea around Okinawa, he added, "was turned into a scene of carnage, and a reconnaissance plane reported that as many as 150 columns of black smoke were observed." In truth, no carriers were hit in the raid, let alone sunk, and American losses, though heavy, were never enough to turn the tide.[8]

14

"Gone? She's gone?"

Light winds were gentling rippling the Inland Sea as the vast superbattleship *Yamato* and her nine escorts weighed anchor off Tokuyama,* at the southern end of Honshu, and headed across the Inland Sea for the Bungo Strait on Friday, April 6, 1945. Captain Hara of the light cruiser *Yahagi* could see "radiant cherry blossoms" dotting the shore and distant mountains sparkling "under the cobalt sky." He had earlier rejected the notion of a suicide mission; now he felt his "beautiful homeland" was "worthy of our sacrifices."[1]

The day before, as his kamikaze pilots prepared for their own operation, Vice Admiral Ugaki had noted in his diary: "The Combined Fleet's issued an order to send *Yamato* and *Yahagi* and six [*sic*] destroyers as a surface special attack unit to the west of Okinawa...with the mission of wiping out enemies there. It may be good, too, as this is the decisive battle." He had been told by Admiral Kusaka, the Combined Fleet's chief of staff, that the movement of the surface ships would not require air cover. "But I couldn't stay aloof," wrote Ugaki who, as the late Admiral Yamamoto's chief of staff, had served on the *Yamato* for a year. "It was only natural to support and cooperate with the friendly force as much as possible to obtain the objective in a related operation." He had, as a result, arranged for a fighter escort for at least part of the voyage.[2]

The primary mission given to the task-force commander, Vice Admiral Itō, was to survive for as long as possible and, in the meantime, attract American carrier-borne planes so as to weaken the aerial defenses of the various task forces off Okinawa. If, by some miracle,

* In preparation for Operation Heaven Number One, *Yamato* had left Kure harbor for Tokuyama on March 29, 1945.

the *Yamato* did get as far as Okinawa, she was to sink as many warships and transports as she could before beaching herself and acting as an immobile artillery battery until her ammunition ran out. Only then would her 2,767-strong crew abandon ship and join the Japanese garrison on the island. That, at least, was the plan.[3]

Acting as the superbattleship's lookout officer as she got under way on the 6th was 22-year-old Ensign Mitsuru Yoshida. "*Yamato* advances inexorably," he noted, "throwing up a bow wave to either side. Thanks to the incomparable seaworthiness of the ship's construction, there is no pitch or roll; even on the bridge we have the illusion of standing on firm ground." A law student at the prestigious Tokyo Imperial University when he was drafted into the IJN, Yoshida had been posted to the *Yamato* after completing an accelerated officer-training program in late 1944. Shortly before departing on what he feared would be a one-way mission, he wrote to his mother: "Please dispose of all my things. Please, everyone, stay well and survive. That is my only prayer."

A couple of hours into the voyage on April 6, the crew of the *Yamato* assembled on the foredeck to hear their executive officer read out a farewell message from Admiral Soemu Toyoda, commander-in-chief of the Combined Fleet. "This task force of the Imperial Navy," said Toyoda, "in cooperation with the army, is about to stake its entire air, sea, and land might on an all-out attack against enemy ships in the vicinity of Okinawa." That attack, he added, was "unparalleled in its heroic bravery," and he urged them to "exalt the glorious traditions of the Imperial Navy's surface forces" and "transmit its glory to posterity." The "fate of the empire," he said, in an easily recognized echo of Admiral Tōgō's flag-signal to obliterate the Russian fleet at Tsushima in 1905, "hangs in the balance." The peroration concluded: "Let each unit, special attack unit or no, fight fiercely, annihilate the enemy task force at every turn, and thereby make secure for all eternity the foundations of the empire." Inspired by these words, the crew bowed in the direction of the emperor in Tokyo, sang the national anthem ("Kimigayo," or "His Imperial Majesty's Reign") and shouted "Banzai!" three times.[4]

At 8:00 p.m., steaming at the center of a diamond of escorting ships, with *Yahagi* bringing up the rear, *Yamato* left the Inland Sea via the narrow and mine-infested Bungo Strait. Barely twenty minutes later, however, the Japanese task force was spotted by two American submarines, *Hackleback* and *Threadfin*, that had been sent to the area after intercepted Japanese radio messages made it clear that an operation by surface ships was under way. They at once reported the sighting to Vice Admiral Mitscher's Fast Carrier Force, describing the number and type of ships and their heading. Mitscher responded by ordering his four task groups to a suitable launching position northeast of Okinawa. From this moment on, the destruction of the *Yamato* was just a matter of time.

For a while, the submarines followed the task force at a safe distance of five miles. Three times a Japanese destroyer tried to drive them away, but never came close enough to make them submerge. As it got dark, the submarines peeled away, having accomplished their task of reporting the movement of surface ships.

At 8:23 a.m. on the 7th, the Japanese task force was located southwest of Kyushu by a search plane from the carrier *Essex*. Its course was 300 degrees—roughly west-northwest—in line with the plan by *Yamato*'s veteran captain, Kōsaku Ariga, to hoodwink his enemies by following a long, circuitous route to Okinawa. But now that it had been discovered, the *Yamato* group was shadowed by relays of American flying boats who gave Mitscher and the other American admirals its real-time location, course and speed. These messages were heard by *Yamato*'s radio operators, but there was nothing Itō could do, short of turning back.

Admiral Spruance's response, meanwhile, was to inform Rear Admiral Deyo of the Gun and Covering Force off Okinawa that the *Yamato* group was fair game for his battleships. At 10:30 a.m., Deyo held a conference of flag officers and captains on Admiral Turner's flagship *Eldorado* at which a battle plan was drawn up for six battleships, seven cruisers and twenty-one destroyers. Aware his ships were outgunned by the *Yamato*, Deyo planned to negate her advantage by force of numbers and by rapidly closing the range.[5]

But first the *Yamato* group had to survive Mitscher's air strikes, the first of which—consisting of 182 dive-bombers with 500- and 1,000-pound payloads, and ninety-eight torpedo-bombers—was launched from multiple carriers at around 10:00 a.m. The first warning of a possible attack was radioed to *Yamato* from a lookout on a Ryukyu island north of Okinawa: "250 carrier-based enemy planes headed due north; keep close watch."

By now the Japanese ships had turned onto their correct course, south-south-west, and were halfway to their target. Despite the threat of attack, Vice Admiral Itō seemed confident. "We got through the morning all right, didn't we?" he said smiling.

It was the first time he had spoken since the mission began. Ensign Yoshida recalled: "The sequence of alerts, the choice of zigzag, the speed, the changes of course—he has left everything to the captain of *Yamato*; and he has merely nodded silently in response to the reports of his chief of staff."

At 12:20 p.m., the ship's air search radar picked up three blips. "Contacts," shouted Petty Officer Hasegawa. "Three large formations. Approaching."

Captain Ariga gave the order to increase speed from twenty-two to twenty-five knots, and to alter course to one hundred degrees. The message was sent to all ships, and they turned simultaneously, as if one.

A light rain had worsened visibility when the first American planes—two Grumman Hellcats—were spotted by a lookout less than two miles away. Then more appeared. "First raid: five planes," shouted the lookout, "…more than ten planes…more than thirty…"

Ensign Yoshida saw the planes peeling off in formation, preparing to attack. Then, dead ahead, another large flight appeared. "More than one hundred planes attacking!" warned the navigation officer.

Ariga had seen enough. "Commence firing!" he ordered, and twenty-four five-inch anti-aircraft guns and 120 machine guns roared into life, followed soon after by the escorts' main batteries. Experiencing his baptism of fire, Yoshida's whole body tingled "with excitement." But the one-sided nature of the clash was soon evident as two Curtiss Helldivers scored bomb hits near the *Yamato*'s aft tower. "A sailor near me is felled by shrapnel," recalled Yoshida. "In the midst of the overwhelming noise, I distinguish the sound of his skull striking the bulkhead; amid the smell of gunpowder all around, I smell blood."

Other ships were also hit. Yoshida watched in horror as the destroyer *Hamakaze*, on the left outer edge of the formation, "all of a sudden seems to expose her crimson belly, then lifts her stern up into the air." She sank in under thirty seconds, leaving behind "a sheet of white foam." Only those crew members above decks were left in the water, "blown off by the impact of the torpedoes and the blast of the exploding ship." To avoid a similar fate, the *Yamato* zigzagged at top speed, her 150,000 horsepower engines at full throttle. She "dodged several torpedoes" before one finally struck her port bow with a huge explosion. It was now that the first wave of attackers departed.

The torpedo had torn a hole in the side of the *Yamato*, flooding the compartments beyond with water. As there were 1,150 of these small compartments—known as flood-control sectors—and all were sealed from each other by metal bulkheads, it was possible to survive even multiple torpedo strikes for a time. But with water pressure building against the bulkheads, it was necessary for the damage-control crews to reinforce them with "great wooden braces." This was done after the first torpedo strike. But henceforth the ship's survival would depend on the crews not being overwhelmed with work.

Informed that the anti-aircraft radar room where he normally worked had been hit, Yoshida raced there from the bridge and found a scene of utter carnage. "It is as if," he wrote, "someone had taken an ax and split a bamboo tube. The bomb, a direct hit, must have sliced its way in at an angle and then exploded." Amidst the debris of shattered instruments, he spotted a "chunk of flesh smashed onto a panel of the broken bulkhead." It was, he realized, "a torso from which all extremities—arms, legs, head—have been ripped off." All around were fragments of "charred flesh," the remnants of comrades "who were alive and at work here until a few minutes ago." The air smelt of burning fat. It was hard for him to process. But even worse was the thought that, without the air search radar, the ship was blind and almost defenseless.

Yoshida returned to the bridge as the second wave of more than a hundred strike planes attacked. "The curtain of anti-aircraft fire *Yamato* throws up," he noted, "is without parallel in our navy. With its carpet of explosions in brilliant red, purple, yellow, and green, it is not an insignificant menace; but its power to intimidate and destroy is far less than we had supposed."

Ignoring the deadly flak, and discarding conventional tactics, the American planes attacked from all angles. Even the torpedo-bombers seemed to "zigzag as soon as they have dropped their payloads and, evading our flak, carry out close-range strafing." They were, as a result, incredibly difficult for the Japanese gunners to hit. "Our percentage of hits," wrote Yoshida, "is very low."

Bombs rained down onto the machine-gun turrets—each equipped with three 25 mm weapons—and, one after another, they were blown to pieces. It was, in Yoshida's words, "a scene or carnage with no place for the living." He saw "white smoke" rising "from the vicinity of the aft flight deck," and near misses off both bows, sending up "a forest of geysers." Water, he remembered, "ten times more than a torrential shower, cascades in, almost shattering the ports of the bridge."

No sooner had the second wave departed than the third swept in "like a sudden rain shower." Yoshida estimated "120 or 130 planes" in the attack from the port beam. Several bombs exploded near the funnel, and reports came in that officer after officer had been killed. Then two more torpedoes hit the port side, causing the needle of the "inclinometer" to begin to move. By that time, many of the damage-control crews were dead or wounded, and it was impossible to shore up all the threatened bulkheads. "Through hatches heedlessly left open for the sailors racing up the companionways," noted Yoshida, "the avalanche of water rushes on. Thus the list increases faster than expected."

To correct the list before it got to five degrees—the level at which the conveyance of artillery shells would be prevented—Captain Ariga ordered the deliberate flooding of adjacent compartments on the starboard side of the ship. That would have let in more than 3,000 tons of water, and stabilized the list. But as the flooding-control station had already been destroyed, the desperate decision was taken to immerse the starboard engine and boiler rooms. There was no time to evacuate the men working there and, as the water rushed in, "the black gang on duty are dashed into pieces." Yoshida added: "At the price of several hundred lives, we barely restore the ship's trim." Reduced now to half power, the *Yamato* was on "one leg and limping."

The next wave of attacks, the fourth, was by 150 planes. They swooped so low that Yoshida could see the "flushed faces" of the American pilots. "Most have their mouths open," he recalled, "and almost ecstatic expressions on their faces." Two sailors beside Yoshida were shot and killed by machine-gun bullets; a fellow ensign was badly wounded in the thigh, his "gushing blood" turning the makeshift dressing "bright red." Though more than half the officers and crew on the bridge were now dead, Vice Admiral Itō remained calmly in his chair, staring straight ahead.[6]

"Aerial torpedoes blew more holes in the port side," recorded the official U.S. naval history, "and at least ten bombs exploded on the decks. The wireless room, supposedly watertight, flooded so completely that thenceforth *Yamato* had to rely entirely on flag and light signals."[7] From 1:45 p.m. there was a brief fifteen-minute respite from attack. But the ship was now listing at fifteen degrees, making barely twelve knots, and was a scene of utter horror. Yoshida wrote:

> Many of the machine-gun turrets are completely destroyed, making the deck a desolation, leaving only pitted lumps of steel... She floats in the water like a chunk of overlogged wood, light brown...The anti-aircraft guns and the secondary guns are completely silent. Only the machine guns remain for the last desperate battle. I understand that many bombs have hit lower down on the bridge, that all medical personnel at the emergency sickbay have been killed.

At 2:00 p.m. the final waves of attack began. Torpedoes hit the stern of the ship, damaging both rudders. More bombs "pour down on the length and breadth of the ship," starting fires below deck. The list worsened to thirty-five degrees, and the speed was down to seven knots. "Don't lose heart!" shouted Captain Ariga from the bridge, but few heard his cry.

Soon after, the executive officer told Ariga: "There's no hope of trimming the list." It was the death knell and, only now, did Vice Admiral Itō rise from his seat and announce: "Stop the operation." He then shook hands with the surviving members of his staff before retiring to "the admiral's quarters directly under the bridge."

For a brief moment, Yoshida considered lashing himself to the bridge and going down with the ship. But he was dissuaded by Itō's chief of staff who ordered the "young ones" to save themselves. Flags were raised to summon the surviving destroyers to take off survivors. Yet the destroyers kept their distance, remembered Yoshida, "fearing either the currents that would follow our sinking or the shock waves from the accompanying explosions."

It was now 2:20 p.m. The deck was nearly vertical and, "fluttering atop the main mast," the battle ensign was about to touch the water. The hull of the ship looked to Yoshida like the exposed belly of a "great whale." Then "the shells for the main batteries fall over in the magazines, slide in the direction of their pointed ends, knock their fuses on the overhead, and explode." Finally, at 2:23 p.m., the huge ship turned belly up and plunged beneath the waves, emitting "one great flash of light" and sending "a gigantic pillar of flame" high into the sky. It was seen from as far away as Kyushu.

Though struck on the head by a piece of shrapnel, Yoshida swam to the surface and used fragments of wood to stay afloat. He was later rescued by the destroyer *Fuyutsuki*, one of only twenty-three officers and 246 sailors out of a total ship's complement of 2,767 to survive. Also sunk or scuttled were the light cruiser *Yahagi* and four of the eight destroyers. In total, the IJN lost more than 4,000 men on this pointless, ill-fated mission. American losses were just ten planes and twelve men.[8]

"My dear *Yamato*," Vice Admiral Ugaki wrote solemnly in his diary, "went down in the China Sea with Commander-in-Chief Ito, Chief of Staff Morishita,* her skipper Ariga, and many fine officers and men. Alas!"[9]

When Emperor Hirohito was told of the disaster, he put his hand to his temple and swayed. "Gone?" he asked in disbelief. "She's gone?"[10]

* In fact, Rear Admiral Morishita, Itō's chief of staff, was the senior officer to survive the sinking.

15

"They just knocked the heck out of us"

The sinking of the world's largest battleship merited barely a line in Lieutenant General Buckner's diary entry for April 7. As the *Yamato* fought vainly for her life in the South China Sea, he was spending his first day on land, visiting in turn the command posts of Hodge's XXIV Corps, and the 7th and 96th Infantry Divisions who, since April 5, had been facing increasingly tough resistance from well-sited outposts to the main Japanese defensive position, known as the "Shuri Line."

On the 6th, the 2/383rd Infantry had braved intense mortar fire to gain the western half of a feature known as Cactus Ridge. "We figured," wrote Staff Sergeant Francis M. Rall, "that the way to get out of that knee-mortar* fire was to get to where it was coming from. So we stood up in waves, firing everything we had and throwing hand grenades by the dozen."[1]

The battalion finished the job on April 7, an action witnessed by Buckner himself as he observed the attack from the hill behind. He then went on to have lunch at Major General Arnold's command post where he was briefed on the progress of the 184th Infantry which, having just captured a rise called the Pinnacle, was advancing toward the main Japanese defenses on Red Hill where the enemy had "made a fortress" by "constructing his usual system of caves and connecting trenches." Private Don Carlton, the Dog Company machine-gunner from rural Minnesota, remembered: "It wasn't a cliff, it was just a big steep hill, and the Japanese were on top, and they had their machine guns and their rifle fire and everything else up there. And we were in a ditch alongside the road, and every time we tried

* "Knee mortar" was the Allied name for a Japanese grenade launcher.

to get up that hill, they just knocked the heck out of us. So they called for tanks."[2]

A total of fifteen tanks—ten medium and five light—were sent through a cut toward Red Hill. But two were disabled by mines and one by a satchel charge* before the others were driven back by artillery and machine-gun fire. This method of "isolating the troops from the tanks with surprise fire followed by close combat tactics" was, noted a Japanese report on the action, "an example in the complete destruction of enemy tanks and will be a great factor in deciding the victories of tank warfare." Only by making a wide flanking attack from the right was the 184th able to capture Red Hill later that day. "Once more," noted the official history, "a Japanese outpost had shown its strength against a frontal attack and its vulnerability to a flanking maneuver."[3]

Having visited Arnold's and Bradley's command posts—the latter in an agricultural school that was "very luxuriously furnished"—Buckner moved on to Kadena airfield which he found "ready for planes except for gas and ground crews which should arrive in a day or so."† He also inspected some "suicide rocket planes" (Ōhkas) with "2,000-lb warheads" that had been found on the airfield.[4]

He did not have time to visit Yontan airfield, but Colonel Vernon Megee did, and found it operational thanks to the "Herculean" efforts of the Seabee engineers. That same day, three squadrons (twenty-four planes each) of Corsairs and one of Hellcats from Marine Air Group (MAG) 31 flew in from support carriers and were put at the disposal of the air-defense commander, Brigadier General Bill Wallace. "The Japanese," noted Megee, "had ample reason to fear these gull-winged fighters, which they chose to call 'whistling death.' The first twelve-plane combat patrol took to the air at 1750 [hours], and the next morning Marine fliers had 'splashed' their first three kamikazes. Henceforth the Marine fliers took over the burden of the close-in air

* A demolition device, primarily intended for combat, composed of blocks of high explosive in a canvas bag with a shoulder strap. The American version was known as the M37 Demolition Kit.

† MAG 33 arrived at Kadena on April 9 and began flying missions the same day.

defense of the objective area, freeing the carrier-based units for operations closer to Japan."[5]

One of the Marine squadrons based at Yontan was VMF (N) 542, flying radar-equipped Grumman F6F Hellcat night fighters. It had been formed at Cherry Point, North Carolina, in August 1944, under Major William C. Kellum, a "popular 30-year-old Californian," and, though it had carried out escort duty at Ulithi, its first proper combat patrol was the night of April 7. Operating in pairs, the Hellcats were "up between dusk and dawn," with each pilot completing a four-hour shift. "This meant that 542 put up four teams (eight aircraft) in two relays each night." Their main point of reference was the tip of land northwest of Yontan known as "Point Bolo." This was the center of the island's radar defenses, and all radar picket ships were deployed in a circle around it.[6]

Part of the ground crew, tasked with keeping 542 Squadron's planes in the air, was 20-year-old Staff Sergeant Donald E. Marpe, a radar expert from a farm near Minneapolis. Arriving on Okinawa with the advance party, Marpe was surprised to find a large A-shaped airfield, with two long runways forming the sides of the letter, and a third, shorter runway as the overlapping crossbar. All were composed of "hard packed gravel" which inevitably became "quite dusty." Marpe wrote: "Our aircraft parking area was just off the south-west side of the left branch of the 'A,' which ran from a south-west to a north-easterly direction, and we made use of several revetments left by the Japanese which gave some of our aircraft a measure of protection. Our working area was next to our aircraft parking and our living area was in the field next to that."

Marpe and his men set up their "test bench radar" in the back of a 6 x 6 truck. Their living area was composed of rows of tattered tents surrounded by moats, to prevent flooding, and "freshly dug" latrines (or "heads" as they were known to Marines) which were "open to the cold wind." Of course, "nobody lived in their tents," preferring the protection offered by foxholes and dugouts. "These living arrangements were made necessary," recalled Marpe, "because when the Japanese bombed Yontan, which they tried to every night it wasn't raining, expended flak fragments fell like rain across the field. This 'friendly fire'...was more to be feared than the actual bomb damage and several of our men were wounded from this."

They lived on "ten-in-one" rations* with options like beans and frankfurters, Vienna sausages, and spaghetti and meatballs. Mail came twice a week, usually with a four- to six-week delay from its posting in the United States. Marpe received the usual home news "about how many lambs had been born, or how the team of mules were being replaced with a team of horses," and occasionally more sobering missives like the death of "Grandpa Marpe." It all helped to keep him on an "even keel" and assure him that there was a life out there that was not just kill or be killed.

There was plenty of water, but "no facilities, so your choice for a shower once in a while was to stand naked out in the rain or take a sponge bath using your steel helmet for your tub." Loss of sleep was also an issue: what with air raids, night duty and living beside an active runway. But despite these privations, Marpe knew he was lucky not to be a line-company Marine: particularly when the first casualty evacuation flights began to take off from Yontan.[7]

On April 8,† while the neighboring 7th Division tackled the strongpoints of Triangulation and Tomb Hills (capturing the former that day, and the forward slopes of the latter on the 9th), the 96th Division advanced toward the start of the main Japanese position on the Kakazu hill mass. It boasted "an ideal combination of defensive features," including a "deep moat, a hill studded with natural and man-made positions," and "a cluster of thick-walled buildings behind the hill." It was, moreover, "an integral element of the Shuri fortified zone and a vital rampart that could expect reinforcements and heavy fire support from within the ring of positions that surrounded the Thirty-Second Army headquarters, only 4,000 yards to the south."[8]

The hill mass stretched northwest to southeast for 1,000 yards, sloping on the west toward the coastal plan, and ending on the east at a highway that spanned the island. It was made up of two hills connected by a saddle. The larger of the two was on the east: 500 yards long and topped by a thin strip of flat land, barely twenty-five

* A food parcel similar to the K-ration, it provided one day's food for 10 men, and included canned meals, jam, evaporated milk, vegetables, biscuits and gum.

† By the evening of April 8, the two divisions of XXIV Corps had suffered 1,510 battle casualties and accounted for 4,489 Japanese killed and thirteen captured.

yards wide, it would become infamous to American troops as Kakazu Ridge. At its western end was a north–south saddle, dotted with tombs (as was the ridge itself), which sloped gently up to a second rise that stretched north to south for 250 yards, forming the head of a "T," and dubbed by the 96th Division "Kakazu West." The whole feature was "not high, nor jagged, nor especially abrupt"; but it would prove to be a fearsome obstacle.

The Japanese had dug mortars into the reverse slope, and zeroed them in on the gorge between Kakazu and the American position, as well as on obvious routes of advance from the gorge to the crest. Several huge 320 mm spigot mortars also protected the hill mass which had machine guns in interconnected pillboxes, tunnels and caves to protect all avenues of approach. Further back, Japanese artillery—both medium and heavy—was in support.

The first American attack on the position was by two battalions of the 383rd Infantry at dawn on April 9: the 1st Battalion assaulted Kakazu Ridge, while the 3rd Battalion took on Kakazu West. Their point companies got as far as the forward slopes of both targets before they were stopped in their tracks by mortar, artillery and machine-gun fire. "Have fifty men on the ridge," Lieutenant Colonel Byron King of the 1st Battalion radioed the regimental commander Colonel Edwin T. "Eddy" May at 8:30 a.m. "Support elements pinned down. Heavy concentrations of mortars and artillery laid down on troops besides MG [machine-gun] crossfire. If we do not get reinforcements, we will have to withdraw."

Having been ordered by Major General James L. Bradley, the divisional commander, to make a "vigorous" attack to the south, Colonel May was unwilling to give up his vital toehold on Kakazu. "Sending G Company to reinforce you," he radioed back. "If the battalion CO is jumpy, have the executive officer take over. Hold the ridge at all costs."

Though sent forward, George Company of the 2/383rd was 1,000 yards to the rear and arrived far too late to help. At 10:00 a.m., taking advantage of a smoke screen, the wounded commander of Alpha Company ordered his remaining men and those of Charlie Company to withdraw. They were joined by the survivors of Baker Company. "For many," noted the official history, "the trip was a nightmare of hair-breadth escapes; the battalion surgeon considered none of the survivors fit for further duty."

It was a similar story on Kakazu West, where Love Company, 3/383rd, held a knoll against repeated counter-attacks by Japanese soldiers throwing grenades and satchel charges. Colonel May ordered George and Item Companies to reach Love's left (east) flank, but they were unable to cross the fire-swept gorge. Observing the carnage below, Harvard-educated PFC Richard Johnson, a 21-year-old flamethrower operator in Item Company, told his platoon sergeant that their mission was not a "good idea."

The sergeant agreed and, letting discretion be the better part of valor, they took cover behind a rock. Johnson had taken off the eighty-two-pound flamethrower and put it behind him as protection. It was a good move because, seconds later, a Japanese mortar exploded just beyond the flamethrower and blew out its napalm tanks. "Fortunately," recalled Johnson, "it didn't explode." But aware they were being targeted, they ran back twenty or so feet to a circular depression and remained there until nightfall. For Johnson, a veteran of Leyte, it was the start of what he would later describe as "a meat-grinder operation" for the U.S. troops involved.[9]

Meanwhile by 4:00 p.m., with only three out of eighty-three men uninjured, and almost out of ammunition, the Love Company commander knew that further resistance was hopeless. He ordered a withdrawal and, once again, it was "expertly handled" by the supporting artillery who used smoke interspersed with high explosives. Even so, it had been a "black day" for the 383rd Infantry which had lost 326 men: twenty-three killed, 256 wounded and forty-seven missing. Worst hit was the 1st Battalion which was now at half strength and "considered ineffective." Moreover, carrying out his threat, Colonel May had sacked the battalion commander, Lieutenant Colonel King, and replaced him with his executive officer. As for the 3rd Battalion, its Love Company had only thirty-eight men left, including company HQ.* Though the regiment as a whole had gained no ground, it had killed more than 400 of the enemy.[10]

Having failed with one regiment, a new "powerhouse attack" was scheduled for the following day using two: this time the 383rd would concentrate on Kakazu Ridge while the 381st tackled Kakazu West.

* Love Company, 3/383rd Infantry, would later be awarded the Distinguished Unit Citation for its tenacity at Kakazu.

The attack was the brainchild of Brigadier General Claudius M. Easley, the 53-year-old assistant division commander from Hood County, Texas. An expert shot and former captain of the infantry rifle and pistol teams, Easley had personally supervised the division's marksmanship training which had borne fruit with the nickname "Deadeyes." At Leyte, he was wounded by a sniper, but not before displays of gallantry and leadership had earned him the Legion of Merit and a Bronze Star.

Unable to support either regiment with tanks, because the ground was unsuitable, Easley ordered a heavy fifteen-minute bombardment from seven battalions of field artillery, later extended to half an hour. One of the artillery battalions was First Lieutenant Chris Donner's 3/11th Marines, loaned from the 1st Marine Division which was carrying out mopping-up duties further north. Assigned as forward observer to the "dogfaces" of the 2/383rd Infantry, advancing on the left of the regimental attack, Donner tried and failed to establish a radio link with his guns before the attack. He went in search of the nearest company commander, but was caught in a barrage of mortars. "One hit almost beside me," he recalled, "and I went down with the blast. Something that felt like a baseball bat had socked my right arm over the biceps. I think I said aloud, 'I'm hit! This is it!' My head was ringing. Someone was helping me sit up, asking me was I OK. I looked at my arm. No blood, but a piece of steel was sticking out of my flannel shirt. I grasped it and pulled it out, almost burning my hand as I did so."

As the wound was not serious, Donner was still with the front-line infantry when the attack began soon after. It was met by Japanese machine-gun fire and "bogged down" almost immediately, even before reaching the cliffs that marked the edge of the gorge. "Several men," noted Donner, "slightly wounded, struggled back calling for medics." When a wide flanking attack was made by one company, Donner followed with his team. But it too was held up at a crossroads by heavy shellfire. When word came back that the "road ahead was impassable," Donner was told to pull back to the start line. "Night was closing in," he recalled, "wind and rain chilled us thoroughly. My arm was throbbing and stiff. Repeated salvos of enemy mortar fire kept us close to the ground." With a fellow officer, he tried to sleep in a tiny foxhole covered with a poncho. But it was quickly swamped. "The water was four inches deep on my side where I sat," noted Donner, "my teeth chattering, and my body involuntarily wracked by shivers as a cold wind began to blow away the rain. It was one of the long[est] nights of my life."[11]

Elsewhere, elements of the 381st and 3/383rd got as far as the northern knoll of Kakazu West where they dug in. But all attempts to take Kakazu Ridge failed, as did renewed attacks by both regiments on April 11 and 12. Of the latter effort, the official history noted: "Three times the troops of the 381st attacked; each time, in the face not only of…mortar fire, but also of machine-gun and rifle fire, grenades, and satchel charges, the attack disintegrated. The battalion lost forty-five men."[12]

Donner—who had spent the previous two nights with wounded GIs in a "pocket" just below the crest of Kakazu Ridge, showered with debris from shellfire, and without water or rations—was finally relieved on the 13th. "We gathered our gear," he wrote, "bid the 96th good luck, and ran single file back through the same route for more than a mile. We were positively overjoyed to see the two Third [Battalion] trucks. Back we headed to the safety of the Battery."[13]

Further to the east, meanwhile, three battalions of the 382nd Infantry had tried and failed to capture a north-east–south-west feature known as Tombstone Ridge. At one point PFC Don Dencker's 3rd Battalion got a foothold on the ridge, but "continual rain, which bogged down the tanks and decreased visibility, combined with heavy enemy mortar, machine-gun and 47 mm fire" forced the battalion to withdraw to its original position. Dencker's mortar section supported Love Company's attack, firing one shell a minute at a distance of 500 yards. When the rifle platoons moved forward, he and his section followed, taking up positions seventy yards to the their rear. At night, he remembered, their job "was to fire a few flares upon request."

By April 11, the attacks had fizzled out and the incessant rain "was making movement very difficult and extremely hard to evacuate casualties." The main threat facing the men was now the huge Japanese spigot mortars whose range was a mile and a quarter. They made, Dencker recalled, "a ringing sound in flight and upon impact blew a hole in the ground about twelve feet deep and thirty feet in diameter." In the air each shell looked like "a flying garbage can with fins."[14]

The 7th Division had a little more success, with the 184th Infantry capturing Tomb Hill on the 9th, and the 32nd Infantry entering the town of Ouki two days later. But this latter force was soon cut off from support and the survivors driven out. By the 12th, the divisional front line had stabilized a few hundred yards north-east of Hill 178, the start of the main Japanese position on the east of the island.[15]

Lieutenant General Buckner was not particularly surprised by the slow pace of XXIV Corps' advance. "All units are doing splendidly," he wrote to his wife on April 8, "but heavy resistance is developing in the south as I anticipated. We have a deep area of concrete and steel to break but we can break it." That same day he also noted in his diary his plans to "land the 27th Div[ision] to give impetus to the [XXIV Corps'] attack and use the 77th [Division] to take Ie [Sh]ima after the 27th lands."[16]

Buckner clearly had a short memory. The 27th Infantry Division was the formation that had made such a poor impression on him and his staff during their tour of inspection of Espiritu Santo. Yet now, just a few months later, he was expecting it to help crack arguably the toughest nut that U.S. forces had encountered in the Pacific. Less one reinforced regiment (which was diverted to the lightly defended islands off the east coast of Okinawa), the 27th duly landed on Hagushi beaches on April 9. A day later, Buckner told Major General Hodge, commanding XXIV Corps, that he should delay any further push until the 27th had reached his front line. He had convinced himself that Hodge's two attacking divisions were outnumbered by the Japanese defenders—in fact the opposite was true—and was also concerned with the XXIV Corps' shortage of artillery ammunition, thanks to bad weather holding up resupply. For all these reasons, he felt that any major attack should wait until troop numbers and shell supplies had reached the sort of level that would guarantee success. To make doubly certain, he assured Hodge that the XXIV Corps would be further reinforced by the 77th Division once it had taken Ie Shima "about 16 April."[17]

If Major General Bruce, the 77th's commander, had had his way he would have followed up the Ie Shima operation with an amphibious landing *below* Naha. "Bruce came aboard [the *Eldorado*] to arrange details of his attack on Ie [Sh]ima," Buckner wrote in his diary on April 11. "As usual, he is rarin' to try a landing behind the main Jap position in southern Okinawa."[18]

In an earlier entry, Buckner had praised Bruce's gung-ho attitude to soldiering. He also knew that his troops had been specially trained for amphibious operations. But he quickly dismissed Bruce's suggestion for a second landing on Okinawa because it would cause difficulties with resupply and there was always the risk it could be isolated and destroyed. He preferred to conduct the type of no-frills, artillery-dominated campaign that was so beloved of U.S. Army doctrine. This meant building up his troop levels and firepower—in the form of artillery batteries—before launching what was bound to be, given the narrowness of the island and the strength of the Japanese defenses, a costly frontal attack on prepared positions. He had said as much to Admiral Spruance when they discussed strategy on the *Eldorado* on April 2. "Spruance is trying to hurry us in the capture of Ie [Shima]," noted Buckner. "This would gain no time in completing the field and would use up the army reserves before the main fight starts."[19]

Buckner's cautious approach was confirmation for Spruance, if any were needed, that he and Admiral Turner had been right to prefer the more aggressive and experienced Lieutenant General Holland Smith as ground-force commander. But ultimately Buckner had been chosen—for reasons that were more political than operational—and Spruance would have to live with the consequences. "I doubt," he wrote to an old friend, "if the Army's slow, methodical method of fighting really saves any lives in the long run. It merely spreads the casualties over a longer period." That of course meant greater naval casualties from air attack, a situation that, in his opinion, Buckner and other army generals were not "allergic to." Spruance added: "There are times when I get impatient for some of Holland Smith's drive, but there is nothing we can do about it."[20]

Spruance was not the only senior officer who was concerned with the slow pace of operations in the south of Okinawa. Brigadier General Oliver Smith, Buckner's Marine deputy chief of staff, deplored the fact that, by 12 April, the enemy's main line of defense had been "probed" but "not attacked in force." This was not entirely fair. The 96th Division, in particular, had fought well and suffered very heavy casualties in its failed attempt to take the Kakazu and

Tombstone ridges.* But Smith was justified in his hunch that delay would be counterproductive. "As the days passed," he later recalled,

> I began to inquire about when the attack [by XXIV Corps] was to be launched. I eventually learned that it was not the intention to launch a corps attack until the corps had assembled four units of fire for the artillery and until the 27th had been committed... The Army apparently did not yet realize what the capture of ground in cave and pillbox warfare costs in casualties; that in the final analysis these caves and pillboxes must be taken by the infantry; that the artillery can blast away the camouflage and keep the enemy underground but cannot take the positions; and that delay only serves to increase total casualties and exhaust the troops. The delay of ten days gave the Japanese the opportunity to get set, whereas continued pressure might have kept them off balance.[21]

Smith had a point. What he was not aware of, however, was that disagreements over strategy by senior Japanese staff officers meant that they were about to throw away some of the advantages that Buckner's caution had handed to them.

* By April 12, the XXIV Corps had lost around 2,900 men: 451 killed, 2,189 wounded and 241 missing. Enemy fatalities were thought to be 5,750.

16

"I want to marry Shigeko"

Even as American forces paused their offensive in the south, their opponents were preparing to take the initiative. The impetus was a radio message sent by General Rikichi Ando, commanding the 10th Area Army on Formosa, to Lieutenant General Ushijima on the evening of April 5. Furious that the attack on the 6th had been postponed, Ando sent Ushijima a "specific command" to recapture the Yontan and Kadena airfields on the night of April 8.[1]

Faced with a direct order, Ushijima felt he had no option but to comply, and Chief of Staff Chō was told to reissue instructions for a general attack on that date. According to Colonel Yahara, the "ill-conceived plan for a counter-attack" involved using all available units, including the bulk of the artillery, "in one massed blow to drive the invaders to the Ishikawa isthmus." The 62nd Division would spearhead the attack in the direction of the Yontan airfield, while the 24th Division continued the advance up the east coast. The 44th Independent Mixed Brigade would be in reserve. Despite the vigorous opposition of Yahara "and other cooler heads among the staff officers" who argued that "even if the attack should succeed initially the Japanese would be at the mercy" of American artillery and air bombardments, the plans were endorsed by Ushijima.[2]

But it was put off once again when American ships were seen moving west of Naha, prompting renewed fears of a landing "near Machinato and an advance toward Urasoe village, behind the left flank of the Japanese main line." Instead Chō downgraded the attack to little more than a night sortie by two companies. When no landings took place, Chō ordered Colonel Yahara to prepare a brigade-strength night attack for April 12. The plan suggested by two young staff officers—Kimura and Kusumuru, both China veterans—was for small groups to penetrate as far as six miles behind enemy lines, and "hide in caves and tombs awaiting a suitable opportunity to attack on 13 April." The main advantage of this plan, according to Yahara, was that it would prevent the use of American artillery because the ground would be "occupied simultaneously" by Japanese and enemy troops. Its disadvantage was that the 22nd Regiment, in particular, "was unfamiliar with the terrain."[3]

The attack took place after dark on April 12, and was preceded by an enormous Japanese artillery bombardment, the heaviest of the campaign so far. Six battalions were involved: three from the 22nd Infantry Regiment, brought up from the 24th Division's area of operations in the Oroku Peninsula, who attacked the eastern half of the American front line and another three reserve battalions from the 62nd Division went forward in the west—their main objective was Kishaba, four miles to the rear.

As Yahara had predicted, the battalions of the 22nd "were bewildered by the terrain and by dawn had made only 500 yards." They were "forced to retire" by units of the 32nd and 184th Infantry (both 7th Division), and suffered "heavy casualties." More headway was made on the left, with infiltration squads from the 27th and 272nd Independent Infantry Battalions getting as far as 1,000 yards behind American lines before the survivors withdrew. Meanwhile the 273rd Independent Infantry Battalion, moving up the west coast, was cut to pieces. PFC Don Dencker's Love Company, 382nd Infantry, was attacked close to the highway that ran along one side of the hill by men of the 272nd Battalion at 3:30 a.m. "We aided in the defense," he recalled, "by firing illuminating shells, which exposed the Japanese to accurate fire by our riflemen. The result was twenty-five enemy bodies left in front of our foxholes as the rest withdrew." Love Company did not have a single casualty.[4]

The most heroic American action of the night was at the lower northern end of the saddle between Kakazu Ridge and Kakazu West, guarded by a mortar squad of the 1/381st Infantry. Spotting the enemy advance at around 3:00 a.m., Technical Sergeant Beauford T. Anderson told his men to stay under cover in a tomb, while he went out alone. Having emptied his carbine magazine and used all his grenades, he could see the Japanese still advancing. In desperation, he grabbed a mortar shell, took out the safety pin, banged the base on a rock to arm it, and threw it at his attackers. Hearing cries as the shell exploded, he repeated the trick, eventually throwing a total of fifteen mortar bombs and forcing his "fanatical foe" to retreat. "Despite the protests of his comrades," read his medal citation, "and bleeding profusely from a severe shrapnel wound," Anderson would not accept treatment until he had reported his action to his company commander.

His "intrepid conduct in the face of overwhelming odds" had "accounted for twenty-five enemy killed and several machine guns and knee mortars destroyed, thus single-handedly removing a serious threat to the company's flank." For this extraordinary act of "conspicuous gallantry and intrepidity above and beyond the call of duty," not to mention his ingenuity in using mortar shells as a close-quarter weapon, Anderson was awarded the Medal of Honor, the first of the campaign.[5]

One Japanese soldier who got back to his lines near Kakazu recorded: "I was leader of the first team of the platoon and started out with four other men. Since the company commander got lost on the way, we were pinned down by concentrated mortar fire before we could cross the hill. Continuous mortar and machine-gun fire lasted until dawn, when we, having suffered heavy casualties, withdrew, taking heavy punishment from concussions...The Akiyama Tai [1st Company, 272nd Battalion] was wiped out while infiltrating."[6]

While Colonel Yahara resented the pointless loss of so many precious troops, the failed attack did have one silver lining: it "strengthened" his position on the staff "as the spokesman of the conservatives." However this would not stop Chō and the "radicals" from lobbying for more offensive action in the weeks to come; nor would it prevent Ushijima from listening.[7]

A few days earlier, in a modest house in the port of Kōzu, fifty miles south-west of Tokyo, 19-year-old Shigeko Araki had barely got to sleep when she was woken by her parents at 11:00 p.m. They said her stepbrother Haruo, a flight lieutenant in the Army Air Corps, had returned on overnight leave. There was a blackout, thanks to an earlier air raid, and the family had to grope in the dark to find their way to the main room. "There's something I have to tell you," announced Haruo, when they were all assembled. "All of you, because we're a family. I've been selected as a group leader of a tokkōtai—or special attack—mission. I don't know when the attack will take place, but it will be soon."

Shigeko knew at once what this meant: every day, dozens of kamikaze planes flew over her place of work, a pressing plant for the navy, and she and her fellow workers would cry because they knew the pilots would not be coming back. Soon Haruo would be joining them.

"I have one request to make, although it's very selfish," continued Haruo. "I want to marry Shigeko, if possible."

At first Shigeko was too stunned by the news to respond. Her parents were also silent. At last she spoke: "I will do as Haruo wishes."

As step-siblings, they had been born into separate families. In fact, Shigeko's "mother" was actually an aunt who had adopted her. The aunt had later married Haruo's father and together they brought up their two children in Tokyo where Shigeko learned traditional Japanese dance and Haruo entered the military academy. When Tokyo was bombed by American B-25s in April 1942, the family was evacuated to Kōzu, in Kanagawa prefecture. Shigeko got work at a factory that produced rice cakes for the navy, and, like all her fellow employees, was trained in the use of long bamboo spears which they were to use if enemy soldiers ever landed on the beaches nearby. "Americans are large and well built," they were told, "so go for the throat. Stab here, drive your spear up into the throat. Don't look at the face. Stab without looking."

"Yes!" they replied in unison.

Shigeko had no compunction about killing the enemy. "It was for Japan," she explained later, "it was to preserve and protect the country. We were sending our loved ones off to die...It was the least we could do on the home front...At that time we had an unbounded faith in Japan. We felt that the Yamato race was unequaled." To be asked to marry her stepbrother before his own samurai death was, for Shigeko, an honor. "At that time," she wrote later, "I thought it was natural that Haruo would die. It would have been shameful for him to go on living."

Their tearful parents were also keen for the marriage to go ahead. "It's decided then," said his father. "Let's arrange for the ceremony."

The wedding took place in a room with "paper walls, with rain shutters outside, so it was pitch-black." With no sake available, they used potato liquor for the three toasts required by the traditional wedding ritual. "My father started to sing the 'Takasogoya' wedding song," recalled Shigeko, "but when he got to the part about living forever, he fell totally silent. We couldn't help crying then. We all wept."

It was almost 2:00 a.m. when Shigeko and Haruo retired to a "Western-style" bedroom with glass windows to spend their only night together. For a long time Haruo was silent. "He probably couldn't say what I should do after his death," commented Shigeko. "I wanted to say something to him, but I couldn't find the words either." It was, nevertheless, a "precious" and "truly wonderful" few hours. Shigeko felt "loved body and soul" and neither slept a wink. Finally Haruo spoke. "If we had a rope," he told her, "we would jump into the sea off Kozū, our bodies tied together."

"What?" she asked, confused.

He knew it was a pipe dream. "I cannot do that now."

They rose at 4:00 a.m. and Shigeko's abiding memory was of her husband "standing in the hall near the window, looking out, dressed in his uniform." After breakfast, she asked if she could accompany him to the train station.

"Walk behind me," he replied.

She did so, her eyes on him as he strode ahead. He did not once look back. At the station she tried to see his ticket, so she would know where he was going. "You can't look!" he snapped.

Her last words to him were: "When can I see you again?"

"I'll be back," he replied, "when it rains."[8]

Meanwhile, eight Ōhka flying-bomb pilots were preparing for the next wave of suicide attacks at their air base in Kanoya, southern Kyushu. They were billeted in an old primary school where, according to the recently arrived Commander Tadashi Nakajima, "the window panes had all been destroyed as a result of air attacks, and the sky showed through holes in the roof." They slept "on a plain wooden floor, and the whole place was indescribably filthy."

On April 12, shortly after eating his final meal, Lieutenant Saburo Dohi, a graduate of a Normal School in Osaka and the lead Ōhka pilot, approached Nakajima and said: "I have ordered six beds and fifteen straw mats. They are supposed to arrive today.

May I ask that you watch for them and make sure they go to the billet?"

Without pausing for an answer, Dohi walked out to a waiting two-engined "Betty" bomber, its Ōhka flying bomb strapped beneath, and climbed aboard. Moments later it lumbered into the air and, accompanied by seven other Ōhka-bearing "Betties," headed for Okinawa as part of a special attack fleet of forty-five Ōhkas, 185 kamikazes and 150 escort fighters. They took "varying courses in order to approach their targets from numerous points, both east and west of the island, at the same time."[9]

The inspiration for the Ōhka—a "piloted rocket-driven projectile" which could be loaded beneath a Type 1 land bomber ("Betty")—had come the previous summer to a young naval aviator, Ensign Ohta, while he was flying transport missions to Rabaul. Ohta's plans, produced in consultation with the aviation research department of Tokyo Imperial University, were submitted to the Naval Aeronautical Depot at Yokosuka, and eventually adopted after the Navy High Command had given its approval. Experiments began, and by late 1944 the weapon—known as Ōhka ("cherry blossom")—was put into production. A small, single-seated wooden glider, just twenty feet long and with a wing span of 16.5 feet, it contained almost 2,645 pounds of explosives and was designed to be carried to within fourteen miles of its target by a twin-engined bomber. Once released at an altitude of around 20,000 feet, it had a range of more than twenty miles, propelled by blasts from its five rockets which could produce speeds of up to 500 knots. "It must have been agony for the young men who were chosen to train and study for Ōhka special attacks," recalled Commander Nakajima, "because it was more than six months after the training started before even the first of them got a chance to die in battle. They were carefully selected from throughout the air force, and all were well qualified."[10]

None more so than Lieutenant Dohi. Shortly after take-off on April 12, Dohi told the bomber's crew that he wanted to nap and be woken when they were thirty minutes from the target area. He then stretched out on a "makeshift canvas cot" and went to sleep. Woken at the assigned time, he smiled and said: "Time passes quickly, doesn't it?"

Having shaken hands with the chief pilot, Dohi climbed through the bomb bay into the cramped cockpit of his Ōhka. He could communicate through a voice tube.

Nakajima, meanwhile, was tracking the progress of the attack through earphones in the radio room at Kanoya. "Attack reports were coming in continuously," he wrote later. "My interest was centered on the progress of the Ōhka-laden bombers."

Eventually he heard the ominous report from Dohi's plane: "Enemy fighters sighted!"

He tensed. The last Ōhka attack, on March 21, had been shot to pieces by Hellcat fighters. Would it happen again? "Time seemed to stop," he recalled. "How could those cumbersome bombers make their way through the screen of enemy interceptors?"

Somehow they did. "We have avoided enemy fighters," the pilot reported.

Messages came in quick succession:

"Standing by to release Ōhka."

"Targets are battleships."

"Let go!"

Nakajima visualized the scene as Dohi "plummeted toward a great battleship, his speed boosted by rocket thrusts, and then the final successful direct hit."

When the mother plane returned—the only one of the original eight to make it back—the crew reported that they had closed on Okinawa from the west and could see "enemy ships in great numbers." A battleship was selected as Dohi's target and at the optimum position—an altitude of 20,000 feet and a distance of thirteen miles—the Ōhka was released. The crew had "watched anxiously as it plunged downward, wavering for an instant." Then, "steadily, and gathering bullet-like speed, the missile quickly grew smaller." They withdrew to the west at top speed, anxious to leave the "enemy-infested sky." Soon after they saw a "column of heavy smoke belching 500 meters high from the general location of Dohi's target."[11]

Was Dohi's attack successful? While Nakajima thought so, it is impossible to know for certain. The circumstantial evidence to the contrary is that no U.S. battleship was hit by an Ōhka on April 12, though one, Rear Admiral Deyo's flagship *Tennessee*, was badly damaged by a conventional kamikaze.* On the other hand, two U.S. destroyers were struck that day by Ōhkas—or "Baka" (foolish) bombs as the Americans dubbed them—and one sank. The lost destroyer, USS *Mannert L. Abele*, was manning Radar Picket Station 14, to the northwest of Okinawa, when she was hit by a conventional kamikaze at around 2:45 p.m. The bomb exploded in the *Abele*'s rear engine room, breaking the keel and the drive shafts, and leaving the ship without power and dead in the water. A minute later, traveling at 500 knots, an Ōhka "hit the ship on her starboard side beneath the forward stack, penetrated No. 1 fire room and exploded." This caused the ship's mid-section to disintegrate, her bow and stern to part, and within minutes "there was nothing on the surface where she had been except wreckage and survivors, who were being bombed and strafed by other Japanese planes."

A bomb exploded close enough to one U.S. ensign to lift him clean from the water. "I heard," he recalled, "several around me scream from pain caused by the blast." Fortunately two support vessels were close at hand, and their gunners were able to shoot down two of the attacking planes while the survivors from the *Abele* were plucked from the sea. The final butcher's bill was six killed, seventy-three missing and thirty-five wounded. It would have been much worse without the assistance of the support ships and the gallantry of men like Lieutenant George L. Way who, having been blown overboard by the Ōhka's explosion, "climbed back to help release life rafts for the men and opened hatches that permitted trapped sailors to escape."[12]

The other destroyer, USS *Stanly*, was struck by an Ōhka at around the same time as the *Abele*. She had been stationed at RPS 2, to the north-east of the island, and was on her way to help the stricken destroyer *Cassin Young* to the west when an Ōhka "suddenly dove out of a melee between CAP and enemy planes, and, although frequently hit by automatic fire, crashed *Stanly*'s starboard bow about five feet

* The *Tennessee* was attacked by five kamikazes at around 2:50 p.m. Four were shot down, but the fifth, a "Val" single-engined navy dive-bomber, clipped the bridge and crashed into a 40 mm gun turret, "scattering flaming gasoline, burning to death many of the gunners, and coming to a shuddering stop abreast fourteen-inch turret No. 3." Its bomb exploded below decks and started a fire. Though her material damage was slight, she still lost twenty-five killed and 104 wounded (thirty-one badly burned). (Morison, *Victory in the Pacific*, pp. 227–30.)

above the waterline, continuing right through the port side, where its warhead exploded." The damage made *Stanly*'s bow "look like the face of a man who had lost his false teeth, but it did not stop her."

Ten minutes later, another Ōhka came in on *Stanly*'s starboard beam, but too high to do any more damage than rip the ship's ensign. As it banked to make a second run, it struck the water, bounced and disintegrated in a ball of flames. The ship's captain, Commander R. S. Harlan, knew he had been lucky. "From the scraps of the jet-propelled plane that were left on board," he reported, "we observed that they are constructed largely of plywood and balsa, with a very small amount of metal, most of that being extremely light aluminum."

Might Lieutenant Dohi have been responsible for either of the destroyer attacks? It is possible. One historian names the *Stanly*'s successful attacker as Flight Petty Officer Second Class Kosai who, like Dohi, took off that day from Konoya. So it is certainly feasible that Dohi carried out the lethal attack on the *Mannert L. Abele*. If so, he would be the only Ōhka pilot to sink an American ship.[13]

17

“Harry, the president is dead”

It was just after 5:00 p.m. on April 12, 1945, when U.S. Vice President Harry Truman arrived at the office of Sam Rayburn, the Speaker of the House of Representatives, to discuss politics over a drink. Truman was nattily dressed in a double-breasted gray suit with wide lapels, white shirt, and spotted dark bow tie. Which was just as well because physically—of medium height, heavily built, and with a round full face and gray hair receding at the temples—he was nothing to write home about. He was also extremely short-sighted and wore thick spectacles.

Beckoning Truman to join his other guests, Rayburn handed him a glass of his favorite tipple, bourbon and water, and mentioned that Steve Early, President Roosevelt's press secretary, wanted to speak to him. So Truman picked up the phone and dialed Early at the White House. “This is the VP,” he said.

“Please come right over,” said Early, his voice strained, “and come in through the main Pennsylvania Avenue entrance.”

Sensing something was wrong, Truman's face drained of color. He hung up, exclaiming: “Jesus Christ and General Jackson! Steve Early wants me at the White House immediately.”

Pausing at the door, his hand on the knob, he added: “Boys, this is in this room. Something must have happened.”

Outside, he broke into a run, his footsteps echoing along the Capitol's marble hallways. Avoiding the secret-service detail that was waiting at his office—the only time he managed to do this in eight years of high office—he went straight to his car and told his chauffeur to drive to the White House and use the main entrance. They arrived at 5:25 p.m. and Truman was taken via the elevator to First Lady Eleanor Roosevelt's study on the second floor. There he found Mrs. Roosevelt, her daughter and son-in-law, and Steve Early. The First

Lady came forward and put an arm around his shoulder. "Harry," she said, "the president is dead."*

Truman was too stunned to speak. On many occasions since their joint victory in the 1944 presidential campaign—Roosevelt's fourth in a row, and Truman's first as his running mate—he had been concerned about the president's health. But he had put that down to the strain of Roosevelt occupying the White House "during twelve fateful years—years of awful responsibility" in which he had borne the heavy burden of leading the United States out of the Great Depression and then during wartime. Truman took solace in Roosevelt's "amazing" powers of recovery, and the most recent word from Warm Springs, Georgia, where the president had gone to rest, was that he was "recuperating nicely." In fact, he was "apparently doing so well," wrote Truman later, "that no member of his immediate family, and not even his personal physician, was with him."[1]

Four words flashed through Truman's mind: *The lightning has struck!* He had hurried to the White House to meet the president, and now he *was* the president. It was only natural to question his ability to replace such a colossus, and to take on the enormous responsibilities that went with the highest office in the land. Moreover, unlike Roosevelt, the 60-year-old Truman came from a humble background and had had little formal education. Born in Lamar, Missouri, he was the elder son of a farmer and livestock dealer. Having completed high school, he enrolled in a Kansas City business school but left after a year. He then took on a series of clerical jobs, farmed for a while and made a number of high-risk investments in mining and oil ventures that did not pay off. His luck turned with service as an artillery officer in the First World War, during which he gained leadership experience and a combat record that would help his post-war political career in Missouri.

After another failed business—this time a haberdashery store—he was elected a county court judge in 1922, and reelected as presiding

* Roosevelt had left Washington DC for his house in the spa town of Warm Springs, Georgia—where the hot natural mineral water was, he believed, good for his paralyzed legs—on March 29, 1945. Two weeks later, he was sitting for a portrait when he suffered a cerebral hemorrhage and never regained consciousness. He was pronounced dead at 3:35 p.m.

judge four years later, helping to transform Jackson County and Kansas City with an ambitious program of public works. This was the springboard for his election to the U.S. Senate in 1934, supported by local businessman Tom Prendergast who was later jailed for fraud. Truman gained national prominence in 1941 when he chaired a special committee on waste and corruption in government military expenditure (the so-called "Truman Committee")—described by *Time* magazine as "one of the most useful Government agencies of World War II"—but was still mystified when Roosevelt chose him as his running mate for the 1944 presidential election with the words, "Boys, I guess it's Truman."[2]

He was a compromise choice: older and less impressive than the other candidates; but with fewer enemies and less likely to alienate voters. So it proved: the Roosevelt–Truman ticket achieved a 432–99 electoral-vote victory in the election, defeating the Republican ticket of Governor Thomas E. Dewey of New York and running mate Governor John Bricker of Ohio. But the job of vice president was hardly an onerous one—he presided over the Senate Chamber and, if the vote was tied, had the casting vote—and Roosevelt kept him at arm's length. During his eighty-two days as vice president, Truman only twice visited Roosevelt on official business.

Now, faced with the shocking news of Roosevelt's death and his own sudden elevation, Truman said to Eleanor Roosevelt: "Is there anything I can do for you?"

She replied: "Is there anything *we* can do for *you*? For you are the one in trouble now."

She was right. "I had been afraid for weeks," wrote Truman later, "that something might happen to this great leader, but now that the worst had happened I was unprepared for it."

Within an hour, Eleanor Roosevelt had left for Warm Springs and Truman had been sworn in as the thirty-third president of the United States in the West Wing's Cabinet Room by the chief justice of the Supreme Court. He then held his first Cabinet meeting, telling its members that the San Francisco conference on the new United Nations peace organization would meet, as planned, on April 25. He added that he hoped all Cabinet members would remain in their posts, and that it was his intention to "continue both the foreign and domestic policies of the Roosevelt administration."

After this short meeting was over, all but one of the members rose and left the room. The exception was 77-year-old Secretary of War Henry L. Stimson who wanted to speak to Truman "about a most urgent matter." A former Wall Street lawyer, and the only Republican in Roosevelt's Cabinet, Stimson was respected on both sides of the political divide as a devoted public servant. There was, he told Truman, an "immense project" under way that he needed to know about. It involved the "development of a new explosive of almost unbelievable destructive power."

Truman had heard rumors of an odd military program that was costing millions; but knew none of the details. He was eager to hear more. But Stimson said that was "all he felt free to say at the time," and Truman was left feeling "puzzled." Only later, when he learned the truth, did Truman recall the time when, as chairman of the Senate Committee to Investigate the National Defense Program, he had received a visit from Stimson who asked him to discontinue checks into two war plants in Tennessee and Washington State. "I can't tell you what it is," said Stimson, "but it is the greatest project in the history of the world. It is most top secret. Many of the people who are actually engaged in the work have no idea what it is, and we who do would appreciate your not going into those plants." Truman, who had long known Stimson to be "a great American patriot and statesman" and a man of his word, said he would order the investigations to be "called off."[3]

The evening he became president, Truman confided his fears to his diary:

> I did not know what reaction the country would have to the death of a man whom they all practically worshipped. I was worried about the reaction of the armed forces. I did not know what effect the situation would have on the war effort, price control, war production and everything that entered into the emergency that then existed. I knew the president had a great many meetings with Churchill and Stalin. I was not familiar with any of these things and it was really something to think about.[4]

Truman was right to be worried. He was, in the words of his biographer, "the prototypical ordinary man." With "no college degree," he had never "owned his own home," governed a state or been mayor of a city. He became president, in his words, "by accident." Small wonder that, according to the *Chicago Tribune*, the whole world was asking two questions: "What sort of man is Harry S. Truman? What kind of president will he make?"[5] They were also mourning the loss of Roosevelt. When Winston Churchill heard the news, he felt as if he had been "struck a physical blow." He wrote: "My relations with this shining personality had played so large a part in the long, terrible years we had worked together. Now they had come to an end, and I was overpowered by a sense of deep and irreparable loss." Josef Stalin, the Soviet dictator, ordered black-bordered flags to be hung in Moscow. Even the new Japanese premier, Suzuki Kantarō (who had replaced Koiso Kuniaki a few days earlier), expressed "profound sympathy."[6] Vice Admiral Ugaki approved of the decision to send a "cable of condolence," confiding to his diary his belief that the success of his kamikaze operations were partly responsible for killing Roosevelt.[7]

On Okinawa, Buckner told his wife that they were "all grieved over the president's death and still feel some concern over his successor's lack of diplomatic experience." On the other hand, they were "relieved" that Henry Wallace, the former VP and a noted pacifist, was no longer in office.[8] Most of the ordinary soldiers were also badly shaken by the news, and Sergeant Harold Moss of the 225th Field Artillery spoke for many when he wrote to his family: "It seems impossible that such a great man, and one so close to the heart of the people, has passed away...[It] will be a long time before history can replace him."[9] Others knew nothing of Roosevelt's replacement. "One Marine would turn to another," recalled a first lieutenant in the 2/1st Marines, and say: "Who *is* president now? Most of us had no idea. We didn't even recognize the name Harry Truman."[10]

Buckner and his men might have been even more concerned if they had known just how uninformed Truman really was about the war situation, and how much he had to learn. Commander George Elsey, who was on duty in the White House Map Room* on the day Truman became president, wrote later:

* The president's intelligence and communications center which received a constant flow of secret information from the War, Navy and State departments, as well as foreign militaries and governments.

> I had met Mr. Truman only once during his vice presidential years, when he was at the White House to meet President Roosevelt and the president brought him to the Map Room… [He] was very ill informed about military and political affairs. He had not been briefed by President Roosevelt or by others in the Cabinet on some of the most major decisions that were coming up; he just didn't know a darn thing about them…[So] he was very, very eager to soak up as much information as he could, as quickly as he could, from the kinds of material we had in the Map Room.[11]

Certainly the Japanese commanders on Okinawa saw Roosevelt's sudden death as a godsend. "The staff officers were ecstatic," noted Colonel Yahara. "Many seemed convinced that we would now surely win the war."[12]

18

"His eyes were rolling in panic"

By the time news of President Roosevelt's death reached Okinawa on April 13, the heaviest fighting had switched from the south to the north of the island where Lem Shepherd's 6th Marine Division was tasked with capturing the main Japanese stronghold in the Motobu Peninsula. "Northern Okinawa," wrote Sergeant William Manchester of 2/29th Marines, "was not defenseless. Motobu Peninsula, steep, rocky, wooded, and almost trackless, was dominated by two mountains, Katsu and 1,500-feet, three-crested Yae-Take. Entrenched on Yae-Take were two battalions under the command of a tenacious officer, Takehiko Udo."[1]

The original plan had been to leave the conquest of the north until after the seizure of southern Okinawa. But as the scale of the Japanese defenses in the south became clear, Buckner decided to tackle both extremities at the same time: not least because it would secure the ports in the north from possible counter-landings by Japanese forces. On April 3, therefore, as the 6th Marine Division approached the Ishikawa isthmus, he removed all restrictions on its further "advance northward."

The 6th's regiments leapfrogged each other as they moved up the isthmus with almost no opposition, bar the odd Japanese straggler. By April 7, the 29th Marines had reached Nago, a medium-sized town at the southern neck of the Motobu Peninsula.* A day later, and the 29th had moved along the southern coast road to Awa, where it

* General Shepherd sited his command post in the grounds and battered buildings of Nago's Normal School. He lived in the headmaster's quarters, a "typical Japanese house with sliding panels and matting for a floor." Its doorways were so low, Americans had to duck as they passed through. (Smith, "Personal Narrative," p. 85.)

faced, for the first time, a proper organized defense. Other Marines had reached the northern coast, thus sealing the peninsula. Their problem now, however, was that they knew virtually nothing about the road network or the layout of the Japanese defenses.

So the 29th Marines spent the next few days trying to fix the enemy's position and, by April 10, the 1st and 3rd Battalions had almost surrounded the rugged Yae-Take feature where Colonel Udo had concentrated his forces. His command post was in a ravine with excellent radio and telephone links to his cleverly sited outposts. His men knew the terrain, were well supplied with machine guns and mortars, and supported by a battery of field guns and emplacements armed with 25 mm naval guns. "Colonel Udo might well have hoped," wrote the U.S. official historian, "to maintain for a considerable time his control of this mountain stronghold."[2]

Gradually, as the 29th's battalions probed Udo's defenses, their intelligence sections began to build up a picture of what they were up against. "There was," wrote William Manchester, "no role here for mechanized tactics; tanks were useful only for warming your hands in their exhaust fumes. This was more like the French and Indian warfare. Each of us quickly formed a map of the peninsula in his mind; we knew which ravines were swept by Nambu* fire and how to avoid them." Manchester's job was to keep the battalion situation map, "drawing red and blue greasepaint arrows on Plexiglas to show, respectively, what the Japs and our forces were doing." It was interesting work for him, and comparatively safe, until his battalion commander asked him to lead a four-man patrol to link up the two regiments assigned to attack Udo's redoubt: his own 29th, and the 4th Marines.[3]

By April 13 it was clear that the main Japanese position was in "an area of some six by eight miles surrounding precipitous Mount Yae-Take." With the number of enemy troops estimated at 1,500, two regiments were scheduled to attack on April 14. The plan was for three battalions—the 1/4th and 2/4th Marines, and the 3/29th Marines—to attack from the west, while 1/29th and 2/29th moved in from the east. Given the difficult nature of the terrain, battalion

* Excellent Japanese Type 96 light machine gun, capable of firing up to 500 rounds a minute from a thirty-round box magazine.

and company commanders were told "to decide methods of approach up the ridges and narrow valleys, and to change those methods on their own initiative when necessary."[4]

Manchester and his men left at dusk and moved "silently down the path, half crouched, passing Japanese corpses on both sides, any of which could be shamming." His main concern was being shot by his own side. "Because the Nips were so skillful at infiltration," he explained, "the rule had been established that after night had fallen, no Marine could leave his foxhole for any reason. Anyone moving was slain." Two nights earlier, a soldier in the 2/29th had been killed by friendly fire when he got up to urinate. With that in mind, Manchester advanced up the trail as quickly as he could, and had just ascended a "little wiggle" and turned a corner when he came face to face with the muzzle of a Browning heavy machine gun. "Flimsy," he croaked, giving the day's password.

"Virgin," replied the gunner with the correct countersign. He seemed to relax and reach for a cigarette. "Have you heard the news?" the gunner asked Manchester. "FDR died."[5]

The attack began the following morning and, by nightfall, the 4th Marines (with 3/29th Marines attached) had seized a 700-feet ridge, 1,200 yards inland from the coast, that dominated the coastal road. But not without cost as the Japanese defenders, operating in small groups from well-concealed positions, ambushed the columns as they moved forward and killed, among others, Major Bernard Green, commanding 1/4th Marines. "It was," noted one Marine, "like fighting a phantom enemy."[6]

The first casualties were in a patrol sent forward by the 2nd Platoon of Baker Company, 1/4th Marines. They were hit as they moved up a small valley that ran "back into the mountains." Ignoring sniper fire, Platoon Sergeant Guide Joe Hiott—a 21-year-old former Marine Raider from Charleston, South Carolina, who had fought at Bougainville and Guam—led forward a party of stretcher-bearers. He recalled:

> We came up on the squad as we rounded one bend...Corp[oral] Red Lindsay had been hit in the upper leg. He had managed to get the squad into cover before he fell. Chester Pas had been killed out in the valley and was still there. Frank Giglio was

> laying on his face on top of his BAR. I carefully moved him and got his BAR. I wanted to make sure that the automatic rifle would not fire in the process. I said, "Giglio is dead." And best I can remember, Red Lindsay said, "Oh, God, no." I looked at Red and I will never forget the pain and torment in his eyes. I said, "It's nobody's fault, Red." One other man was dead. I think Stevenson. And Walter Hipp, the corpsman, was wounded as he tried to help.[7]

The advance from the east, by the 1/29th and 2/29th Marines, came up against much tougher opposition and failed to clear the Itomi–Toguchi Road. So it was reorientated to move in a south-westerly direction "to take advantage of the high ground." Even then it made little headway and, by late afternoon, the two battalions were ordered to dig in for the night.[8]

The offensive resumed on the 15th, and again the two battalions of the 4th Marines took the bulk of the casualties as they came up against well-sited caves and pillboxes. Corporal Melvin Heckt from Grundy Center, Ohio—a young assistant machine-gunner attached to the 1st Platoon, Baker Company—recorded in his diary:

> Moved out at 7:30 up steep valley. Mountains were on each side. Around noon we ran into sniper and Nambu fire and at the day's end we had lost thirty men—Lt Quirk was killed [and] Tuttle, Kaercher, Arrowsmith, Godwin and one communication man were [also] killed. Banker and Bohman hit out of MG [machine-gun] section…I never had so many close shaves in all my life and only have God to thank for being alive. Maffesoli was hit in buttocks crossing in front of me; when Banker was hit I went to him…We finally realized we were sitting in a fire lane after a Nambu burst just missed my arm and chest. We took off as if we were running the hundred-yard dash. Another time I got up to run and a Nip fired at me, but hit Red McDonald who was sitting along the trail. He cussed me at first and then realized he was only hit in the finger and could get the hell out of this Hell and thanked me as he was being evacuated…Wonder what tomorrow will bring?[9]

Despite heavy losses, the two battalions of the 4th Marines ended the day on their objectives—high points to the west of Yae-Take—while the 3/29th Marines were "on favorable ground" slightly to the rear.* Little progress, however, was made by 1/29th and 2/29th Marines on the far side of Yae-Take. When General Shepherd arrived at the command post of the 29th Marines to find out why, he discovered the regimental commander, Lieutenant Colonel Victor F. Bleasdale, in a "highly agitated" state.

New Zealand-born but raised in Janesville, Wisconsin, the 49-year-old Bleasdale was, according to Sergeant Manchester, the type of "colorful hard-charger that the Marine Corps has always valued highly." The years "had shrunk his slabs of muscle to gristle, and he had a grooved, wind-bitten face with wattles that turned crimson when he was enraged, which was often." There was no doubting his physical bravery: he had been awarded two Silver Stars, a Navy Cross and a Distinguished Service Cross for repeated acts of heroism while serving as a Machine Gun officer in the First World War; in Nicaragua, in 1927, he won a second Navy Cross. More recently he had fought at Guadalcanal before overseeing the formation and training of the 29th Regiment at Camp Lejeune.

Bleasdale was also something of a ladies' man—or "swordsman" as Manchester put it—and, the evening before sailing to the Solomons, he was seen in the lobby of San Diego's U. S. Grant Hotel, surrounded by young women, "wearing dress blues and all his decorations," and "striking the lordly pose of a czar carefully choosing tonight's bedmate." In the field he adopted a piratical pose, with his "bleached khaki fore-and-aft cap pushed rakishly to the back of his head, his hands on his lithe hips, his chin tilted up aggressively." He looked, wrote Manchester, "every inch the gifted commander. Alas he wasn't." Why? Partly because he had "never led a large body of troops" in action before Okinawa; and partly because he was not very bright. "Inside his second-rate mind, one felt, a third-rate mind was struggling toward the surface."

* During the fight, 19-year-old PFC Harold Gonsalves, a forward artillery observer from L Battery, 4/15th Marines, fell on a live enemy grenade, saving his comrades and sacrificing his own life. A veteran of the Marshall Islands campaign and Guam, Gonsalves was awarded a posthumous Medal of Honor.

Bleasdale was infamous for pointless utterings such as: "Eat lots of food and plenty of it," "Here in Dixie we're in the Deep South," and "Sunrise will come at dawn." He once invented a fiendishly complicated flytrap and ordered his men to build it. It failed to snare a single fly so his XO, fearing Bleasdale's wrath, told all enlisted men to capture ten flies each and put them in the trap. When he saw them, a delighted Bleasdale suggested a second opening to catch twice as many. But if there were two, protested the XO, the quarry could "fly in one and out the other." The idea was quietly shelved. Like Buckner, Bleasdale was convinced that athletes made the best fighters. So during training on Guadalcanal, despite a stony outfield and a temperature of 103 degrees, he challenged the commander of the 4th Marines to a game of football. It ended scoreless, shut down at the end of the first quarter by navy doctors who were worried by "the incidence of heat prostration."[10]

Put this insanely brave, gung-ho Marine in charge of a battle, however, and he was all at sea. Asked by General Shepherd on April 15 where his three battalions were, he admitted that he "wasn't aware of, familiar with, or apprised of where nearly 3,000 men might be located, found, or situated."* He was relieved of his command by Shepherd and replaced by Colonel William J. "Wild Bill" Whaling, a veteran of the Pacific War who had served as the 1st Marine Division's operations officer on Guadalcanal and commanded the 1st Marines in New Caledonia. "Whaling," commented Manchester, "had fought well on the Canal; we had confidence in him."[11]

With the command rejigged, Shepherd ordered a three-pronged assault on Udo's stronghold for April 16: the 29th Marines would resume its advance from the east; the 4th Marines, with 3/29th attached, would attack from the west and south-west; while strong combat patrols from the 1/22nd Marines would strike north into the gap between the 4th and 29th, and "effect a juncture between the two regiments." Each attack would be supported by a battalion of artillery.[12]

* According to Brigadier General Oliver Smith, "Vic [Bleasdale] was a weapons enthusiast and had thoroughly trained his regiment in the use of their weapons. Vic, however, tried to run everything and when his battalions were scattered in the central part of the peninsula he practically lost control of his regiment." (Smith, "Narrative," p. 99.)

Preceded by a heavy bombardment from planes, artillery and naval guns, A Company of the 1/4th Marines moved up the wooded slopes of Yae-Take until they reached "steep bare rock one hundred yards from the crest." Their first attempt to storm the crest was driven back by Japanese mortars and hand grenades. But joined by C Company, which had worked its way up a draw to the right, A Company charged over the crest and took the ridge. Prominent in C Company's charge was 20-year-old Corporal Richard Bush, a 3rd Platoon squad leader from Glasgow, Kentucky, whose pre-war job was driving a tractor on a tobacco farm. Bush "fought relentlessly in the forefront of the action until seriously wounded and evacuated with others under protecting rocks." Lying there, he heard a thud and saw that a Japanese grenade had landed amongst them. Without hesitating, he "pulled the deadly missile to himself and absorbed the shattering violence of the exploding charge in his own body, thereby saving his fellow Marines from severe injury or death." Incredibly, he survived his multiple injuries and was later awarded the Medal of Honor for "conspicuous gallantry and intrepidity at the risk of his life above and beyond the call of duty."[13]

The grenade that almost killed Bush was probably thrown in the desperate counter-attack launched by the Japanese defenders at 6:50 p.m. It was beaten off with heavy losses—the official history estimates one hundred Japanese killed—and the 1/4th Marines had to survive the night "with very little water" and no "chow."[14]

The 29th Marines took a more prominent part in the fighting on the 17th. Inspired by their new colonel, who "unhesitatingly exposed himself to direct hostile fire among the most advanced elements of his Regiment" and "skillfully maneuvered elements of his command through rugged and precipitous mountain terrain," they took the northeast heights of Yae-Take, capturing five 25 mm guns in the process.[15]

That same day the 4th Marines swept north, killing 700 Japanese and capturing Colonel Udo's command post, complete with telephone switchboard. Corporal Mel Heckt celebrated by reading five letters from his family and sweetheart Jean, and eating "delicious chow" that included "fresh bread, pineapples, peaches, hot meat and spaghetti." He was less enamored by the news that, the following day, his regiment would be going over the next ridge. "More mountains," he noted in his diary. "Damn it."

All organized Japanese resistance in northern Okinawa was now over, though fleeing soldiers would fight as guerillas for weeks to come. Since landing, the 6th Marine Division had "moved eighty-four miles, seized 436 square miles of enemy territory, counted over 2,500 enemy bodies and captured forty-six prisoners." Its losses, meanwhile, were "236 killed, 1,016 wounded and seven missing." The successful execution of its first mission was "conclusive evidence," stated the 6th's special action report, "that a Marine division is capable of extended operations ashore."[16]

During the final stage of the battle for Yae-Take, a remarkable confrontation took place between Sergeant Manchester and a Japanese sniper. Manchester's battalion, the 2/29th Marines, was moving forward with Baker Company, 1/29th Marines, on their left and a unit of 1/22nd Marines on their right. Manchester had taken cover with one of his "Raggedy Asses," Barney Cobb, on the extreme left of the battalion perimeter, and was scanning the ground ahead when he noticed a little hut on a rise. It was between him and Baker Company, and as he looked he saw two American soldiers drop, and knew "from the angle of their fall" that "the firing had to come from a window on the other side of the hut."

He also realized that if the sniper changed position, and fired from the window facing Manchester, he and Cobb would be sitting ducks. He had to act, and fast. For a brief moment he thought of ordering Cobb to take out the hut. But he knew that if he "ducked this one," his men would never let him forget it. He also "couldn't be certain that the order would be obeyed." He was, by his own description, a "gangling, long-boned youth, wholly lacking in what the Marine Corps called 'command presence'"—in other words "charisma"—and he commanded "nineteen highly insubordinate men." So instead he asked Cobb if he had any grenades. The answer was no. Finally, taking a deep breath, he told Cobb: "Cover me."

With that, Manchester took off for the hut "in little bounds, zigzagging and dropping every dozen steps," remembering to roll as he hit the ground. He was almost there when he realized he was not wearing his steel helmet; all he had on was his cloth Raider cap.

Reaching the threshold of the shack, his mouth dry and his heart pumping, Manchester paused to flick off the safety on his Colt pistol.* Then he kicked open the door and leapt inside. The room was empty. There was another door opposite, which meant the sniper was in the next room, and probably forewarned of his presence. Manchester considered flight. But it was too late for that and, careering onwards, he burst through the second door and saw a blur to his right. He wheeled that way, pistol gripped in both hands, and saw a "robin-fat, moon-faced, roly-poly" Japanese soldier, his "thick, stubby, trunklike legs sheathed in faded khaki puttees." The soldier was trying to turn toward him, but was trapped by his rifle harness. "He couldn't disentangle himself from it," recalled Manchester. "His eyes were rolling in panic. Realizing he couldn't extricate his arms and defend himself, he was backing toward a corner with a curious, crablike motion."

Manchester fired, and missed. He fired again, and hit the soldier in the left thigh, severing his femoral artery. "A wave of blood gushed from the wound; then another boiled out, sheeting across his legs, pooling on the earthen floor. Mutely he looked down at it." More shots struck the soldier's chest until he "slumped down, and died."

Shocked by his first killing, Manchester stared in horrified fascination as the corpse's eyes glazed over and a fly landed on one eyeball. He reloaded his pistol to distract himself; but he could not stop his body trembling. Eventually he sobbed: "I'm sorry."

Overcome by what he had done, he threw up "half-digested C-ration beans." Just then Cobb burst in, carbine at the ready, and checked the sniper was dead. Satisfied, he approached Manchester, but quickly backed away. "Slim," he said, "you stink."

Only now did Manchester realize he had pissed his pants.[17]

* Manchester had bought the Colt after his own pistol was stolen by a "demented corporal" shortly before the invasion. He was, he reckoned, the only Marine "who had to buy his own weapon." (Manchester, *Goodbye, Darkness*, p. 11.)

19

"Three bullets had ripped into his temple"

In the evening of April 16, 1945, as the fighting on Yae-Take was nearing its conclusion, Ernie Pyle got drunk with his fellow war correspondents in the rear area near Hagushi beaches. "He seemed," wrote one, "to have a load on his chest and appeared to be glad to get it off. He said he was disappointed because he went in with the Marines and failed to see any major action. As a matter of fact, we gathered from his general attitude that he hated the Pacific—that the climatic conditions seemed to sap his strength. He indicated he was fed up with the whole mess and that he would go along on the Ie landing, return to Okinawa, move around with the Army divisions for a few weeks and then head home."[1]

Pyle had spent the first ten days or so of the campaign with Able Company, 1/5th Marines. It was, in some respects, an unfortunate choice because the 1st Marine Division was occupied chiefly with mopping-up duties in the center of the island. Assuming he might think less of them because they had not shown him "a bloodbath," the Marines were "continuously apologizing" for the campaign starting out "so mildly." Pyle told them he "could not have been happier," and that it was the "kind of campaign" that suited him. They said it suited them too.

Pyle was not being entirely honest. He had heard a lot about the warlike qualities of Marines and was keen to see them in action. "I had," he wrote, "conjured up a mental picture of a marine as someone who bore a close resemblance to a man from Mars, I was almost afraid of them." Having met them, he realized they were much like other soldiers: "They had fears, and qualms, and hatred for the war the same as anybody else. They wanted to go home just as badly as any soldiers I've met." They were "confident" and intensely "proud" to be

Marines, but "not arrogant" and with a "healthy respect for the infantry." Yet Pyle knew all too well that the "major part of the battle" on Okinawa "was being fought by the Army" and that, thus far, "the Marines had it easy."[2]

Which is why Pyle had asked for, and been granted, permission to join the troops of the 77th Division on D-Day + 1 of their landing on Ie Shima, an island barely three miles off the western tip of the Motobu Peninsula. Rectangular in shape—two miles by five—and lying east to west, Ie had airfields that could be used to support the assault on Okinawa and raids against the Japanese home islands. It was not thought to be a tough nut to crack: its southern beaches, in particular, were sandy and free of obstacles; its terrain, apart from a 600-foot high feature known as "the Pinnacle," was mostly a flat plateau; and it was guarded by a garrison of barely 2,000 men, many of whom were not front-line troops. Yet the defenders, commanded by a Major Igawa, had constructed formidable defenses on and around the Pinnacle and the nearby town of Ie in the central east sector of the island.

Two regimental combat teams duly landed unopposed on April 16: the 305th RCT on Red 1 and 2 on the south coast; and the 306th RCT on Green Beach in the south-west. Once ashore, both regiments moved inland before swinging east. By nightfall, faced with minimal opposition, they had captured the main airfield and two-thirds of the island.[3]

That evening, before his drinking session, Pyle was told at a journalists' briefing not to be fooled by the apparent ease of the landings on Ie Shima. The fighting would be bitter* and, once ashore, he would need a guide "as the island was heavily mined and there were many snipers." He set sail on LST *647* the following day, and landed on Ie in the afternoon with WLW Radio's correspondent, Milton Chase, who recalled: "Ernie was dressed in khakis and the officers in the area suggested that he grab some jungle greens because he would be a

* That night, the warning was vindicated when the Japanese counter-attacked the 3/305th Infantry with small arms, sharpened stakes, hand grenades and satchel charges. More than 150 attackers were killed, including a number of who blew themselves up with their charges. One American soldier had his arm broken by a suicide bomber's flying leg. (Appleman et al., *Okinawa*, p. 159.)

logical target for some snipers and there seemed to be quite a few in the vicinity of the road leading to the forward OP [observation post]. Ernie borrowed a jungle green coat and then we started out."[4]

Pyle spent the night in an abandoned Japanese dugout near the beach. Next morning, he had a brief chat with Major General Bruce, commanding the 77th Division before joining Lieutenant Colonel Joseph B. Coolidge, the new commander of the 305th Infantry, for the move up to his new regimental command post. The day before, Coolidge's men had fought through intermittent mortar, rifle and machine-gun fire to get as far as the outskirts of Ie town. But it was clear that the Japanese defense was stiffening and, to direct the battle more effectively, Coolidge needed to be closer to the front.

That morning, April 18, Pyle was wearing the cotton khaki uniform of a war correspondent, steel helmet, and sunglasses. For some reason he did not cover the distinctive khaki uniform—which set him apart from most combat soldiers—with the borrowed jungle green coat. He got in beside Coolidge and three others in a jeep that was easily recognizable as a command vehicle because of its long whip antenna. Part of a column of 2.5-ton trucks and other jeeps, they drove down a road which ran parallel to the coast, and had been cleared of mines. As it approached a junction, Coolidge's jeep was fired on by a Nambu machine gun hidden in the terraced coral slopes to their left front, at a distance of about 500 yards.

The driver slammed on the brakes and all five occupants took cover in narrow ditches on either side of the road: Pyle and Coolidge in the ditch furthest from the machine gun. "After getting to safety," recalled the colonel, "both of us, Ernie and myself, raised our heads to look around for other members of the party. A short conversation with [one of them] assured me that all men were safe though scattered. The Jap then let go at us. Some shots ricocheted over my head but I knew that it had been a close one. After ducking I turned around to ask Ernie how he was and found him lying on the ground and quivering. He was lying face up."

At first, seeing no blood, Coolidge wondered what was wrong. But then blood began to flow from Pyle's mouth and he noticed three bullet wounds in his left temple. "He must have lived unconscious for a minute or two," wrote Coolidge. "It was then that I called to some soldiers nearby if the Medico was near."

It was too late. Pyle was dead. Leaving one of his men to keep an eye on the newspaperman's body, Coolidge crawled back to report his death. Later that day, an army photographer executed "an almost unbelievably slow, laborious, dirt-eating, fifteen-minute crawl" forward to take pictures of Pyle's corpse. "Three bullets had ripped into his temple," the photographer remembered. "Except for the thin trickle of blood that had escaped from the right corner of his lips, it would have been easy to assume he was asleep." A few hours after that, his body was retrieved for burial by an army chaplain and four volunteers.

A clue to the way he had been killed was just above Pyle's helmeted head where "the soft dirt of the ditch line had been literally eaten away in a half moon design, about thirty-six [inches] long and eighteen [inches] deep...which better than anything else attested to the viciousness and the intense concentration of the machine-gunner's fire." In other words, Pyle was probably shot *through* the bank of earth as he lay on his back. This, in turn, would explain why the three bullets lacked the velocity to pass through his head. There were entry wounds; but no exits. The final detail noticed by Roberts was that the right lens in Pyle's sunglasses was missing, as if blown out by flying dirt.[5]

Pyle was buried on Ie Shima between an infantry private and a combat engineer. Where he died, a monument was erected that reads: "At this spot the 77th Infantry Division lost a buddy, Ernie Pyle, 18 April 1945."

That evening, General Bruce wired his superiors: "I regret to report that War Correspondent Ernie Pyle, who made such a great contribution to the morale of our foot soldiers, was killed in the battle of Ie Shima today." As word spread, tributes poured in from the great and the good. Former First Lady Eleanor Roosevelt, who often quoted Pyle's dispatches in her newspaper column "My Day," wrote: "The sad news has just come to us that Ernie Pyle has been killed at the front with our boys on Okinawa. To thousands and thousands of people all over the world, his column has brought the best understanding of the human side of our fighting men...I shall never forget how much I enjoyed meeting him here in the White House last year, and how much I admired this frail and modest man who could endure hardships because he loved his job and our men."[6]

In office for just a few days, President Truman said in a statement: "The nation is quickly saddened again by the death of Ernie Pyle. No man in this war has so well told the story of the American fighting man as American fighting men wanted it told...He deserves the gratitude of all his countrymen."[7] Similar messages were released by Secretary of War Henry L. Stimson, U.S. Army Chief of Staff George C. Marshall, and senior commanders such as Dwight D. Eisenhower and Mark W. Clark.

Perhaps the worst affected by Pyle's death, however, were the ordinary soldiers on Okinawa. "Shame about Ernie Pyle, huh?" said one Marine to his corporal. "Guy getting killed like that, after all the shit he'd been through. Makes ya wonder, huh? Don't even know why he was here, when he didn't have to be." The corporal wrote later: "It really was a shame...The only newsman to truly earn his stripes in combat was killed on his first jaunt to the Pacific. We all applauded him coming, and when we found out he was killed, to be honest, some Marines took it harder than the president's death."[8]

Shortly before Ernie Pyle's death, Yoshiko Sakumoto, the 14-year-old schoolgirl who had narrowly survived the naval bombardment on March 29, was hiding with her family in a cave near the village of Seragaki when she heard a dog barking and "conversations in a strange language." Fearful her father would be accused of working for the Japanese army—as many men of his age had been forced to do—she urged him to flee. He did so by climbing through a small opening in the back of the cave.

Twenty minutes later, noises heralded the arrival of "seven or eight American soldiers" into the cave. "Don't cry," said an old man, Mr. Uezato, to Yoshiko and the other children. "Keep still. Pretend you're sleeping."

They all lay down on the tatami mats. Resting closest to the cave entrance, Mr. Uezato was poked by an American soldier's rifle. "Get up!" shouted the American.

He did so, and calmly instructed the others: "Children, get up slowly, and go outside."

One by one they moved along the narrow passage to the entrance. Yoshiko delayed long enough to mess up her hair "like a bird's nest," smear soot on her face and walk with a limp as if she were a cripple. It was her response to a terrifying ordeal, a week earlier, when an American wearing civilian clothes had intercepted her on the beach near the cave and, waving a long knife, tried to get her to go with him. But for the arrival of her friend's father, she was convinced the American would have raped her. Now, she was trying to prevent a repeat by making herself as unattractive as possible.

Outside the cave she saw that her father had also been captured, and that some American soldiers had dogs. Two of them, noticing her limp, gestured that they would take her to a hospital. When she ignored them, a second-generation Japanese-American (known as a *nisei*), told her in Japanese that she would get better if she got proper treatment. She told him she did not want to be separated from her family. "Still they would not give up," she recalled, "so at last I abruptly straightened out my legs and walked ostentatiously in a normal way. When they realized what I was up to, they all burst out laughing."

They were eventually driven to a civilian refugee camp in Ishikawa. "Tents covered a large field," wrote Yoshiko, "where thousands of refugees were held. Children were without shoes, and looked as if they hadn't bathed for many days. Older people in torn and dirty clothes sat with dazed expressions as if they had lost their souls...The camp was surrounded by barbed wire."

As soon as they got off the truck, Yoshiko's father was separated from his family, handed a jacket marked "PW" on the back, and assigned to the construction team that was building sheds under the supervision of American soldiers. The others were taken to a different section of the camp, closer to the sea, where they were put in a grass-thatched house. "Compared to the tents," noted Yoshiko, "it looked clean and tidy. Nearby was a well with clean water." Later, when she was less fearful of Americans, Yoshiko got a job at the nearby headquarters of the U.S. Military Government on Okinawa, run by Brigadier General W. E. Crist, the deputy island commander. Her father, meanwhile, was allowed to build a small house for his family with "surplus materials that the U.S. military did not need."[9]

Yoshiko and her family were among the tens of thousands of Okinawans who were interned in refugee camps—in Ishikawa, the Katchin Peninsula,* Koza, Shimabaku and Awase—for their own

* More than 40,000 civilians were interned in the Katchin Peninsula where, noted General Buckner, they were "left practically to their own devices." (Buckner Diary, April 17, 1945.)

safety. There they were given the basic necessities to survive—food, water, clothing, shelter, medical care and sanitation—and encouraged to harvest crops on a communal basis and tend to farm animals that had been rounded up by the invading troops. The camps had originally been designed for no more than 10,000 occupants, but this quickly rose until many had double that number. By the end of April, more than 125,000 were under the control of the Military Government.[10]

"We felt lucky to have been captured," noted Yoshiko, "and taken out of harm's way." She appreciated the fact that the Americans were feeding thousands of refugees with "flour, sugar, salt, oil, powdered egg, dried cabbage, potatoes, ham, and corn-beef hash as well as jam and peanut-butter." But their survival was chiefly down to geography: Okinawans in the center and north of the island had a good chance; those living in the south, trapped behind the front line, were in a much more precarious position. Then there were those who refused to come in, like Yoshiko's cousin Koga, a member of the Blood and Iron Corps, who was hiding out with remnants of his unit on Onna Mountain. She later heard he had been shot and killed running from American soldiers, while his friend surrendered and survived. "Those split-second-decisions," said Yoshiko, "determined their fates."[11]

Having heard the stories of mass killings in the Keramas, Lieutenant General Buckner was relieved that so many Okinawans had decided to surrender. "The Jap soldiers told the Okinawans to kill their women," he wrote to his wife, "rather than let us take them. A few of them did so and, after finding that we treated civilians well, they are most hostile to the Japs...I passed streams of them on the road today carrying their babies and their few household possessions. Many of them smiled and waved at us."[12]

Not all Okinawan refugees had reason to thank the Americans, though. Corporal Sterling Mace, a 21-year-old fire-team leader in King Company, 3/5th Marines, came across a field of forty dead civilians, including a little girl still clutching her wooden toy. "Close by," noted Mace, "a woman lies on her stomach—probably the child's mother. Her arm reaches out toward the baby girl, fingers splayed wide, as if she were trying to protect her dead child...The side of the woman's face is mashed to the ground. An almost black pool of blood has thickened below her pursed lips." Around the victims were their scattered belongings: "baskets filled with clothes and crude household goods, lacquered boxes shattered by bullets and the impact of their falls." They had all been shot in the back, Mace concluded, by a U.S. fighter plane on a ground strafing attack. "Never," commented Mace, "not even for a second, does it cross our minds that the Japanese did this. The Japanese have only one purpose in the air, and that is to get to our ships."[13]

The strafing attack might have been a mistake, but some American soldiers were capable of casual brutality toward the Okinawans. Twenty-eight-year-old Tamaki Matsu was hiding with her two children and others in a cave near Nago Town, at the base of the Motobu Peninsula, when she heard voices shouting "*Detekoi! Detekoi!*" ("Come out! Come out!"). Afraid of being killed, she left the cave with her children and saw ten American soldiers with guns. They told her and the others to sit in a circle, and quickly singled out a "Mr. N" who was wearing Western clothes and gaiters, "so maybe they regarded him as a Japanese soldier." He was led away and shot.

Then two Americans began to inspect each of the captives. Convinced they were looking for a young woman to satisfy their carnal desires, Tamaki "hunched over to avoid their notice." But they spotted her and tried to take her away. She went mad, "screaming, shivering, and struggling against them." In desperation she grabbed hold of the trunk of a cherry tree. Seeing their mother struggle, her children both burst into tears and started screaming. Only then did the soldiers let her go.[14]

20

“Progress not quite satisfactory”

Lieutenant General Buckner’s diary entry for April 18 did not mention Ernie Pyle’s death. The two men had never met and, in any case, the general was preoccupied with other business that day: the movement of his command post from *Eldorado* to its new location south of Kadena airfield;* and preparations for the XXIV Corps’ big offensive the following day that Buckner hoped would crack open the Japanese defensive line. “All set for tomorrow’s attack,” he scribbled in his journal. “Took [Major] Hubbard forward to 7th Div CP [command post] to spend night so as to watch jump off tomorrow from forward OP [observation post] in that Div. One of our 155 mm gun batteries fired over our tent all night but after a couple of hours I got used to it and it ceased to keep me awake.”[1]

Designed to break through the “enemy’s intricate defense system around Shuri and to seize the low valley and highway extending across the island between Yonabaru and Naha,” the attack was made by three infantry divisions: the recently arrived 27th would assault the town of Machinato and the Kakazu hill mass on the right; the 96th would take on the Tombstone and Nishibaru ridges, and the Tanabaru escarpment, in the center; and the 7th would tackle Hill 178 and the town of Ouki on the left. H-hour was fixed for 6:40 a.m., and for forty minutes prior to that the guns of twenty-seven battalions of artillery (including nine of Marines)—324 pieces in all, ranging from 105 mm to eight-inch howitzers—would fire a huge

* His new command post was a pyramidal tent in “a pleasant spot,” he told his wife, “with a lovely view except on occasions when unpleasant things are dropping into it from guns and planes, at which time I have a dugout to retire into.” (Buckner to his wife Adele, April 17, 1945, “Private Letters,” p. 84.)

bombardment. "It is going to be really tough," commented corps commander General Hodge. "There are 65,000 to 70,000 fighting Japs holed up in the south end of the island, and I see no way to get them out except blast them out yard by yard."[2]

This was music to Buckner's ears, believing as he did that artillery held the key to the battlefield. Others were not so convinced. A couple of days earlier, Brigadier General Oliver Smith had warned correspondents not to expect rapid gains. "I pointed out," wrote Smith,

> that the concentration of artillery behind the XXIV Corps (twenty-seven battalions), for the narrow front on which it was attacking, was greater than that employed on the western front in the First World War. But I also pointed out the limitations of artillery employed against an enemy dug in as the Japanese were. The artillery was capable of destroying any enemy not underground, but in the final analysis it would be the infantryman who would have to dig the Japanese out of his caves.

Needless to say, it was the amount of artillery that was mentioned in the press dispatches, not Smith's "qualification regarding its effect." Shortly before leaving the *Eldorado* on the 18th, Smith told Admiral Turner that he thought the army "overconfident regarding the effect the artillery would have in the forthcoming attack." Turner agreed, but said there was "nothing anybody could do about it at that late date." His parting words, as Smith turned to leave, were "God bless you."[3]

Buckner rose at 4:35 a.m. on the 19th and went to a forward observation post with General Arnold to watch the start of the 7th Division's attack. He thought the "preparation and later use" of the artillery was "beautiful," but that the 7th's troops did not "advance quite fast enough," though there was little opposition to begin with. Shortly before 10:00 a.m. he moved across to the 96th Division and saw that "resistance was much stiffer there." He then continued on to the 27th Division before returning to his own CP. He noted in his diary: "Result of day's operations: a gain of about 800 to 1,200 yds on right and left leaving a salient in the heavily fortified escarpment area in the center. Expect to work on flanks of Jap salient tomorrow.

Progress not quite satisfactory." To hammer home the point, he visited corps commander General Hodge before supper and told him the 7th Division had been "too cautious" and that he was to "speed up the advance."[4]

Brigadier General Smith also noted "moderate gains, up to 800 yards, were made." In the west the 27th Division had captured the town of Machinato; but elsewhere the attack had been "brought to a stop by intense mortar and machine-gun fire." Yet even the gains, in his mind, were illusory because for some days prior to the attack the front-line divisions had often reported their patrols proceeding up to 800 yards without being fired on. In other words, they were in places—chiefly on the extreme right and left—some distance from the real Japanese front line, which meant that a "good part of the tremendous artillery preparation" had fallen into no man's land. "The net effect of the first day of the attack," wrote Smith, "was to gain possession of the ground over which our patrols had previously been operating."[5]

If Smith was exaggerating, it was not by much. Which is probably why the least progress was made by the 96th Division in the center where the proper Japanese front line was much closer.* Observing the initial attack against Tombstone Ridge—the feature his regiment had failed to take ten days earlier—was PFC Don Duncker of Love Company, 3/382nd Infantry. First there was the "typhoon of steel" as 19,000 shells were aimed at Japanese positions across the island. Then, "promptly at 6:40 a.m., smoke-signal shells landed ahead of our front lines and the attack by our 1st and 2nd Battalions moved forward, supported by tanks, heavy machine guns and mortar fire."

His battalion was in reserve, waiting to follow "behind and slightly to the east of the 1st Battalion" in the assault on Tombstone. Their assignment was to "mop up any enemy strongpoints bypassed, kill left-behind snipers, and blow caves shut with demolitions." They thought it inconceivable that any Japanese troops could have survived

* The front line was also close on the right of the 27th Division's sector, opposite Kakazu Ridge. A pincer attack round the ridge by thirty tanks and self-propelled guns (on the left) and the 1/105th Infantry (on the right) was cut to pieces by anti-tank, machine-gun and mortar fire, mines and satchel charges. Many of the tanks were destroyed in and around the village of Kakazu; only eight returned. They were the worst armor losses of the campaign.

the "murderous shelling." Yet within minutes Japanese Nambu machine guns and mortars were dropping American troops.

By early afternoon, with the 1st Battalion pinned down on the northern half of Tombstone Ridge, Dencker's Love Company moved up in support, losing a platoon sergeant and a number of men as they destroyed a Japanese pillbox. They dug in behind the 1st Battalion's Baker Company, though Dencker found it almost impossible to penetrate the rocky ground. Eventually, by turning the shovel blade to ninety degrees from the handle, and using it as a pick, he and another mortarman managed to hack out a small hole, and then extend its depth slightly "by placing rocks around the perimeter." They set up the mortar nearby, and prepared to fire high-explosive and illuminating shells in case the Japanese counter-attacked.[6]

The verdict of the official historian was withering: "The big attack of 19 April had failed. At no point had there been a breakthrough. Everywhere the Japanese had held and turned back the American attack. Even on the west, where the front lines had been advanced a considerable distance by the 27th Division, the area gained was mostly unoccupied low ground, and when the Japanese positions on the reverse slopes of the escarpment were encountered further gain was denied." XXIV Corps' casualties numbered 720 dead, wounded and missing.[7]

But not all was doom and gloom. According to Colonel Vernon Megee, the air support for the attacks was a great success as his controllers "put some 375 combat aircraft over the XXIV Corps front, handling without incident as many as seven individual strikes simultaneously." It proved "beyond further challenge," he believed, "the thesis of close air-support control by the ground commanders on the spot, rather than by some distant naval commander."[8]

The offensive was resumed on the 20th but, again, made little headway. "Visited 27th Div in the morning," noted Buckner in his diary, recalling a conversation that was characteristic of his hard-nosed leadership style. "Saw Col. Stebbins of the 105th. He was slow in getting his attack off this morning. Jap art[iller]y concentration and shot out bridges given as the reason. Too many reasons and not enough advance. Told him so. Also saw Col. Kell[e]y of the 165th

Inf[antry] and urged him toward a faster pace. To go where the going is good and pinch out pockets of resistance."[9]

This was wishful thinking, particularly of a division that had not performed especially well in battle before. Attacking on the extreme right near the coast, the 165th Infantry's objective was Machinato airfield, a mile ahead. Its XO, exuding confidence, had announced they would rename it "Conroy Field"—after the 165th's former commander killed on Makin—when they reached it that evening. In the event, both battalions were stopped well short of their objective by the fierce Japanese defense of a series of small fortified ridges.[10]

Only modest gains were made elsewhere: two companies of the 3/382nd Infantry—Item, and Don Dencker's Love—managed to reach the southern end of Tombstone Ridge. But when Love Company's 3rd Platoon tried to take a small tree-covered knoll just east of the south tip of Tombstone, it became the site of a "furious battle." Even before the attack began, First Lieutenant Bob Glassman, Love Company's commander, was shot in the chest and seriously wounded by a Japanese sniper as he and other officers observed the ground they would cross. Dragged to safety, he was "given plasma, blood, and a shot of morphine," and then carried on a stretcher back to the aid station. Half conscious, he heard the mess sergeant call out, "They got Hoagie!" (the code name used for the company commander in combat).

A short while later, the artillery barrage began and was augmented by Dencker and his comrades firing high-explosive shells from their 60 mm mortars. "The firing rate," he recalled, "with me dropping the shells down the tube was about three per minute. We tried to saturate the area over which Company L was to advance, stopping at 7:30 a.m. for the start of the mission." The experience of being a mortarman while his company was making an attack was, wrote Dencker, a little like "being just outside a large football stadium when an important game is going on. You hear lots of noise, but you have little idea of what is actually going on."

The intensity of the firing in both directions on April 20 was proof, if Dencker needed it, that it was going to be a tough fight. This was confirmed when some Sherman tanks, firing in support of the attack from a point a hundred yards to his rear, were narrowly missed by a high-velocity 47 mm anti-tank shell. "A minute later," noted Dencker, "another anti-tank shell roared overhead, like the sound of a freight train...Again a near miss. But this time the tanks had started to move, as a third shell roared by."

By noon the rifle platoons were moving down the ridge, with Dencker and his mortar team following along a terrace below the summit. A shot rang out, then more, narrowly missing Dencker. Desperate to escape the sniper, he ran toward some cover, but misjudged a curve in the terrace and fell six feet on to some rocks, badly injuring his knee. Luckily he was out of the line of fire and, though in pain, he managed to catch up with his team. They provided supporting fire for the assault on the little knoll, but it still suffered numerous casualties, including both platoon leaders, one of whom was killed. With the officers and most of the senior NCOs out of action, Communications Sergeant House took command of the platoons and succeeded in repulsing several ferocious Japanese counter-attacks. The mortars moved up in support, as did the remaining platoon, and Dencker volunteered to collect a five-gallon can of water from the battalion dump on Tombstone Ridge. Returning to the knoll, he had just placed it next to his foxhole when a Nambu machine gun opened up, puncturing the can. "I started to laugh," he remembered, "at the sight of my hard-obtained water trickling over me."

Love Company had spilled blood—literally—to win the knoll. But as they took it, they found it was highly exposed and open to fire from three directions. So the replacement company commander, Lieutenant Young, requested and was given permission to rejoin the rest of the battalion on Tombstone Ridge. They pulled back under the cover of a smoke barrage and dug in on the ridge as it was getting dark. "We had lost our rations and water," noted Dencker, "but had withdrawn without further casualties. April 20th had been a bad day for Company L. We suffered thirty-five battle casualties, including ten men killed or died of wounds. Our strength had been reduced to 101 men from the 168 who had landed on April 1st."[11]

Also badly hit were the Sherman tanks of Sergeant Bob Dick's Charlie Company, 763rd Tank Battalion, who were supporting the attack on Nishibaru Ridge by the 381st Regiment. Dick's *Cutthroats* was following the tank of his platoon leader Lieutenant Schluter—a small, softly spoken regular who had started out as a private in the horse cavalry in Texas—when a shell blew a hole in the dirt between them.

"OW,"* said Dick to his tank commander, Sergeant Ovid W. French, a lobster fisherman from Rumbly, Maryland, "did you see that?"

"What...see what?"

"Something just hit the ground between the lieutenant's tank and us...!"

"You sure?"

"Hell yes I'm sure."

They were moving down a valley, with a small ridge on their left. Soon they turned that way, passed the ridge and eventually reached the far end of the valley. Their job, as agreed with the infantry, was to scour that area for Japanese positions and knock out any they found. But as Schluter's tank came level with an intersecting gulley it seemed to Dick as if it was "coming apart." He could see its tow table "flying through the air, stretched out straight as string." Realizing Schluter was under fire, Dick tried to maneuver his tank so that his gunner could get a clear shot. He nosed forward, and got a quick sight of a 47 mm anti-tank gun at the end of the draw. Two shells in rapid succession hit the ground in front of *Cutthroats*, causing Dick to back up in a hurry. They then fired smoke to try and cover Schluter's tank which was trying to turn around. But it was too late. Shell after shell penetrated the Sherman's hull, causing some of the crew to bail out and run back down the valley. "I guess in the confusion," wrote Dick, "they didn't realize that we were sitting right there a few feet away, waiting to pick them up."

Told by OW to "get the hell outta here," Dick drove to the far end of the valley from where they had an easy shot to take out the long-snouted 47 mm gun. It was, he knew, a "wonderful weapon" that could be fired almost in semi-automatic mode: "That is, as fast as the gunner could pull the lanyard, the weapon would spout them off."

Dick heard later that Schluter's tank was hit by eleven shots, "and that nine had penetrated." Those shots were fired within a matter of seconds and Dick had witnessed it all from a distance of just twenty yards. It was a sight, he wrote, "I'll not soon forget."[12]

* Pronounced "oh-dub-ya."

21

"All Kaitens prepare for launch!"

"We don't know when we'll encounter the enemy," said the captain of the submarine, "so this will be our farewell party. I wish you a most satisfying dash against the enemy."

The four Kaiten pilots responded by raising their glasses of sake, and downing the contents. Among them was young Yutaka Yokota who had been part of the aborted mission in late March. This was his second mission and, he hoped, his last. They had left Hikari on April 20, as part of a flotilla of submarines carrying Kaiten human torpedoes, and were nearing American ships off Okinawa.

Next morning, with their launch imminent, Yokota and his fellow pilots were told to change into their battle clothes. He paused to say goodbye to the reserve officers who had taken such good care of him, and by the time he reached the ready room the others were changed. "Hey, guys, look the other way. I have to change my F-U*," said Yokota, referring to his loincloth.

"Yokota, there's nothing to be ashamed of," replied Warrant Officer Yamaguchi, who liked a joke. "No cute girls here. What's the matter, your main gun just a water pistol?"

Yokota turned his back to change, but Yamaguchi sneaked a look. "You stingy bastard!" he exclaimed. "Your cannon looks even smaller than my 'sidearm.'"

"Yamaguchi, you've got two?" asked another pilot.

"Naw. I call it a 'sidearm' when things are peaceful."

They laughed uproariously, grateful for the salve of humor, a respite from the growing tension they all felt. They were young and preferred bawdy jokes to more serious discussions about "loyalty,"

* Short for Fundoshi, the traditional cotton undergarment worn by all Japanese males.

"bravery" or "the nobility of the soul." Only one pilot, Commander Kakizaki, had a girlfriend and carried her picture. Yokota kept one of his mother who had died when he was four. "Ma," he would whisper, "I'll soon be there with you."

Minutes later the submarine's speaker blared: "Kaiten pilots! Board! Prepare for Kaiten battle!"

With hearts thumping, they fastened their *hachimaki* headbands and made their way to the ladders that led to their craft, muttering, "I'm going now."

Their stomachs were churning as they climbed through the open hatches and into their cramped cockpits. To calm himself, Yokota thought of his mother and how he would soon be joining her. "Absolute success!" he vowed to himself. That's all I can accept. If I do not succeed, I cannot die in peace. Even if my life is gone, I will not rest."

His thoughts were interrupted by Warrant Officer Nao who looked after his Kaiten. Nao gripped his hand, and said: "I pray for your success."

With the hatch closed, Yokota's only means of communication was by telephone. "All Kaitens prepare for launch!" came the instruction. "We will launch number one and number four Kaitens! Others await orders!"

The Kaitens named were piloted by Kakizaki and Yamaguchi. Yokota heard their restraining belts being released, and then the roar of their propellers as they moved away. Through his periscope he would see "only the pure white bubbles left behind."

After an agonizing wait of twenty minutes, there was a dull boom, "*GUWAAAANNNNN!*"

It was the unmistakable sound of the Kaitens exploding. "When am I going?" pleaded Yokota down the telephone. "What am I supposed to do?"

The controller replied: "Only two enemy ships sighted."

"What, can't you find more?"

"Wait."

"What do you mean, wait? There must be more of them. Search harder!"

Yokota was desperate to share his comrades' glorious deaths. Surely he would not be cheated a second time.

"Kaiten number two," said the controller, "prepare to launch."

That was Furukawa. Once he had been dispatched, only Yokota was left. He pleaded some more, but it was not to be. There were no more ships.

He was ordered back into the submarine. "*That* was the moment," he recalled, "I really wanted to die."[1]

Even before XXIV Corps began its offensive on April 19, the Japanese 62nd Division manning the front line had lost thirty-five percent of its troop strength and almost forty percent of its artillery. After four more days of fighting—during which time it was forced to relinquish the Nishibaru and Tombstone ridges in the center—the division was down to half its original strength and barely operational in the sector facing the U.S. 27th Division. Colonel Yahara, Ushijima's operations chief, estimated that for every soldier, field gun and mortar that the 62nd Division had on the line, its opponents had four, not to mention a total of a hundred tanks and 640 aircraft.

The obvious solution was to move up the troops guarding the southern coastline. But if he did that, Yahara reasoned, it would open the back door to an amphibious landing. He estimated that the Americans now had six divisions ashore in Okinawa—in fact it was five, though a sixth, the 77th, having finally taken Ie Shima, was due to land—and that only three were attacking the main Japanese defenses above Naha. It seemed logical to him that the Americans would try to land at least a division on Okinawa's south-east coast of Minatoga. That would force the defenders to fight on two fronts.

But if he left the dispositions as they were—with the 24th Division and 44th IMB facing the south-west and southeast coasts respectively—the 62nd was bound to disintegrate. Instead he came up with two alternatives: move both formations north to reinforce the 62nd; or abandon the northern defenses and withdraw the whole Thirty-Second Army to three strongpoints in the south. Yahara's preference was for the former, but he feared an amphibious landing in the rear. Unable to make up his mind, he consulted Chief of Staff Chō—the only time he did this during the battle—who backed the move north. "If we don't reinforce the 62nd Division immediately," argued Chō, "the whole army is finished."

As for an amphibious landing, they would deal with that problem if it happened. "A man who chases two rabbits," said Chō, quoting the Japanese proverb, "won't catch either."

With his decision made for him, Yahara still had to choose how best to use the extra troops. His solution was genius. He would straighten out the front line by abandoning any salients and withdrawing to pre-prepared positions about half a mile to the rear. The left half of this line would continue to be held by the 62nd Division, while the remainder was taken over by part of the 24th Division. The balance of the 24th and the 44th IMB would hold the right and left respectively of the final defensive position, about a mile to the rear, known as the "Shuri Line." This would allow, noted a study of the Japanese battle strategy, "defense of the forward line to be continuous and, at the same time, provide a still unencroached defensive position in the rear into which retreating forces could fall back gradually." Meanwhile the whole of the southern coast would be defended by a force of 5,500 men, mostly from rear-area supply units. In the event of a landing, it would be expected to hold the Americans up until main-force units could deploy from the north.[2]

During the night of April 23–4, in line with Yahara's plan, a massive Japanese artillery bombardment masked the withdrawal of front-line units to a new unbroken defensive position half a mile to the rear. For five days, Japanese soldiers had fought doggedly to defend the Machinato–Ouki line, limiting American gains to "yards daily and in some places, such as Kakazu, denying any gain." But with the line perforated, it now made sense to pull back a little. The final diary entry of a Japanese superior private, fighting in the Nishibaru–Kakazu area, dated April 23, captures the desperation that Japanese infantrymen were beginning to feel:

> Although nearly a month has passed since the enemy landed, a terrific battle is still going on day and night. I am really surprised at the amount of ammunition that the enemy has. When friendly forces fire one round, at least ten rounds are guaranteed to come back. There is not one of our friendly planes. If some come, I think we can win the fight in a short while. We want planes! We want planes![3]

"The Japs here seem to have the strongest position yet encountered in the Pacific," wrote Lieutenant General Buckner to his wife Adele on April 22, "and it will be a slow tedious grind with flamethrowers, explosives placed by hand and the closest of teamwork to dislodge them without very heavy losses."[4]

Knowing this, it seems astonishing that Buckner did not reconsider his earlier decision to veto a second landing in the south. While he could not know the extent to which the Japanese had denuded their protection of the southern beachheads, he was soon made aware—from intelligence gleaned on the battlefield—that troops of the Japanese 24th Division had been moved north. He was also receiving advice from a number of people that a landing was advisable. They included General Bruce who, with the Ie Shima battle drawing to a close, again offered to land his 77th Division on the beaches north of Minatoga with a view to linking up with American forces north of Shuri within ten days. Bruce's men had had success performing such a landing behind the Japanese line at Ormoc on Leyte, and he felt they could repeat the trick. But Buckner and his staff rejected the offer on the same grounds as earlier: that the beaches were too restricted for resupply and might result in a second Anzio.*

Buckner also felt, from his observation of the battle thus far, that the 27th Division was performing poorly, and that the other divisions of XXIV Corps were badly depleted and needed a rest. Moreover, he had been warned by Nimitz not to commit either the 1st or 6th Marine Divisions to the battle because they might be needed for other operations, while the 2nd Marine Division was back in Saipan, pending a landing north of Okinawa. It seems logical, therefore, that he wanted to use the 77th Division to bolster XXIV Corps. Yet this imperative disappeared on April 26 when Nimitz informed him that Phase III of Operation Iceberg, the occupation of islands north of Okinawa, had been postponed indefinitely by the Joint Chiefs of Staff in Washington, "thus freeing the III Amphibious Corps for full use on Okinawa."[5]

* In January 1944, in an effort to outflank German defenses in southern Italy, part of General Mark Clark's Anglo-American Fifth Army had landed at Anzio south of Rome. They failed to break out of the beachhead for more than four months.

Nimitz had warned Buckner that this might happen when he flew into Okinawa with Admiral Spruance to discuss strategy on April 22. Buckner recorded after the visit that the third phase might be canceled, "if sufficient fields can be found here to fulfill air-support requirements...Adm. Nimitz presented me with a bottle of liquor which I told him I would open when all organized resistance here had ended."[6]

It was also around the 26th that General Hodge, commanding the XXIV Corps, urged Buckner to attempt a landing in the south on the basis that soldiers of the Japanese 24th Division had been identified in the front line, leaving the south more thinly defended than hitherto. But Buckner rejected the proposal, arguing that a major landing could not be supported logistically. A day later he issued orders for the 1st Marine Division to move south and replace the disappointing 27th Division in the front line. This was typical of Buckner's cautious, artillery-dominated approach to battle. It was a missed opportunity of untold proportions, and one that would have costly consequences.[7]

According to his Marine deputy chief of staff Oliver Smith, Buckner "had hoped to complete the campaign in the south without committing the [III Amphibious Corps]." This was partly U.S. Army pride, and a belief that the rotation of his four army divisions would do the job. But when the 27th Division quickly wore itself out "mentally and physically"—losing 3,500 men in fifteen days—he knew it had to be relieved. The excuse he gave to war correspondents was that the 27th's original assignment was as a non-combat garrison division and, with the fighting over in the north, he could now revert to that plan. He said much the same thing to General Greiner, the 27th's commander, who was "obviously relieved." But Smith was not fooled. Buckner relieved the 27th, he wrote, "because he had lost confidence" in it.[8]

Meanwhile, Buckner was finding the sights and sounds of battle from the vantage point of forward observation posts oddly exhilarating. "It really was a superb spectacle," he informed his wife of one attack, "plane strikes, artillery concentration, smoke screens, flame-throwers, tanks and the steady determined advance of the infantry closing with the enemy. Along with this were the crash of bombs, the screech of projectiles, the whistle of shell fragments, the sputter of machine guns and the sharp crack of rifles. I shall never forget it. It was really stirring."[9]

What was missing from his description, of course, was the horror of close combat on Okinawa: the screams from the badly wounded, the sweet smell of decomposing flesh, and the sight of close friends disemboweled by shells or mortars. This was the reality of war in the Pacific for both sides.

22

"The most terrible weapon"

On April 24, President Harry Truman received a brief note from Secretary of War Henry Stimson. "Dear Mr. President," it began, "I think it is very important that I should have a talk with you as soon as possible on a highly secret matter. I mentioned it to you shortly after you took office but have not urged it since on account of the pressure you have been under."[1]

Truman knew at once the subject that Stimson was referring to. When they had last spoken about it, on the day of Roosevelt's death, Stimson had referred only cryptically to a "new explosive of almost unbelievable destructive power." The following day, April 13, Jimmy Byrnes, Roosevelt's former director of war mobilization, had told Truman they were "perfecting an explosive great enough to destroy the whole world." It was so powerful, said Byrnes, it would put the United States in a position to dictate its own terms at the end of the war. But it was only when Dr. Vannevar Bush, head of the Office of Scientific Research and Development, came to the White House to explain the technical aspects of the bomb that Truman began to understand its awesome potential. Not that everyone was convinced. "That is the biggest fool thing we have ever done," said Fleet Admiral William D. Leahy, Truman's chief military adviser and de facto chairman of the Joint Chiefs of Staff, who also heard the briefing. "The bomb will never go off, and I speak as an expert in explosives."[2]

Keen to hear Stimson out, Truman scheduled a meeting for April 25. Stimson arrived at the Oval Office at noon and was joined, soon after, by Major General Leslie R. Groves, a large barrel-chested army engineer who had supervised the building of the Pentagon. They were both holding memorandums which they gave to Truman. He read Stimson's first. "Within four months," it began, "we shall in all probability have completed the most terrible weapon ever known in human history, one bomb of which could destroy a whole city." It added:

> Although we have shared its development with the UK, physically the U.S. is at present in the position of controlling the resources with which to construct and use it and no other nation could reach this position for years. Nevertheless it is practically certain that we could not remain in this position indefinitely... As a result, it is indicated that the future may see a time when such a weapon may be constructed in secret and used suddenly and effectively with devastating power by a willful nation or group...The world in its present state of moral advancement compared with its technical development would be eventually at the mercy of such a weapon. In other words, modern civilization might be completely destroyed.

Yet, continued the memo, if properly handled the weapon might be a force for world peace.[3]

Groves's memo, on the other hand, concentrated on the science. "An atom," it read, "is made up of neutrons, electrons and protons. When a free neutron from outside the atom, strikes an atom of U-235 [uranium], the collision causes the atom to break into two parts freeing more neutrons and releasing a relatively large amount of energy." This would enable an atomic bomb to explode with the power of 5,000 to 20,000 tons of TNT, said the memo, if everything worked. It continued:

> The successful development of the Atomic Fission Bomb will provide the United States with a weapon of tremendous power which should be a decisive factor in winning the present war more quickly with a saving in American lives...If the United States continues to lead in the development of atomic energy weapons, its future will be much safer and the chances of preserving world peace greatly increased.[4]

The pair then explained how the largest industrial and scientific enterprise in history had come about. It began with a letter from the theoretical physicist Albert Einstein to President Roosevelt in August 1939, explaining how "the element uranium may be turned into a new and important source of energy in the immediate future," which in turn could be used to build bombs. Fearful that Hitler and the Nazis might get there first, Roosevelt told an aide: "This needs action."[5]

That autumn, the federal government had made $6,000 available for the purchase of special materials, including uranium. The following June, Roosevelt created the National Defense Research Committee,* with Vannevar Bush, president of the Carnegie Institution, as chairman. Other members included Dr. James Conant, president of Harvard; Dr. Richard Tolman of the California Institute of Technology; and Dr. Karl Compton, president of MIT. Their job was to gather the best minds in physics and see if they could build an atomic bomb. Stimson was brought on board in November 1941, just a month before Pearl Harbor, when Bush let him into the secret. "For nearly four years thereafter," recalled the Secretary of War, "I was directly connected with all major decisions of policy on the development and use of atomic energy, and from 1 May 1943...I was directly responsible to the president for the administration of the entire undertaking."[6]

Known as the Manhattan Project, it was being run by the then Brigadier General Groves who, in June 1942, appointed physicist J. Robert Oppenheimer as scientific director of the new secret laboratory where the bomb would be built. Oppenheimer chose the isolated village of Los Alamos in New Mexico as the site for the laboratory. "My two great loves," he had once said, "are physics and New Mexico. It's a pity they can't be combined." Now they could. At the same time, Groves supervised the construction of two other secret facilities: a forty-four-acre building in Oak Ridge, Tennessee, where uranium would be enriched for the bombs; and a massive site, twelve miles by sixteen, in Hanford, Washington, where the world's first full-scale plutonium-production reactor was built.[7]

Everyone involved knew it was a race against time. "The original experimental achievement of atomic fission," wrote Stimson, "had

* Superseded in 1941 by the Office of Scientific Research and Development, also headed by Vannevar Bush.

occurred in Germany in 1938, and it was known that the Germans had continued their experiments. In 1941 and 1942 they were believed to be ahead of us, and it was vital that they should not be the first to bring atomic weapons into the field of battle. Furthermore, if we should be the first to develop the weapon, we should have a great new instrument for shortening the war and minimizing destruction."[8]

In August 1943, at the first Quebec conference, Roosevelt and Churchill agreed to share their respective work on the atomic bomb but to concentrate the research and manufacture in the United States (the so-called "Tube Alloy" memorandum). But their fear of what the Germans were doing was stoked by an article in the *New York Times* on December 4, 1943. It quoted a senior Nazi official saying they "intended by one fell, drastic stroke" to retaliate against the Allies. He added ominously: "Mankind is not far from the point where it can at will blow up half the globe."[9] In truth the German efforts to build nuclear weapons—code-named "Uranverein"—were never effectively coordinated and were further hampered by a lack of uranium ore. By 1945 they remained a long way from achieving their goal.

The opposite was the case for the Manhattan Project and, by the spring of 1945, the moment of truth was fast approaching. "By the nature of atomic chain reactions," noted Stimson, "it was impossible to state with certainty that we had succeeded until a bomb had actually exploded in a full-scale experiment; nevertheless it was considered exceedingly probable that we should by midsummer have successfully detonated the first atomic bomb." His last conversation on the subject with Roosevelt was on March 15. The president had received a memo from Jimmy Byrnes that the project—which had cost an astonishing $2 billion to date—"might be a lemon." Could Stimson reassure him? The answer was yes. He explained that the scientists included four Nobel Prize-winners, and all were convinced that the success of the project was near.[10]

Listening intently to all this, Truman asked how quickly the bomb might be ready. "Within the next few months," said Stimson. To prepare, therefore, Stimson suggested setting up an interim committee to advise the president "on the various questions raised by our apparently imminent success in developing an atomic weapon." Truman agreed. "I thanked him for his enlightening presentation of this awesome subject," recalled the president, "and as I saw him to the door I felt how fortunate the country was to have so able and so wise a man in its service."[11]

23

"Corpsman!"

Corporal Jim Johnston of Easy Company, 2/5th Marines, knew it was a bad sign when trucks arrived to move his battalion south. "This wasn't good," he wrote. "They needed us too badly to wait for us to walk."[1]

Since the bloodless landing on Love Day, Johnston's unit—like the rest of the 1st Marine Division—had had a relatively easy time of it. Having crossed the island, their job was to ferret out local resistance. But it was almost nonexistent. "In a more or less static position," noted the 1st's official history, "the division devoted its time to patrolling, mopping up, sealing caves and handling civilians. The combat teams lost few men during this period."[2]

For Johnston, the worst experiences of those first few weeks on Okinawa were witnessing the needless deaths of civilians. "They were," he recalled, "afraid to come out of their hiding places during the day, when we could easily have identified them." Instead they came out at night and were shot by trigger-happy Marines who, wary of Japanese infiltration tactics, would shoot "whatever moved in on us at night." To see the bodies of civilians, particularly children, was "abhorrent" to the Marines. For a time they let people get close so they could identify them. That was a mistake, as it allowed Japanese soldiers to move through their lines, tossing grenades as they went. The Marines, as a result, "resumed killing whatever approached them at night."

Not surprisingly, Johnston kept such gruesome details out of the regular letters he wrote to his parents in Wauneta, Nebraska, where the family had moved from his birthplace in southern Kentucky when he was very young. "I'm on Okinawa in the Ryukyu Islands," he confessed on April 18, "so you guessed right. It isn't far to Japan from here. It has been easy going so far—big surprise to me. Guess we surprised them hitting this close to home. Lots of bombing. May get rough a little later."[3]

He was right. On April 30, the 1st Marine Division began its relief of the 27th Infantry Division on the extreme right of the American front line. Among the 1st Marines who took over from the 165th Infantry on the west coast that day was 24-year-old First Lieutenant Bruce "Watts" Watkins from Manchester, Connecticut. A married graduate of Tufts College, Watkins had served on Peleliu—where he won a Silver Star—and at the start of the Okinawa campaign as a platoon commander in the 2/1st Marines' Easy Company. He felt close to his men, and "objected strongly" when the 2/1st's commander, Lieutenant Colonel James C. Magee Jr., told him he was being reassigned to battalion headquarters as assistant operations officer. But it was to no avail. Soon after, they were in action. "As we moved up to relieve the 27th," recalled Watkins, "they passed us in bedraggled lines. They had what we call the 'thousand-yard stare.' Their casualties were everywhere and as our rifle platoons took over their foxholes, they hastened wordlessly to the rear. There was heavy incoming fire. Mortar and artillery shells were landing all around us, and we started to take casualties. The mournful cry of 'Corpsman!' was heard once again."[4]

A similar scene was playing out in the neighboring sector where the 3/1st Marines attempted to straighten the front line by pushing south of the village of Miyagusuku. Moving across a narrow, rising plain, they had just crossed a low ridge when they received incoming fire from machine guns and mortars. "Immediately," recalled Private Robert Neal, a battalion runner from the small farming community of Eagle Lake, southern Minnesota, "guys I had been calling *buddies* began to fall to earth. Some of them were making sounds that I knew meant they were badly hurt, others were even more strangely not making any sound at all. I hit the deck as I'd been taught to do in a rolling motion and I came up with my carbine spitting death from my shoulder but no enemy was visible."

Spotting an injured comrade, he crawled forward to help him. "I pulled his sulfa unit from its pouch and yelled for a corpsman as I covered the wound. I opened the sulfa packet and poured the [antiseptic] powder into the wound. The corpsman was there before I could finish the bandage." Neal was not surprised: no soldiers were more "highly honored and respected" by Marines than U.S. Navy medical corpsmen who "continually expose themselves to enemy fire while trying to keep life in the body of the guys laying on the ground in front of them."[5] The area that Neal's battalion was trying to advance over had been patrolled earlier without incident by the 2/165th Infantry. But the Japanese had reoccupied it since then and, having inflicted almost thirty casualties, they stopped the 3/1st Marines in their tracks.[6]

A day later, the 5th Marines moved into the line beside the 1st Regiment, replacing units of the 105th and 106th Infantry. Corporal Jim Johnston's 2/5th Marines were assigned to the left of the regimental sector. As Easy Company marched in with full packs during a heavy enemy mortar and artillery barrage, Johnston saw a young soldier sitting by the trail, his hand bleeding profusely from a shrapnel wound. "Lad," said Johnston, "you'd better get that patched up."

"I don't know how," replied the bewildered boy.

"Where's your corpsman, your medic?"

"I don't know."

"Corpsman!" hollered Johnston.

Before long, Doc Lindemann appeared. He was tall and slim, and among the best medics that Johnston had served with. He quickly bandaged the kid's hand with a compress and sent him back down the road. Meanwhile, Johnston and his machine-gunners continued on to the front lines where they were shocked to find strewn about the decomposing bodies of young Americans. The smell was repulsive. So they set to work collecting dog tags to send to the Graves Registration unit, and then burying the corpses "where at least the fucking flies couldn't work on them."

The army troops they were relieving were so disorganized that Johnston asked one of them if he had an officer. The soldier pointed at one of the rotting bodies and said, "That's our lieutenant."

"So who's in charge?"

When no one responded, Johnston asked if a corporal was present.

"I am," said one young fellow.

"What's the word?" queried Johnston, referring to the situation "past, present, and expected."

The army corporal did not know what he was talking about. "He was a good boy," recalled Johnston, "as I know they all were, and he wanted to help. But, like his fellow soldiers in that division, he hadn't been given the consideration and respect he deserved. He hadn't gotten the teaching he so badly needed in the place he found himself."

Fishing for information, Johnston asked the corporal if the artillery fire was always that fierce. "It has been for some time," the corporal replied.

"Isn't there something we can do about it?"

"I sure as hell don't know what."

"Have you tried to advance?"

"Not lately."

Off to the flank, Johnston could see one of the army machine-gunners firing burst after burst from a heavy Browning "at nothing." Johnston, aware that the gunner made a "good sighting point" for the Japanese artillery, told him it would be a good idea to quit. He did, and before long the artillery and mortar fire had eased off.

Searching for a good firing spot, one of Johnston's squad leaders, PFC Lamm, was shot in the leg. As he cut away Lamm's trousers so the corpsman could get to work, Johnston saw that the leg was badly mangled. He tried to raise the man's spirits by talking up his "twenty-five-dollar wound—a ticket home—but his color was bad." The soldier died on the way to the aid post.

Once the guns were sited, Johnston set up his headquarters in a little straw-covered pigsty riddled with shrapnel holes. Directly ahead, running parallel to the front line, was a gently sloping valley. The ground fell away forty or fifty yards to the valley bottom, and then rose the same distance the other side. At its base was an abandoned tank. The valley extended to the right for a distance of about 500 yards, "the ground then rising rather quickly to a prominent rocky hill." Beyond the ridge, directly in front, was a "great, deep gorge" known as the Awacha Pocket. From there a valley ran west all the way to the sea. "We came into that area not knowing what was going on there," remembered Johnston, "and we spent the lives of a lot of good men finding out."[7]

Also moving into the line on May 1, a little to the west of Johnston's position, was Corporal Sterling Mace of King Company, 3/5th Marines. Born in the back of a hardware store in Queens, New York City, Mace had endured a tough upbringing in Little Italy, wearing clothes from a handout store and shoes that were always too small.

But it was good training for what would come. "We didn't know it then," he wrote later, "but the kids of the Great Depression, a deprived generation, were preparing for war."

A veteran of Peleliu, he was now commanding a fire team of four men: himself, a BAR man, his assistant, and the scout, PFC Bob "Wimpy" Whitby, 32 years old and married with two daughters. "All of them were untested in combat," wrote Mace. "They relied on veterans to give them the skinny on what combat was like—but short of giving them a line of bullshit, it was a difficult thing to describe." They were about to find out.

Moving forward on May 1, Mace and his team were "nervously scanning the bombed-out hills" before them when the "ground felt like it had been lifted a foot." As artillery shells screamed in, they broke into a zigzagging run, clods of earth bouncing off their helmets. Mace saw a foxhole and dived into it. Others did the same, "peeking out of the rims of their holes, and *flash*!" A shell erupted, sending a wall of brown earth into the air. When the shelling stopped, it was replaced by a thick carpet of smoke, "swirling over the ground, and shrouding us in a fog."

"Sonofabitch!" cursed his BAR man, PFC Eubanks, a 19-year-old hick from the Appalachians. "These guys aren't fucking joking!"

"No, they're not," said Mace.

The shattered terrain reminded him of the black-and-white photos of Flanders during the First World War: "muted earth tones, scant vegetation, pitted and pocked ridges from the constant shelling—and in the many shell holes along the muted ground lay the detritus of war in its myriad forms. Empty cases of ammunition, spent shell casings, burned-out military vehicles of all types, discarded personal equipment." At one spot, during the journey down, they had passed rows of army dead, covered in ponchos, most of them bootless, "their buddies having scavenged the best pairs for their own use."[8]

By May 2, three U.S. divisions were facing the Japanese in southern Okinawa: from west to east, the 1st Marine, 77th Infantry (which had replaced the 96th Division on April 30), and 7th Infantry. Lieutenant General Buckner visited the commanders of both new divisions—Pedro Del Valle and Andrew Bruce—and got the impression that they expected "to show their superiority over their predecessors by a rapid breakthrough of the enemy position." They quickly realized the Japanese defenses were a much tougher nut to crack than they had imagined.[9]

Both divisions attacked that day and the next: the 1st Marine in the direction of the Asa River, north of Naha; and the 77th up the Maeda escarpment, a "huge, forbidding, sheer cliff" named after the village just over the crest on its southern slope. "They were promptly stopped," jotted Buckner in his diary, and "learned some valuable lessons...From now on they will be more valuable as all-round fighters."[10]

The terrain over which both divisions would have to fight was particularly formidable. "The Japanese," noted the official historian of the 1st Marine Division,

> had carefully prepared all the terrain leading into Shuri and utilized every mound, hummock, hill, and ridge to emplace troops and weapons. In some instances the burial vaults of Okinawans were opened up to make positions for machine guns, 47 mm anti-tank guns and mortars. Caves were dug with connecting passageways so that ammunition could be brought up for emplaced weapons. Special emphasis was placed on coordinated fields of fire. By carefully using the natural arrangement of the hills and ridges, gun positions were made mutually supporting. On the reverse slope[s]...the enemy dug caves for protection of mortar squads, to store food and ammunition, or to provide places of safety for defenders of the hills when our artillery, naval gunfire and aerial bombing made the forward slopes and crests untenable.

The Japanese were further helped by the fact that "each piece of defensive ground was higher progressively and afforded the enemy excellent observation of all troop movements and activities to his front." As the pressure intensified, the Japanese commander was able to "withdraw his troops to prepared positions on the next hill," thus contracting his defensive perimeter and making his fortress ever more formidable. "Nowhere on the island," noted the divisional historian, "could be found more suitable ground for a real war of attrition."[11]

During the 5th Marines' attack on the left of the divisional line, one of the more remarkable feats of courage was by a corpsman, 18-year-old Hospital Apprentice First Class Robert E. Bush from Tacoma, Washington. The son of a lumberjack and a nurse, Bush dropped out of high school and was working as a logger when he decided to enlist in early 1944. Trained at the Naval Hospital Corps School in Farragut, Idaho, he was later assigned as a corpsman to the 3rd Platoon of George Company, 2/5th Marines. On the day of the attack, May 2, he was moving "constantly and unhesitatingly" from one casualty to another when he saw his platoon officer lying badly wounded on the skyline. As the attack swept on, he stopped to administer blood plasma. Just then, the Japanese counter-attacked, and with the plasma bottle "held high in one hand," he "drew his pistol with the other and fired into the enemy's ranks" until he was out of ammo. He then grabbed the officer's discarded carbine and used it to shoot six Japanese soldiers who were "charging point-blank over the hill." Badly wounded by grenade shrapnel, and unable to see out of one eye, he refused treatment until the lieutenant had been evacuated. Even then he insisted on walking to the aid station, and collapsed en route. Hailed for his "daring initiative, great personal valor, and heroic spirit of self-sacrifice," Bush became the war's youngest naval recipient of the Medal of Honor.[12]

Every day of combat was, according to First Lieutenant Bill Looney, the XO of Charlie Company, 1/5th Marines, the same: "The order is 'Take that hill' and every evening it is 'Set up a defense and be sure you are tied into the unit next to you on your right and left, and give us your coordinates.' Attacking 'that hill' means you try to move down into the valley, with the enemy firing sometimes at you from the caves on the downhill slope as well as from the hill you want to take."

People were constantly getting hit, and Looney dreaded the words: "They just got so and so." In early May he heard, "They just got [Jack] Kimble." The young second lieutenant had survived a wound on Peleliu only to die on Okinawa. The day before, a parcel had arrived for Kimble at company HQ, containing a new watch from his parents. But before Looney could get it up to him, he was killed. Looney's first thought was: who will take over the platoon? "Sometimes it's you," he noted, "other times you know the sergeant is there and capable, and then you suck in your gut and keep going. Believe me, it is a lousy way to live."[13]

For Corporal Jim Johnston of Easy Company, 2/5th Marines, the many attempts his battalion made to capture the Awacha Pocket were a "study in futility and frustration." He and his machine-gunners had two options: man the forward defensive positions, or stay so close to the riflemen in assaults that they could bring their firepower to bear "in a matter of seconds." Either way they were in the enemy's "direct line of sight" and, as a result, "took a hell of a beating from small-arms fire, mortars and artillery." Nor did they have the compensation of shooting against massed targets, as they had on Peleliu. With mainly individual targets, they tended to hold their fire as they would only give away their position, inviting immediate retaliation. Apart from acting as insurance against counter-attacks, he and his men would have been better off armed with rifles and BARs. "Instead," he noted ruefully, "we carried the heavy machine-gun shit all over the island and never did get the chance to use the guns effectively."[14]

Perhaps the most valuable troops in this costly attempt to root the Japanese out of their well-dug-in positions were the four-man demolition teams, part of each Marine battalion's Assault Platoon. They were composed of a leader, demolition specialist (armed with a twenty-four-pound TNT satchel charge), flamethrower man and bazooka man. Private Paul "Pop" Ison, a 28-year-old married man with four children from Ashland, Kentucky, was the demolition specialist for a team attached to Love Company, 3/5th Marines. On May 3, Ison's squad—made up of his and two other teams—was ordered forward to help Love Company secure a small hill in front of their lines.

When they got there, Ison recalled, the company was under "heavy fire" from enemy machine guns, snipers and mortars, and losing men fast. Spotting a Japanese firing position in a cave nearby, Ison and his team leader, Corporal Ralph Boschke, "crawled out to try to place a satchel charge of TNT* on top of the cave in order to drop the roof…

* Described by one Marine officer as "a cloth carrier with pockets for about six 'sticks' of 'composition C' linked together by 'primacord,' which would cause all blocks to explode at the same moment when a detonator cap was activated." (Carrell, "King One," p. 27.)

in on the enemy." But they were spotted by a Japanese machine-gunner who opened up, the bullets striking Boschke in the chest and "killing him very quickly."

Someone shouted, "Look out!"

Ison did, and saw to his horror a shell from a Japanese knee mortar heading directly for him. "It was," he remembered, "like someone throwing a baseball at me."

As he dived for cover, the shell hit a small tree behind him and blew it apart. Unscathed, Ison scrambled back to the company position and dropped into a foxhole. By now, with most of the men killed or wounded, the surviving officer radioed back to the battalion CP: "We cannot hold this hill any longer."

Permission was eventually given by the 3/5th's commander, Lieutenant Colonel John C. Miller, for Love Company to destroy its heavy equipment and pull back as soon as possible. Before it did so, Ison and four men went out to retrieve Boschke's body, throwing smoke grenades as they went. Unfortunately the corpse was in too exposed a position, just over the crest, and they were forced to leave it, much to Ison's dismay. But they were able to recover the dead man's Thompson sub-machine gun, which was handed to Ison. He gave his carbine to another soldier.

To mask the withdrawal, two young Marines threw grenade after grenade "over the hill toward the enemy." When they had emptied two cases, they ran down the hill as Ison provided covering fire with his Tommy gun. They were the last three off the hill.* By now the enemy mortars were falling like rain, and Ison and two of his team took cover in a shell hole. But one of them got jumpy and suggested moving to the base of a nearby hill. "OK," said Ison. "Let's go."

They had just reached their new refuge when another trio of Marines jumped into the hole in which Ison and his men had been hiding. "A few seconds later," recalled Ison, "a Japanese mortar shell made a direct hit into that shell hole, killing all three Marines," and showering the ground nearby with their body parts.

As they moved back, one of Ison's comrades spotted a brand-new M1 rifle on the ground. "Pop," he said, "do you want this M1?"

* For their heroism that day, the two Marines were awarded Silver Stars, and Ison the Bronze Star Medal.

Ison ran his hands over its stock and replied: "I sure do!" He swapped it for the Tommy gun. Arriving back at battalion headquarters, a short distance behind the lines, Ison was told to report to the Assault Platoon leader, Lieutenant Ellington. "I want you to take over the four-man demolition team," said Ellington. "Corporal Boschke told me a few days ago that if anything should happen to him, he wanted you to replace him."[15]

24

Hacksaw Ridge

Dominating the ground in front of the 77th Division was a "huge, forbidding, sheer cliff" known as the Maeda escarpment, or "Hacksaw Ridge" to the soldiers who fought there. They would remember it as "all hell rolled into one."

At its eastern point, the ridge ended abruptly in a large sentinel-like monolith, "Needle Rock," where the summit was barely a few yards across. But as it ran west it widened gradually to a depth of fifty yards. The reverse slope was also steep, though not as high as the northern face, and riddled with an intricate network of caves and tunnels that connected with pillboxes on top. East of the ridge, a 200-yard saddle dipped toward Hill 150, and 400 yards beyond that, across another saddle, was Hill 152. This was the point at which the high ground of the Urasoe–Mura feature turned at right angles to the south-west.

The first attempt to take Hacksaw Ridge was made on April 26 by the 381st Infantry of 96th Division. They had few problems advancing to the face of the ridge, but as they clambered up the sheer face toward the crest, with some men forming a human ladder, they were shot down by machine guns. Further east, men from the 383rd Infantry reached the crests of Hills 150 and 152, and were able to fire down the reverse slopes onto hundreds of exposed Japanese soldiers. One BAR man claimed to have killed thirty on his own. Meanwhile tanks and armored flamethrowers got as far as Maeda village where they caused havoc. This prompted General Ushijima to issue the following order: "The enemy with troops following tanks has been advancing into the southern and eastern ends of Maeda…The 62nd Division will dispatch local units…[and] attack the enemy advancing in the Maeda sector and expect to repulse him decisively." Soon after, Ushijima ordered adjacent units of the 24th Division to "crush the enemy which has broken through near Maeda."

With Japanese reinforcements rushing to the area, the 96th Division made very little further progress, except on the east flank where Love Company, 383rd Infantry, advanced to within a mile of the town of Shuri. Hacksaw Ridge, however, remained firmly in Japanese hands when the 307th Infantry of the 77th Division took over the sector of the front line facing the Maeda escarpment from the 381st Infantry on April 29. A day later, the relief of the 96th Division was completed when the 306th replaced the 383rd Infantry on the left. The 381st was now down to around forty percent of its original combat strength, having suffered 1,021 casualties, 536 of them in the attempt to take Hacksaw Ridge. Now it was the 307th's turn.[1]

Moving back with the 96th was the remaining armor of the 763rd Tank Battalion which had been on the line for thirty days straight. They were warned on April 29 that at noon the following day they would be "replaced by fresh troops and tanks and given a ten-day rest and resupply period." It was not a moment too soon for Sergeant Bob Dick, the driver of Charlie Company's *Cutthroats*, who had reached the point where he "knew" that sooner or later he would be hit. "The only question left in my mind," he recalled, "was how bad it would be...My nerves were just about shot. I think I was hanging on more by force of habit than anything else. And I think the rest of the crew were pretty much in the same state."

For some time Dick's tank commander, Sergeant Ovid "OW" French, had been vomiting blood and was unable to keep his food down. So during the afternoon of April 29, French was sent to the field hospital for a check-up, and was replaced by a Lieutenant Bomax who had yet to experience combat. That evening, Bomax and Anderson, the gunner, compared photos of their young daughters and talked for several hours. Dick felt "good for them."

Next morning, they boarded their thirty-ton Sherman and moved up in support of the infantry, taking position behind some cover a little to the rear. "As we sat and watched," recalled, Dick, "fresh infantrymen relieved the combat-weary 96th Division Deadeyes, one man at a time, foxhole by foxhole. Amazingly, even though the Japanese could see all of this going on, not a shot was fired."

Then the radio crackled into life. It was an order to move the tank ahead of the lines, at the base of a "fairly high ridge." Their task was to fire into the caves and emplacements on the ridge face. Once in position, Anderson began firing the 75 mm cannon, its shells exploding in a sheet of flame and smoke, as great chunks of coral and concrete were blasted into the air. Another tank, away to their right, was doing the same. Then suddenly Dick could hear explosions just behind them, almost certainly from Japanese heavy mortars or artillery. Anticipating an order to withdraw, Dick grabbed the shift lever with his right hand and prepared to put the tank in reverse.

The tank shook from a direct hit. Badly concussed, Dick did not hear or feel a thing. But he knew that something was wrong. "Everywhere I looked, it was as if I had red goggles on." Gazing back up into the turret, he could see someone's foot disappearing out of the commander's open hatch. He then looked to his right and saw his assistant driver, Kahn, "frantically jerking" at the hatch lever.

"We're on fire," yelled Kahn, "and the hatch is jammed!"

Dust clouded the air so thickly that it obscured Dick's vision. He realized it had been thrown up by the explosion, and was not smoke from a fire. "Calm down!" he yelled. "There is no fire!"

Kahn seemed to heed Dick's words, but then reached up, opened the hatch and was gone. Dick was the last of the crew of five still in the tank. He felt strangely calm and, noticing the engine was still running, tried to put the tank into gear. But all he could hear was the grinding of metal. The shell must have hit the back deck, he reasoned, and messed up something in the shift mechanism. As he tried again without success, he could hear Anderson yelling at him to get out. He shouted back, "I'll be right out."

He reached for the Tommy gun that, every morning, he put in the space behind the dash panel. But it seemed stuck and would not budge. Leaving it, he stood up so that his head was just above the hatch entrance. Suddenly his head jerked back involuntarily—yanked by the intercom cord that he had forgotten to unplug—just as a bullet struck the edge of the hatch. His error probably saved his life. Having now unplugged the wire, he grabbed the hatch opening with both hands and launched himself out and over the side of the tank, "landing in a heap in the dirt" before scrambling round to the far side where Anderson and Bomax were crouching by the front-left drive socket. The air was full of small-arms fire, the "dry branch-like snap" of bullets making them flinch repeatedly.

"We'd better get out of here," shouted Dick. "Those guys are bound and determined to get us." With that he took off running, zigzagging as he went, before taking cover in a shell hole. Moments later Anderson joined him as, all around, bullets were sending up little geysers of dirt. Dick was pondering his next move when he saw the other tank moving back. He ran over to it and motioned for the crew to drop the escape hatch. While he waited, crouching low, he was joined by Anderson and Bomax, who had now appeared. To lessen the chances of being shot, Dick slid under the rear of the Sherman and wiggled through the narrow escape hatch. He could see Anderson through the hatch and asked him what was wrong.

"The lieutenant's been hit," replied Anderson. Bomax had tried to slide under the front of the tank and was shot in the back just two feet short of the hatch. Anderson was trying to manhandle him into the tank, but it was impossible. Meanwhile the tank commander, Sergeant Boggs, had spotted a Japanese soldier with a satchel charge on the bank above. His gunner tried to shoot the soldier with the .30 caliber coaxially mounted machine gun, but that jammed. So Boggs opened his hatch and let rip with his pistol. When that ran out of ammo, he used his Tommy gun, eventually hitting the enemy soldier. Anderson was still trying to get Bomax in the tank. But at 185 pounds Bomax was just too heavy.

Worried he might lose a second tank, the company commander ordered Boggs to leave Bomax and withdraw. He would see to it that the infantry recovered the lieutenant's body after dark. By the time they got back, Anderson was a mess: he was sobbing and could not feel his legs, though there was no sign of a wound. Dick was not much better. "My nerves were so shot," he recalled, "I was shaking all over." He asked the company medic to give him something to calm him, and was handed "green pills, a super aspirin." It was, he thought, a "lousy way to end our first thirty days of fighting."[2]

The new battalion tasked with capturing Hacksaw Ridge was the 1/307th Infantry. During the night of April 30–May 1, Cooney's men attached four fifty-foot ladders and five cargo nets, the latter borrowed from the navy, to the northern face of the ridge. The following day, Able Company attempted to scale the ladders close to Needle Rock, but every man who got to the top was killed or wounded. A little farther to the west, using the cargo nets, Baker Company got two platoons onto the edge of the ridge by nightfall. But they were driven off by a midnight counter-attack.

Both companies tried again the following day, and got men up to the lip of the summit. But faced with machine-gun fire so intense that one GI was decapitated, they could go no further. On May 3, they fought a desperate grenade battle for control of the ridge. Meeting a storm of shrapnel from Japanese grenades, knee mortars and 81 mm mortars sited on the reverse slope, some "Dogfaces" withdrew to the northern edge, refusing to go back into the fight. Yet they quickly regained their courage, noted one platoon leader, and were soon "back in there tossing grenades as fast as they could pull the pins."[3]

Next morning, Able and Baker Companies were ordered to extend their perimeter by knocking out a big cave-tunnel and pillbox network that was 200 feet west of Needle Rock. Before Baker's 2nd Platoon moved off, First Lieutenant Cecil L. Gornto of Live Oak, Florida, told his men: "OK, fellows, we're going up on top again today. You have plenty of ammunition. Do your best, men."[4]

As they got ready, the platoon medic PFC Desmond T. Doss, 26, asked to speak to Gornto. Born in Lynchburg, West Virginia, Doss and his two siblings had been raised by their mother Martha, a shoe-factory worker, as devout Seventh-Day Adventists. This meant a strict adherence to the Bible (the "Word of God"), keeping Saturday—the Sabbath—as a rest day, nonviolence and a vegetarian diet. So when Doss was drafted into the army in 1942—from his job as a joiner at the Newport News shipyard—he asked for a non-combat classification. "There's no such thing," said the draft officer. "You'll have to go in as a conscientious objector. If you go in as any other classification, you'll be court-martialled if you refuse to do ordinary work on the Sabbath or refuse to bear arms."[5]

Doss took this advice and, knowing that his religion allowed him to take care of sick or hurt people on the Sabbath, had opted to train as a medic. He learned how to sprinkle sulfanilamide powder on open wounds, bind them with battle dressings, inject syrettes of morphine to alleviate pain, and make splints for broken limbs from saplings and rifle stocks. He was also instructed "how to give blood plasma on the battlefield, what to do for shock, when to administer water and when to withhold it."

After marrying another Seventh-Day Adventist, the "pretty, blonde" and "serious" Dorothy Schutte, he was assigned to Baker Company of the 307th Infantry, part of the 77th "Statue of Liberty" Division, and dominated by New Yorkers to whom Doss's flat Southern drawl sounded distinctly alien. Slim and gawky, with brown wavy hair, Doss's habit of praying by his bedside soon earned him the derisive nickname of "Preacher."[6]

But gradually they came to accept and even admire Doss, particularly after he proved himself in the Guam and Leyte campaigns, receiving a Bronze Star for treating wounded soldiers under fire. He kept up the good work on Okinawa. A couple of days before the May 3 attack, he went up Hacksaw Ridge in the dark to assist a man who had been wounded by mortar fire. "As soon as it was light enough," recalled Gornto, "I observed him lowering the wounded man over the cliff on a rope to evacuate him. The man had both his legs blown off." A day later, Doss went in to no man's land to bring in a wounded man "under very heavy rifle and knee-mortar fire."[7]

So when a medic as courageous as Doss asked to speak to him on May 3, 1945, Lieutenant Gornto was ready to listen. "What is it Doss?"

"Lieutenant," said the medic, "I believe prayer is the best lifesaver there is. The men should really pray before they go up."

Gornto agreed. "Fellows," he told his platoon, "come over here and gather around. Doss wants to pray for us."

This was not Doss's intention. He had assumed that each soldier would pray individually. But faced with all those expectant faces, he began: "Dear Lord, bless us today. Be with the lieutenant and help him to give the right orders, for our lives are in his hands. Help each one of us to use safety precautions so that we all might come back alive. And, Lord, help all of us to make our peace with Thee before we go up the net. Thank You. Amen."[8]

With the prayer over, they and the rest of Baker Company went up the cargo net and were almost immediately pinned down. "Company A was fighting on our left," recalled Doss, "and they were so badly shot up we were ordered to take the whole escarpment by ourselves. We started forward and knocked out eight or nine underground Japanese positions. The amazing, miraculous thing was that no one in our company was killed and only one man was injured—by a rock that hit his hand." An estimated 600 Japanese soldiers were killed by the 307th Infantry on "Miracle Day."[9]

Next morning, Baker Company had to consolidate its hold on Hacksaw Ridge by advancing down the reverse slope. This time Doss asked the company commander, Captain Frank L. Vernon, if he could say a prayer with the men before they left. "Sorry, Doss," replied Vernon, "we're all ready to start off."

They all assumed, after the success of the previous day, that it would be a "mop-up job." But they could not have been more wrong. The advance went wrong from the start. "We threw all kinds of high explosives [satchel charges] onto the Japanese position," recalled Doss, "and they would pull the fuse out before it went off." Eventually they decided to use gasoline, emptying thirty-five gallons on to the underground bunker, followed by a phosphorus grenade. There was an enormous explosion, and earth, concrete and flames flew through the air. "The whole mountain seemed to quiver and you didn't think anyone could survive such a thing."

But they did. Realizing it was now or never, hundreds of Japanese emerged from camouflaged trenches and charged the 1/307th Infantry. Outnumbered, Baker Company withdrew to the northern edge of the summit. "The captain [Vernon] was just a little ways behind the platoon," remembered 25-year-old Elwyn Gaines from Marsing, Idaho. "We were on this small knoll and in come those mortar shells and Japanese just all over the top, you know, so the sergeant said, 'Retreat. Get out of here.' And so we started running."[10]

It was supposed to be an orderly retreat, but it ended in a panicked rush down the cargo nets, leaving scores of wounded behind. One man stayed with them: Desmond Doss. "Some of my men were married with families," he said later, "and they had so much confidence in me that I couldn't leave them, even if it cost me my life."

He did not have a clue how to save them all. The Japanese were keeping their distance, assuming the American foxholes were still manned. But as soon as they realized there was no opposition, they would advance and kill everyone. Doss had to work fast. With only one stretcher, he tied one of the more serious casualties into it and, using a tree stump as an anchor, lowered him down the thirty-five-foot drop to the bottom of the ridge where Baker Company men were waiting. "Take him to the aid station pronto!" yelled Doss from the summit. "He's hurt bad."

Once they had unfastened the stretcher, Doss pulled up the rope and used the bowline knot he had learned at church school to create two loops in the end. He put the next casualty's legs through the loops, tied the rope off round his middle, and lowered him over the cliff. Then he dragged another injured man to the edge and repeated the trick. And so on. "How I was going to get all those men down I didn't know," recalled Doss. "I just kept praying, 'Lord, please help me get one more.'"

With his luck holding, Doss worked feverishly for five straight hours, lowering man after man. Finally, and incredibly, there were no more casualties left, or none he could get to. "After I got the last man off, I came down," he said. "My clothes were bloody. I'd been soaked to the skin by the blood of the men." Back at the bivouac area, covered in flies, he was given a clean pair of fatigues and looked uncommonly spruce when divisional commander Major General Andrew Bruce, who had heard of his exploits, came to offer his congratulations. He told Doss he would recommend him for the Medal of Honor, or "nothing less" than a Distinguished Service Cross.

Some thought Doss saved a hundred lives that day. He put the true number closer to fifty, so they split the difference on his Medal of Honor citation to seventy-five. Such details were, to Doss, irrelevant. He was just glad he could help. "The medic's work," he insisted, "is the most rewarding of all."[11]

On May 6, two days after Doss's heroics, the remaining Japanese were killed or entombed in their pillboxes and tunnels on the reverse slope, and Hacksaw Ridge was finally in American hands. Doss's 1/307th Infantry had lost more than half its original strength of 800, including eight company commanders. Japanese fatalities in the battle were estimated at "upward of 3,000."[12]

25

"We will fight to the last man"

During the morning of May 4, the Japanese launched an all-out counter-attack on Okinawa that its architect, Major General Chō, hoped would turn the tide of the campaign. The final decision to leave their "safe cave fortresses" and advance in the open had been taken a few days earlier in Chō's office, part of the Thirty-Second Army's huge headquarters tunnel that ran 1,280 feet north to south through the hillside, with side chambers and a side shaft angling to the left. Chō's room, faced with sawn planks and supported by square beams, was situated with the other senior officers' rooms in the northwestern extremity of the side shaft, at least a hundred feet below Shuri Castle.[1]

It was a fractious meeting, oiled by large quantities of sake. Present were all the Thirty-Second Army's senior commanders and staff officers bar Lieutenant General Ushijima. True to form, he would wait to hear the result of their deliberations before making his own decision. The meeting was led, therefore, by Chō who argued that the Americans held the upper hand and, if the Japanese did nothing, the enemy would sooner or later break through the Shuri Line and wipe out the Thirty-Second Army. On the other hand, with the bulk of the Japanese forces still intact, the time was ripe to strike a "decisive" blow.[2]

As before, the main opponent of aggressive action was Colonel Yahara who felt his defensive strategy was working well. Despite the Americans' big advantage in firepower and men, they were being held to gains of just a hundred yards a day. Moreover, by the end of April, the Thirty-Second Army had become the only Japanese force "to maintain organized resistance to an American island landing for over thirty days." Under the circumstances, they needed to continue what they were doing. "To take the offensive with inferior forces," he insisted, would be "reckless" and "lead to certain defeat." It would leave the 32nd Army "unable to hold Okinawa for a long period and unable to delay the U.S. invasion of Japan." This, in turn, would be a failure of duty.

But Yahara was backed by only a small minority of those present, mostly staff officers. The majority had grown gloomy at the constant reports of lost men and positions, the ever closer explosions of American shells that were killing sentries and sending clouds of noxious fumes into the ventilator shafts, and were prepared to risk all in a sudden attack. Better that than certain defeat and death. Chō's most vigorous supporter was the conservative Lieutenant General Takeo Fujioka, commanding the 62nd Division, who "expressed the general desire of his men to fight the decisive action in the [division's] zone of defense." With Chō and a majority in favor, Ushijima ordered an all-out offensive for May 4, referring to it as an "honorable death attack."[3]

The final plan was ludicrously ambitious: to devote the bulk of the remaining ground, air and amphibious forces in a coordinated attack on the American XXIV Corps and the Allied fleet offshore. Despite General Fujioka's enthusiasm, most of the initial fighting would be done by General Amamiya's relatively intact 24th Division. First it would drive two strong spearheads through the center and left (east) of the American lines. With the front broken, more Japanese troops would pour through the gaps to destroy the XXIV Corps in a series of day and night battles. Meanwhile troops in barges, armed only with satchel charges and light arms, would land behind American lines on both coasts to seek out and destroy artillery and tanks. The offensive would be coordinated with yet another tsunami of kamikaze attacks against American ships.

Ordered to draft the attack plan, the reluctant Colonel Yahara made one vital change by shifting the 44th IMB from its reserve line to a position north-east of Shuri, from where it would join the attack, not on May 3, as originally intended, but a day later. This meant it would not be in a position to join the assault on the 4th, and thus reduced the attacking force by a third. His intention, of course, was to keep the 44th IMB out of the battle and reduce casualties. The final orders for the offensive stated: "Display a combined strength. Each soldier will kill at least one American devil."[4]

Kamikazes began the attack on American shipping at dusk on May 3, with seven suicide planes hitting the destroyer *Aaron Ward* at Radar Picket Station 10, killing forty-five and wounding another forty-nine. But thanks to the heroics of her crew, who put out fires amidst exploding ammunition, the *Ward* stayed afloat and was eventually towed to Kerama for repairs. "We all admire a ship that can't be licked," wired Admiral Nimitz to the *Ward*'s captain. "Congratulations on your magnificent performance."[5]

That night, several hundred men of the 26th Shipping Engineer Regiment, armed with anti-tank guns, heavy machine guns, light arms and thousands of satchel charges, boarded barges near Naha and headed in darkness for landing places at Oyama, well behind the front line. But miscalculating their position, they headed in to shore at Kuwan, a point just behind the front line and heavily defended by men from Baker and Charlie Companies, 1st Marines. At 2:00 a.m., the defenders spotted ten barges offshore and opened fire with machine guns. Assisted by naval flares, the Baker Company mortar officer fired more than a thousand 60 mm mortar rounds, "sinking one barge, killing many of the enemy and causing them to disperse." They were shot down by a platoon from Baker Company that "burned out six machine-gun barrels and one gun and used fifty boxes of ammunition." Then, according to a fellow officer, Lieutenant Lee Height of Easy Company "charged his platoon through fifty yards of knee-high palmetto and met the Japs on the beach. Few Japs made it that far...Lee's platoon finished off the rest." Those Japanese not killed were mopped up the following day. "The whole thing was a godsend," commented a Baker Company officer. "If the Nips had landed above us, they would have faced no opposition, but they headed in where we were and we cut them down."[6]

A second attempted landing on the east coast, by the 23rd Shipping Engineer Regiment, was destroyed by American fire from the coast and ships in the bay. The two amphibious attacks had been a fiasco, costing the Japanese at least 500 men and almost all their landing craft.[7]

At dawn on May 4, Japanese howitzers and field guns began a huge bombardment of the American front lines, eventually firing more than 13,000 shells. Thirty minutes later the infantry moved forward and, for a time, made some headway. On the far right the

89th Regiment advanced more than 2,000 yards before it was blocked by the U.S. 7th Infantry Division and cut to pieces by land, naval and air bombardment, losing half its strength. In the center, the 22nd Regiment was delayed laying smoke and, when that unexpectedly cleared, it presented an easy target for machine guns and artillery fire. Further to the left, the 32nd Regiment and supporting tanks were supposed to penetrate the American lines east of the Maeda escarpment, and then sweep forward and secure the Tanabaru escarpment. But the attack became entangled with the rightmost unit of the 62nd Division, and was further blunted by American artillery fire.

The 44th Mixed Brigade was now in a position northwest of Shuri to begin its drive to the western coast behind the 1st Marine Division. But when its commander, Major General Suzuki, asked for permission to enter the fray, he was told by Yahara that "Maeda hill was not sufficiently occupied for the 44th move." To do so "would only heighten the needless sacrifice and still not achieve a strategic breakthrough."

The Japanese air attack on May 4 was more successful, sinking four ships—including two U.S. destroyers *Luce* and *Morrison*—and damaging thirteen others. The casualties included the destroyer *Shea*, hit by a Baka bomb; Admiral Deyo's flagship *Birmingham*, struck by a kamikaze bomb that penetrated to the sickbay, killing and wounding 132 men; and the escort carrier *Sangamon* which lost twenty-one planes and had her entire hangar deck gutted by fire. A total of 660 U.S. sailors were killed and more than 500 wounded.[8]

Two hundred miles south, the battleships and cruisers of the British Pacific Fleet had just begun a bombardment of Japanese airfields on the Sakishima Islands when kamikaze planes, taking advantage of the weakened anti-aircraft screen, attacked the aircraft carriers. One crashed into the fleet carrier HMS *Formidable*'s steel flight deck, sending splinters into the central boiler room that reduced her speed to just eighteen knots, and another narrowly missed the carrier HMS *Indomitable*. "The *Formidable* was hit by 'suicider' in the island," noted a British sailor in his diary. "A blazing plane slid along the deck on *Indomitable* and into the sea, no damage was done. Fifteen planes were shot down today." The *Formidable* lost eight men killed and forty-seven wounded, and eleven planes destroyed, but, thanks to its armored flight deck, was operational again by evening.

PFC Don Dencker, a good student whose hobby was racing pigeons, during training with the 3/382nd Infantry at Camp Luis Obispo, California. Raised in Minneapolis, Dencker had completed three terms of a chemical engineering degree at the University of Minnesota when he was drafted into the US Army in 1943.

Private Howard Arendt (top right), 20, from Louisville, Kentucky, with five tent mates from the 3/22nd Marines. None came through the battle unscathed: three were killed and three wounded (including Arendt who was shot in both legs after crossing the Asa River on May 10, 1945).

A landing ship firing rockets onto Japanese positions on Okinawa, as part of the softening-up process, in late March 1945.

Marines climb into a landing craft on Love Day, April 1, 1945.

Landing craft and ships off Hagushi beaches on Love Day, April 1, 1945.

Private Salvatore Giammanco, a 20-year-old Italian immigrant from Brooklyn, was the first ground casualty of the campaign. Shot in the chest by a sniper as he moved inland with the 3/4th Marines on Love Day, he was transferred to a hospital ship and saved by a blood transfusion.

Major General Lemuel Shepherd (center, with his arm in a sling), the commander of the 6th Marine Division, with his staff on Okinawa. His aide-de-camp, Lieutenant Benjamin S. Read, is far right.

An American intelligence officer questions a Japanese prisoner.

The celebrated war correspondent Ernie Pyle (sitting 3rd from the left) enjoys a cigarette break with men from the 1/5th Marines on April 8, 1945, a week after the Okinawa landings.

The body of Ernie Pyle, lying in a roadside ditch on Ie Shima. Pyle had been travelling with the commander of the 305th Infantry when their jeep was ambushed by a Japanese machine gunner on April 18, 1945. Both took refuge in a ditch, but Pyle was killed when three bullets passed through the dirt bank and struck him in the left temple. "No man in this war," said President Truman, "has so well told the story of the American fighting man."

Lieutenant General Mitsuru Ushijima, 57, commanding the Japanese Thirty-Second Army on Okinawa. A former head of the Imperial Japanese Army Academy, he preferred to leave "all operational details to his subordinates."

Ushijima (far left) and staff plot the battle. In the center, holding a pointer, is Chief of Staff Isamu Chō, a hawkish ultranationalist who wanted to fight the Americans on the beaches; next to Ushijima is Colonel Hiromichi Yahara, the operations chief and architect of the Japanese defensive strategy, who survived the war and later wrote a book that remains the most authoritative Japanese account of the battle.

A Japanese light tank with two of its dead crewmen in the foreground.

Marines follow two M4 Sherman tanks into action. The lead Marine is armed with a Thompson sub-machine gun.

American troops use a flamethrower to flush out Japanese snipers on a beach.

US Marines assaulting a former Japanese barracks at Shuri in late May 1945.

Soldier (left) firing a .30 caliber Browning automatic rifle (BAR) on May 2, 1945.

A rifleman looks for a target, while his officer talks into his battery-operated walkie-talkie. Both are wearing the Marine standard-issue Ka-Bar utility/fighting knife.

Standing atop the Maeda escarpment ("Hacksaw Ridge"), remembered by the soldiers who fought there as "all hell rolled into one," is PFC Desmond Doss, 26, a Seventh Day Adventist from Lynchburg, West Virginia, who had joined up as a medic to avoid the need to kill. Doss is standing at the point from where, in early May 1945, he lowered by rope more than 50 casualties of the 1/307th Infantry in an astounding act of gallantry that earned him the Medal of Honor.

Colonel Francis Fenton kneels beside the body of his son PFC Mike Fenton, a 19-year-old scout/sniper in 1/5th Marines who was killed in the fierce fighting for the Awacha Pocket on May 7, 1945.

Ensign Kiyoshi Ogawa, the pilot of one of two kamikaze planes that struck the aircraft carrier USS *Bunker Hill*, Vice Admiral Mitscher's flagship, on May 11, 1945.

Smoke and flames pour from the USS *Bunker Hill* after the kamikaze attacks. Almost 400 men were killed (including 14 of Mitscher's staff, most by smoke inhalation) and 264 wounded, the worst naval casualties of the battle.

Sugar Loaf Hill, near Naha, the seemingly insignificant feature at the apex of a triangle of defensive positions that were mutually self-supporting. The week-long battle in mid-May to capture the hill—described by one combatant as an "ugly hive" that was 300 yards long and 100 feet high—would cost the 6th Marine Division more than 2,600 casualties, including three battalion commanders and nine company commanders, and a further 1,200 cases of combat fatigue.

American soldiers collecting supplies dropped by air during the fierce fighting for Shuri Castle in late May 1945.

Japanese schoolgirls wave cherry blossoms to bid a kamikaze pilot farewell as he leaves on his suicide mission from Chiran Air Base, Kyushu, on April 12, 1945.

US Marines evacuate a wounded colleague.

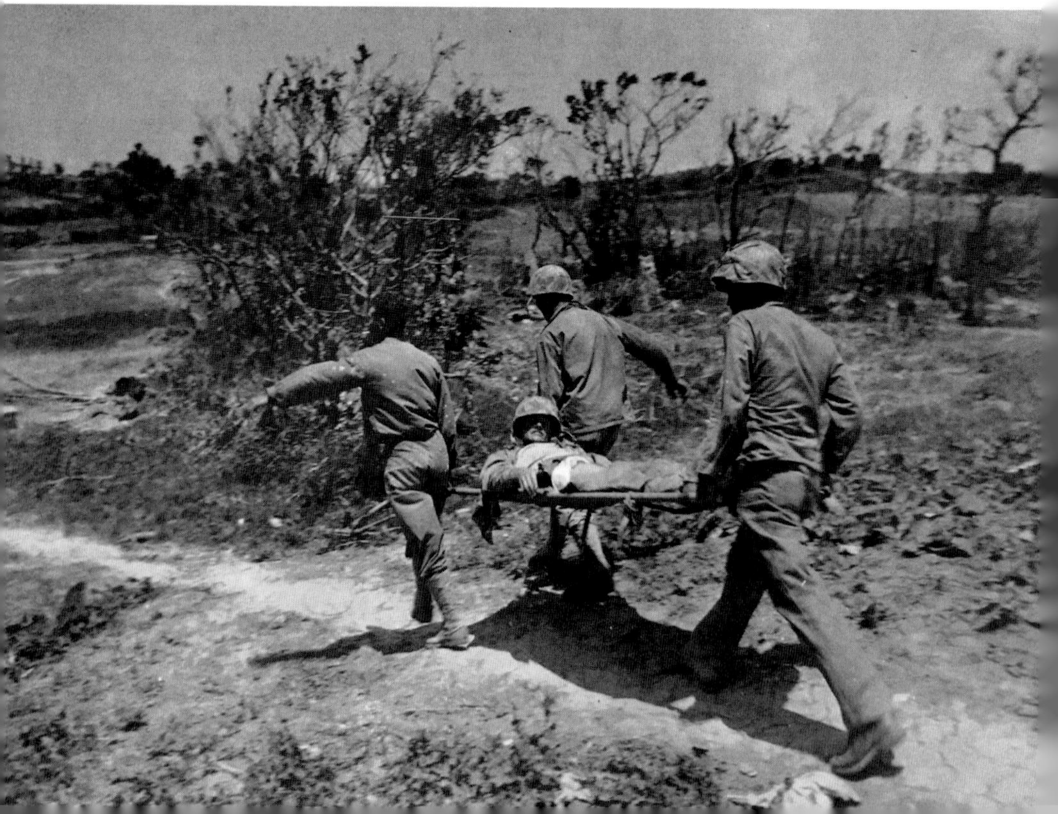

Two soldiers cover a Japanese sniper hidden in a wrecked church.

Major Bruce Porter DFC, the commander of 542 (N) Squadron, walking away from his Grumman F6F Hellcat night fighter. Porter shot down two Japanese planes during a sortie over Okinawa on June 15, 1945, making him an "Ace," and was the only Marine Corps pilot to score multiple victories in both the Hellcat and the Vought F4U Corsair.

A US Marine removes grenades from the corpse of a female Japanese soldier killed in the fighting.

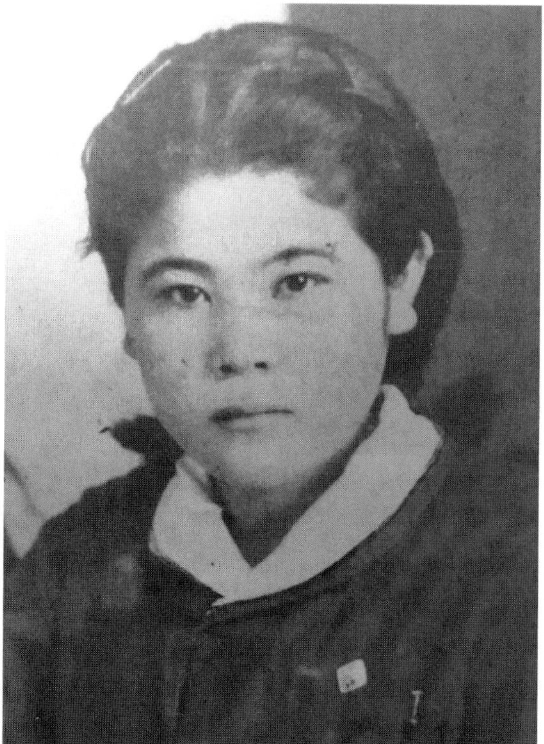

Miyo Takaesu, one of the 118 student nurses of the Himeyuri Corps—recruited from schoolgirls between the ages of 15 and 19—who perished in the battle for Okinawa.

The last photograph of Lieutenant General Simon Buckner (right), shortly before the commander of the US Tenth Army was mortally wounded by a Japanese shell in an OP on the forward slope of Hill 52, near Mezado Ridge, on June 18, 1945. Standing behind Buckner are (from right to left) Colonel Clarence "Bull" Wallace and Major Bill Chamberlin of the 8th Marines.

Men of the 6th Marine Division raise the Stars and Stripes to signal the end of organized Japanese resistance as they reach the sea at the end of the Kiyan Peninsula on June 21, 1945.

Japanese soldiers surrendering to US forces during mopping-up operations in late June 1945.

An aerial view of the "Little Boy" atomic bomb exploding over Hiroshima on August 6, 1945. It detonated with the force of 20,000 tons of TNT, destroying four square miles of the city and killing an estimated 80,000 people. Eight days later, after a second bomb had been dropped on Nagasaki, the Japanese government agreed to surrender unconditionally. "I have had no regrets," Truman wrote later, "and, under the same circumstances, I would do it again."

With a wooden flight deck, the *Sangamon* suffered far more serious damage, losing more than 160 killed and wounded, and never returned to operations.[9]

Overall, the Japanese attack on May 4 had been a costly failure. A rare exception was the feat of the 1/32nd Regiment, under Captain Koichi Ito, which got as far as the Tanabaru escarpment, a mile to the rear of the American front line, during the night of 4/5 May. But unable to communicate his success to his commanders, Koichi remained unsupported and isolated. Despite constant attacks by the U.S. 17th Infantry, Ito and his men held on until the evening of May 6 when the survivors withdrew to their own lines, abandoning 462 casualties.[10]

At 6:00 a.m. on May 5, Colonel Yahara was working in his office in the Thirty-Second Army's underground headquarters when he was summoned by General Ushijima. He found the general sitting cross-legged, as usual, on the worn tatami floor. "Colonel Yahara," said Ushijima softly, "as you predicted, this offensive has been a total failure. Your judgment was correct. You must have been frustrated at the start of this battle because I did not use your talents and skill wisely. Now I am determined to stop this offensive. Meaningless suicide is not what I want."

Ushijima admitted that, before leaving Tokyo in 1944, he had been urged by both War Minister Anami and Army Chief of Staff Umezu "not to be hasty in ordering a last suicidal charge." Now he was going to heed that advice. The main force was "largely spent," but some of the fighting strength was left, and they were getting "strong support from the islanders." He added: "With these we will fight to the southernmost hill, to the last square inch of land, and to the last man. I am ready to fight, but from now on I leave everything up to you. My instructions to you are to do whatever you feel is necessary."

Yahara felt a mixture of anger and frustration. How could Ushijima say such a thing! Only now that their forces were exhausted did he recognize what Yahara had been saying all along. It was "outrageous" and, worse, "too late to accomplish anything." Yet Yahara appreciated the general's "sincerity and the fact that he could admit the truth."

Yahara was also prepared to acknowledge—at least to himself—that he was partly to blame. Believing in his own defensive plan, he should have "staked his life on it." Instead he allowed himself to be browbeaten by others, notably Chief of Staff Chō whose office was next door. He knew that Chō could hear every word of the conversation, and could only imagine what he must be feeling. After all, Chō had "staked his life" on the offensive, and it had been a "complete failure." Yahara "felt sorry for him, but the results had been predictable." Henceforth the chief of staff would have to play second fiddle to a subordinate, but he retained his sense of humor. "Hey, Yahara," said Chō a few days later, "when will it be OK for me to commit hara-kiri? Is this a good time?"

Yahara summarized the cost of the failed two-day Japanese offensive as follows: the 24th Division had lost two-thirds of its "fighting strength"; the 5th Artillery Group's ammunition was "almost expended," with each gun limited to just ten rounds a day for the rest of May; two Shipping Engineer regiments had been "totally annihilated"; the Thirty-Second Army had lost "5,000 seasoned soldiers, killed and wounded"; and, if the offensive had not gone ahead, they could have "prolonged the Okinawa battle for another month and saved thousands of lives."[11]

To staunch the bleeding, Yahara reverted to his original strategy. This meant the 24th Division canceling its offensive and returning to its "original entrenchments," while all other forces did the same. To replace some of the losses, service and support troops were converted into combat infantrymen. "One man in ten," stated one order, "will continue with rear-echelon duties. The remaining nine men will devote themselves to anti-tank combat training." But the outlook was far from rosy. "Arai, the prefectural police chief, visited our headquarters," noted Yahara, "and confirmed that everyone on the island—military and civilian—had suffered a loss of morale as a result of our failed counteroffensive."[12]

The view was echoed by one Japanese lieutenant who wrote in his diary: "We realized we were doomed when we heard of the failure of the 24th Division."[13]

In truth, the morale of Okinawan civilians drafted into the Japanese armed forces had already been irreparably damaged by a month of vicious fighting. Stationed in the underground wards of the army field hospital at Haebaru, 16-year-old Kikuko Miyagi and her fellow student nurses had had to deal with an unceasing flow of casualties. "They were carried in one after another," recalled Kikuko, "until the dugouts and caves were filled to overflowing, and still they came pouring in. Soon we were laying them out in empty fields, then on cultivated land. Some hemorrhaged to death and others were hit again out there by showers of bombs. So many died so quickly."

Even those inside the caves were far from safe. With dressings changed only once a week, their wounds quickly became infected and riddled with maggots. Pus would squirt in the student nurses' faces as they tried to clean their patients. "Gas gangrene, tetanus, and brain fever were common," noted Kikuko. "Those with brain fever were no longer human beings. They'd tear their clothes off because of the pain, tear off their dressings. They were tied to the pillars, their hands behind their backs." At first the nurses wept to see so much "suffering and writhing," but they soon got used to it.

The older student nurses were assigned to the operating rooms where they would hold limbs as they were "chopped off without anesthesia." Kikuko and the younger girls helped to dress wounds, and carry out excrement, limbs and corpses. "One, two, three!" they chanted, as they threw another body in a shell hole, before crawling back to the cave. There was "no time for sobbing or lamentation." They were also sent outside to collect food rations and water from the well. When a shell exploded, they would throw themselves into the mud, "but always supporting the barrel because the water was everybody's water of life."

They had been drafted as nurses, wrote Kikuko, "but in reality we did odd jobs."[14]

Inevitably, the nurses themselves became casualties. The first of the 222 Himeyuri student nurses to be killed was Yoneko Sakugawa, the victim of an American strafing attack near the entrance to the First Surgical Cave on April 26. Her fellow students were heartbroken. But many more would follow her to the grave. On May 1, with the front line getting ever closer, 17-year-old Yoshiko Yabiku and fourteen other student nurses were sent to the Itokazu Clinic Cave, two miles southeast of Haebaru, where twenty medical personnel were caring for 700 patients. "The stench," she remembered, "was unbearable, so it was almost impossible to nurse the wounded... I can still hear the cries and shrieks of those in the throes of death during operations. It was hell itself. We didn't have enough anesthetic so doctors administered just enough to ease the patient's tension."

At the end of his tether, one patient begged: "That's enough! Doctor! Kill me! Just kill me now."

"Shut up!" screamed the surgeon. "You're a Japanese soldier, aren't you? You can't put up with this much pain, and you still call yourself a Japanese soldier?"[15]

Some coped better. Hisa Kishimoto, 17, was present at Haebaru when a sergeant who had been shot through the shoulder was operated on without anesthetic. Using a special pair of scissors, the surgeon made a series of cuts at least an inch deep and four inches long. Not once did the sergeant scream, though his brow was wreathed in sweat and "tears streamed down his face." Hisa tried to hold his hand, "but he wouldn't let me and instead held his own hands to bear it. I bet it hurt him to death."[16]

Other young Okinawan girls were working in the Thirty-Second Army's underground headquarters. They included 17-year-old Masako Shinjo, sold as a young girl to a Naha brothel by her impoverished father, who had been assigned as a comfort girl to the staff of the 62nd Division. Fortunately, as a friend of chief of staff Colonel Ueno's mistress, she was not expected to "service the soldiers" with the other girls; instead her duties included "taking meals" to Colonel Ueno and some of the other officers. She remembered:

> The size of the shelter was overwhelming...The corridors, lighted by electricity, seemed to go on forever. There were many rooms off the main corridors, and more corridors leading to more rooms. There was much confusion as we were moving in. Soldiers were carrying things this way and that, and we were trying to stay out of their way. There was a large kitchen with a storeroom loaded with food and many sacks of rice. All of the girls were assigned to one large room where we were to stay and sleep. Inside our room we had no water for bathing and no toilet, so at night we would go outside to look for some way to wash and for a dark place to relieve ourselves. When we were outside, we could hear bombing and gunfire and we could see distant fires.

At one point she was making her way along a corridor when a group of soldiers came the other way, "leading a blindfolded man who was bent over and had his hands tied behind him." As she squeezed against a wall to let them pass, she saw that the captive had red hair. She was told later he was an American pilot.*

On another occasion, she tried to protect a "very young teenaged girl" who was being preyed upon by a Japanese lieutenant. "I talked with her," remembered Masako, "and advised her that she was too young and should stop seeing the lieutenant. She told him what I had said. Later, he called me to a remote place in one of the tunnels. He put his pistol against me and said that if I continued advising the girl he would kill me. I was so scared that I bowed with my head against the floor of the tunnel as I apologized. After that I never told her anything."[17]

* Yahara insisted that four American pilots were captured and sent to Tokyo for interrogation. He added: "No POWs were reported to Thirty-Second Army HQ during the operation; if any were taken they were dealt with on the spot." In other words, executed. (Yahara Interrogation, August 6, 1945, in Yahara, *The Battle for Okinawa*, p. 10.)

26

"Doc, this one is worth saving"

Dominating the high ground north of the Asa River was Hill 60, a "small hump" that sat between the main north–south railroad and the Dakeshi Plateau. It was commanded by Japanese positions on Dakeshi Plateau and Ridge, Wana Ridge, and the high ground south of the river. It was also protected by Japanese positions that were still holding out in caves and tunnels on the reverse (southern) slope of Nan Hill, a hillock 200 yards to the north.

On May 6, the 2/1st Marines attempted to capture Hill 60 after a preliminary bombardment by mortar, artillery and naval fire. But assailed by fire from front, flank and rear, the attacking platoons of Fox Company became separated and their supporting armor was knocked out by anti-tank guns. One platoon got as far as the crest of Hill 60, but was then hit with "grenades, satchel charges, white phosphorus shells," and "carloads of knee-mortar shells." Shortly after midday, battalion commander Lieutenant Colonel Magee ordered Fox Company to pull back, supported by machine-gun fire from George and Easy Companies. Fox had lost three killed and thirty-two wounded.

Magee's new plan was for George Company, which held the crest of Nan Hill, and supporting tanks to destroy the positions on the reverse slope of Nan *before* Easy attacked Hill 60. The attack was due to begin at 8:50 a.m. on May 7. But it was raining heavily and, with poor visibility and slippery ground, the tanks could not be used. So George delayed its attack, preferring to concentrate its fire on the reverse slope of Hill 60 where a company of Japanese soldiers had been spotted. Four battalions of artillery and a fire support ship joined in the bombardment, plastering the foot and crest of Hill 60 with shell bursts, so that when Easy Company went forward at 1:15

p.m. it had "little difficulty" reaching its objective. But it was largely confined to the right side of the hill, which was protected from enfilade fire from Nan by a razor-backed fold in the ground. Even so, the platoons on Hill 60 were under extreme pressure from the Japanese on the reverse slope. "We used two machine guns effectively," noted one 1st Platoon soldier, "to drop those Japs who attempted to rush over the summit of the hill, returned satchel charges that the Nips threw at us, and clubbed them with rifle butts."[1]

During this vicious hand-to-hand fighting, 22-year-old Private Dale Hansen, one of a pair of 1st Platoon twins (his brother Don had earlier been evacuated with a leg wound) from a farming community in Wisner, Nebraska, "crawled to an exposed position" and used a bazooka to destroy a Japanese pillbox. Seizing a rifle, he leaped over the crest of the hill and opened fire on six Japanese, killing four before his weapon jammed. Attacked by the other two, he used the butt to defend himself as he retraced his steps. Rearmed with another rifle and more grenades, he crossed the crest a second time to destroy a mortar position and kill eight more Japanese soldiers. He was later awarded the Medal of Honor for his "indomitable determination, bold tactics, and complete disregard of all personal danger."[2]

Watching all this through his field glasses from the battalion command post was Lieutenant Bruce Watkins, the assistant operations officer and former commander of 1st Platoon. When Easy's commander Lieutenant Robert W. "Smitty" Schmidt was wounded and evacuated, Watkins went forward to see if he could help. "Upon arrival," he recalled, "I found that there was considerable confusion and that they were receiving fire from the left rear (this was the [reverse] slope of the hill where G Company held the crest)." He could also see his friend Lee Height "directing the Second Platoon, often standing upright, heedless of his own danger from flanking fire." Watkins told him "to get his butt down, but he paid little heed."

The biggest problem, however, was the state of the lieutenant who had taken over from Schmidt as company commander. He seemed "to be in a daze, not knowing what to do." Watkins took charge, grabbing the handset for the company radio and calling the battalion. "This is Easy Six," said Watkins, using the company commander's call sign, "calling Vulcan Six."

When Magee came on the line, he assumed he was talking to the replacement lieutenant. Happy to continue the deception, Watkins outlined the dire situation and suggested using tanks "to suppress the fire from our left rear."

"There won't be any available," said Magee, "until tomorrow."*

"In that case, sir," replied Watkins, "I recommend withdrawing the company until we can make a coordinated attack with tanks."

Magee OK'd the move, and Watkins gave the necessary orders. He was the last man off the hill, partially protected by smoke fired by the battalion's 81 mm mortars. "The Company got off in good shape," noted Watkins, "and I came scurrying after, taking advantage of whatever cover I could find. Bullets snapped around us and kicked up dirt. Just ahead of me, Frank Carey stood up and fired a full clip back at them with his Tommy gun, more or less in defiance. Almost at once he went down with a bullet in the chest."

Knowing he could not carry the 200-pound Carey on his own, Watkins scrambled over the rise that separated him from the rest of Easy Company, grabbed a stretcher and ordered the nearest Marine to follow him. When they got back to Carey, he was in a bad way. "But there was no time for thinking," remembered Watkins. "We rolled him on the stretcher and made a frantic dash up the slope, sliding and tumbling down the far side. We then carried him to the hastily set up aid station only to find he was dead."

Amidst the rows of casualties was another platoon leader, with a serious leg wound. Watkins had just stopped to chat with him when a "horrendous mortar barrage came in." To try to protect him, and "acting on some paternal instinct," Watkins covered his body with his own. When the barrage lifted, he "got up somewhat embarrassed" and made his way back to the battalion CP.

With bad weather delaying the new attack by twenty-four hours, Watkins went forward again at noon to brief Easy's replacement commander. They were talking when word arrived that Lee Height had been hit. Watkins raced over to the 2nd Platoon to find Height "laid out on a stretcher, unconscious." He had, Watkins learned later,

* In fact, twelve Shermans from the 4th Marine Tank Battalion did manage to burn "several caves" on the reverse slope of Nan Hill on May 7, but others remained. (Stockman, *The First Marine Division on Okinawa*, pp. 14–15.)

been hit in his foxhole by a bullet aimed at the platoon sergeant who had just jumped in beside him. The bullet had made a small groove above Height's left eye that did not, at first sight, appear that grievous. But when Watkins saw "gray matter" in the wound and foam at the corner of Height's mouth, he knew he had to get him help, and fast.

Radioing back to Battalion the seriousness of Height's wound, Watkins and three others grabbed the stretcher and ran the half-mile back through the mud as fast as they could go, never once stopping though they were all "exhausted in nothing flat." An amtrac was waiting for them. Once the stretcher was placed on its steel deck, Watkins climbed in beside it for the ride to the regimental aid station. There Height was transferred to a chest-high cot. Watkins put his hand on his friend's shoulder, and could feel "a ragged pulse near his neck."

A doctor was inspecting the wounded. When he got to Height he said: "I guess you're his friend."

Watkins nodded. "Doc, this one is worth saving."

"Don't worry, we'll take good care of your friend."

Watkins stayed with Height for another thirty minutes, but he remained unconscious. "I took his wallet and personal effects," remembered Watkins, "and headed back to the front, hopeful but depressed. There were so many wounded. I just said a prayer they would get to him soon."

From Spring Lake, New Jersey, Height had joined Easy Company as a platoon leader replacement in July 1944, and he and Watkins quickly became friends. "Lee," wrote Watkins, "was an outstanding young man and we found that our values in life were much the same." After Peleliu—where Height was wounded and Watkins the only company officer to come through unscathed—they spent all their time together on and off duty. Height had a serious side, and Watkins would often find him reading his Bible. But he was also "full of fun and something of a daredevil," which worried his friend. "To be reckless in battle," noted Watkins, "is to ask for trouble."

Shortly before leaving Ulithi for Okinawa, Watkins noticed a change in his friend: "He became very quiet and didn't join in the good-natured rough-housing anymore. He never said so, but I believe he had a premonition of his own death. I couldn't seem to cheer him up, nothing worked." A few days after his desperate attempt to save his friend's life, Watkins was informed by the battalion doctor that Height had "died aboard a hospital ship on the operating table." By then Watkins was commander of Easy Company and, with responsibility for the lives of 200 men, did not have time to grieve. That would come later.[3]

On May 9, Easy made its second attempt to capture Hill 60. Only this time, as well as a synchronized attack by George Company on the remaining Japanese occupied caves on Nan Hill, and support by armor, Easy's advance was made easier by the 1/1st Marines' simultaneous attack across the Dakeshi Plateau. The new strategy worked. By 1:00 p.m. the 1/1st Marines had reached their objective, though not without cost: both Lieutenant Colonel James C. Murray Jr., the "eager beaver" battalion commander, and the commander of Baker Company were wounded and evacuated. Acting as a forward observer for the 1/1st Marines that day was Lieutenant Chris Donner:

> I could see bursts of action. Our men pinned down halfway up the opposite hillsides, grenades tossed into caves. Japs jumping up and running but riddled with bullets before going fifty yards. The valley was cleared within two hours. The demolition men came in with satchel charges to seal the cave entrances. I had fired at two Jap machine-gun positions as my share of helping the action.

Called forward by Murray, Donner was told that he could find a "fine observation point right at the apex of the new line." So Donner went back to get his team, and as they came forward, laying telephone wire, they passed Murray "being taken out on a stretcher. He had been nicked while taking a look from our good OP."[4]

Meanwhile Easy Company—supported by a platoon of tanks—had taken Hill 60, and George Company the remaining enemy caves on Nan Hill. "This time it was a breeze," noted Watkins, who accompanied the attack, "and we secured both forward and rear slopes of this hill in minutes, sealing a cave with Jap holdouts on the far side." The four-day battle for Hill 60 was over. Watkins' reward, when he returned to the battalion CP that night, was to be told by Lieutenant Colonel Magee that he was the new commander of Easy. "It seems," wrote Watkins, "that the lieutenant in charge had a chat with him and told him that I had been running the Company." Watkins, who had had enough of the battalion staff, was delighted.[5]

* * *

Further to the west, on the left of the 1st Marine Division's zone of action, the 5th Marines were having just as much trouble reducing the "Awacha Pocket." It took a week to do so, with all three battalions, 1/5th, 2/5th and 3/5th Marines, supported by tanks and heavy weapons, doing their share of the fighting. One of the keys to taking the pocket was a north–south valley on its eastern flank—known to the Marines as "Death Valley"—and an oblong feature beyond called "Wilson's Ridge."

During one attack toward the ridge, on May 7, Captain Julian Dusenbury, commanding Able Company, 5th Marines, the quiet but well-liked officer who had so impressed Ernie Pyle during their brief time together, "repeatedly braved intense hostile fire to ensure the success of his company's advance" against "strongly fortified enemy positions." After one of his platoon leaders was seriously wounded, he "reorganized the platoon and, in the face of intensified enemy fire, led it in continuing the attack." He moved fearlessly across the company front, coordinating the advance with armor, and "personally directed the fire of tanks in destroying several Japanese strongpoints." Although "painfully wounded" early in the attack, he "refused to be evacuated and continued to direct the attack until Japanese resistance was broken and the positions overrun." By his "initiative and indomitable fighting spirit," he was an inspiration to his men. For this second outstanding act of gallantry—he had won a Silver Star on Peleliu—he was awarded the Navy Cross.*[6]

A day later, with his battalion due to assault Wilson's Ridge the following day, demolition man PFC Paul Ison and other members of the 3/5th Marines' Assault Platoon were sheltering from the rain in an Okinawan burial tomb when their commander, Lieutenant Ellington, appeared at the door. "Ison," he said, "get up early in the morning and take your squad up on the line. Captain Smith has a job for you."

Next morning, after breakfasting on cold C-rations, Ison and his team went to the ammunition dump to get their satchel charges, one per man. They were turned away by the sergeant in charge. "I've

* The U.S. Navy and Marine Corps' second-highest award for gallantry, after the Medal of Honor. Equivalent to the U.S. Army's Distinguished Service Cross and the USAAF's Air Force Cross.

already sent a working party up to the front line," he told them, "with all the TNT charges they will need."

So Ison and his men moved out, and eventually came to the "draw, between 2 hills" that was known as Death Valley. Some of the Assault Platoon were already on the far side. Spotting Ison, one of them called out: "Send one man at a time across." With machine-gun and mortar fire raking the valley, Ison knew this made sense and did just that. When it was his turn, he ran with shoulders hunched, clutching his new M1 in his right hand. He was just nearing the far side and safety when he noticed, out of the corner of his right eye, someone in a foxhole raise a camera and click the shutter. Moments later he joined two "good buddies" in another foxhole. "Hey, Ison," said one, "that guy took your picture as you went past."

"Well," replied Ison. "I'll never live to see it."*

Shortly after, heading along the side of the valley, Ison and his men were taking cover from bursting shells in a communication post when they watched a young Marine dash across the valley, trying to find a break in the wire. "He disappeared in that exploding hell of smoke and hot steel," recalled Ison. "His fellow Marines were yelling for him to stop and come back. I do not know if that brave Marine made it or not, as things were happening so fast, but I sure hope he did."

Reaching the front line, Ison reported to Captain Smith, commanding Love Company, who briefed him on his mission. "Did you receive the TNT that was sent up, sir?" asked Ison.

"No."

Not bothering to explain, Ison returned to his men and said: "Come on, fellows, we have to go back to the ammo dump and get our TNT."

So back they went across Death Valley, channeling their anger into what they would say to the ammunition sergeant when they got there. Fortunately for him, there was another sergeant on duty, so they "just grabbed our TNT satchel charges and *again* had to cross Death Valley," the third time that day. "How we made it," wrote Ison, "I will never

* The picture, taken by Marine combat photographer Private Bob Bailey, became one of the most famous of the Pacific War and graces the cover of this book. Documents seen by the author in the USMC Archives in Quantico, Virginia, confirm that the subject is PFC Paul E. Ison.

know. All this was accomplished under intense enemy fire and reports show that we suffered 125 casualties in one eight-hour period."[7]

Next day, May 10, the 1/5th and 2/5th Marines attacked the pocket with armor and, at one point, three companies had gained a foothold on Wilson's Ridge while another cleared out many of the caves along the face of the ridge. But casualties were heavy and, by nightfall, the companies had withdrawn to their starting points. They completed the job the following day. By sending tanks and infantry "around the left flank," recalled Corporal Jim Johnston of Easy Company, they were able to get "to a position where they could bring fire to bear on the Japs in the valley caves, the ones that had stopped the advances on our flanks." Thus the infantry and tanks on the right "could get over the brink of the hill and knock out the gun positions behind it." As they were doing that, Easy Company moved through Death Valley. By nightfall on the 11th, the Awacha Pocket was finally overrun and the 5th Marines were given a few days' rest.[8]

It was not a moment too soon. All three battalions had suffered heavy casualties and were badly depleted.* After the inconclusive fighting on May 9, mortarman PFC Eugene "Sledgehammer" Sledge, 21, of King Company, 3/5th Marines, had been met with the "same tragic sight of bloody, dazed and wounded men benumbed with shock, being carried or walking to the aid station in the rear. There were also the dead, and the usual inquiries about friends. We were all glad when the word came that 3/5 would move into reserve." That night, keeping watch across Death Valley, Sledge received a letter from his parents with the news that his "beloved spaniel" Deacon had been hit by a car, dragged himself home, and died in his father's arms. "There," noted Sledge, "with the sound of heavy firing up ahead and the sufferings and deaths of thousands of men going on nearby, big tears rolled down my cheeks, because Deacon was dead."[9]

Six of Jim Johnston's machine-gun section had died in the pocket:

* Among the many fatalities was PFC Michael Fenton, a 19-year-old scout-sniper in Baker Company, 1/5th Marines, who was killed beating off a Japanese counter-attack in the Awacha Pocket on May 7. One of the more heart-wrenching images from the battle is that of Colonel Francis I. Fenton, division engineer, kneeling beside his son Michael's flag-draped body before it was buried (see picture insert). Getting back to his feet, and noticing the corpses of other young Marines, the colonel said: "Those poor souls. They didn't have their fathers here."

one by mortar fire and the others killed by small arms. Johnston himself, shortly before leaving the area, suffered a "series of convulsions" as he lay under an artillery barrage. He tried everything he could think of to make them stop, all to no avail. Eventually he gave up "and let the convulsions run their course." They were, as Johnston well understood, a nervous reaction to the strain he was under. Battle "is unbelievably depleting both mentally and physically," he wrote later, "and the nature of our circumstances was starting to take its toll on me." But he refused to report sick, and preferred to die there "rather than leave because of the convulsions."[10]

While the vaunted 1st Marine Division—the "Old Breed"—was coming to terms with the bitter nature of the fighting on Okinawa, and the severity of the task ahead, news reached the island of Germany's unconditional surrender to the Allies on May 7, 1945, and the formal signing on the 8th (known as Victory in Europe, or VE Day). "At noon," wrote Lieutenant General Buckner in his diary, "every gun of our land and ship support batteries fired one round at the enemy. We then tuned into the Jap radio frequency and announced in Japanese that the volley was in celebration of the victory."[11]

The reaction of the ordinary soldiers was mixed. Some were convinced it would shorten the Pacific War. "It is hard to believe that there is actually peace in Europe," wrote an artilleryman to his parents on May 9, "for it has lasted so long and been so much on our minds, that when it ended so suddenly it will take a while to really soak in. Now of course I hope it won't be long until the full weight can make itself felt against Japan. The surrender has also raised our hopes for returning home...I wonder how long Japan can last now."[12] Corporal Joe Kohn, a forward artillery observer in the 6th Marine Division, was thinking the same thing, telling his family: "Now that Japan can be concentrated on, we hope to be home in a year or a year and a half."[13]

Others were not convinced it would make any difference. "After all," noted Corporal Sterling Mace of the 3/5th Marines, "the news didn't change the position of our lines, or the texture of the mud, the tint of the sky, or the amount of ammunition each of us carried in our pouches. Nor did it change what we knew was coming—that we'd be making another assault on the Japanese soon, and more Marines would surely die in the process."[14]

27

"The happy dream is over"

Flight Lieutenant Haruo Araki's hand shook as he composed a last letter to his wife of just a month:

> Shigeko,
>
> Are you well? It is now a month since that day. The happy dream is over. Tomorrow I will dive my plane into an enemy ship. I will cross the river into the other world, taking some Yankees with me. When I look back, I see that I was very cold-hearted to you. After I had been cruel to you, I used to regret it. Please forgive me.
>
> When I think of your future, and the long life ahead, it tears at my heart. Please remain steadfast and live happily. After my death, please take care of my father for me.
>
> I, who have lived for the eternal principles of justice, will forever protect this nation from the enemies that surround us.
>
> Commander of the Air Unit Eternity
> Haruo Araki

The letter was written at Chiran Air Base, Kyushu, on the evening of May 10. Haruo had already penned a note to his father, mentioning that he had flown over the family house at the end of April, circling many times in the hope that his father might see him. But he had not looked up from his work in the fields. "Father," wrote Haruo, "I was unable to catch your attention." Having sealed both letters, Haruo handed them to a visiting journalist who had promised to deliver them in person.

Early the following morning, the journalist had taken some pictures of the airman before he left on his mission. One was with his two group leaders: all three were 21 years old and had graduated from the Military Academy in the 57th Class. Another showed Haruo giving the final address to his fellow kamikazes. He was smiling, "conscious of the camera." On his forehead he was wearing a white headband with Japan's rising-sun emblem. The students at the girls' school near the base had "cut their fingers and filled in the red sun with their own blood." Copies of these photos were later given to Haruo's wife.[1]

Finally, at 6:00 a.m., Haruo took off in the lead plane, one of 150 aircraft to take part in the sixth mass kamikaze attack against Allied shipping near Okinawa on 10–11 May. Haruo's fate is unknown. It is just possible, however, that his plane was one of two that struck Vice Admiral Mitscher's flagship *Bunker Hill* on the 11th, causing extensive fires and killing 396 men (including fourteen of Mitscher's staff, most to smoke inhalation) and wounding 264, the worst casualties since the *Franklin*. Though still afloat, the *Bunker Hill* was out of action for the rest of the war, forcing Mitscher to transfer his flag to *Enterprise*.[2]

There is no better account of the ordeal faced by U.S. sailors at Okinawa, living every moment in fear of kamikazes that fell from the sky, than one written by Alexander Burnham, a radio operator on the repair ship USS *Romulus*. The tension aboard these ships was, Burnham noted, "extreme, with sailors with little sleep or rest sometimes near the breaking point." Small wonder that one captain felt compelled to tell his crew: "We have Jap planes en route heading directly for us. If you characters ever want to sleep with a blonde again, you had better shoot down these bastards as soon as they come up."

Topside, the sailors could see bandits "winging in from every different direction, first as small dots miles away, then within minutes as recognizable aircraft getting nearer and nearer." Warships did their best to frustrate the attackers by assuming "flank speed" and adopting "evasive maneuverability," while the gunners opened up with everything they had. They shot down many, but not all, and "when an aircraft smashed into a ship the impact was "defiling." Sweeping over a vessel were "death, fire and destruction," power was lost and "radar and radio communications destroyed."

Below decks, "sealed off in hot watertight compartments," unaware of how the battle was going, hearing only the muffled sounds of the ship's guns', they were only too aware that death could strike at any moment if the hull was "penetrated by a suicide plane, allowing the sea to rush in and drown them all."

Their biggest nightmare was multiple attacks, likened to a "swarm of wasps." While one came in "low over the water headed for the bridge," another was "high up but nose down aiming right for dead center, a third with its right wing torn to bits by the ship's guns but still on target," then more. After the impacts, the "entire deck" was smashed, fires raged from stem to stern, the engine room was flooded, the ship was not moving, but the guns were still firing. Corpses, wounded and dismembered bodies "litter[ed] the wardroom, mess hall, sickbay, gun positions, fantail, passageways," while out in the water "men blown over the side struggle[d] to stay afloat and pray that nearby ships will pick them up before they're eaten by sharks."

The battle over, the ship often resembled "a floating junk-pile" and, with luck, was "towed to a safe Okinawan harbor." By then her decks had been cleared of bodies and debris: the dead buried at sea and the wounded "taken to somebody else's sickbay." The scene of battle, meanwhile, had reverted to "Homer's wine-dark sea," unvisited by veterans from either side because "there will be no monuments, no crosses, nothing to view but an ocean forever anonymous."[3]

A few days after the failed counteroffensive, Colonel Yahara was working in his underground office when a liaison officer handed him an order from generals Ushijima and Chō. Aviation staff officer Major Jin, it stated, was being sent back to Tokyo. When Yahara asked why, he was told: "We are sending him to Imperial Headquarters to request approval for our air forces to attack the enemy fleet in strength, force their withdrawal, and thus end the Okinawa operations."

Yahara was mystified. He knew—as did the generals—that kamikaze pilots from the navy and army air forces were already doing everything they could "to destroy enemy shipping from the air." The fliers, as a result, were claiming that "*they* were the main strength" in the Okinawa operation, "with the Thirty-Second Army being merely a bunch of stagehands." Yet, despite this, American air strength over the island was far superior. It was also clear to Yahara that, with six infantry divisions ashore, the enemy was not about to up sticks and leave.

The other issue was the security of Japan's home islands. Yahara had long argued that the correct strategy on Okinawa was "to hold the enemy as long as possible, drain off his troops and supplies, and thus contribute our utmost to the final decisive battle for Japan proper." To request more air assets would be to weaken Japan's defenses. For all these reasons Yahara opposed the idea of sending Jin to Tokyo.

He was also concerned that Jin, who naturally favored the use of air power, would "misconstrue or even ignore" Yahara's views when he gave an assessment of how best to conduct the Okinawa campaign to Imperial General Headquarters. "If that happened," commented Yahara, "my position would be lost forever." But as the order to send Jin was "already signed and sealed" he knew there was no way to stop it. So he sent him on his way with a notebook that Jin promised to deliver to Yahara's father-in-law, a retired lieutenant general.

The plan was for Jin to go south to Mabuni and take a seaplane to Tokyo. But when bad weather delayed the plane's arrival, Jin set out by night in a fishing boat. He eventually reached Tokyo and reported to Imperial HQ. But, as Yahara had suspected, the appeal for a massive air attack on the American fleet was impossible to satisfy.

At Shuri, meanwhile, Colonel Yahara had ordered all "women occupants (nurses as well as comfort girls)" to leave the underground headquarters and head south. Conditions in the cave were "miserable"—sanitation had collapsed, food was scarce, and morale was "deteriorating"—and it had become clear that, sooner or later, everyone "would die in battle." Yahara, as a result, wanted to get the women out of this "depressing situation and send them to rear areas." But the women, when they were told, did not want to go. "You order us out," they objected, "because you think of us only as women. We are no longer just women. We are soldiers, and we wish to die."

Despite their pleas, Yahara told them "they had to go." At dusk on May 10, as the enemy artillery fire began to slacken, they were waved off from the cave entrance, carrying rucksacks with a few donated mementoes, such as General Chō's "precious teapot." A soldier shouted after one beauty: "You may get yourself killed, but don't let anything happen to that fabulous face."[4]

Former prostitute Masako Shinjo was among the girls forced to leave. "We knew that the battle was raging beyond the relative safety of our tunnel shelter," she recalled, "but we had no real understanding of where the enemy troops were or what the Japanese army was doing... When orders came that we must leave the tunnel and make our way southward toward Itoman, we departed much as sheep to the slaughter."

She had one word to describe what they went through: *jigoku* (which roughly translates as "hell"). Moving out at night, in the rain, they had "no idea of direction or distance," and simply followed the flow of humanity. "Mostly," she remembered, "we used the main road only at night. The paths and roads were quagmires of mud. Beside the road were bodies of the dead, wounded, and others who were just too exhausted to go farther." At one place she saw "a dead woman with her baby, still alive, strapped to her back." She tried to help the child, but a soldier ordered her to keep moving. They finally reached Itoman City, in the south of the island, where there was hot food waiting for them. But Masako was so exhausted, she lay down and slept.

Before long, it was time to move on. Marching by day, the sound of a plane would cause the girls to run for the roadside ditches and pretend to be dead. "At last," wrote Masako, "we reached Komesu village, and our shelter was nearby, deep inside a cliff...There were radio communication soldiers above us and other soldiers near the front of our shelter. Now there were only nineteen of us girls left." Conditions in the cave were pitiful: it was knee-deep in water, there was "little food, no change of clothes, and no water to drink except for a small pond not far from the shelter entrance." Assigned as *hancho*, or leader, of the remaining girls, Masako gave them their tasks, "the main one being nightly forays into the surrounding fields in search of food." They would "scour the area for anything to eat," and depended mostly "on finding sweet potatoes, a few of them having escaped the villagers' harvest on our previous searches."[5]

Change was also afoot for 16-year-old Shigetomo Higa. Since joining the First Prefectural Middle School's Blood and Iron Corps Unit in late March, Shigetomo and his comrades in No. 2 Platoon had been carrying out support duties for the Japanese army from their shelter in Shuri. During that time, much had happened: the unit suffered its first casualties when two boys were killed by an air raid;

Shigetomo received an emotional visit from his father who was serving in the home guard (it would be their last meeting); and the First Prefectural Middle School building was destroyed by shells fired from a U.S. warship. "Sheets of flames leapt out of the second-story windows," recalled Shigetomo, "and lit up the early evening sky as the dazed students lined up in front of the building. A place of learning boasting sixty years of tradition, the building crashed to the ground, its final gasps sounding like cries of help."

By May, it was obvious to Shigetomo that the Japanese front line was beginning to crumble. On the 12th, Shigetomo's No. 2 Platoon shelter was invaded by a Japanese second lieutenant and some of his men. "Get out of here, you lot!" they screamed at the Okinawans.

A teacher intervened. "This is the Blood and Iron Student Corps' shelter."

"What the hell's that?" snapped the officer. "Anyway, we're using this shelter now."

As the officer was shooing the boys outside, their commander Lieutenant Shinohara appeared. More senior in rank, he slapped the interloper. "You prick," he said. "You're nothing but a second lieutenant."

The new officer beat a hasty retreat, followed by his men.

But a couple of days later it was Shigetomo's turn to leave. With front-line casualties mounting, he and the rest of his unit had been assigned to a combat role. "During war," said Principal Norio Fujino at their leaving parade, "circumstances are always changing, hour by hour, minute by minute. Things can become extremely difficult, and don't necessarily continue in our favor. Keeping all of you together has become impossible."

After the address, Shigetomo and twenty-six others were taken to their new unit, the No. 1 Heavy Field Artillery Regiment, based at Kochinda, five miles to the south. Shigetomo was disappointed. "I thought that this would put me in harm's way," he wrote, "and, compared to that, the survey unit was far more attractive. I was really envious of them." In fact, unbeknown to Shigetomo, the work of the field survey unit was extremely dangerous as, not unlike the role of an American forward observer, it involved spotting the fall of artillery shells and relaying the information to the guns. Not one of the twelve boys assigned to the survey unit survived the war.

Shigetomo, on the other hand, was well behind the lines with only the occasional naval shell falling in the vicinity. He and the other boys slept on two- and three-tiered bunks in a tunnel where life, apart from the constant dripping of water, was relatively comfortable. Issued with a steel helmet, a combat knife and a Type 38 Arisaka rifle (with fifteen rounds), he now thought of himself as a proper soldier.[6]

28
Sugar Loaf Hill

"Attack started at 7:00 a.m.," wrote Lieutenant General Buckner in his diary on May 11. "Progress all along the line. Visited both corps CPs and put a little pressure on corps commanders."[1]

It was the start of the first general offensive by both corps—Major General Roy Geiger's III Amphibious Corps having taken over the right sector of the front on May 5—with the intention of enveloping Shuri from both east and west, while a strong holding attack was maintained in the center. Buckner's staff was convinced that the Japanese defenses were particularly weak in the western half of the island, and that the fresher Marine divisions there had a real opportunity to break through. "It will be," he explained on May 10, "a continuation of the type of attack we have been employing to date. Where we cannot take strongpoints we will pinch them off and leave them for the reserves to reduce. We have ample firepower and we also have enough fresh troops so that we can always have one division resting."[2]

The four divisions attacking were, from west to east, the 6th Marine Division, 1st Marine Division, 77th Infantry Division and 96th Infantry Division (which had relieved the 7th Division in the most easterly sector on May 9). The newest arrival was the 6th Marine which had begun the long journey south from the Motobu Peninsula on May 5. Having helped to capture Mount Yae-Take, Sergeant William Manchester and his "Raggedy Asses" had expected a "respite, hot chow, and a few days in the sack." Instead they and the rest of the 6th Marine Division were told they had to change places with the 27th Division because it "couldn't keep up with the other army units." Their tiny revenge was to teach the kids in Nago to chant loudly: "Twenty-seventh Division eats shit! Twenty-seventh Division eats shit!"

The journey south in six-by-six army trucks took two days. During the second, they became aware of a "grumbling on the horizon, which turned into a thumping, then a drumming, then a rumbling, and then an enormous thudding." It was the sound of artillery fire pounding a front line that was packed with more soldiers than any First World War battlefield: in that earlier conflict, most battalions had fought on a front of 800 yards; here it was barely 600. Manchester's first glimpse of the front came when his truck stopped in traffic and he jumped out to take a look. Climbing a small hill, he had a bird's-eye view of the whole battlefield. "It was," he recalled,

> a monstrous sight, a moonscape. Hills, ridges, and cliffs rose and fell along the front like the gray stumps of rotting teeth. There was nothing green left; artillery had denuded and scarred every inch of ground. Tiny flares glowed and disappeared. Shrapnel burst with bluish white puffs. Jets of flamethrowers flickered and here and there new explosions stirred up the rubble. While I watched, awed, an American observation plane, a Piper Cub, droned over the Japanese lines, spotting targets for U.S. warships lying offshore so that they could bring their powerful guns to bear on the enemy. Suddenly the little plane was hit by flak and disintegrated. The carnage below continued without pause.[3]

Manchester enjoyed a brief respite from battle when his 29th Marines began the new offensive in reserve. Most of the initial fighting was left to another of the 6th Marine Division's regiments, the 22nd Marines. On May 8, the 22nd Marines relieved the 7th Marines (1st Marine Division) on the bluffs north of the Asa River. Due to take part in the general offensive on the 11th, their task was to ford the river and attack the Japanese positions beyond. "The enemy held ground," noted the official history, "rose gently to the horizon 2,000 yards away. To the west barren coral ridges formed a barrier to the sea; to the south a long clay ridge dominated the road to Naha; to the southeast a group of low grassy hills, set close together, commanded the ground between the Asa River basin and the Asato River corridor. On the east were the rough folds of Dakeshi Ridge, Wana Ridge, and Wana Draw, positions toward which the 1st Marine Division was driving."[4]

In the early hours of May 10, two battalions of the 22nd Marines began crossing the Asa River, most by a small footbridge which had been hastily constructed by engineers as soon as it got dark. They went with the advice of their divisional commander, Lem Shepherd, ringing in their ears: take advantage of cover and camouflage, use maneuvers to outflank the Japanese rather than try to "outslug" them, and keep driving forward. "Your enemy," concluded Shepherd, "can't think as fast as you can and he is no match for a determined aggressive Marine who has confidence in himself and his weapon."[5]

Among the first troops over the river was 20-year-old Private Howard Arendt from Louisville, Kentucky. Enlisting in the Marines in 1943, straight out of high school, Arendt completed his training in San Diego before being assigned to 2nd Platoon, King Company, 3/22nd Marines in Hawaii. "This was," he recalled, "a real gung-ho outfit, most were teenagers just out of high school or who had left high school to join the Marines." Arendt saw action with it at Eniwetok in the Marshalls and Guam, experiencing the sheer terror of banzai attacks at night and the gruesome sight of "two screaming Japanese soldiers with their bodies engulfed in flames" after a cave had been hit with a flamethrower. One Marine had suggested shooting them, to put them out of their misery, but others said, "No, let them suffer."

Let them suffer they did. Only minutes earlier, the popular platoon leader Lieutenant Raines, a schoolteacher from Texas, had been shot in the head and killed by a bullet from the cave.

Although Arendt had made it through both campaigns without a scratch, on Guam he "came down with dengue fever, had a bad case of jungle rot (skin ulcers) and numerous planter warts" on his feet, caused by "constant walking in mud, rain, through swamps, jungles, etc." He returned to duty on Guadalcanal after surgery to remove the warts. The largely bloodless landing on Okinawa had been a "wonderful feeling but was short-lived."

In the morning of May 10, Arendt's King Company was the first over the footbridge, followed by Item Company, while Able Company of the 1/22nd Marines waded across the stream a little further to the east. Arendt had forded the stream a day earlier on a reconnaissance patrol which lost one man killed—Franklin Coomer, a dirt-poor cotton picker from Texas—and three wounded when they ran into an ambush. Arendt had helped to carry Coomer's body back to their starting point, "followed by the rest of the squad with the Japs shooting at us." Now, moving down the coast in broken terrain, 2nd Platoon were in the vicinity of the previous day's ambush when they "again ran into unseen Jap rifle and machine-gun fire." Arendt recalled:

> We ran toward a small ridge hoping to take some cover behind it. However as we approached the top of it our bodies were silhouetted against the sky, making us excellent targets. [Ray] Gillespie was leading, I was behind him and behind me were three other Marines. As we got to the top a Jap machine gun opened up. I saw a bullet rip through Gillespie's back and he fell forward over the ridge. I too had been hit.

The force of the bullets lifted Arendt off his feet, spun him around, and sent his rifle flying. Still on the exposed side of the ridge, his first thought was: thank God Gillespie is on the other side, "out of the sights of the machine gun." Though feeling no pain, he feared a chest or stomach wound. But there was no sign of blood or holes in his dungaree shirt. His trousers, however, were in shreds and it was obvious he had been shot in both legs. Fortunately he could move his legs and toes a little, and concluded that no bones were broken.

Looking around, he saw the other three Marines all hugging the earth, but unwounded. All four of them were pinned down by the Japanese machine gun that continued to spray bullets on the ground directly in front of them. Their only hope, Arendt decided, was to get over the ridge. He called to see if anyone was over the other side and, to his surprise, a Marine shouted back "and said that part of my platoon was there and that Gillespie had been hit bad." Arendt explained their predicament, and asked for smoke to give them cover. Moments later, several grenades were lobbed over which "enveloped the immediate area in a dense screen of smoke."

Shouting for the other Marines to follow, Arendt "stumbled and crawled to the top of ridge" as the Japanese machine gun continued to rake the area. He made it to safety, as did the other Marines. "I was," he recalled, "very, very lucky and the Lord had indeed been very good to me again." He was evacuated to the rear and did not rejoin his outfit until the campaign was over. By then, only a single member of his platoon had come through the entire operation unscathed, all the rest either dead or wounded. Among the unlikely survivors was Ray Gillespie who eventually made a full recovery from the two bullets that hit his back and "exited through his chest."[6]

The situation got worse for the 3/22nd Marines when two Japanese "human demolition charges" destroyed the south end of the footbridge at around 6:00 a.m. But 1/22nd Marines relieved the pressure by making ground to the east and, by dusk, the assault companies of both battalions had secured a bridgehead over the Asa that was 1,400 yards long and 350 yards deep. That night engineers built a Bailey bridge over the Asa that could carry tanks to support the attack on the 11th, though the first one would not cross until after 11:00 a.m.

By nightfall on the 11th, the 3/22nd Marines had advanced as far as the high ground overlooking the Asato estuary and, beyond, the devastated capital of Naha. Watching from the regimental OP, General Shepherd sent the battalion commander, Lieutenant Colonel Donohoo, a message commending "every single officer and man who participated in this assault for his personal bravery and the fine team work exercised by all units in capturing this precipitous and strongly defended terrain feature."[7] Further to the east, the 1/22nd Marines also made ground, as did the attacking troops of the 1st Marines, and 77th and 96th Infantry Divisions. It was on this day, May 11—as we have seen—that the last organized Japanese resistance in the Awacha Pocket was eliminated. The fighting continued across the front on May 12 and 13, but progress was generally slower.

On the 12th, for example, George Company of the 2/22nd Marines tried to take a seemingly insignificant feature on the left of the 6th Marine Division's sector. "I guess the best way to describe it," noted one Marine, "was if you took a watermelon and cut in half, the upper half would be similar to the type of hill it was . . . it wasn't really that high."[8]

Nicknamed "Sugar Loaf Hill" by the 2/22nd's commander, Lieutenant Colonel Horatio C. Woodhouse, the rectangular hump was one of a number of hills in this part of the island that were "so small," according to the official history, "they did not show up on the standard military map with its ten-meter contour interval." Yet they would present a formidable obstacle.[9]

Perhaps the best description of the "undistinguished mound now known to history as Sugar Loaf Hill," and the challenge it presented its attackers, was provided by Sergeant William Manchester whose own 2/29th Battalion would lose so many lives on its seemingly innocuous slopes:

> Sugar Loaf, which was actually shaped more like a bread loaf, was a height of coral and volcanic rock three hundred yards long and one hundred feet high. It was vital because it was almost impregnable. Not in itself; few summits are unscalable if attackers can reach their slopes. But this ugly hive was supported on the southeast by another mound, Half Moon Hill,* and to the south by yet another, Horseshoe Ridge. Thus Sugar Loaf, a spear pointed at the advancing 6th Marine Division, was merely the most visible feature of a triangular system connected by hidden galleries.

Not only were the three peaks mutually self-supporting, but "a deep trough of ground within Horseshoe Ridge gave the Japanese mortar positions which could be reached only by grenades and small-arms fire, and our riflemen couldn't get that close because the three hummocks rose abruptly from a bare plain, providing no defilade." Troops attacking one peak would be "cut down by converging interlocking fire from the rest of the triangle." Furthermore the whole complex "could be raked by Jap artillery, mortars, and machine guns emplaced in Shuri Hill, to the east, which had stopped the 1st Marine Division in its muddy tracks." Shuri was bigger, but it was the Sugar Loaf complex that, in Manchester's estimation, "cracked the whip" of the whole Japanese defensive system.[10]

When Captain Owen T. Stebbins of George Company, 2/22nd Marines, first saw the torn shrubs, tree stumps and shell craters on Sugar Loaf Hill's steep coral slopes on May 12, he did not consider the feature any more formidable than "other draws, ravines, or steep inclines" he and his men had "faced in previous combat actions." He added: "We didn't think we were going to have too tough a time."

Two platoons began the attack at 8:00 a.m. on May 12, supported by four Shermans from Able Company, 6th Marine Tank Battalion. But they soon came under heavy fire from mortars, artillery and 47

* Also known in some accounts, and marked on contemporary maps, as Crescent Hill.

mm anti-tank guns. Two tanks were knocked out, and one bogged in a ditch. When the tank commander, Platoon Sergeant George Beranek, got out to arrange a tow, he was shot in the throat, the wound gushing blood "as if from a garden hose...[it] squirted up all over my tank and everything else," remembered Captain Morell in the fourth Sherman.

With the forward platoons pinned down on the slopes of Sugar Loaf Hill, Stebbins was about to arrange support when he was shot in the leg and evacuated. Up on the hill, meanwhile, First Lieutenant Edward Ruess of 1st Platoon tried to identify the source of incoming fire by bravely making a target of himself, "skipping back and to his left, now firing from the hip instead of the shoulder." But his luck could not last and he was hit by a burst of machine-gun fire in the lower abdomen. "His face turned ashen," remembered PFC Mezo, "and I didn't feel he would suffer long."*

By now, First Lieutenant Dale W. Bair, the company XO, had arrived to take command. A six-foot two-inch, 225-pound former enlisted man, Bair split the reserve platoon and its light-machine-gun section into two, leading fifteen men up the right of the valley that led to the hill, while Platoon Sergeant DeMar took the balance up the left. "As we advanced," said DeMar, "enemy weapons of all kinds opened up. Their fire, already intense, now increased in volume, men going down everywhere."

When one machine-gunner was hit, Bair took his gun and fired "burst after burst at the Japanese positions." He was standing on the crest of the hill, a perfect target, and his men could not fail to be inspired by his courage. "It was impossible to be afraid," said one, "when you saw him standing up there." Hit by three bullets—in the arm, leg and across the chest—Bair kept firing until a corpsman insisted on treating his wounds. Covered in bandages, his cut trousers looking like a "bathing suit," he continued to provide covering fire until he was shot again. "Down he went," noted a Marine, "he just couldn't take any more."

Platoon Sergeant DeMar got as far as the crest of the hill before he was shot in the leg. "Enemy fire was tearing up the ground around

* Ruess was evacuated but died of his wounds. He was awarded a posthumous Navy Cross for his gallantry.

me," he recalled. "My rifle stopped firing...then it occurred to me that I was alone on Sugar Loaf with a bum leg." Fortunately he was rescued by Corporal Howard Perrault, the driver of one of the knocked-out tanks, who got him back to the remaining tank before he, too, was wounded. As the tank withdrew with the wounded on its deck, it was raked by more bullets and Perrault was killed.

By nightfall the last of George Company's survivors were off the hill. Of the 151 who had gone forward, only seventy-two were still on their feet. The casualties included the company commander, executive officer, two platoon leaders and two platoon sergeants. "We'd been shot up so bad," remembered one Marine, "that the 3rd Pl[atoon] no longer existed, and our squads and fire teams were gone because the company was short of people."[11]

On May 13, the 3/29th Marines entered the fray to the east of the 22nd Marines and made small gains in the hilly terrain overlooking the upper Asato River. A day later, the 2/22nd was ordered to seize the high ground west and north of Sugar Loaf, and then attack the hill itself.

During the officers' briefing, Lieutenant Colonel Woodhouse referred to three objectives: Hills One (the closest, north of Sugar Loaf), Two (Sugar Loaf) and Three (west of Sugar Loaf). "The operation," said Woodhouse, "is to take Hill One, then Hill Three, and then all assemble and take Hill Two. Any questions?"

"Yeah," said one of his company commanders, "why don't you order the hill numbers in the order they're going to be taken? Hill One on the left, then Hill Two on the right, and Hill Three the fore one."

"No, I've already given the regiment my attack order. It's going to be Hill One, Hill Three, and then Hill Two."

With the summary over, he asked if there were any more questions. "How 'bout that hill numbering," persisted the captain. "What can we do?"

"All right, the heck with it," said Woodhouse. "We're going to call it like this: Hill One on the right, Hill Three on the left, and the fore hill is going to be called Sugar Loaf."*

* This is how Sugar Loaf Hill got its name: to avoid confusing the officers of 2/22nd Marines.

With George Company down to a reinforced platoon, the two companies due to attack were Fox on the right and Easy on the left. They jumped off at 7:30 a.m. and were able to capture the forward slopes of the two hills protecting Sugar Loaf—One and Three—but intense fire met them whenever they tried to move around or over these hills. Easy Company on Hill Three was particularly vulnerable as it was well ahead of the forward line of the neighboring 1st Marine Division, and as a result could be enfiladed from both flank and rear. "There were very few people left that were still in fighting condition," said First Lieutenant Ed Pesely, acting commander of Fox Company, "because they were being attacked hard from the left side."[12]

At 3:00 p.m., Woodhouse received orders from division to take Sugar Loaf "regardless of the consequences" and, to help him do it, he was being sent King Company, 2/29th Marines.[13] As it was getting dark, and Sugar Loaf had still not been captured, the battalion XO, Major Henry A. Courtney Jr., appeared at Fox Company's CP. A 29-year-old lawyer from Duluth, Minnesota, Courtney had been commissioned into the Marine Corps Reserve in 1940, and served at Guadalcanal as a company commander. He was, wrote William Manchester (who knew him well), "a fair, handsome man who looked like what we then called a matinee idol. No man bore less resemblance to John Wayne. There was something faintly feminine about Courtney, a dainty manner, almost a prissiness."[14]

With a determination that belied his appearance, Courtney told Pesely—a pre-Pearl Harbor Marine who had been commissioned from the ranks—that they needed to get men over to Sugar Loaf. Spotting people on the hill, and assuming they were Americans, he said: "You've got troops up there so let's go join 'em."

Pesely knew that none of his men were on the hill. "They were all Japanese," he said later, "not our troops. If they had been our troops they would have waved us to come on top." But Courtney was so determined to move men to Sugar Loaf that Pesely got swept up by his enthusiasm. The only problem were the flares that were lighting up the hill as if it were day. "When the flares stop," said Courtney, "we'll attack. Maybe we'll have some safety in darkness."

As the last flare died away, Fox Company's battered platoons moved toward Sugar Loaf with Courtney leading the way. They were joined at the base of the hill by some George Company men who had come from Hill Three. Once they were gathered together, Courtney warned them to be careful because the Japanese were still manning caves and tunnels on the face. Then he barked the order: "Take off."

They did just that, scrambling up the face of the hill. As they approached the crest, spread out in a long skirmish line, Japanese grenades started to explode among them. They hit the ground and started throwing grenades back. "They were coming up the far side of the hill," recalled Pesely, "and we were on top."[15]

Soon Japanese knee mortars were adding to the carnage and casualties began to mount. "Little puffs of dust appeared as we ran from shell hole to shell hole," remembered 20-year-old Corporal Joe Kohn from Metuchen, New Jersey, part of a four-man artillery forward-observer team accompanying the attack. "The lieutenant ran ahead and found a large mortar hole near the top. We followed and the [communications personnel] men started to string the wires back to the lines." But no sooner had a telephone link been established with the gun battery than the lieutenant was shot in the back and killed. "He slid down between us," said Kohn. "We all looked at each other. All hell was breaking loose outside and I couldn't get base on the phone. Either the wires got cut or something happened."

No longer able to call in artillery support, Kohn told the other men to move down the hill and spread out so that one shell would not kill them all. They did that, digging separate holes over a distance of about fifty yards. "We could yell to each other," noted Kohn, "but I said not to do it except in case of an emergency."[16]

Further up the hill, where they were running out of men, grenades and bullets, Courtney turned to Fox Company's commander: "Pes, we're out of ammunition. Go back and get some." As Courtney had climbed the hill without a weapon, bar his pistol, he asked Pesely if he could borrow his carbine while he was gone. The lieutenant handed it over. Pesely then set off and, as he passed one of his "shot up" platoons on the left side of the hill, was joined by the officer who said: "You'll never make it by yourself. I'm going with you."

As they skirted Hill Three, jittery Americans fired at them but missed. They hollered back the password, and the firing ceased. Eventually they got back to the battalion command post and told Lieutenant Colonel Woodhouse what was going on. "OK," he replied,

"I just got a load of ammunition from regiment, and it's on that vehicle over there. Is there anything else you need?"

"Yes," said Pesely. "there's so few of us up there. Maybe about ten or fifteen left."

Woodhouse nodded. "OK. I just got twenty-two reinforcements from regiment. Do you want them?"

"Yeah, we'll take them."

Ordering the replacements to mount the amtrac, Pesely and the other officer climbed in beside the driver. Then they headed at speed for the base of Sugar Loaf, and stopped near the entrance to the trail. Each man carried a box of ammunition—bullets and grenades—up to Courtney and the few men remaining near the crest of the hill. There they used bayonets to break the metal bands sealing the ammunition boxes, and made sure every foxhole was well supplied. Once that was done, and Pesely had recovered his carbine, Courtney announced: "Let's clean out the top of the hill so we can get some rest."

As the two officers began their sweep, grenades began to explode behind them, near their original firing line. Coming up the hill, firing and throwing grenades as they went, was a long line of Japanese. "We started pulling the pins," remembered Pesely, "and throwing them down on them, and they were screaming and tumbling, and full of dust and everything." Then flares revealed "columns of Nips" coming up the reverse slope, a force later estimated at battalion strength. Pesely used his radio phone to call for artillery support. "Put it out there five hundred yards."

Shells began to explode, killing and maiming some of the attacking Japanese. But the majority kept coming, so Pesely reduced the range: "Four hundred yards ... Three hundred yards ... Two hundred yards."

When he said, "One hundred yards," the officer on the other end replied: "Hey, some of those rounds are going to land right with you if you lower them to a hundred yards!"

By then, the attack had been beaten off by a combination of artillery, mortar and small-arms fire. It was around this time, as the Japanese retaliated with knee mortars, that the gallant Courtney was struck in the neck by shrapnel and killed. Taking command of the mixed force of around fifty men, Pesely "ran back and forth" between the foxholes, making sure the defenders stayed alert. At 2:00 a.m. on

May 15, he received a call from Colonel Woodhouse who wanted to know why it was so quiet.

"Because," replied Pesely, "there aren't very many of us left."

"I have a company from another battalion," said Woodhouse, referring to King Company, 2/29th Marines, "could you use them?"

"Sure," replied Pesely.

About half an hour later, with Pesely giving instructions over the radio, First Lieutenant Reginald Fincke led the three officers and ninety-nine men of King Company up the slope of Sugar Loaf. As they neared the summit, and began to deploy, the Japanese fired another salvo of knee mortars. One of them struck a machine-gun post that Fincke was directing, killing the gunners and mortally wounding the company commander. Moments later, Pesely heard a voice. "Where's Fox Company?"

"This is it," replied Pesely. "What's left of it anyway. I'm the skipper, Ed Pesely."

"I'm Jim Roe, King Company exec," said the voice. "Lieutenant Fincke just got killed, so I'm in charge of the company now. How do you want us to deploy?"

"Just spread out on top of the hill and dig in as quietly as you can and wherever you can. You guys're damned brave to climb into a mess like this, but we're happy as hell to see you."[17]

The King Company men were just in time. At 4:00 a.m., the Japanese launched another attack up the hill, killing and wounding more of the defenders, but failing to overrun their position. Huddled in his foxhole a little further down the hill, flinching from each mortar explosion, Joe Kohn "could hear screaming and yelling" and knew men were being "wounded or killed." One was pleading for his God to intervene, but most just yelled "for their mother." It was, he remembered, the "longest night and it seemed to last forever." When dawn finally came, Kohn looked for the other men in his team. Only one was left. Kohn motioned to the rear and the two took off, stumbling and falling in their haste.[18]

The many casualties on Sugar Loaf—including Lieutenant Pesely, wounded by grenades fragments in the throat and chest—were evacuated by amtrac at daybreak. Roe assumed command. But with his numbers shrinking by the minute, he made the difficult decision at 8:30 a.m. to abandon the hill they had fought so hard to capture.

To try to recover the situation, Woodhouse ordered a platoon from Dog Company, 2/29th Marines, to retake the crest. Led by First Lieutenant George Murphy, a former Notre Dame football star, they attacked the hill with fixed bayonets and, once on top, were drawn into the now familiar grenade battle with the Japanese on the reverse slope. But they were soon out of grenades and, realizing the position was untenable, Murphy asked his company commander, Captain Howard L. Mabie, for permission to withdraw. Mabie refused. Murphy was "to hold the hill at all costs."

But with mortars falling all around, and his command reduced to a fragment, Murphy told his surviving men to fall back. He tried to cover their retreat down the hill, but was killed by a mortar blast as he stopped to help a wounded Marine.

When Mabie saw that Murphy's platoon was pulling out, he advanced his company to protect the survivors. He also sent Woodhouse a message: "Request permission to withdraw. Irish George Murphy has been hit. Has eleven men left in platoon of original sixty."

"You must hold," responded Woodhouse.

But it was too late. "Platoon has withdrawn," said Mabie. "Position was untenable. Could not evacuate wounded. Believe Japs now hold ridge."

The Japanese continued to attack along a 900-yard front, and by noon had recovered much of the ground lost to Woodhouse's battalion the day before. It was around that time, as the Japanese assault fizzled out, that the battered 2/22nd was relieved by its sister battalion, the 3/22nd. Since May 12, it had lost 400 men in its heroic but vain attempt to capture Sugar Loaf Hill.[19]

29

"Hell's own cesspool"

"Today," wrote Lieutenant General Buckner to his wife Adele on May 13, "I spent five hours in a forward observation post watching a regiment take a hill, all in plain view. It was a most inspiring sight."[1]

He was referring to the attack by Colonel May's 383rd Infantry on the 500-foot high "Conical Hill," the eastern anchor of the Japanese main line of resistance. Having studied the terrain prior to the attack, divisional commander General Bradley had been convinced that the hill could be taken only from the northwest, "by advances down the ridge line of the chain of hills." But when nearby villages and a part of the hill's northern spur were captured on the 11th and 12th, the corps commander General Hodge phoned Bradley and ordered him to make a frontal attack on Conical Hill from the north. "We'll have the key to the Shuri line if he can make it," Hodge told a member of his staff.

Directing the advance on the 13th, May ordered the 2/383rd Infantry to send two companies with tanks up the northern slopes. Two platoons of Fox Company got halfway up the north-east spur with "surprising ease" and, on their own initiative, continued on up to the north-east crest which they reached at 1:00 p.m. Realizing they had been outflanked, the Japanese counter-attacked fiercely, but were beaten back, and by nightfall Fox had been reinforced by Easy and George Companies. By using a "naturally stronger but less heavily defended avenue of approach," May's men had driven a vital wedge into the Japanese defenses.[2]

Buckner was understandably delighted, noting in his diary that May's "handling of the Reg[imen]t was a beautiful piece of troop leading" and he deserved promotion to brigadier general.[3] In his letter to his wife, he admitted to visiting "both corps and four front-line command posts and three observation posts overlooking the entire battle front" the day before. "By gaining intimate familiarity with the problems of front-line troops," he added, "and of the terrain features, I find it much easier to direct the battle than I could possibly do otherwise."

He then explained his methodical and unspectacular approach to combat. "We are making," he told his wife, "slow but steady progress and killing lots of Japs. It is tough going and will continue to be for some time, but I feel that we have control of the situation and are ready for any counter-attack. We repulsed the last large one with heavy losses to the enemy and light losses to our men."

He was, he admitted, "eager to get this island completely cleaned up so as to move on to other battlefields, but it can't be hurried without heavy losses." As for his own role in future operations, it was "difficult to predict" since General MacArthur's appointment as commander of all U.S. Army forces in the Pacific in early April. "He has his own group of generals that he has been working with," wrote Buckner, "and my chances can scarcely be as good as those of Krueger and Eichelberger." Yet, he consoled himself with the knowledge that, with the invasion of Japan to come, there was enough "fighting in prospect to satisfy the most ravenous appetite."[4]

Buckner might not have been so upbeat about his future prospects if he had known just how low MacArthur's estimation of him was, an opinion that seemed in part to be influenced by Buckner's willingness to serve on Okinawa under navy command. Only a few days earlier Lieutenant General Robert Eichelberger, one of MacArthur's senior commanders, had written to his wife: "Big Chief says if Buck[ner] ever comes under him he would bust him because he has sold out to one of our sister services."[5]

The 6th Marine Division—in the form of Dog Company, 2/29th Marines—finally captured Sugar Loaf Hill on May 18 and held it that night against one last desperate Japanese counter-attack. The week-long battle for the hill had cost the division 2,662 casualties, and another 1,289 cases of combat fatigue. The two regiments involved—the 22nd and 29th Marines—had lost no fewer than three battalion commanders and nine company commanders.[6]

For Sergeant William Manchester, it was a nightmare experience for which a "structured account of events" was impossible to piece together. Instead he was left with a "kaleidoscopic montage" of incidents and impressions, and in no particular order. They included the "Truce of the Fucking Dogs," when an American "war dog" got loose, "ran out on the killing ground north of Sugar Loaf, somehow met an Okinawan pye-dog, and mounted her while both sides, astounded by this act of creativity in the midst of annihilation, held their fire." He also remembered an incident involving "a supercilious pair of army officers" who appeared at the front and asked to be directed "to the best view of the battle." A gunnery sergeant "pointed toward the Horseshoe [Hill], and off they went, covering about thirty feet, before they were slain."

More traumatic for Manchester personally was the time he and one of his "Raggedy Asses," a former Colgate athlete named Chet Pryzastawaki, went on a routine tour of the line companies. He recalled: "Chet and I had covered the companies, Fox to Easy to Dog, as smoothly as Tinker to Evers to Chance.* Positions around Sugar Loaf were in constant flux—at one time or another nine Marine battalions fought on the hill—and we had been told to skirt enemy lines on our way back, scouting every dip, crease, cranny, and rut in the ground that might be useful in combined attacks."

They had almost completed their patrol, and were moving down a rock gulch they had christened "Windy Alley," when they were fired on by a sniper who was between them and safety. A crack shot, Manchester was armed with only a carbine and a .45 pistol, "both useless in a sniper's duel," so he borrowed Pryzastawaki's M1. While his comrade threw a grenade to distract the sniper, Manchester darted out from his rock, "rolled over on the deck, into the prone position, the M1 butt tight against my shoulder." Ignoring a mortar explosion that parted the air overhead with a "shredding rustle," Manchester kept his eyes locked onto the "jagged edge of rock" the sniper was hiding behind. "I had," recalled Manchester, "taken a deep breath, and let a little of it out, and was absolutely steady when the

* A famous double-play in baseball by three Chicago Cubs that helped their team win the World Series. It was the subject of the 1910 poem by Franklin Pierce Adams, "Baseball's Sad Lexicon."

tip of his helmet appeared, his rifle muzzle just below it...I was in plain view, but lying flat, head-on, provides the lowest possible profile, and his vision was tunneled to my right. Now I saw a throat, half a face, a second eye—and that was enough."

He pulled the trigger.

It hit the sniper in the cheek, and more shots finished him off. Manchester turned to his comrade "and stifled a scream. He had no face, just juicy shapeless red pulp. In all likelihood he had been peering out curiously when that last mortar shell burst. Death must have been instantaneous." The news of Pryzastawaki's demise deepened the intelligence section's numbness, wrote Manchester, "but the days of cathartic grief, of incredulity and fury, were gone. One by one the Raggedy Ass Marines were disappearing." The deaths included that of one marine, a "strong candidate for his family's stock-exchange seat," who "crawled out on a one-man twilight patrol up Sugar Loaf" and had just cleared the American wire when he was "eviscerated" by a burst from a Nambu machine gun. "There was no way that any of us could reach [him]," recalled Manchester, "so he hung there, screaming for his mother, until about 4:30 in the morning, when he died."

After the war, Manchester visited the soldier's mother who told him she had spent that night praying for her son. "God didn't answer my prayers," she said.

Manchester replied: "He didn't answer any of mine."

Newsweek later described Sugar Loaf as the "most critical local battle of the war," but for Manchester there was little pride in what he and his fellow Marines had achieved. "My father had warned me that war is grisly beyond imagining," he wrote, "now I believed him." The battle was the moment his "puerile" dream of war and glory was exposed for what it was. "As I look back," he recalled, "it was somewhere on the slopes of that hill, where I confronted the dark underside of battle, that passion died between me and the Marine Corps...I saw through the Corps' swagger, the ruthless exploitation of loyalty I had guilelessly plighted in that Springfield recruiting station after Pearl Harbor. On Sugar Loaf, in short, I realized that something within me, long ailing, had expired." Though he would continue to fight, he "now knew that banners and swords, ruffles and flourishes, bugles and drums, the whole rigmarole, eventually ended in squalor."[7]

On May 19, the "bleeding remnants" of Manchester's 29th Marines were relieved by the 4th Marines who, over the next two days, expanded the 29th's footholds on Horseshoe Hill. The fighting was no less ferocious than it had been on Sugar Loaf Hill. Corporal Mel Heckt of Baker Company, 1/4th Marines, had just set up one of his machine-gun teams in a ditch between Sugar Loaf and Horseshoe hills when it received a direct hit by a mortar on May 21, killing three. "Poor Red McGee was blown all over the side of the hill," noted Heckt in his diary.

> Only his red hair and scalp remained where he had been sitting. Jennings, a devout Catholic and one of the most religious among us, said before his death, "It will be only by the grace of God for those who remain to walk today." He never knew what hit him for it was concussion. I could hardly recognize the body for it was blown up twice the normal size.

By May 24, with the 6th Marine Division advancing toward the outskirts of Naha, Heckt's machine-gun section had only five men left: eight were dead, nine wounded, and one sent to the rear with battle fatigue. "The strain," wrote Heckt, "has been too much. We need a rest. I hope and pray we will receive it or many more will crack up. I know I've had enough and am ready to go stateside or back to Guam. War is hell. The battle for Guam was a picnic compared to Okinawa."

When Heckt's Baker Company was relieved on May 28, it was down to eighty-nine of its original 240 men. "It rained like hell all night," wrote Heckt on the 29th, "but [Ray] Courtney and I put up our pup tent in time. This morn we all took a shower and shaved and put on new clothes. For the first time in ten days I felt tired but at least clean. It is really a wonderful feeling to be clean and alive."[8]

The gruesome task of recovering dead Marines from the slopes of Sugar Loaf Hill was left to volunteers from the 29th Marines' HQ and Service Company. One of them, Nils Andersen from Brooklyn, remembered bodies so decomposed they had started to turn green and were falling apart. In a cave he slipped on the stinking remains of three Japanese soldiers and got up "covered in maggots and parts of their flesh and skin." His colleague threw up after he tried to pull the body of a Marine and its arm came off at the shoulder. Unable to know for certain which limb belonged to which body, they put a "head, torso, two arms, two legs" on each poncho and left it to Graves Registration to "sort out the pieces later."

A special task was to locate the body of Major Courtney, the man who had "led a reverse banzai charge with fifty men." On finding the major's corpse, they put it on a stretcher. But as Courtney was "too long, too tall," they "made the decision to break his legs under him and compact his body" so they could get him down the hill. At the collecting point, they placed Courtney's body to one side. The other Marine corpses were stacked like logs: four one way, three the other, then two, then one. "So they were pyramid-style," remembered Andersen. "We started to build up quite a few of these piles."

For the journey back to the regimental CP, Andersen drew the short straw and traveled in the back of the amtrac with around twenty corpses. On one steep slope, the pile slid on top of him and he was drowning in "water, maggots, and bits of flesh, blood." His desperate screams of "Enough, enough, enough!" could not be heard over the roar of the engine. Back at the CP, before he could shower and change, a Marine said to him and the other volunteers: "God you guys stink and you look like death. Don't come near us."[9]

Buried initially in the 6th Marine Division Cemetery on Okinawa, Major Courtney's remains were reinterred in his home town of Duluth, Minnesota, in 1948. A couple of months earlier, his parents were presented with the Medal of Honor that had been awarded posthumously to Courtney for his "astute military acumen, indomitable leadership and decisive action in the face of overwhelming odds."[10] William Manchester visited Courtney's widow after the war to offer his condolences. "Apart from our shared grief," he wrote, "I was still trying to understand why he had done what he had done. I thought she might know. She didn't. She was as mystified as I was."[11]

If the 6th Marine Division's nadir on Okinawa was the desperate fighting for Sugar Loaf Hill, the same could be said for 1st Marine Division's three-week battle to take the "Shuri Heights." The term was coined by the Marines to include not only Shuri Castle, and the headquarters of the Thirty-Second Army that lay in tunnels and caves beneath, but also the Japanese positions that were dug into the key features of Dakeshi Ridge, Wana Ridge, Wana Draw and Hill 55, and the ruined towns of Dakeshi and Wana, all of which protected Shuri from the northwest.

So vital were the strong points in the Dakeshi–Wana area that General Ushijima had ordered the defending troops of the 62nd Division to hold them "without fail." He also bolstered the shattered 63rd Brigade with airfield construction troops, a cannon unit, and a suicide-boat group, bringing its strength up to 6,700 men; and sent part of the 44th Mixed Brigade to defend the Dakeshi sector with instructions to fight to the last man. They did just that, but it was not enough to prevent the 7th Marines from capturing the ridge and town in three days of vicious fighting from May 11 to 13. A day later, in concert with the 1st Marines, which were advancing on their right flank, the 2/7th Marines tried to capture Wana Ridge, a "long coral spine" lined on both sides with fortified tombs, that ran west from the northern outskirts of Shuri town. Though some of the 1st Marines, attacking from the west, got part of the way up the ridge, the 2/7th Marines were unable to cross the shell- and bullet-swept low ground between Dakeshi and Wana ridges, and the Marines pulled back to lower ground under the cover of smoke.[12]

On four successive days—May 16–19—the 1/7th Marines and 3/7th Marines assaulted Wana Ridge without success. Leading one of the assault platoons on May 17 was Second Lieutenant "Jep" Carrell of King Company. "We moved out under an artillery barrage," he wrote, "and arrived at the bottom of the slope, under considerable enemy fire: small arms, knee mortars, and a good deal of heavier stuff." Losing men along the way, Carrell's platoon got as far as a "flat area just below the top of the ridge" where, for a time, they were supported by tanks. But they and the other assault platoon did not stay long. "The ridge was untenable," recalled Carrell, "and we received not only heavy fire from the front, but a good deal of fire from the left rear, out of our immediate area. We had lost about ten men from each of the two platoons, bringing our rifle-platoon numbers down to about twenty each, for a total of about forty. We had landed with 129."

Next day, Carrell watched Item Company move right and attack the nose of the "steep, rugged, almost shell-proof" ridge, "honeycombed with tunnels and many, many small openings for firing." The "exasperating problem" for the attackers was that "it was almost impossible to spot the fire ports until you were about ten to fifteen yards from them." Listening on Item Company's radio frequency, Carrell heard one platoon leader tell his skipper: "There appear to be two machine guns firing down the ridgeline toward us, but at the moment, we are in defile. When we attack, we'll be going right into that. There is no other route forward."

The company commander replied: "Hold in place until our artillery has laid down a barrage, then move out."

"Roger, and out."

But Carrell was not convinced that the barrage would do much to immobilize defenders buried so deep in tunnels and caves, and he was right. Within five seconds of the barrage ending, the platoon leader moved forward and was killed, as were two of his men. "The defensive fire," noted Carrell, "was overwhelming."[13]

On May 19, the 7th Marines were relieved by the 1st Marines. Having lost more than 1,000 men since May 10, the 7th were later awarded the Presidential Unit Citation for their part in the Battle for the Shuri Heights.[14]

Meanwhile the 5th Marines—having taken over from the 1st Marines on May 14—were making progress in their flanking attack on Hill 55 and the neighboring Wana Draw. Supported by tanks and 105 mm self-propelled guns, one platoon of Easy Company got a foothold on the western slope of Hill 55 on 17 May. Three days later, an all-out attack by Easy Company seized the rest of the hill, while tanks and fire teams "moved up into Wana Draw and with point-blank fire flushed out numerous enemy dug-in on the reverse slope of Hill 55."[15]

It was during this fighting that Corporal Jim Johnston witnessed an extraordinary act of self-sacrifice when a "tall, slim, stoop-shouldered" Marine from one of the Carolinas smothered a Japanese grenade with his body, "killing himself but saving some of his friends." Well aware that several Medals of Honor had been "given posthumously for exactly the same well-defined, selfless, and brave act of sacrifice," Johnston tried to get someone to acknowledge the man's deed. But he failed. "Everyone was too occupied," wrote Johnston, "or indifferent to the man personally, or unapproving of something he had done that didn't fit the corps' mold."

It was yet another reason for Johnston to condemn the process of awarding medals for valor as "an unqualified miscarriage of justice and a spurious practice." The implication was "that men with medals for valor are valorous and men without them are not." Yet in his experience that was demonstrably untrue. "No man," he argued, "or group of men, can make awards for valor with any degree of consistency or regard for worthiness. Everyone with any real experience in war realizes that fact." In Johnston's mind, courage was "in a man's own heart," and only God had the right to compare it with others.[16]

Once in possession of Hill 55, the 5th Marines were able to seize more ground to the south from where they could observe Shuri Ridge, the last natural feature protecting Shuri Castle to the west. But it would still take another two days of costly advances—May 20 and 21—for the 1st Marines to gain a foothold on the northern slope of Wana Ridge, while the 5th Marines extended the front line from the lower crest of the ridge to Wana village. Forming the spearhead of the 1st Marines' attack was Lieutenant Bruce Watkins' Easy Company. Approaching the draw up a railway cut, amidst sporadic sniping and the occasional mortar explosion, Watkins noticed his battalion commander Lieutenant Colonel Magee come striding up in full view of the enemy. He yelled: "Get down, sir! Colonels get hit just as easy as privates!"

Magee ignored the advice. He "wasn't used to ducking and diving like the rest of us," recalled Watkins. "He was a proud man and I'm sure his intent was to give us incentive and show courage. Fortunately, he wasn't hit." Shortly after the Magee incident, Watkins witnessed two Shermans get knocked out by high-velocity anti-tank rounds as they advanced to his right. Several crew members were killed as they ran for cover, prompting Watkins and some of his men to run forward and drag the wounded to safety. It was hard for him "to watch it happen and be powerless to help effectively," but Easy Company gained revenge soon after by disabling the anti-tank gun with flamethrowers and satchel charges.

Watkins and his men finally reached the crest of Wana Ridge in the afternoon of May 22, provoking a storm of mortar and small-arms fire. "It was," recalled Watkins, "the most intense mortar barrage I had experienced. Large 90 mm rounds were landing all around, mixed with smaller knee mortars. They had that crest really zeroed in.

Nevertheless, we dug in as best we could and hung on…I had just jumped into a 2nd Platoon foxhole when a very intense barrage hit. We were piling ammunition boxes around us to help catch the shrapnel. One round hit on the edge of the hole, knocking down the boxes and covering us with rocks and dirt."[17]

The previous night it had began to rain, the start of a downpour that continued, on and off, for the rest of the month. "Wana Draw was filled with mud and water until it resembled a lake," noted the official history. "Tanks bogged down, helplessly mired. Amphibian tractors were unable to negotiate the morass, and front-line units, which had depended on these vehicles for carrying supplies forward in bad weather, now had to resort to hand-carrying of supplies and of the wounded."

Inevitably the offensive ground to a standstill, and living conditions for the front-line troops became almost unbearable. Foxholes flooded and collapsed. Men were constantly wet and cold. "The bodies of Japanese killed at night lay outside the foxholes, decomposing under swarms of flies. Sanitation measures broke down. The troops were often hungry. Sleep was almost impossible. The strain began to take a mounting toll of men."[18]

Mortarman Eugene Sledge, whose 3/5th Marines took over a section of the front on Half Moon Hill from the 4th Marines on May 23, was appalled by what he found. "As we approached our destination," he recalled, "the Japanese dead, scattered about in most areas since May 1, became more numerous." Even more depressing, however, was the sight of so many Marine corpses. It was a strong Marine tradition, he knew, to recover their dead, "sometimes even at considerable risk, to an area where they could be covered with a poncho and later collected by the Graves Registration people." But so incessant were the Japanese artillery and mortar bombardments that this had not been possible. As Sledge and the rest of King Company trudged through the mud to their new position, they could see six Marine corpses "lying face down against a muddy slope where they apparently had hugged the deck to escape Japanese shells." Lying side by side, scarcely a foot apart, they were clutching rusted rifles and showed every sign of being "new replacements, fresh to the shock of combat." Bizarrely, one was wearing a shiny gold watch, an oddity when most combat soldiers made do with "plain, simple luminous-dial, waterproof, shockproof wristwatches" with green cloth wristbands. How odd, thought Sledge, for a Marine to wear such a "flashy, conspicuous" watch; and odder still that "some Japanese hadn't slipped out during a dark night and taken it."

While artillery shells swished and whined overhead in both directions, Sledge and the mortar section dug in below the ridge line, a hundred yards back from the rifle platoons in the front line. After siting the mortar, registering in on the aiming stakes, and preparing ammunition, Sledge had a good look around. "It was," he wrote, "the most ghastly corner of hell I had ever witnessed. As far as I could see, an area that previously had been a low grassy valley with a picturesque stream meandering through it was a muddy, repulsive, open sore on the land. The place was choked with the putrefaction of death, decay, and destruction." In a shallow defilade to his right, lay the corpses of twenty more Marines, each on a stretcher and covered with a poncho. Other bodies lay in shell craters, "half submerged in muck and water, rusting weapons still in hand." Swarms of flies hovered around them.

"Why ain't them poor guys been covered with ponchos?" asked Sledge's foxhole buddy. The answer came in the form of a loud explosion from a Japanese 75 mm shell, fired from gun positions on Shuri Ridge. If anyone moved from their holes, the shelling began immediately. "Thus it was perfectly clear," noted Sledge, "why the Marine dead were left where they had fallen." He added:

> For several feet around every corpse, maggots crawled about in the muck and then were washed away by the run-off of the rain. There wasn't a tree or bush left. All was open country. Shells had torn up the turf so completely that ground cover was nonexistent. The rain poured down on us as evening approached. The scene was nothing but mud; shellfire; flooded craters with their silent, pathetic, rotting occupants; knocked-out tanks and amtracs; and discarded equipment—utter desolation.

All around was the stench of death. Sledge's only escape from the "monstrous horror of it all" was to look up and "watch the leaden gray clouds go scudding over, and repeat over and over" to himself that the "situation was unreal"—a nightmare—and that he would soon awake and find himself "somewhere else." He had been depressed by the waste of human life on Peleliu; but this was far, far worse. "We were," he wrote, "in the depths of the abyss, the ultimate horror of war... Men struggled and fought and bled in an environment so degrading I believed we had been flung into hell's own cesspool."[19]

30

"I still hear those cries today"

Staff Sergeant Don Marpe had just made the last radar checks in the two Grumman Hellcat fighters that would fly that night from Yontan airfield when the air-raid sirens went off. It was 10:00 p.m. on May 24, a clear, moonlit night that was perfect for Japanese bombing raids. Marpe and the other men on the flight line went straight to their slit trenches from where they could see anti-aircraft fire to the north and west, but nothing overhead. "It wasn't long," recalled Marpe, "before we could hear (and feel) bomb explosions from hits not too far away, but none of the searchlights seemed to pick anything up."

The wave of bombers was the first of seven sent that night against American airfields on Okinawa and ships offshore. Planes in at least four of the first six waves got through to bomb Yontan and Kadena airfields, with one strike igniting 70,000 gallons of aviation gasoline in a fuel dump not far from Marpe. Shaken by the huge explosion, he was forced to duck in the slit trench when several bombs hit "close enough to rain dirt and rocks down on us and on our parked aircraft." But as no one was injured, and the aircraft did not appear to be damaged, they stayed put. All around them the anti-aircraft fire seemed to intensify in volume, with bright tracer criss-crossing the sky.

Soon the Marine anti-aircraft battalion near the end of the south-west–north-east runway—not far from Marpe's squadron area—began firing and, from the tracer trajectories, Marpe knew the targets must be low-flying planes. "All of a sudden," he wrote, "there was a flash and a big ball of fire when the plane they were firing on exploded just off the end of the runway, crashing into one of the anti-aircraft weapon revetments and, we found out later, killing the gun crew." The low-angle firing continued over the approach to the runway, but a plane got through and made a belly landing, skidding on the gravel and coming to rest just 200 feet from Marpe's slit trench. Shortly after it had "skittered to a stop," a dozen men got out and "huddled around in a group." Marpe could hear them "shouting to each other as if they were getting last-minute instructions, or maybe last-minute inspiration."

They either did not see 542 Squadron's dark blue Hellcats parked nearby, "or the line-up of the many larger aircraft which were parked off to the opposite side of the main runway was a better target for them," and they made straight for the latter, though they were farther away. Using incendiary grenades and charges, the Japanese commandos began destroying planes as fast as they could. Marpe and his colleagues were powerless to intervene. "None of us in our slit trenches," he recalled, "had any weapons other than a few screwdrivers, or maybe a pocketknife or two, so there was nothing we could do except stay where we were and keep our heads down." It was just as well, since Marpe's men were outnumbered and "probably couldn't have stopped them anyway."[1]

A few hundred meters away, in the squadron camp, Marpe's new commanding officer, Major Bruce Porter, was resting in his tent after an uneventful night patrol when he heard the sound of explosions. A former varsity water-polo player at the University of Southern California, Porter had entered the U.S. Navy flight training program in 1941 and was already a veteran of Guadalcanal and the Russells, flying thirty missions in Corsairs and shooting down three confirmed Japanese planes (and another four probables). Retrained as a night fighter, he had taken over 542 Squadron the day before the Japanese attack on Yontan airfield because the previous CO, Major Kellum, had, at his own request, been "removed from flight status." This was a blow to the whole squadron. "Pride is taught in the Marine Corps," wrote a staff sergeant, "I think, by all the training that demands excellence and perfection, so when your commanding officer 'opts out,' as it appeared, it's like a low blow, or stab in the back." Porter, however, had quickly repaired morale by personally speaking to the whole squadron: cooks, parachute riggers, armorers, mechanics, anyone who helped to keep the planes flying. "You could see a big change right away," recalled Porter. "All it took was for someone in authority to show a little interest in what the guys were doing."

With the attack on Yontan under way, Porter got a call on his command phone saying the "Japanese were landing airplanes." He ordered his men to grab their weapons and take cover in their foxholes. "It was chaotic," he wrote, "because we really did not know what was going on." Nor did his men know how to use their Thompson sub-machines properly and, with "bullets flying all over the place," it was fortunate that the action was on the far side of the airfield.[2]

Marpe, meanwhile, could hear gunfire coming from beyond the burning aircraft and "knew some effort was being made to counter what the suicide troops were doing." Marine tanks and infantry had finally arrived to tackle the intruders. Eventually the firing died away and, as dawn broke, "it was found that all but a couple of Japanese had committed suicide and those who didn't were taken prisoner."[3] In fact, according to Joe Sama, another member of 542 Squadron, one commando hid nearby and ambushed four men as they came to view the damage in the morning. "As they were bent over a Jap [corpse]," noted Sama in his diary, "a live one who was hidden thr[ew] a grenade & hit all but Jerry who was at a distance. He killed the Jap. Leehy lost an eye, Vince got a bad leg wound & Stan a few pieces of shrapnel… We expect a repetition…soon. It's really nerve-wracking."[4]

The plane that crash-landed at Yontan was the only one of nine two-engined Sally bombers sent on a suicide mission from the Japanese mainland to reach an Okinawa airfield. The other eight were all shot down en route: four by the perimeter anti-aircraft guns at Yontan airfield. They each contained fourteen heavily armed "Giretsu" commandos whose mission was to cause as much havoc as possible. In the event, the commandos from just one bomber destroyed or damaged no fewer than thirty-three American planes, including a liberator bomber, four C-54 transports, three Hellcats and twenty-four Corsairs. They also killed two American servicemen and wounded eighteen before their rampage came to an end.[5]

Lieutenant General Buckner witnessed two of the bombers crash in flames from his nearby command post, and later noted that the commandos were found with "maps and photographs of the field with arrows and circles marking points to be attacked." He was relieved that the damage was not worse, noting in his diary that of the eight planes totally destroyed, most were "transports." This was true, but it was still quite an achievement for such a small team of commandos.[6]

Watching the fires at Yontan from Shuri Castle, Colonel Yahara "imagined that our special-attack squadrons had struck a mighty blow on our behalf." Such attacks gave him and his colleagues on the Thirty-Second Army staff the "assurance that we were not alone in our desperate battle," and he was "deeply moved."[7]

A couple of days earlier, aware that the defenses in front of Shuri could not hold out for much longer, Colonel Yahara had managed to persuade Lieutenant General Ushijima and Chief of Staff Chō to agree to a fighting withdrawal to the south of the island. But as this flew in the face of his original strategy to fight it out at Shuri—a point that he knew Chō, in particular, would be quick to make—he ensured that the original suggestion was made not by him but by Major Nagano, Chō's deputy, who also felt it was the best course to take.

Yahara and his superiors at the Thirty-Second Army's headquarters had known for some days that they were "losing" the battle. They had even sent a message to Imperial Headquarters for more air support: "We have wrought havoc on three enemy divisions," it read, "which are disintegrating. Three other enemy divisions are under heavy attack. We have lost many elite troops, but still believe in the immortality of the empire. We are surrounded by the enemy but our fighting spirit remains strong. Please continue air operations to destroy all enemy naval forces in the Okinawa area."

The commando mission against the airfields on Okinawa, and the huge kamikaze attack that day by 165 planes—the seventh mass strike since the start of the battle—was partly in response to this request, but Yahara knew deep down that such desperate measures would not turn the tide. The appeal, he admitted, was little more than an effort to raise morale. His main concern now was how best to prolong the struggle. There were, he felt, three options. They could remain at Shuri, but there was a danger the army would soon be outflanked and destroyed. They could withdraw to the Chinen Peninsula in the southeast of the island, a compact position that would be protected by water on three sides and was favorable for anti-tank warfare. On the other hand it was too small to accommodate all the remaining Japanese troops, was vulnerable to enemy bombardment from all directions, and did not have good road links for a rapid and orderly withdrawal. Or they could move to the Kiyan Peninsula at the bottom of Okinawa which was protected by natural fortifications facing north. It also had the advantage of good road communications, many natural caves, and a number of underground bunkers and tunnels. This was Yahara's favored option, but he knew he needed to tread carefully. So after he had drawn up the paper outlining the pros and cons of each option, he persuaded Major Nagano to put his name to it.

Asked his opinion of the paper by Major General Chō on May 22, Yahara replied: "I have long considered the option of remaining at Shuri, so it is difficult to relinquish it. Nevertheless, I feel that retreat, especially to Kiyan, is the most desirable."

In reality, he felt that Kiyan was the *only* option, but "did not want to appear too enthusiastic." Nor did he want Chō to think that he was making a snap decision, so he added: "Since last year when the 9th Division was moved to Taiwan, we have mapped our war plans for southern Okinawa. Some division commanders feel that it would not be right to offer their opinions. In making this crucial decision, which may determine the fate of our entire army, may I suggest that you ask each division commander for his opinion?"

Chō agreed and, that evening, the chief of staff and his deputy from each major formation—24th and 62nd Divisions, 44th Mixed Brigade, 5th Artillery Group and Naval Base Force—came "through heavy rain and enemy bombardment' to the headquarters cave where they met with Yahara and the other army staff in the officers' quarters next to General Ushijima's office. Chairing the meeting, Yahara could see the strain on each of the familiar faces before him. Yet they "treated each other with a kind dignity and kept up an air of calm." Refreshments had been provided and, as the visitors tucked in to canned pineapple, clams and sake, Yahara "described the overall battle situation" and asked for "frank opinions regarding the three options."

Colonel Ueno, the 62nd Division's chief of staff, was first to respond, and the first to acknowledge their desperate but determined position. "After all we have endured," he said, speaking rapidly with a hoarse voice, "we cannot retreat. Our division dutifully followed your directives and prepared Shuri's formidable fortifications. Even if we abandon them and try to withdraw to the rear, our transportation is inadequate. There is no way to transport 1,000 wounded soldiers and stores of ammunition. Our division determined from the beginning to fight to the death at Shuri. We cannot leave behind thousands of dead and wounded who dedicated their lives to our motherland. We want to die here."

The next two speakers—the chiefs of staff of the 24th Division and 5th Artillery Group—both endorsed the Kiyan option, while Major Kyoso of the 44th Mixed Brigade wanted to move to the Chinen Peninsula. Lieutenant Colonel Nikao of the Naval Base Force was the only one not to state a preference. It thus became clear to Yahara that, as he put it, "each command insisted on sticking to its own territory," or at least to terrain they were familiar with from earlier deployments.

To avoid endless debate, Yahara declared: "I do not know General Ushijima's decision but it may be the Kiyan Peninsula." He then ran through the arguments for each option, adding that the transport of casualties and ammunition would be the responsibility of the transport regiment. The whole withdrawal of front-line forces could be completed, he insisted, in just five days.

With the meeting over, the participants drank more sake before returning to their posts. The tipsy Yahara went to his office where he told his deputies what had been said and boasted: "When I was in the military academy, instructors praised my skill in tactics and strategy. My judgments and decisions were outstanding." Glancing at Ushijima, who was reading in the adjacent office, Yahara continued: "Our last stand must be at Kiyan."

As he spoke, he could see Ushijima's mouth break into a half-smile. The lieutenant general had not said a word, yet Yahara knew that he had his support. Thrilled, he went to report the result of the meeting to Major General Chō. "The 62nd Division wishes to die here," said Yahara, "This is understandable, but it is impossible for all troops to assemble at Shuri. If we are to contribute to the homeland battle we must continue to fight. Thus, to remain at Shuri is unthinkable, and Kiyan is the most realistic option. It suits the goal of army operations."

When Chō promptly accepted this advice, Yahara assumed he must have already considered the options. With the decision made, Yahara devised a plan for the withdrawal on May 29, or "X-Day." It aimed to combine a "total retreat toward fortifications in Kiyan" with a "German-army-style, local prolonged resistance, taking advantage of the rugged terrain and numerous caves along the twelve kilometers between the Shuri line and the new front line." The carefully worked timetable was as follows: the Thirty-Second Army headquarters would withdraw first to Tsukazan—its previous underground location, a few miles due south of Shuri and not far from the army field hospital at Haebaru—on X-Day minus 2 (May 27), and continue on to Mabuni Hill, at the base of the Kiyan Peninsula on the night of X-Day itself; the Artillery Group would move on X-Day minus 1 (May 28), with some of the guns deploying on the route to assist the retreat, and others moving direct to Kiyan; the main strength of the 24th Division and the 44th Mixed Brigade, the best of the remaining troops, would pull back on the night of X-Day, while a few remained in their present position to block any enemy pursuit (themselves retreating on the night of X-Day plus 2, May 31); the Naval Base Force on the Oroku Peninsula would move east to positions on the southern bank of the Kokuba River to assist the Thirty-Second Army's retreat; and, finally, the surviving troops of the battered 62nd Division would, in line with its commanders' wishes, "continue its present mission and, if possible, repulse the enemy in the Yonabaru area," making "every effort to block pursuit by the enemy."

Characterizing his plan as an "offensive retreat," Yahara fantasized that it would be remembered by generations to come in the same vein as "Napoleon's Battle of Marengo, France's counter-attack on the Marne in World War I, the Polish army's counter-attack against the Soviets in 1920." Once the plan was approved by Ushijima, Chō and the senior staff, all that remained was to move tens of thousands of civilians south first. That these Okinawans would be heading into a trap—penned into the southern tip of the island where many were bound to perish as the Thirty-Second Army fought its desperate last stand—was not something that concerned the Japanese military in the slightest, for it was not only a duty, but also an honor, to die for the emperor.[8]

For the Himeyuri student nurses, the grim forced retreat began in the early hours of May 26 as they left the hospital caves in pouring rain and headed south, "walking with ambulatory patients and carrying their injured classmates on stretchers and medical supplies and documents on their backs."[9] When 16-year-old Kikuko Miyagi and her colleagues got the order to leave, one asked a soldier what they were going to do with the seriously wounded. "Don't worry," he replied, "I'll make it easy for them." Only later did Kikuko discover that the patients were offered condensed milk laced with cyanide as their final drink, and told to achieve their "glorious end like a Japanese soldier." Others were left grenades so that they could kill themselves. "Would it have been so terrible if they had been captured and revealed the Japanese army's situation?" wrote Kikuko, lamenting the extreme measures taken to prevent that. "Instead they were all murdered to protect military strategy."

The route south to Ihara in the Kiyan Peninsula was, wrote Kikuko, "truly horrible, muddy and full of artillery craters with corpses, swollen two or three times normal size, floating in them." They could move only at night, and even then the Americans sent up flares to identify targets for their artillery. Ironically they provided the fleeing civilians "with enough light to see the way." Walking beside Kikuko, using her shoulder as a crutch, was an injured friend; another student had night blindness and kept stumbling over corpses and crying. "We'd become accustomed to the smell of excrement, pus, and the maggots in the cave," noted Kikuko, "but the smell of death there on that road was unbearable. And it poured rain every day."

They were part of a mass exodus of tens of thousands of civilians "moving like ants." Among them were grandparents and mothers with children on their backs, "scurrying along, covered in mud." If a child was injured, it was simply left by the roadside to fend for itself. "Those children," recalled Kikuko, "could tell we were students. They'd call out, '*Nei, nei!*' and try to cling to us. That's Okinawan dialect for 'Older sister!' It was so pitiable. I still hear those cries today."

Kikuko and her friends—mostly 15- and 16-year-olds—hid by day in whatever cover they could find, crying out to their teachers, "I'm afraid!"

"Bear up!" the teachers replied. "You can take it!"[10]

Another student nurse moving south was Shizuko Oshiro, also just 16 years old, who had been assigned to the First Surgical Unit at Haebaru. Soon after leaving she noticed a "legless soldier desperately crawling along." She recognized him as one of the seriously wounded soldiers they had left behind. Somehow he had followed them. "I was afraid he might notice me," admitted Shizuko, "so I looked away and went on."[11]

For 18-year-old Nobuko Kinjo, originally part of the 2nd Surgical Unit, the march was a nightmare experience. "During the daytime," she remembered, "fighter planes and hydroplanes would sweep down from the sky, strafing the crowds. Each time they strafed, many people in the crowd fell down, but people didn't care. They just kept on walking. They no longer seemed to have any fear."[12]

31

"The entire enemy line appears to be crumbling"

As dusk was falling on May 27, Colonel Yahara destroyed the last documents in his office before wading through knee-high flood water to the entrance to Tunnel 5 where he found a scrum of soldiers patiently waiting their turn to leave the Thirty-Second Army headquarters' cave. They were fully armed and weighed down with heavy packs containing up to 130 pounds of extra ammunition and provisions. Yahara forced his way through the crowd, shouting, "This is Senior Staff Officer Yahara. Let me pass."

As Yahara neared the opening to the cave he could see General Ushijima leaving with an escort of soldiers. Shell explosions forced a number of them back inside, but not Ushijima. Yahara "regretted not departing with him and hoped that he was safe." Twenty minutes later, during another break in the bombardment, Yahara exited with General Chō and two other staff officers. "We at once turned left," he recalled, "and climbed a gentle slope for about thirty meters. We had almost reached the top when a massive explosion shook the hill. We ducked into bushes and hit the dirt. I looked back at [Captain] Sakaguchi, who was saying, 'Quick, sir, come up here,' as he helped General Chō up the slope. Chō passed me without a word."

Badly shaken by the near miss, Yahara scrambled back to the cave entrance where Major General Suzuki of the 44th Brigade joked, "Hey, brave Yahara, are you back again?"

An hour later, having recovered his composure, Yahara left a second time with some other staff officers and was guided by duty soldiers along the muddy route to Tsukazan. Glancing back, he could see the "solemn outline of Shuri Castle hill" through the gun smoke. He said goodbye to the place where he thought he would die.

Further along the track they passed a "dead soldier, fully armed, at the side of the road," a sight Yahara found "especially heartbreaking." Enemy flares lit the way, and some naval shells exploded nearby, but none of Yahara's party was injured. After resting in a farmhouse, they continued on through intermittent shellfire and eventually reached the entrance to Tsukazan cave. A few hundred meters inside they found generals Ushijima and Chō enjoying a meal with Paymaster Sato. "I'm glad to see you again," said Chō to Yahara. "When I didn't see your face I was worried. I was just telling these gentlemen that if anything happened to you, I would have to do your work."

After congratulating the generals on their safe arrival, Yahara went next door to his own small room. Four meters square, it contained two beds and a table, and was lit by a single candle. There he was joined by Major Nagano who brought sake and three cans of pineapple. As they ate and drank, a tipsy Yahara voiced his regret that the Thirty-Second Army had ever gone on the offensive. "Only fools and madmen dream of victory in a battle against a superior enemy," he told Nagano. "Where we had only two and a half divisions, the enemy had six. While we had no way of replenishing troops and supplies lost in battle, the enemy has a constant resupply of soldiers and ammunition. The enemy divisions are being continuously reinforced by sea and air. Our army should have faced the fact that we could not win this battle. We should have concentrated on a strategy of attrition for the defense of Japan."

Looking up, Yahara was shocked to see the two generals standing in his doorway. "Is everything OK with both of you?" asked Chō.

Assuming they had heard his outburst, but were "too gracious to show their displeasure," Yahara reddened with embarrassment. "We're both fine," he replied, before saying it was nearly dawn and there were intelligence reports to check. He retired soon after, and "went to sleep to the lullaby of distant gunfire."[1]

As one pessimistic report after another was received from the front-line units the following morning, Yahara realized that his "great retreat-and-attack dream was dead." The 62nd Division commanders, he believed, "did not really want to go into offensive action" and had deployed their troops "only to be ready for a retreat." He could hardly blame them. Most of their best troops were dead and the officers were "totally exhausted." All that could be asked of the 62nd Division, noted Yahara, "was to block the enemy from sneaking up behind us. That would help our entire force to retreat safely to the south."

Endorsed by Ushijima, Yahara made one other key decision on May 28: he agreed to General Suzuki's request to leave the bulk of the 44th Mixed Brigade's troops in their present positions until the night of May 31, when they would retreat "all at once to Kiyan Peninsula."[2] Meanwhile the Naval Base Force, which had wisely ignored army plans by retreating to Kiyan two days before, had on Rear Admiral Ōta's orders returned to the Oroku Peninsula, south of Naha, in a fateful move. Ōta had listened to his officers who, unconvinced by the defenses at Kiyan, lobbied for a return to Oroku "to fight and die at the place where we built positions and…in that one part of the island which really belonged to the navy."[3]

At midnight the following day, May 29, Ushijima, Chō, Yahara and the rest of the headquarters staff boarded trucks at Tsukazan for the night drive to Mabuni. En route they passed the 24th Reconnaissance Regiment, which had fought on the army's right flank, marching silent and "in good order." They had been, noted Yahara, "in a desperate position to attempt a retreat, but here they were and it was going as well as I had planned it."

At a bridge further on, heavy shelling had left the area "strewn with shell craters and soldiers' corpses." The stench was unbearable. But of more concern to Yahara and the others on the truck were the near misses from enemy shells, one of which demolished a nearby house. At one point on the road Yahara saw "a girl of 7 or 8 carrying baggage on her head," her tiny hands cupping her face and tears streaming down her cheeks. As the truck stopped beside her, he asked if her mother was dead, or merely lost, but his words "were lost in the noise of guns and her sobbing." He started to lift her into the truck, but the others said, "No, don't do it. She might find her parents nearby and, even if we get her to Mabuni, we can't care for her." They left her and drove on, passing more corpses, fleeing civilians and troops digging in.

At last they reached Mabuni where they found the village "completely intact." On top of the nearby Hill 69 was the entrance to their new army headquarters cave. "We climbed down the ladder of the central shaft to a level passageway," recalled Yahara. "After sixty or seventy meters, we turned right and were at the western cave opening. In some places it was difficult to squeeze past the rock formations of this natural cave. Low-hanging stalactites dropped water, and it was dangerous to walk without a helmet. It was an awful place."

Crammed into a muddy room at the north end of the shaft, the two generals and their staff officers were not happy. "What's the meaning of this?" Chō shouted at Adjutant Kutsuno. "You came here to prepare for our arrival, but nothing has been done."

Kutsuno looked mortified. "I'm sorry, sir," he replied. "We just couldn't get enough furniture and equipment."

At daybreak, Yahara went to see the hilltop view. "At the end of gentle slopes rising northward to Shuri" he could see the Yaeju-Dake and Yuza-Dake hill masses. They were at the northern extremity of the Kiyan Peninsula, an area barely five miles by two and a half, and were protected by steep escarpments that were "ideal for use as natural fortresses." It was the site of the Thirty-Second Army's "final showdown" and Yahara prayed to the "holy spirits of the hills and rivers who would witness the last battle." An American reconnaissance plane appeared briefly overhead, but there was no sign of warships in the sea to the south. Yahara paused to take in the serenity around him. "Because of our swift retreat," he noted, "and the enemy's slow advance, we briefly enjoyed this paradise, which would soon become a violent battlefield."[4]

Despite many indications that the Japanese Thirty-Second Army was carrying out a strategic withdrawal, Lieutenant General Buckner and his staff took some time to cotton on. On May 26, for example, reconnaissance planes reported the extensive movement of troops and civilians from the front lines to the southern tip of the island. The columns were targeted by strafing attacks and naval bombardment, and Buckner ordered both his corps to "initiate without delay strong and unrelenting pressure to ascertain probable intentions and keep him [the Japanese] off balance."

Yet this was precautionary, and on May 28 the Tenth Army intelligence chief, Colonel Louis B. Ely, told a staff meeting that it "now looks as though the Japanese thinks holding the line around north of Shuri is his best bet." At the same meeting, Buckner voiced his concern about a possible Japanese assault on the 7th Division at

Yonabaru. "What has [General] Arnold got in reserve against counter-attack?" he asked.

A day later, Buckner said at another staff meeting that it looked as though the Japanese were trying to withdraw to the south, but had made the decision too late. Only during the evening of the 30th, however, after discussions with his opposite numbers in the III Amphibious and XXIV Army Corps, did Ely conclude that the "enemy was holding the Shuri lines" with a light covering force, and that "the bulk of the troops were elsewhere." There were, he estimated, around 5,000 troops in what he hoped would be the Shuri Pocket; but he was unaware of the exact whereabouts of the bulk of the Japanese forces. At another staff meeting on May 31, Buckner insisted that General Ushijima had "made his decision to withdraw from Shuri two days late."[5]

This was, as we have seen, far from the case. The main movement of the remaining Thirty-Second Army combat units out of the inner Shuri defense zone had taken place in late May—with some setting off as early as May 26—and by early June a new defensive line had been established, unbeknown to Buckner, on the Yaeju-Dake and Yuza-Dake hill masses. The retreating Japanese suffered casualties from strafing attacks and naval bombardment, while some of their rearguard troops were eventually overwhelmed, but the movement itself was largely unmolested by ground forces because Buckner and his staff failed to acknowledge it was taking place until it was too late to intervene.

According to Brigadier General Oliver Smith, Buckner "chafed at the slow progress being made" by his troops during the period May 22–30 "when the southern front was engulfed in mud." He was, at this time, "under considerable pressure" to finish the campaign as quickly as possible "as the navy was sustaining heavy casualties by being forced to remain in the vicinity of Okinawa." Losing patience, he sent Smith to find out why the III Amphibious Corps was making such slow progress. The corps commander, Major General Geiger, was unimpressed. Okinawa, he told Smith, was his "first experience at being heckled" by a general who "was constantly calling him up on the telephone and urging more speed." If this continued, said Geiger, he would do "some frank talking to General Buckner." When Smith spoke to General Hodge, he found that he was "also being heckled" and that Buckner believed the XXIV Corps was "not trying."[6]

But Smith's mission was not until June 3. Buckner's diary entries and letters for late May, on the other hand, show little sign of any real urgency. On May 26, for example, he noted that rain "continued all day" and the 7th Division made "slight progress." That evening, while some of his combat troops wallowed in flooded foxholes surrounded by corpses, he had supper with the visiting General John DeWitt "in an embellished Okinawan house with three navy nurses and danced after supper to the accompaniment of Radio Tokyo and artillery fire."

The following day he found that the troops were "still bogged down in the mud with no advance, tanks unable to move and supply difficult" because of "six inches of rain in forty-eight hours." On May 28, the Japanese put up "stubborn resistance against all advances except on the extreme flanks where some progress was made."[7] He wrote to his wife that day:

> We continue to be deluged with rain . . . This came at an unfortunate time, since I had caught the Japs napping and shoved a division [the 7th] past their right flank. The mud slowed down the movement of our heavy weapons to such an extent that I was unable to take full advantage of the initial success, thus giving the enemy a chance to man previously constructed, but at the time, unoccupied defensive positions. However, the move has considerably extended the Jap line, thus weakening it for his depleted force. The Jap garrison appears to have considerably exceeded our initial estimate, but we have killed over 55,000 and we still have the privilege of exterminating a lot more.

Japanese air attacks were continuing with "great desperation," he added, forcing him to pause his letter-writing to go to his "foxhole" during one raid. But, he assured his wife, no damage had been done by the near miss of an anti-aircraft shell, "other than to blow up a lot of mud and cause a certain amount of merriment among those who watched the others trying to dodge it."[8]

On May 29, he finally noted significant progress in his diary, writing that the "Naha and Shuri fronts have apparently been deserted permitting the 6th and 1st Mardivs [Marine Divisions] to advance from 1,000 to 1,800 yds, giving most of Naha to the 6th and Shuri Castle* to the 1st with almost no opposition." He added: "It looks as though the envelopment by the 7th [Division] had forced a withdrawal but the Japs made the decision to withdraw after it was too late."

In fact, it was a combination of factors—but chiefly the erosion of key positions in front of Shuri—that prompted the Japanese withdrawal. That they were able to do so in an orderly manner, and with minimal interference, was because, as the official history put it, "the Americans had underestimated the scope of the enemy's tactical plan and the extent to which it had been executed."[9]

Buckner noted in his diary on May 31: "The entire enemy line appears to be crumbling." It was only now that he displayed some vigor by ordering Hodge's XXIV Corps to drive southeast to the coast to "prevent the enemy from retiring" to the Kiyan Peninsula. That day he also urged Geiger's III Amphibious Corps to "secure the port and airfield of Naha," and complained incessantly when there were delays (hence the dispatch of Oliver Smith to Geiger's CP). But it was too little, too late.[10]

The Japanese were already manning their new defenses, and would be joined by the surviving rearguard troops over the next couple of days. Their fighting strength before the retreat was estimated by Colonel Yahara at 40,000 men. Of these, 30,000 got back to the Kiyan Peninsula. They were: 24th Division—12,000; 62nd Division—7,000; 44th Mixed Brigade—3,000; 5th Artillery Group—3,000; Others, including Okinawan home guard—5,000. Yet Yahara knew all too well that mere troop numbers did not tell the whole story. The Thirty-Second Army's main strength—the 24th and 62nd Divisions, and 44th Mixed Brigade—"had lost eighty-five percent of its original complement" and was now made up chiefly of "untrained, rear-area soldiers and Okinawan defense conscripts." The Artillery Group had

* At 10:15 a.m. on May 29, the remnants of Shuri Castle were occupied by Captain Julian Dusenbury's Able Company of the 5th Marines. A native of South Carolina, Dusenbury is credited with hoisting the Confederate flag on the castle's shell-torn ramparts. "When we learned that the flag of the Confederacy had been hoisted over the very heart and soul of Japanese resistance," recalled PFC Eugene Sledge, "all of us Southerners cheered loudly. The Yankees among us grumbled." (Sledge, *With the Old Breed*, p. 300.)

lost half of its guns, while the infantry had only a fifth of its machine guns and one tenth of its heavy weapons. Just as serious was the total lack of cable and radio communications, and the loss of all construction equipment to improve the new defensive positions. The Thirty-Second Army had also lost touch with the Naval Base Force which, after its premature retreat, had returned to the Oroku Peninsula where its 2,000 remaining men would fight their own last stand.

But Yahara was undismayed. "Our defense policy," he wrote, "was to fight to the end with all our strength at the main defense fortifications of the Yaezu and Yoza hills. If the enemy launched landing operations on the southern beach, we would destroy them there."[11]

32

"It is terrifying to think about"

"Good morning, gentlemen," said Secretary of War Henry L. Stimson, "and welcome to the fourth meeting of the Interim Committee. The committee was appointed by me, with the approval of the president, to make recommendations on all matters to do with the Manhattan Project, including war-time controls, public announcements, legislation and post-war organization."[1]

It was just after 10:00 a.m. on Thursday, May 31, 1945, and the men were gathered round a long conference table in Stimson's suite, in the newly constructed Pentagon building in Arlington, Virginia, just across the Potomac from downtown Washington, DC. Beside Stimson, at the head, sat seven other members of the committee, including Vannevar Bush, James Conant, Karl Compton and Jimmy Byrnes. Also present were U.S. Army chief of staff General George Marshall, Manhattan Project director Major General Leslie Groves, and four physicists who had played a key role in the development of the atomic bomb: Robert Oppenheimer, scientific director of Los Alamos; Italian-born Ernico Fermi, who had created the first controlled nuclear chain reaction in 1942; Arthur Compton, who, with Fermi and others, had designed the first plutonium-producing reactor at Hanford, Washington; and Ernest Lawrence, the inventor of UC Berkeley's cyclotron who worked out how to enrich uranium. All the physicists bar Oppenheimer, were Nobel laureates.[2]

"First," continued Stimson, "I would like to give high praise to the brilliant and effective assistance rendered to the Manhattan Project by the scientists of this country, and particularly to the four present today whose great contributions to the work and willingness to advise on the many complex problems that the committee has had to face is much appreciated."

Stimson then gestured toward Marshall. "The U.S. Army chief of staff is here today because I share with him the responsibility for making recommendations to the president on this project with particular reference to its military aspects. It is, therefore, highly desirable that he hears at first hand the views of the scientists. But, make no mistake, we both agree that the project should not be considered simply in terms of military weapons, but as a new relationship of man to the universe. It might, in this sense, be fairly compared to some of the other great scientific discoveries of history, such as the Copernican theory and of the laws of gravity; and yet it is far more important than these in the effect it will have on the lives of men."

After a brief pause, Stimson continued: "I'm sure I don't need to remind any of you that the implications of the project go far beyond the needs of the present war. For that reason, it needs to be controlled effectively to make it an assurance of future peace rather than a menace to civilization."

With the introduction over, they discussed future stages of development, including the prospect of creating a bomb within three years with the explosive force of 10 million to 100 million tons of TNT, whereas the existing bomb had a force of *only* 2,000 to 20,000 tons. They also looked at the need to continue the domestic program after the war, building up a stockpile of bombs and bomb-making material; the possibility of sharing some information with the rest of the world; and the setting up of an international control body with the right of inspection. It was during the latter exchange of views that Dr. Bush assured the committee that democracies would always trump totalitarian states with regard to any future arms race because of their "system of teamwork and free interchange of information." The proof of this, he added, was information just in from Germany that revealed that Hitler's regime "was far behind us in the technology" of atomic weapons and other scientific fields.

After a short break for lunch, the committee reconvened at 2:15 p.m. to discuss the possibility of using the new atomic bomb against Japan. Though the effect of using a single bomb on a military arsenal would, said Robert Oppenheimer, not be "much different from the effect caused by any Air Corps strike of present dimensions," the visual effect would be "tremendous." A tall, thin man with a striking face—prominent cheekbones, thick black eyebrows and bright blue eyes—Oppenheimer was a mesmerizing presence. Such an explosion would, he said, "be accompanied by a brilliant luminescence which would rise to a height of 10,000 to 20,000 feet. The neutron effect of the explosion would be dangerous to life for a radius of at least two-thirds of a mile."

Then began a spirited debate on the use of warnings, the type of target they would go for, and its possible effect. Eventually Stimson summed up their common ground: "We should not give the Japanese any warning prior to dropping the bomb. We cannot concentrate on a civilian area. And we should seek to make a profound psychological impression on as many of the inhabitants as possible." Agreeing with Dr. Conant, Stimson said the "most desirable target would be a vital war plant employing a large number of workers and closely surrounded by workers' houses."

The only remaining question was whether to drop more than one bomb at the same time. Oppenheimer said it was possible. But General Groves poured cold water on the idea by pointing out three objections: they would "lose the advantage of gaining additional knowledge concerning the weapon at each successive bombing"; multiple drops would "require a rush job on the part of those assembling the bombs" which might, therefore, be "ineffective"; and the effect would "not be sufficiently distinct from our regular Air Force bombing program."[3]

The following day, having met with four leading industrialists involved in the project, the Interim Committee made the historic recommendation that the atomic bomb "should be used against Japan as soon as possible; that it be used on a war plant surrounded by workers' homes; and that it should be used without prior warning." It was, moreover, the committee's assumption that the "small bomb" would be used for the test explosion—scheduled for mid-July—and the "large bomb (gun mechanism)" kept for the "first strike over Japan."[4] To follow any other course, argued the committee, would be to put at risk the "major objective of obtaining a prompt surrender from the Japanese." This view was mirrored by a panel of distinguished atomic physicists—including Oppenheimer—who reported: "We can propose no technical demonstration likely to bring an end to the war; we see no acceptable alternative to direct military use."

Given that the committee's function was "entirely advisory," the ultimate responsibility for the recommendation to President Truman rested with Stimson as Secretary of War. The conclusions of the committee were "similar" to Stimson's own, though the latter had been arrived at "independently." In Stimson's opinion, the only way to "extract a genuine surrender from the [Japanese] emperor and his military advisers" was by administering "a tremendous shock which would carry convincing proof" of the United States' "power to destroy the empire." Such "an effective shock" would, he felt, "save many times the number of lives, both American and Japanese, that it would cost."[5]

In fact, it was Jimmy Byrnes who told President Truman about the Interim Committee's recommendations in an unscheduled meeting in the White House later that day. Truman was shocked. A short while later, Truman voiced his fears to his publicity adviser, Leonard Reinsch. "Leonard," he said, "I have just gotten some important information. I am going to have to make a decision which no man in history has ever had to make. I'll make the decision but it is terrifying to think about what I will have to decide."

He added, more than once: "I wish I could talk to you about it." Of course he could not.[6]

33

"There is NO tactical thinking or push"

At 1:15 p.m. on June 3, a Boeing B-17 "Flying Fortress" bomber touched down at Yontan airfield and out stepped General Joseph W. "Vinegar Joe" Stilwell. Officially he was conducting an inspection tour of troops in the Pacific in his capacity as commanding general, U.S. Army ground forces. But the real reason for the trip was to lobby Doug MacArthur for a command in the forthcoming invasion of Japan.

Born in Florida but raised in Yonkers, New York, the 62-year-old Stilwell was the eighth-generation descendant of an English colonist who had arrived in America in the early seventeenth century. Known to his family by his second name of Warren, he was a talented student and athlete who eventually rebelled against his strict religious upbringing by making friends with a group of gamblers and troublemakers. The response of his father, a medical doctor, was to insist he attended the U.S. Military Academy at West Point rather than Yale University as originally planned. He passed out thirty-second of 124 cadets in the class of 1904 (though first in French), played varsity football and captained the cross-country running team.

He served as a liaison officer to the French Army during the First World War, and later worked on the staff of the U.S. Army's IV Corps, helping to plan the successful Saint-Mihiel offensive and winning the Distinguished Service Medal. His soubriquet, "Vinegar Joe," was earned during his time as chief of tactics (under Assistant Commandant George C. Marshall) at the Infantry School at Fort Benning, Georgia, where he often gave harsh critiques of his students' performance in field exercises. It was also between the wars, during three tours of China, that he mastered spoken and written Chinese. He returned from a stint as military attaché at the U.S. Legation in

Peking in 1939 to become assistant commander of the 2nd Infantry Division, and, a year later, commander of the reactivated 7th Infantry Division.

Initially selected by his mentor General Marshall to plan and command the Allied invasion of North Africa (Operation Torch), he was diverted instead to China in 1942 when it became necessary to keep that country fighting the Japanese. He acted as chief of staff to Generalissimo Chiang Kai-shek, commander of U.S. forces in the China–Burma–India theater, and later as Lord Louis Mountbatten's deputy in the South East Asia Command. He generally had a low opinion of his British and Commonwealth allies, and was prejudiced against foreigners in general, referring to the French as "frogs," the Germans as "huns and squareheads," the Chinese as "chinks," and the Japanese as "ugly, moon-faced, buck-toothed, bow-legged bastards."

Having helped reform the Chinese Nationalist army, he fell out with Chiang in 1944 and was recalled to the United States. Meanwhile his replacement as commander in North Africa, the then Major General Dwight D. "Ike" Eisenhower, had become the Supreme Allied Commander in Europe and one of the architects of Hitler's downfall. Small wonder, then, that in June 1945 Stilwell was looking for one last hurrah as the commander of an American field army.[1]

Before leaving Washington, Stilwell saw General Marshall who "had nothing to offer, except that I could go & make my own arrangements." From this he concluded: "Doug [MacArthur] obviously out of control; WD [War Department] afraid of him. So I'll go out and look around." He did just that, meeting MacArthur in Manila on May 26 but extracting no promises from him about his future employment. Having inspected some of MacArthur's troops, Stilwell flew on to Okinawa. At Yontan, he cadged a lift in a commodore's jeep, and found the new network of roads "ambitious," but the muck "terrible." He arrived at Tenth Army headquarters "unannounced" at just after 3:00 p.m., and had a "long talk" with Buckner. Next morning he began his tour of the front-line troops.[2]

The situation on June 4 was still very fluid. A day earlier two of the 6th Marine Division regiments—the 4th and 29th Marines—had crossed the Asato estuary from Naha in amtracs and landed on the northern shore of the Oroku Peninsula which was defended by the remaining 2,000 men of Rear Admiral Ōta's Naval Base Force. Yet it would still take more than ten days for the Marines to subdue the "half-trained enemy force, poor in standard weapons, organization, and hope of eventual success, but possessed of abundant automatic fire power, a system of underground positions...and a willingness to die in those positions."[3]

While the 6th Marine Division cleared the Oroku Peninsula, the plan was for Geiger's other division, the 1st Marine, to keep pace with the two forward divisions of Hodge's XXIV Corps as they advanced south toward the new Japanese stronghold on the Kiyan Peninsula. At first it was unable to do so because its supply system had collapsed in the poor weather, forcing it to rely upon air drops and carrying parties to get food and ammunition to its front-line troops. This inevitably slowed its advance and, by the end of June 3, the gap between it and the neighboring 96th Division was 3,000 yards, thus exposing the 383rd Infantry to harassing fire from its right flank. To fill the void, the corps commander Hodge sent forward the 77th Division's 305th Infantry. But the 1st Marine Division—stung by Buckner's complaints—also made ground on June 4 when the 2/5th Marines attacked south-west and captured Hill 57 and the high ground south of Gisuchi. This reduced the gap to the XXIV Corps to 1,000 yards.

Further east the 7th Division, Stilwell's old command, had advanced the farthest on June 3 by reaching the southeast coast near Hyakuna at the base of the Chinen Peninsula. Buckner was delighted, telling a staff conference that it was a "magnificent achievement." He was particularly pleased to receive from General Arnold that day "a bottle of seawater and beach sand and a picture of two soldiers bathing their feet on the southern shore."[4]

Stilwell, of course, had responsibility only for U.S. Army troops and therefore confined his inspection on June 4 to XXIV Corps. He first visited Hodge at his command post in an old fort, and then headed toward the headquarters of the 7th Division, his old formation. Bogged by deep mud at a crossroads, he continued in an "M-5 tractor with two trailers of artillery ammunition," reaching General Arnold's command post in time for "chow." He then continued his tour of the forward troops in a variety of vehicles and craft—including a two-and-a-half-ton truck and an LVT landing craft—meeting a number of regimental and battalion commanders. "Recognized everywhere," noted Stilwell, "& got friendly greeting." Back at Arnold's CP by 9:00 p.m., he had a late dinner before turning in.

He saw a little more of the eastern coast the following day before returning to Yontan for a flight over the island. He wrote in his diary:

> 1:30 took off in a cub [light plane]. Down to Naha & across the island to Yonabaru. Looks like Verdun. Escarpment must have been tough. Caves, holes, & tombs everywhere. The poor Okinawans have had even their ancestors blown to pieces. Complete destruction in center of island. Naha harbor blocked by sunken ships. 6th Marine [Division] fighting on hill just S. of inlet. Went around the SE peninsula on sea side & came in at south port. 7th [Division] behind a smoke screen, apparently having a hard time.

Later, back at the Tenth Army headquarters, where news had just arrived of the battlefield death of Colonel Eddy May of the 383rd Infantry,* Stilwell found Buckner "tiresome." He wrote: "I tried to tell him what I had seen but he knew it all. Keeps repeating his wise-cracks. 'The Lord said, Let there be mud, & there was mud.' Etc., etc."

Just two days into his tour, Stilwell was distinctly unimpressed by the way Buckner was conducting the campaign. There were, he noted, an "estimated 15–20,000 Japs left, & two weeks to finish them. They are holing up in SW corner...Tactics—All frontal. 6th Marine landing S. of Naha only attempt to go by. No thought of repeating it. Buckner laughs at [Major General] Bruce for having crazy ideas. 'Two out of fifteen are OK. The rest are impossible.' It might be a good thing to listen to him."

Next morning, June 6, Stilwell ignored the warnings of Buckner's staff—"You probably can't reach the 96th or 77th," "May get stuck all night"—to visit the command posts of generals Bradley and Bruce. Undeterred by a "sea of mud two feet deep," he walked the last half a

* Colonel May, 48, from Cleveland, Ohio—the man Buckner had praised for his "beautiful piece of troop leading" in the capture of Conical Hill in mid-May—was shot and killed by machine-gun bullets in front of his CP. He was awarded a posthumous Distinguished Service Cross.

mile to the 96th Division's headquarters, and thought Bradley "looked well." During lunch, Bradley complained that the 1st Marine Division, which should have been protecting his right flank, was lagging behind. "They don't know how to keep their supply going," said Bradley. Stilwell had less trouble reaching the headquarters of the 77th Division, and had a long talk with General Bruce who was, he noted, the "only man I've met who remembers his tactics."

Back at Tenth Army headquarters that evening, Stilwell recorded his low opinion of Buckner and his staff, particularly his operations chief Brigadier General Dumas and intelligence chief Colonel Ely. He wrote in his diary:

> [Dumas] and the nut Ely put on a daily show at the GS [General Staff] conference, which is a kindergarten affair... This is merely an admin staff, with no influence on the operation. Buckner is obviously playing the navy. He rec[commended] Geiger as Army Comdr. Nimitz is perfect. His staff is perfectly balanced. Cooperation is magnificent. The Marine divs are wonderful. In fact, everything is just ducky...It is all rather nauseating. There is NO tactical thinking or push—No plan was ever discussed at the meetings to hasten the fight or help the divs. The 96th had the whole escarpment, & the 6th Mar. Div. is to be "pinched out."[5]

This last sentence referred to Buckner's recent decision to shift the XXIV Corps' axis of attack to the south-west, thus giving the 96th Division the responsibility for tackling both the Yaeju-Dake and Yuza-Dake hill masses. They were, noted the official history, "physical barriers which, together with Hill 95 on the east coast, formed a great wall across the entire XXIV Corps sector from Gusichan to Yuza." The highest point of the four-mile-long cliff was Yaeju-Dake, which rose 295 feet from the valley floor. Yuza-Dake "stood at the west end of the line and then tapered off into Kunishi Ridge, which extended across the III Amphibious Corps' sector."[6]

Buckner's decision was clearly one that Stilwell did not agree with, as it left the bulk of the heavy fighting to army troops, while the Marines had the lesser task, in his view, of capturing Oroku (6th Division) and assaulting the Kunishi Ridge (1st Division). With no operational authority, Stilwell was powerless to intervene. In public, he was fully supportive of Buckner, telling reporters at a morning press conference on June 7 that they had "under-publicized and failed to appreciate this campaign either in hardship overcome, ferocity of fighting or colorful events." But his diary entries confirm the contempt for Buckner's handling of the campaign that he was determined to share with MacArthur at their next meeting in Manila. He left Okinawa by plane at 11:15 a.m. on the 7th, with Buckner blissfully unaware that the older general wanted his job.

With Stilwell out of the way, Buckner took a flight of his own in a cub, following the front lines and reconnoitering the "plateau positions" defended by the Japanese. The enemy's new stronghold would be, he jotted in his diary, a "tough nut to crack," particularly the escarpment facing the army divisions approaching from the southeast. Yet he felt better about the Marines, noting that the 1st Division had broken through to the west coast below the Oroku Peninsula and had its "tails up again." He added: "Geiger also feels better. After riding both somewhat I gave them a little praise today."[7]

34

"I lost damn near all of them"

Corporal Jim Johnston's luck finally ran out in the late afternoon of June 3 as Easy Company, 2/5th Marines, led the attack on Hill 57, a prominent feature a mile south of the Thirty-Second Army's former headquarters at Tsukasan. Having made a wide flanking movement that, for a time, crossed the corps boundary, the company then advanced several hundred yards west until they came to Hill 57, "a rather prominent knob of land" directly to their front.

"We need a couple of strongpoints up there," said the commander of 1st Platoon to Johnston. "Do you think you can make it?"

"I think we can make it."

Taking two teams of machine-gunners, and some riflemen as an escort, Johnston began to climb the ridge, passing various cave openings en route. One looked "especially foreboding": a fairly large hole in the bank, from which you could "see to the back of the cave," and tunnels going right and left. As some Marines threw grenades into the cave opening, they could hear the Japanese soldiers inside "working themselves into a frenzy."

Suddenly a "black, acrid smoke started to roll thickly from the cave opening." Thinking it was about to blow, Johnston told his men to back away. But before they had gone a few yards, the earth shook and then erupted as a massive explosion blew off the side of the hill, taking many of Johnston's men with it. He was thrown forward onto his belly. With pieces of rock and earth raining down around him, he checked for injuries. "In my back," he recalled, "there was a tingling numbness but I seemed to be able to move all right in spite of it, so I started checking the men." Three had been killed, two on either side of him.

Johnston helped patch up the injured. One was blind, another had lost part of his arm, a third a leg from just below his knee, and a fourth soldier was paralyzed from the waist down. Several more had a variety of wounds. Once they had been treated by a corpsman, Johnston helped to get them back to company headquarters where the first sergeant asked him if he needed treatment as well.

"I do."

"What's wrong? Need a rest?"

"Hell, yes, I need a rest," said Johnston, resenting the inference, "but that's not why I'm turnin' in. I got hit in the side." As he was fully dressed and equipped, the sergeant had assumed he was just weary.

It was 3:00 a.m. by the time his men had all been treated in a rear-area aid station. The doctor turned to Johnston: "What's your problem?"

"I don't know, sir, but something is starting to hurt pretty bad in my back and side."

"Peel off your gear and I'll have a look."

Johnston was still holding his carbine, and wearing his pack, minus the shovel which had been lost in the explosion. He put the weapon down, took off his pack and cartridge belt, which had a hole in it, and undressed.

The doctor inspected his torso, and said, "Son, lie down on the stretcher on your belly and don't move until I tell you to."

As Johnston lay there, he thought of the "bunch of kids" and "old man" Wiley Brown in his section. For the last seven months he had done his best to take care of them. At times they had pissed him off, acting lazy or indifferent, but mostly he was "so very proud" of them. Desperate to teach them how to survive, he felt he had done a "pretty good job," mothering them "through some pretty tough spots without losing too many." Until, that is, they got to Hill 57, where he "lost damn near all of them." Feeling both helpless and futile, he "took a deep breath and fell sound asleep."

Taken by ambulance to an army field hospital, Johnston had an operation to remove shrapnel from his back and side. A day later, he wrote to his parents in Nebraska: "I am in hospital now but will be out soon. I got a very little wound—nothing to worry about. It is just a scratch on my side and back. I'll only be in hospital a couple of days, and then back to duty."[1]

* * *

That morning, June 5, Sergeant William Manchester of the 2/29th Marines was standing in the courtyard of an Okinawan tomb when he heard the "familiar shriek" of a shell. A day earlier his battalion had crossed into the Oroku Peninsula from Naha, and Manchester had sited his intelligence section in the tomb because it was on the reverse slope of a hill, and well protected from the enemy. The chances of a shell clearing the top of the hill and hitting the courtyard were, he calculated, a thousand to one. Even so, he moved instinctively toward the doorway of the tomb where he would have a little more protection than two of the remaining "Raggedy Asses," Izzy Levy and Rip Thorpe, who were cooking over "hot boxes" in the open.

Beating the odds, the eight-inch shell landed in the center of the courtyard, blasting Thorpe's body into tiny pieces. "It disintegrated," recalled Manchester, "and his flesh, blood, brains, and intestines encompassed me. Izzy was blind. So was I—temporarily, though I didn't know that until much later. There was a tremendous roaring inside my head, which was strange, because I was also deaf, both eardrums having been ruptured."

His more serious injuries included "chunks of shrapnel and Rip's bones" in his back and left side, and a severe concussion. Rising to his feet, he staggered out of the scene of horror, and collapsed. For four hours he was left for dead. Luckily a corpsman checked him and found he was "still hanging on." He gave him two shots of morphine and arranged for Manchester's evacuation to a landing ship that was serving as a "clearing house for casualties."

Three days earlier, as his battalion moved through the southern outskirts of Naha, close to the Kokuba estuary, Manchester had suffered a "superficial gunshot wound" to his right thigh. "Will I get a Purple Heart?" he asked a corpsman.

He nodded.

Manchester was elated. At last he had his "million-dollar wound, the dream of every infantryman." Moved back to a field hospital, he had the chance to sit out the rest of the campaign, enjoying clean sheets and hot chow. But when he heard his battalion was going to land behind Japanese lines on the Oroku Peninsula, he left his dry bunk, "jumped hospital, hitchhiked to the front, and made the landing on Monday." A day later, he was almost killed.

Why did he do it? He was, he admitted, gung-ho at the start of the war, but "quickly became a summer soldier and a sunshine patriot," indifferent to rank and seeking no glory. He "hadn't published a short story, fathered a child, or even slept with a girl." He wanted, therefore, to "stick around," so he became "the least intrepid of warriors, a survivor, not a hero, more terrier than lion." So why return to the front and almost certain death when he did not have to? "It was," he realized many years later, "an act of love. Those men on the line were my family, my home. They were closer to me than I can say, closer than any friends had been or ever would be. They had never let me down, and I couldn't do it to them. I had to be with them, rather than let them die and live with the knowledge that I might have saved them." Men, he understood, "do not fight for flag or country, for the Marine Corps or glory or any other abstraction. They fight for one another."[2]

Advancing fast at the extreme eastern end of the American line, with its flank on the coast, was Private "Slim" Carlton's 1/184th Infantry. "The enemy was retreating rapidly now," he recalled. "Our progress was measured in parts of a mile now instead of feet. 'Hey, we got the bastards on the run,' was a joyous remark heard often. Well it was far from being over. The Japs were just pulling back to another defense line where we would have to dig them out again."

Faced with destroyed bridges and difficult terrain, their main problem was getting supplies. This was partially solved by air drops. Late one afternoon, dug in on a ridge, Carlton and his machine-gunners heard the sound of aircraft. "Over the hills to our right," noted Carlton, "appeared six navy torpedo bombers... The first pass was a fly-by to get their bearings. On the second they came in low with their torpedo bays open. Out came a parachute that pulled the big bundles of supplies from the plane's bellies. A few got tangled and the bundles contacted the ground before the chutes opened fully. When this happened the bundles landed with tremendous force and bounced along the ground for many yards before coming to a stop."

On this occasion, however, the "complete drop" landed in no man's land. One or two "brave souls" went forward to retrieve some supplies, but were driven back by small-arms fire. "As it grew dark," remembered Carlton, "we could see our food and water supply a few yards away, but were forced to visualize it only. It was not the first time that we went hungry." By morning, every scrap had disappeared, taken by the Japanese who had "silently slipped to within a few yards" of Carlton's "not too alert" guards. A second drop the following day was more accurate, but some of the supplies were "thoroughly mangled" when the parachutes failed: "water cans burst open, food scattered all over the ground, and in one case the pointed ends of 250 rounds of machine-gun ammunition were driven through the side of the case making a nice sieve."

As patrols moved forward, Carlton's job was to provide covering fire with his machine gun, keeping up a "steady stream of bullets over their heads and toward the crest of the hill" in front. One morning, as a team probed the ground ahead, Carlton and his fellow machine-gunner opened up. "Our tracers," he recalled, "flew in a graceful arc well over the men's heads and into the jungle ahead of them. The patrol was hiking along the top of a ridge that had dense jungle on both sides. They had only traveled a couple of hundred yards when I saw a knee-mortar round erupt from the brush on the right side of the column. Instead of its normal flight, it was tumbling end over end. I yelled, 'Look out!' at the top of my lungs, but I was way too far away to be heard."

Carlton watched in horror as the mortar descended on the unsuspecting patrol. "Oh, my God!" he muttered. "It's going to land right in their midst!"

The shell came down on the officer leading the patrol, striking the top of his helmet and driving him to his knees. But it did not explode. "Luck?" wondered Carlton. "An angel looking out for him? That surely got the patrol's attention. They immediately began raking the jungle with their weapons." Years later, a member of the patrol told Carlton that "the officer prized his damaged helmet, and had earned the nickname of 'Dent.'"

A day or two later, Carlton was just below the crest of a small hill when he was ordered to take cover as Marine Corsairs were about to drop napalm on a Japanese position ahead. With no time to dig a proper foxhole, he frantically scraped a shallow depression and lay in it. The sound of planes caused a soldier on his right to scream: "Here they come! Hope the bastards know what they are doin'! They look awfully low!"

Looking up, Carlton saw the "long streamlined tank of jelly-gas" fall from the first plane. It seemed like it was coming straight for him and he froze, "expecting to be burned to death in the next few seconds." Yet by "some miracle" the projectile "swooshed" over him and the crest of the hill, and exploded beyond. "Dark red flames and black smoke erupted in the jungle below," wrote Carlton. "It must have been right on target judging from the screams that were heard...When we moved forward the next day we witnessed the carnage that the napalm had wrought. Bodies burned black and already beginning to bloat were strewn about, some still smoldering. The stench was overpowering."

Most of the troops picked up souvenirs as they went—including flags and Japanese weapons—while a few of the more callous, like Carlton's "good buddy" Frank, collected gold teeth from Japanese corpses. Frank kept his in a large pouch. One morning, Carlton was eating a tin of cold C-rations in his foxhole when Frank returned from checking a booby trap. "Any luck?" asked Carlton.

"Yeah, got two last night," replied Frank, before tucking into his own can of rations. Normally, his friend was "full of jokes," but this morning he seemed preoccupied.

"What's eating you, Frank? You don't seem normal today," said Carlton.

"One of them sons of bitches had a nice gold bridge. When I tried to pull it out of his mouth, it came loose and fell down his throat."

"Shit, Frank," responded Carlton in jest, "he's dead. Just reach down his throat and pull them out."

Taking the suggestion seriously, Frank put down his can and spoon, got up and left. A minute later he returned holding a "slimy bridge with four gold teeth" between his index and middle fingers. His face was wreathed in smiles. "I had to rip his jaw off to get them," he said, matter-of-factly, "but it was worth it."

Frank picked up his can and spoon, and resumed eating, but Carlton stopped. He had lost his appetite.[3]

As the fighting moved south, some rear-echelon troops took the opportunity to do a bit of sightseeing. They included Technical Sergeant Harold Moss, 22, from Minatare, Nebraska, who had just entered his freshman year of university when he was called up in September 1941. A veteran of Saipan and Tinian, his job on Okinawa was running the personnel office of HQ Battery, 225th Field Artillery Battalion, part of the XXIV Corps artillery.

A prolific writer, Moss penned more than 340 letters to his family during his four-year war service. The final batch was written on Okinawa, and one sent in June includes a graphic description of the devastation wrought on the island's two main towns. "On my travels today," he wrote,

> I saw Shuri and Noha including Shuri Castle or what is left of it. You know the struggle it has been to take those places. I couldn't describe to you the desolation and wreckage. Hardly a structure stands and everywhere there is rubble of stone and wood. Only a long two-story brick building remains of what was a city of 65,000—Noha. Bulldozers nudge around through the debris clearing roads and cleaning up, and preparing areas to live in.
>
> Shuri is equally wrecked. [It] sits in a valley surrounded by hills and ridges that shelter catacombs of interlocking caves and emplacements. Every ridge is specked with these holes. From a high view the fields are pitted with circular shell holes and occasionally a huge crater of a bomb or a large naval shell. And I saw our burned out tanks, many of them, stopped in a low place where the Japs probably used their suicide tactics of planting satchels on the tanks and blowing themselves up. Shuri Castle has a few remaining pillars still standing. They immediately remind one of the Greek ruins.

He added that the last Japanese troops had been "pushed into a very small pocket" where they would probably "repeat their banzai charge and the remainder dive into the sea as they did on Saipan."* They had, he wrote, beliefs about the value of life that were "entirely alien" to those that Americans held dear. To illustrate the point, he said that

* In July 1944, toward the end of the Saipan battle, more than 1,000 civilians responded to an order by Emperor Hirohito to commit suicide by jumping from cliffs to their deaths. Around the same time, the surviving garrison of 4,000 men, including many wounded, charged forward in a final attack. They surged across the American lines, killing and wounding more than 650 men of the 1/105th and 2/105th Infantry (part of the 27th Division) before they were shot down. It was the largest banzai attack of the war.

he had seen four "freshly killed" Japanese soldiers in a cave, and one had "apparently held a grenade to his chest at the last minute for his chest was blown open and his face gone." It made him reflect on how, in peacetime, the U.S. authorities "will spend thousands of dollars to find the murderer of one man but here a life seems worth little."

Referring to matters closer to home, he agreed with his parents that his sister Nancy should go to the same university as him, and have "every advantage of graduating." He regretted not taking his own studies seriously, and hated to think that he would "never get a degree."

As he wrapped up his letter, Moss admitted that, at times on the island, he felt as "nervous as hell."[4]

35

"You're just going to have to hang on"

On June 5, the day before Easy Company went back into the line, Lieutenant Bruce Watkins wrote to his wife June for the first time in a month. "A bunch of her letters had come in," he recalled, "and I read them over and over. I gave my letter considerable thought as I knew the odds on my survival had been running down, and I wanted desperately to say the right thing. This could well be my final letter. I had no premonitions, I just knew the sands were running low in the glass."

Even with replacements, Easy numbered barely a hundred men, well down from its pre-campaign strength of 235. But with better weather, and only the odd sniper to contend with, Watkins' men made good progress as they spearheaded the 2/1st Marines drive south toward Kunishi Ridge. One night they heard activity to their front and sent up flares that revealed Japanese civilians. Fortunately Easy's fire discipline was good and nobody was shot. "There were maybe thirty of them," wrote Watkins, "and they jabbered to us, obviously trying to get a point across. One of them was visibly pregnant and the others kept pointing at her until we got the message. She was about to give birth." So Watkins got some of his men to rig a pup tent and she crawled inside.

"Doc," said Watkins to his corpsman, "you've gotta help this lady."

The medic was far from keen, and vehemently protested his "lack of obstetrical experience." Luckily some of the other women helped out, and the new mother soon emerged from the tent carrying her newborn. "With much smiling and bobbing of heads," recalled Watkins, "they thanked us and continued on to our rear. It was a special moment and I know there was no Marine so tough that he wasn't moved by this event."

Almost in sight of Kunishi Ridge, they killed twenty or thirty Japanese soldiers after a "sharp, short fight" on a plateau divided by a railway embankment. Watkins moved his two forward platoons up to the high ground ahead, and kept the other in reserve near the embankment. Since landing two and a half months earlier, Watkins' one chance to wash properly was a swim near Kadena airfield. "We were," he admitted, "a raunchy lot. We must have been so used to unwashed odors that they went unnoticed. Besides, the odor of death was always with us, overpowering everything else. The days were now hot and sticky, speeding the decay of the thirty or more dead Japanese lying about."[1]

By June 10, the two forward regiments of the 1st Marine Division—the 1st on the left and the 7th on the right—were barely 1,500 yards north of Kunishi Ridge and subject to observation and harassing fire from Yuza-Dake peak to the east. That day, the 1/1st Marines lost 125 men killed and wounded in an assault on a small hill west of Yuza town. The 7th Marines had far fewer casualties as it reached high ground near the town of Tera on the 10th, while the 2/1st Marines took Hill 69, west of Ozato, a day later.

The problem, now, was the nature of the ground. Only 1,000 yards separated the 1st Marine Division's front line between Tera and Ozato from Kunishi Ridge. But the intervening terrain was generally low and flat, offering an attacker little cover as he advanced. The 7th Marines were the first to move forward on June 11, but heavy Japanese machine-gun fire promptly drove back the two assault battalions. That night they tried again, with Charlie and Fox Companies leading off. Both reached the western edge of Kunishi Ridge with little difficulty. But as dawn broke on June 12, their foothold was targeted by a storm of mortar, shell and machine-gun fire. Colonel Edward W. Snedeker, the regimental commander, tried to reinforce the men with two tanks, but one was knocked out and the other driven back. When two support companies tried to cross the open ground under the cover of smoke shells, they were also forced to retire with heavy casualties.

It was then that Private Bill Niader of the 7th Marines' Headquarters and Service Company volunteered with three others to brave the enemy fire to bring in a man who had been shot in both legs and was lying in the open. Born in Pennsylvania and brought up in Clifton, New Jersey, Niader had left his job at the Trowridge Conveyor Company to join the Marines only six months earlier. On Okinawa he wrote a number of letters to his parents, the last on May 28, the day after his nineteenth birthday:

> Just a few lines to let you know that I'm fine & am in the best of health & hope that you are all the same...We should have this island secured in about a week & a half or two...I could get all kinds of souvenirs yesterday—Jap helmets, rifles, bayonets, gas masks, uniforms, money, caps, shells, penknives, & many other things. I have some of them—but don't have any place to put it because I only have the pack that I live out of...
>
> Guess people back there are celebrating VE Day over Germany. That's good news, but my war's over here. The German isn't half as smart as the Japs or tricky or as strong. They're in solid strong caves over forty feet in the ground, and we have to dig them out. People back there celebrating and & we out here in a foxhole half full of water & mud. I got flooded out of my foxhole the other night. Another ten minutes & I'd drown, but I got up. They get you so mad that you don't care what happens. But I'm making out OK. I only have to keep my head down & my ears & eyes open. But tell Dad not to worry because I'm OK. It will be over in a short time.[2]

A couple of days before the attack on Kunishi Ridge, Niader was sharing a foxhole with his buddy Private Harry Switzer. "One of us was sleeping," recalled Switzer, "and the other one was awake to see that the Japanese did not infiltrate during the night. About midnight, I woke up and Bill and the fellows in the foxhole next to ours were involved in gunfire. Eight Japanese soldiers had come up and if they weren't stopped, they would have given us a bad time." When dawn broke, there were seven bodies within twenty-five feet of the two foxholes. Niader had fired first and killed at least two.

Switzer was also part of the rescue mission on the 12th with Niader and two others. Loading the casualty onto a stretcher, they got back "OK and breathed a sigh of relief." Just then, wrote Switzer, a "well-placed mortar shell landed and Bill and I were both hit. The impact knocked Niader unconscious and he never came to. Five minutes after being wounded, he was in an aid station, and the doctor was doing all he could for him." But it was not enough and Niader died without regaining consciousness. Unable to take off his Marine ring, they cut through the metal and sent it home with his personal effects.[3]

After Niader's death, more tanks were used to ferry plasma, water and ammunition to the men on Kunishi Ridge. They also took reinforcements—six to a tank, fifty-four in total—and brought back twenty-two casualties. The same method of transporting supplies and men was used throughout the fighting for the ridge. That night, two more companies moved up in support, including Second Lieutenant "Jep" Carrell's King Company. "We darkened our faces," he remembered, "and moved down the forward slope of Tera sometime after darkness...We were instructed to hold our fire, keep voices to a whisper, and watch where we put our feet. We glided out of the rubble of our ridge into the flats. The moon was bright, and we could see with some clarity for a hundred yards or more. This meant, of course, that if the Japanese happened to look our way, they would have no difficulty in seeing *us*."

Fortunately they did not and, after crossing a bridge, the two companies made it to a point near the top of the ridge where they were told to dig in. At daylight—by which time there were elements of six companies occupying the lower end of Kunishi Ridge—the firing began. "The Marines ahead of us were pinned down," wrote Carrell, "and we got many of the bullets fired at them. There were a number of casualties. About noon, tanks came up and did some good work, taking some of the pressure off. We expanded our toehold a little, then a little more. By this time, all of us were engaged."[4] The 7th Marines lost 140 men on June 13: the seriously wounded were returned in tanks, men with light wounds stayed where they were, and the dead were collected near the base of the ridge.[5]

Most of the 7th Marines' incoming fire was from the front and left flank. To relieve the pressure, therefore, the 2/1st Marines were ordered to seize the higher, eastern end of Kunishi Ridge. Lieutenant Bruce Watkins' Easy Company was "well dug in" and hoping for a "quiet night" when Lieutenant Colonel Magee radioed at 9:00 p.m. on June 13 with new orders. Easy and George Companies would attack the ridge at 3:00 a.m., with Watkins in overall command. "For some reason," noted Watkins, "I asked Col. Magee how come I got elected. He said, 'Colonel [Russell E.] Honsowetz [the divisional chief of operations] specifically asked for you.' I had two thoughts about this. One was that Col. Honsowetz was still unhappy about his order that I had refused to carry out on Peleliu.* The other more optimistic thought was that he really thought I was the best man for the job."

They moved out in single file with Easy Company's 3rd Platoon in the lead, followed by 1st Platoon, Watkins and his headquarters staff, 2nd Platoon and then George Company. At roughly half strength, they numbered about 240 men. Despite an order to the contrary, naval flares were constantly bursting overhead, forcing Watkins and his men to freeze in their tracks, and slowing their progress. They had barely reached the foot of the ridge when dawn broke and the Japanese opened fire. One of the first fatalities was a replacement officer, Second Lieutenant White, who had taken over the 3rd Platoon only the previous day. "He lasted," wrote Watkins, "about five minutes in combat."

Despite a number of casualties, all three platoons got to the top of the ridge where they were supported on their left by a single platoon from George Company. Watkins stayed at the base of the ridge and set up his company CP behind a four-foot drop-off. The hundred feet that separated him from his men "soon became a no man's land. Even to stick your head up over the drop was to invite immediate fire." His bigger problem, however, was that there was a sizable gap to the 7th Marines lodgement away to his right, leaving the Japanese defenders "in front and on both flanks in protected positions where they could shoot at almost anyone in our perimeter." Casualties "mounted alarmingly," and were "carried down in ponchos like sacks of meal" and left behind the shelter of the drop-off.

Watkins called for tanks and tried to evacuate the wounded on their hulls. But they were picked off by snipers "in the long grass to

* Then commanding the 2/1st Marines, Honsowetz had ordered Watkins to take his platoon "back up the hill from which we had been blasted." It was, wrote Watkins, "an emotional moment for me and the only time I ever refused to carry out an order. I told him that I would not order my men up there again until the gun that blew us off was silenced. However, I would personally go up with him if he felt that was a solution. He gave me a long look and then turned away." (Watkins, "Brothers in Battle," p. 27.)

our flanks and rear," so he loaded them instead through the escape hatch. "This was a rough way to handle badly wounded men," recorded Watkins, "as the tank had to straddle them and then they were pulled through a small hole about eighteen inches square. However it was the only way." It helped, too, that the Japanese had no more anti-tank guns.

At noon, Watkins tried to check on his platoons. Ducking and dodging the small-arms fire, he got as far as the 1st Platoon where he agreed with Second Lieutenant LeFond that "any further movement in daylight was impossible." He returned to his CP, aware that casualties were about thirty percent and the situation was "desperate."

Shortly before dark, he radioed Lieutenant Colonel Magee, asking for more troops to extend the line. "Without a longer front," said Watkins, "we'll continue to receive fire from both flanks and rear."

"Negative," replied Magee, "there's no help available."

"Sir, if we pull back we'll at least save a few lives."

"I'm sorry, Watts. You're just going to have to hang on. We'll send you an air drop."

"We don't need an air drop, sir, we need more men."

The air supply of ammunition and water came anyway—but two-thirds of it landed on the Japanese side of the ridge. Watkins recalled: "I was a little bitter at this point. Our situation had all the elements of Custer's Last Stand. Facing up to the situation, I went forward at dark and tried to encourage the men as best I could. No one was joking, but they were all disciplined fighters and there was a bulldog attitude about them." Watkins tried to encourage his platoon commanders by saying reinforcements might arrive the following day. In fact Fox Company did come forward in the night, but Watkins chose to "spread them out as a secondary line in the flat behind us." Then, if the Japanese broke through, they could fall back on this line. He consoled himself with the thought that the situation would have been far worse if the Japanese had been able to bring their 90 mm mortars and artillery to bear. "As it was," noted Watkins, "knee mortars and hand grenades fell among us throughout the night."

The darkness was "lit with flares and sporadic gunfire," and at one point an attack on George Company pushed it back several hundred yards. By dawn the defensive position had contracted into a "semicircle bowed toward the front with a diameter of about 150 feet."

Meanwhile the Japanese had moved into better firing positions, and many of Watkins' men were "shot in their foxholes half asleep before they could find better cover." But still the remnants of three platoons "hung doggedly to their position, unable to move either forward or back." Two men brought back everyone's canteens in a poncho to refill them from the tank's supply. But it was very hot and thirst was a constant problem. The men ate very little, living on "canned lunch crackers and water."

Watkins felt lethargic and sluggish of mind. He knew they had to hang on and, if necessary, would do so to the last man. Late that afternoon, June 15, he tried to make "one more check of the lines if only for the men's morale." But a long burst of machine-gun fire—ricocheting off a rock face in front of him with frightening velocity—sent him scurrying for cover. Surprised not to be hit, he "didn't have the courage to go over that rock again."

Salvation came in the form of a radio message from Magee that they would be relieved by the 2/5th Marines that night. "I passed the word down the line," remembered Watkins. "About midnight they did arrive and I met my counterpart in the 5th Marines, Lt Dick Strugerik. He was a classmate of mine in the Reserve Officers Class and a welcome sight. We went up and down the line checking each foxhole and replacing my men. I emphasized to Dick that he should try to extend the line if he had enough men and, if not, to demand them. He was killed the next morning."

By then, Watkins and the remnants of his command had recrossed the open ground to safety. The last man out, he found Colonel Magee waiting for him. "Watts," he said, "I never expected to see you alive again."

Taken by trucks a mile to the rear, Watkins did a head count: Easy Company had just three officers and fifty-two men. They had landed, he noted, "with 235 men and, with replacements, had carried about 450 men on our roster. Of this remnant, perhaps half had been wounded and returned to action." Which meant that the casualty rate for the campaign was about 185 percent of the original roster, with only twenty-five men or so—Watkins included—coming through unscathed. He was proud that they had won a foothold "on the last Japanese defense line, but it had been at a terrible cost."[6]

36

"We were so gullible, so innocent"

"Will drop offer of surrender to Japs tomorrow," noted Lieutenant General Buckner in his diary on June 9, "with little hope of results but largely at the behest of psychological 'experts.'"[1]

The letter was duly dropped behind enemy lines on the 10th. Addressed to General Ushijima, it stated in Japanese:

> The forces under your command have fought bravely and well, and your infantry tactics have merited the respect of your opponents...Like myself, you are an infantry general long schooled and practiced in infantry warfare...I believe, therefore, that you understand as clearly as I, that the destruction of all Japanese resistance on the island is merely a matter of days.

Buckner then invited Ushijima to enter into negotiations for surrender. There was no response. Two days later, planes scattered 30,000 leaflets emphasizing Ushijima's selfish determination to sacrifice his entire army, and calling upon his officers and men to quit of their own accord. A similar appeal was made on the 14th. They fell mostly on deaf ears, though there was a noticeable increase in surrenders after June 12 as the hopelessness of the Japanese position became evident.

As it happened, Ushijima did not receive Buckner's letter until June 17. He and Chō found it very entertaining, and completely at odds with their duty as samurai to fight to the finish and then take their own lives.[2] "The enemy," commented Ushijima with a smile, "has made me an expert on infantry warfare."[3]

For the previous fortnight or so, one piece of bad news after another had reached the Thirty-Second Army headquarters cave at

Mabuni. On June 5, for example, Ushijima received a radio message from Rear Admiral Ōta whose Naval Base Force was engaged with the 6th Marine Division on the Oroku Peninsula. "Under your command," said Ōta,

> our naval forces fought bravely to the last man at Shuri, as you are well aware. They aided your successful retreat from Shuri to Kiyan Peninsula. I have discharged my duties, and have nothing to regret. I will command my remaining units to defend Oroku Peninsula as brave warriors unto death. My deepest gratitude, Excellency, for all you have done for us. May our fortunes in war last forever.
>
> Though I die on the desolate battlefield of Okinawa, I will continue to protect the great spirit of Japan.

Colonel Yahara, for one, was bitterly disappointed. He had hoped to deploy Ōta's men in the Kiyan Peninsula, and "could not bear to think of the navy being crushed in isolation, while we stood by as mere spectators." Feeling the same, Ushijima made a final appeal. "I must express my heartfelt gratitude, Admiral Ōta," he replied,

> for the honorable performance of your duty. The naval forces under your command and my army troops have fought together audaciously and contributed greatly to the Okinawan campaign. We truly admire the completion of your naval mission and your fight to the death to defend Oroku Peninsula. I cannot bear, however, to see your forces perish alone. It is still possible for you to withdraw. I hope that our forces may be joined so that we may share the moment of death.

Ōta, however, was determined to remain at Oroku. Late on June 6, moved by the plight of the Okinawan civilians, he made an extraordinary plea to the Naval Ministry in Tokyo:

> Since the attack began, our army and navy has been fighting defensive battles and have not been able to attend to the people of this prefecture. Consequently, due to our negligence, these innocent people have lost their homes and property to enemy

> assault. Every man has been conscripted to take part in the defense, while women, children and elders are forced into hiding in the small underground shelters which are not tactically important or are exposed to shelling raids and the harsh elements of nature. Moreover, girls have devoted themselves to nursing and cooking for the soldiers and some have gone so far as to volunteer in carrying ammunition or join in attacking the enemy...
>
> Now we are nearing the end of this battle but they will go unrecognized, unrewarded. Seeing this, I am deeply depressed and am at a loss of words for them. Every tree, every plant life is gone...By the end of June, there will be no food. This is how the Okinawan people have fought the war and for this reason, I ask you to give the Okinawan people special consideration, this day forward.[4]

It was a plea that would fall on deaf ears.

Ōta's troops, meanwhile, were fighting "remarkably well at Kanegusuki, Tomigusuki, and in the Oroku hills." Yet by June 11, with the remnant surrounded by three Marine regiments in a pocket barely 1,000 yards square, the end was near. Late that evening, Ōta sent a final message to Ushijima. "The enemy has begun an all-out assault on our headquarters. This is our last chance to contact you. 2330 [hours], June 11."[5]

Trapped on flat ground near the Naha Inlet, the last of Ōta's men were killed or committed suicide on June 13, though 159 did surrender, the first large group to do so. They included a lieutenant commander and his wife, both wounded. Ōta's body and those of four members of his staff were found "still warm" in a room in his underground headquarters, an elaborate 450-meter-long tunnel complex near Tomigusuki at the northern base of the peninsula. They had committed *seppuku*—ritual suicide by disembowelment—before being shot. A further 200 bodies were scattered throughout the tunnels which were "well ventilated, equipped with electricity, and reinforced with concrete doorways and walls." Private Thomas McKinney, 18, of the 2/4th Marines recalled:

> The stink was getting real bad, and we turned the corner and looked down this one tunnel [and] there was nothing but dead Japanese sailors and soldiers stacked along both walls... We went just a little further, and here is this room. It was carved out of coral and here laid [on] a big platform, tatami mats on it... [were] five officers. The one in the center... was a rear admiral. The two on each side were navy captains. They were in full uniform, except they didn't have any shoes on... Each of them had a ceremonial hara-kiri knife an inch or so below the belt buckle. The blade was buried all the way into their abdomens. Each one of them had been shot in the temple.[6]

The ten-day battle for the Oroku Peninsula had cost the 6th Marine Division an astonishing 1,608 casualties and thirty tanks, a higher rate than they had lost at the Shuri Line where they were opposed by Ushijima's infantry.[7]

Less successful, however, was the defense of the right—or eastern sector—of the new Japanese line at Kiyan by the exhausted remnants of General Suzuki's 44th Mixed Brigade. On June 9, the 3/17th Infantry secured a lodgement on the southern end of Yaeju-Dake escarpment, just north of the town of Asato. That day, the 1/32nd Infantry attacked Hill 95, the eastern anchor of Ushijima's defenses, and finally took it on the 11th. Yahara had sent reinforcements from the 62nd Division to counter-attack, but they could not recover the lost ground. Their task was made much harder by the fact that, thanks to better weather and firmer ground, the Americans could deploy more armor. "Flame tanks became the American solution to the Japanese coral caves," noted the official history. "Interference from enemy shells became less with the destruction of each Japanese gun; and, more important, through experience the infantrymen and tankers developed a teamwork that neared perfection. The battle for the southern tip of Okinawa blazed with orange rods of flame and became a thunderous roar of machine guns, shells, rockets, and bombs."[8]

Further inroads were made by the U.S. 7th Division during the night of June 11–12 when the 17th Infantry expanded its foothold on Yaeju-Dake, including the capture of the peak itself. Meanwhile the 381st Infantry (of the 96th Division) had reached the saddle between the Yaeju-Dake and Yuza-Dake peaks, and on June 12 it linked up with the 17th Infantry on the escarpment itself. Ushijima tried to respond by ordering the annihilation of all enemy units on Yaeju-Dake, the Main Line of Resistance. But it was wishful thinking and the counter-attacks were beaten off.[9]

On June 15, Colonel Yahara received an unexpected visit from Major Kyoso, the 44th Mixed Brigade's chief of staff. Formerly so healthy and vigorous, Yahara was shocked at how "completely drained" his friend looked, with "lines of sorrow and suffering" evident on his dirt-streaked face. He told Yahara: "The brigade is finished. Our right flank has collapsed. We can fight no more. I regret to report that unit commanders are crying aloud as they watch their men die in vain. Whatever we do we cannot stop the enemy. Imperial Headquarters never gave us adequate support. Our commanding officers are asking if Japan will follow the fate of Okinawa. Why? Is there no alternative?"

Yahara knew what Kyoso was trying to say: that it was pointless dying for nothing. But the decision had been made. They ate tinned pineapple and drank sake before the helmet-less Kyoso "disappeared in the pre-dawn darkness."

It was around this time that a last message reached army headquarters from the 44th Brigade commander, Major General Suzuki. He wrote:

> Flowers dying gracefully on Hill 109,
> Will bloom again amid the Kudan trees.*

To try to shore up his crumbling defenses, Ushijima gave Lieutenant General Fujioka of the 62nd Division responsibility for the eastern sector. But he could do nothing to retrieve a situation that was hopeless.[10]

"I'll be back when it rains," Flight Lieutenant Haruo Araki had said to his wife Shigeko as they parted at Kōzu railway station, Honshu Island, on April 10.

* The Kudan ambassadorial residence is close to where the Yasukuni shrine—the spiritual resting place for Japanese warriors—is located in Tokyo.

On every day that it had rained since, Shigeko had said to her parents: "He'll be back today."

They would leave the door open, so that he could come in at any hour, and would often wait for the last train. But he had not returned. Meanwhile, suffering from nausea, Shigeko went to see the family doctor. "Do you have anything to tell me?" he asked.

"No."

"Are you married?"

"Yes."

"Well, it seems you may be carrying a child."

Shigeko was stunned. They had slept together only once, but it was enough. "From that moment on," she recalled, "I wanted to see him and tell him. We searched and searched, but we had no clue."

Finally, in mid-June, they were visited by a well-known author and journalist. "At Chiran," he said solemnly, "I was entrusted with the last will and testament of Haruo Araki together with some clippings of his hair and nails. He was killed in action on May 11."

Shigeko broke down sobbing. Her unborn baby was now her sole reason to live. It was the same for her parents. Later, having read Haruo's last brief letter to her, she was grateful that it was addressed simply to "Shigeko," his wife, and not to "Dear Miss Shigeko" as he usually wrote. In the note he asked her to forgive him for being "cruel" and "cold-hearted." Why, she wondered, "did a man who was going to die have to beg my pardon? I was the one who wanted to be forgiven."

The most heartbreaking thing for her was that there was "no way to respond to his plea." She could only pray, and "feel sympathy and misery."

As for his sacrifice, she wanted to believe that it had not been in vain, and that he had sunk an American ship. "Otherwise," she wrote later, "he still lies at the bottom of the cold Okinawan sea for nothing."

Family friends, when they heard of Haruo's death, would say: "That's good; congratulations."

"Yes, it is," Shigeko replied, putting on a brave face. Back home, she would burst into tears.[11]

* * *

The nightmare of the long retreat to the Kiyan Peninsula had ended for young Kikuko Miyagi and her fellow student nurses on June 10 when they finally reached Ihara. But conditions in the new hospital caves were so cramped and unsanitary that it was little consolation. "If you put your hand into your hair," she remembered, "it was full of lice. Our bodies were thick with fleas. Before we had been covered in mud, now we were covered with filth. Our nails grew longer and longer. Our faces were black. We were emaciated and itched all the time."

Most meals consisted of "moldy, unpolished raw rice" which they would boil outside the cave in a mess tin. But it was always risky to leave the cave because of bombing from the air. On one occasion, Kikuko returned to the smell of blood. She could hear her classmates crying: "I don't have a leg!," "My hand's gone!"

Descending into a "sea of blood," she saw that a number of nurses, students and soldiers had been wounded and killed by an explosion. A friend of hers, Katsuko-san, was injured in the thigh, and crying, "It hurts!"

Another senior student, desperately trying to push her intestines back into her stomach, whispered: "I won't make it, so please take care of other people first."

Meanwhile weeping teachers were cutting locks of hair from their dead students and putting them in their pockets. At a loss what to do, they kept saying, "Do your best! Don't die. You absolutely mustn't die."

They had believed the Japanese soldiers when they told them: "Victorious battle!," "Our army is always superior!"

Now they knew the truth. "We were so gullible," said Kikuko, "so innocent."

37

"We are down to the final kill"

"I spent the day at the front," wrote Lieutenant General Buckner to his wife Adele on June 14,

> looking over the enemy position which showed signs of weakening. But for the rain when we broke the Shuri position which bogged down our heavy weapons in the pursuit, the Japs would never have reached their present stronghold on a plateau almost surrounded by cliffs. However, we pressed today's attack from a quarter that seemed to surprise the enemy and got two battalions and some tanks on top of the [Yaeju-Dake] plateau. If we can hold on tonight we can probably break this position tomorrow or next day and the Japs will be forced to a final ridge at the southern tip of the island and soon destroyed.[1]

Buckner's impatience to end the campaign had been heightened by recent adverse reports in the American press: first a dispatch in the *New York Herald Tribune* by experienced war correspondent Homer Bigart that criticized his rejection of a second landing and described his tactics as "ultra-conservative"; then two even harsher pieces by syndicated columnist David Lawrence that highlighted Buckner's inexperience and incompetence, insisting an amphibious assault would have saved American lives.[2] In response, Buckner assured his wife: "We have had splendid relations here between the Army, Navy and Marine components of my command, in spite of unpatriotic attempts on the part of certain publicity agents at home who are trying to stir up a controversy." He had, he told her, seen an article by Lawrence saying that he had "made a monumental fiasco of the whole campaign by not doing it the 'Marine way.'" Yet in the same mail was a letter from the Army–Navy Staff College "saying that their studies of the campaign indicated that it had been handled beautifully. Take your choice."[3]

The following day, June 15, Buckner held a press conference at army headquarters to defend his generalship. The purpose of taking the island, he told the correspondents, was to use its airfields to bomb mainland Japan and build up a base for the forthcoming invasion. This mission and the geography of southern Okinawa made a second landing inadvisable. Reefs would have caused problems for an amphibious landing and the hilly terrain made it easy to contain forces on the beach. "If we'd scattered our forces we might have got licked," he said, "or it might have unduly prolonged the campaign, or we might have been forced to call on additional troops, which we did not want to do." Any more troops on the island would have slowed down construction of the airfields. "We didn't need to rush forward," he explained, "because we had secured enough airfields to execute our development mission."

None of these arguments is convincing, and it is odd that Buckner chose not to mention the chief reason his staff had ruled out a second landing: the difficulty of resupply. He did, however, receive support from Admiral Nimitz who released a statement describing Lawrence's article as "badly misinformed" and unpatriotic. "Comparisons between services," noted Nimitz, "are out of place and ill-advised." Yet, in private, many in the U.S. Navy and Marine Corps—and even some U.S. Army men like General Bruce—acknowledged it was a mistake not to have attempted a second landing. Homer Bigart agreed. It was, he wrote, "absurd" to call the campaign a "fiasco," as Lawrence had done—Bigart had covered the Anzio and Cassino campaigns in Italy, and knew what a fiasco looked like—yet he still believed "that a landing on the south coast of Okinawa would have been a better employment of the Marines."[4]

Buckner, meanwhile, told a Tenth Army staff meeting on June 15: "We have passed the speculative phase of the campaign and are down to the final kill."[5] He was now making daily visits to battalion outposts at the front to urge his troops to finish the job. "I have just made a careful personal reconaisance [*sic*] of the enemy's present position," he wrote to his 18-year-old son Claiborne, who was a cadet at West Point, on June 16. "It is a strong one surrounded by coral rock cliffs on most of the front and heavily fortified by tunnels, caves and concealed-rock gun and machine-gun emplacements...I don't think he can stand our pounding much longer and, unless something unexpected happens, I believe we should be able to destroy the last organized remnants of the Japanese Thirty-Second Army within a week. It has been a tough fight, but our men have fought superbly and killed Japs at the rate of twelve of them to one of ours which is remarkable considering the formidable character of their defense." His hope, once his men had recovered from "nearly three months of continuous fighting," was for "nothing more glorious than to be with the spearhead of the final assault on Tokyo."[6]

Even as the fighting on Okinawa was nearing its endgame, the kamikaze attacks on Allied shipping off the island continued. By mid-June, there had been nine major attacks,* involving a total number of 1,420 planes (830 navy and 590 army). Intermittent, smaller-scale attacks brought the total number since the start of the campaign up to around 1,850. These planes had sunk more than twenty American ships and damaged a further 150, with other types of suicide attacks and conventional bombing accounting for another eleven sunk and sixty damaged.[7]

With reserves of aircraft dwindling, and air chiefs keen to preserve stocks for the coming battle on Japan, the number and frequency of these attacks were diminishing. Yet they were still a constant concern for the American pilots whose job it was to protect the fleet. Those pilots included Major Bruce Porter, commanding the Marine Corps' 542 Squadron of Grumman F6F Hellcat night fighters. Porter had inherited his Hellcat from the previous squadron commander, Bill Kellum, and rechristened it "Black Death." The name was appropriate.

At 9:00 p.m. on June 15, Porter was flying a routine solo patrol in the Ie Shima sector, which was the closest to Japan's home islands, when he received a radio alert that a "bogey"—an unidentified plane, possibly hostile—was inbound for Okinawa on an easterly heading at 13,000 feet. He changed course to intercept and, soon after, saw a

* The major kamikaze attacks took place on: April 6–7 (355 planes); April 12–13 (185); April 15–16 (165); April 27–8 (115); May 3–4 (125); May 10–11 (150); May 24–5 (165); May 27–8 (110); June 3–7 (50). (Appleman et al., *Okinawa*, p. 364.)

blip on the outer edge of his radar screen. Reducing speed for a "slow closure rate," to ensure he did not miss the plane, Porter made visual contact at 9:15 p.m. He recognized the aircraft as a twin-engined Kawasaki Ki-45 fighter known as a "Nick," moved into position on its tail and gave it a "short burst" with his four .50-caliber machine guns and two 20 mm cannon. The noise and effect of these guns was like a buzz saw. "I could see the tracers," recalled Porter, "mark a true line to and into the airplane and it was all over with it in just a few seconds. The airplane broke right, then nosed down, as if the pilot had fallen on the stick. It went down in flames. The radar operator confirmed the kill a few minutes later."

The adrenaline was still coursing around Porter's body when the same radio operator called again: "I've got another bogey for you."

"Oh God," said Porter, taken aback. "Really?" Double contacts in one mission were unheard of, and no 542 pilot had shot down two planes on the same sweep.

"Bogey at Angels one-four [14,000 feet] indicated 180 knots," continued the operator. "Vector 145 at Angels one-three [13,000 feet]."

Climbing through clouds, Porter was concerned that he might not reach the intruder before it reached the island's anti-aircraft defenses. He knew from the southeasterly vector that the bogey was nearing its target, and he could see searchlights flicking on as he approached the west coast of Okinawa. If he did not make visual contact soon, he would lose his quarry. Increasing his speed to 260 knots, Porter strained his eyes for a sight of the plane. Suddenly a twin-engined Betty bomber seemed to leap out of the darkness. Once it was framed by his illuminated gunsight, he fired another short burst with all guns. "I could see the tracers light up the night," he said, "as they exploded forward and into the ship. Like the one before, the airplane burst into flames, peeled right, then nosed down. Radar also confirmed this kill."* It was 10:25 p.m.

Back at base, Porter celebrated with brandy provided by the squadron doctor. Only later, thinking about the action, did he get the "cold

* According to one source, this Betty bomber that Porter shot down "was carrying an Ōhka (a piloted flying bomb) which released and crashed when the mother ship exploded." (Tillman, "Hunter in the Dark," p. 15.)

chills." Next morning, Porter was in the flight line when a friend drove up in a jeep and asked him how it felt to be the newest Ace, the term of distinction given to pilots who had shot down five or more enemy planes. "What do you mean?" asked Porter.

"Well the two you got last night makes five, doesn't it?"

Porter just stood there, open-mouthed. It had not occurred to him before, but he was delighted. Not only was he an Ace, he was also the first Marine Corps pilot to score multiple victories in both the Corsair and Hellcat. He was rewarded with the Distinguished Flying Cross.[8]

Anxious as Buckner was for an end to the fighting, the Japanese were not finished yet. This became abundantly clear to PFC Don Dencker when his Love Company, 382nd Infantry, returned to the line on the XXIV Corps' right flank directly south of the village of Ozato, on June 16. With a company of the 2/5th Marines immediately to their right, Dencker and his men dug in their mortars behind the ruins of some houses and prepared for the "big push" the following day.

At 7:30 a.m. on June 17, the American artillery opened up on Japanese positions in the Yuza-Dake escarpment to their front, and was soon joined by 4.2-inch howitzers and 81 mm mortars. Shortly before 8:00 a.m., jump-off hour, Dencker and his men joined in by firing high-explosive shells from their 60 mm mortars. "We had," he recalled, "plenty of shells, so starting at a range of 150 yards we advanced our shelling to the south every few minutes, each mortar firing about a hundred shells."

At the appointed time, Sherman tanks and armored flamethrowers moved forward, closely followed by two of Love Company's rifle platoons whose job was to protect the tanks from suicide attacks. Dencker and his team also advanced, as did Item and King Companies to his left and the Marines to his right. Dencker captured the action of the day, writing: "The terrain was rough, with many scattered rock outcroppings and boulders that hindered our advance. About a hundred yards forward, the Japanese started to respond with machine-gun and rifle fire. We took casualties from this fire, with our tanks blasting and roasting the Japs. Our infantrymen cut down the few enemy that ran from the flamethrowers."

The defenders were from the Japanese 24th Division, the best formation still intact. "They did not surrender," recorded Dencker, "but died where they fought. All morning we were shelling, burning, grenading, and blasting Japanese positions with satchel charges as we slowly advanced." By noon they had advanced 300 yards and secured their objective: a small hill to the side of the Yuza-Dake escarpment. But the fighting had been "costly" for Love Company, with a new replacement officer killed and the company commander, First Lieutenant Ferguson, wounded and evacuated. First Lieutenant Harry Johannis took over, the sixth Love Company commander since April 1. The rifle platoons were similarly depleted: 1st Platoon, for example, had just two survivors from the landing.[9]

Also attacking on June 17 were the 3/7th Marines and a battalion of the 22nd Marines (6th Division) which had moved south from the Oroku Peninsula to relieve the 2/7th Marines. Spearheaded by King Company, the 3/7th angled south-west from Kunishi toward the Mezado Ridge, crossing 1,600 yards of open valley almost unopposed apart from stray sniper bullets. Once on the ridge, King Company moved east to attack Hill 69, led by Second Lieutenant "Jep" Carrell's 1st Platoon. "There was a high point," recalled Carrell, "a kind of jutting cone in our line of advance, and Van Daele's men (a squad) had it in their territory. They approached it gingerly, since we had plenty of hard experience with coral outcroppings of that nature."

Shots rang out from a hidden gun port, and one of Van Daele's riflemen was hit. "Van Daele had been close to him," noted Carrell, "saw the source of the shot, fired into the port, and ran over to the wounded man. A hand grenade flew out of the port, and Van Daele threw himself over the wounded rifleman to protect him." Then, with his men giving covering fire, he helped the casualty to safety before silencing the bunker by throwing two grenades into the slot. A second bunker, which also caused casualties, was knocked out by a combination of hand grenades, demolition charges and flamethrowers.[10]

As King Company advanced on Hill 69, it was supported by Item and Love Companies. Commanding Item's 2nd Platoon was Second Lieutenant Marius Bressoud, 21, the Roman Catholic son of a French businessman who had settled in New Jersey. Having joined the Marines after his junior year at Syracuse University, Bressoud was married by the time he shipped out to Pavavu in late 1944 and was assigned to Item's mortar section. But high casualties since the start of the campaign had seen him take over one of only two remaining rifle platoons. Of the attack on June 17, Bressoud recalled: "K and L Companies were digging in on high ground at the forward limit of their advance when I arrived with the 2nd Platoon of I Company close to their left flank...We were on high ground with good visibility to the front. I had time before dark to organize the platoon, tie in the machine guns, and coordinate the defense with adjacent platoons leaders."

Bressoud went forward with a runner to scout for defensive positions and reached the peak of Hill 52 on the Mezado Ridge. From there, he could see all the way to the southeast coast, three miles away. To his immediate right, in the direction of Hill 69, was a platoon commanded by his friend and former Special Officer Candidate School classmate Ken Phillips. But his left flank was open because the 5th Marines had failed to capture Hill 79 that day. "I talked to Ken on the radio,"* wrote Bressoud, "found out exactly where his left flank was, and we agreed on placement of our machine guns. I could not raise anyone by radio on my own left flank, probably because no one was there."

Telling his runner to bring forward the platoon, Bressoud was keeping low when Phillips radioed him back. "Be careful, Bress, I've just spotted Japs in your area."

Raising himself a little to look, Bressoud could not see anyone directly ahead or down the slope. There was, however, a Japanese soldier in the valley at a distance of around 300 yards. He raised his carbine to take a pot shot, but then lowered it "with a little laugh at the absurdity of trying to hit so distant a target with so light a weapon." It did not occur to him to look behind. He had, after all, come from that direction, the runner had just returned through it, and the platoon itself was barely a hundred yards to his rear.

It felt like he had been hit in the back with a baseball bat. The blow had knocked him forward and, regaining his senses, he could see his

* Handheld, battery-operated and short-range radios—also known as "walkie-talkies" that were carried by the company commander, the executive officer, and the platoon and section leaders.

left arm spread out at an unnatural angle. He pulled it closer to his body with his right hand, and was relieved to find it still attached. But there was a spreading stain of blood on his upper left sleeve, so he put pressure on his left armpit to try to stem the flow. "I was," he remembered, "reluctant to use the radio to call for help because I thought [the assailant] might be searching the area and would hear me. I half expected him to find me, stand over me, and finish the job." Fearing he might bleed to death, he made "a battlefield confession, an act of contrition, and felt confident of God's forgiveness and love."

Eventually the platoon arrived and Bressoud was helped back to the battalion aid station, the first stop in a long journey to a field hospital where they gave him blood and properly assessed his wounds. They were more serious than he had thought. The bullet had entered his upper back, just to the left of the spine, and exited through his left armpit before shattering the bone in his upper arm. He was lucky to be alive.[11]

That night, the 1/7th and 3/7th Marines were relieved by the 8th Marines of the 2nd Marine Division on Kunishi and Mezado ridges respectively. "Jep" Carrell and his men cheered when they heard the news, and hoped they would be sent to the rear out of harm's way. In fact they were moved a mile to the east, to clear out an "as-yet-untouched area," and it was while they were doing this that Lieutenant Colonel Edward Hurst, the battalion commander, was shot in the neck by a sniper, shortly after Carrell had warned him to "get down!" He survived, as did Carrell, one of only five of the original forty-three members of 1st Platoon to fight through the campaign unscathed. Carrell, moreover, was the only rifle-platoon leader out of twenty-seven in the 7th Marines to last through the operation. "I was bucking," he wrote, "some pretty high odds."[12]

38

"I haven't come up to the front to hide"

At 11:00 a.m. on June 18, General Joe Stilwell finally got to speak to Doug MacArthur in Manila about his role in the anticipated invasion of Japan. Offered the post of MacArthur's chief of staff, Stilwell turned it down. "I fancy myself," he declared, "as a field commander."

"How about an army?" asked MacArthur. "Would you be willing to step down?"

"Yes. I'd take a division to be with troops."

MacArthur then asked about Buckner's handling of the Okinawan campaign, and Stilwell did not pull any punches. Buckner had not performed well, he said. He lacked drive and imagination, and had used costly head-on tactics, instead of considering a second amphibious landing, as some of his subordinates had urged. He was, moreover, far too cozy in his relations with the navy. This merely confirmed MacArthur's low opinion of Buckner. "Told me," Stilwell noted in his diary later, "he would rather have me as an army commander than anyone he knew, and if GCM [General George C. Marshall, U.S. Army chief of staff] was willing, he was."

Stilwell left the meeting highly satisfied. MacArthur wanted him and not Buckner to command an army in the invasion of Japan, and once Marshall had been apprised of this fact, there was a good chance he would relieve Buckner. But Marshall would have the final say. "If Navy gives [up the Tenth Army] and Buckner is not relieved," noted Stilwell, "I get nothing."[1]

Unaware of these machinations playing out in Manila, 900 miles to the south, Lieutenant General Buckner was making yet another visit to the troops at the front. He had left army headquarters with his aide Major Hubbard and an escort at 8:30 a.m., telling his chief of staff E. D. Post that he wanted to see how "his boys" were doing. He was, according to Post, "particularly keen" this day because he was "enthusiastic about the prospect of decisive gains."[2] He chose to visit the Marines as they had made the biggest leap forward on the 17th, whereas the "doggies" of XXIV Corps had made "no progress."[3]

Passing through Naha, he stopped briefly to speak to Major General Del Valle at the 1st Marine Division's headquarters, before continuing south. En route he met Colonel Bob Roberts, commanding the 22nd Marines, who advised against visiting the front at that particular point. His regiment and the neighboring 8th Marines had made such a rapid advance that morning, explained Roberts,* that they would have "bypassed a good many Japanese, and, further, there was considerable flanking fire coming from the high ground in front of the 96th Division." Buckner responded "that if his men were there he too would go, for he wanted to see first-hand what they were up against."[4]

The regiment he chose to visit was the newly arrived 8th Marines. One of the 2nd Marine Division units that had so impressed him during his inspection tour of Saipan in early February, the 8th had arrived on Okinawa only two days earlier and, according to Del Valle and Roberts, was already making "rapid progress."[5]

Buckner reached the vicinity of the 8th Marines' regimental CP, on the reverse slope of Mezado Ridge, at around noon. Getting down from his jeep, he found himself among the men of Captain Fred Haley's Able Company which was in battalion reserve. Buckner stopped to talk and shake hands with some of the Marines, a gesture that "meant a great deal" to them. The presence of a three-star general on the front line, commented Haley, "gives a tremendous boost to morale."

After pausing for several minutes, Buckner and his entourage were escorted to Able Company's CP where Haley and his officers were discussing supply problems with Lieutenant "Duke" Davis, the battalion logistics officer. They stood to attention as Buckner approached. "It was apparent," wrote Haley, "the general had not lost any of his Command Presence...since his visit to Saipan. He was an impressive and

* An hour after this conversation, Colonel Roberts was moving forward to observe his own regiment's advance to the Kuwanga Ridge when he was shot in the heart and killed by a Japanese sniper.

commanding figure." More worryingly, Buckner was wearing the same steel helmet with three highly visible silver stars. Haley noted: "The thought occurred to me, 'Why did not someone suggest to the general that he change helmets so as to conceal his rank on the front lines?'"

Unbeknown to Haley, Brigadier General Oliver Smith had made just such a suggestion. But the compromise position for generals—to wear a helmet liner with small painted white stars when in the front line—was not one that Buckner adhered to.

If Buckner recognized Haley from the Saipan parade fiasco, he did not mention it. Instead they shook hands and, when Buckner had explained what he was there for, Haley radioed through to the battalion CP for instructions. As the battalion commander had gone forward with the assault companies, he spoke to Major Don Kennedy, the XO. "Take General Buckner and his party to the regimental OP," said Kennedy. "I will let Colonel Wallace know that the general wants to meet him there."

As they were leaving Haley's CP, Buckner stopped next to the body of a young Baker Company officer who had been killed earlier that day. Told his name and background—he had been a famous all-round athlete at the University of Iowa—Buckner seemed moved and asked for his address so that he could write to his family. Kneeling briefly next to the body, he wiped a "small clod of mud" from the dead officer's forehead.

Accompanied by two runners and his radio operator, Haley led Buckner and his party up a steep path toward the regimental OP which was sited on the forward slope of Hill 52—close to where Marius Bressoud had been shot the day before—"with a commanding view of the valley between Mezado Ridge and Ibaru Ridge." Yet it was also "exposed to Japanese field glasses scanning north from the northerly crest of Ibaru Ridge" and there was "scant natural cover" for camouflage.*

Covering a circuitous route of about 1,000 yards, they arrived to find Colonel Clarence R. "Bull" Wallace, the regimental commander, and Major Bill Chamberlin, his operations officer, waiting for them.

* Captain Haley wrote later: "The 8th Marines' Observation Post was too 'up front' and should have been placed in a more secluded, concealed, camouflaged position with some thought given to the safety of its occupants." (Haley, "The General Dies at Noon," p. 28.)

Wallace—an aggressive and fearless officer, with "very little compassion or understanding of the frailties of his charges"—sent Haley back to his company, and led Buckner, Hubbard, Chamberlin and the two runners over the crest to the OP. So as not to attract too much attention, the other members of Buckner's party were dispersed in foxholes just behind the crest.[6]

The observation post was composed of two coral boulders with a gap of about a foot separating them. Buckner stood behind the gap, and watched the "whole panoply of war" as riflemen from the 2/8th Marines moved up the valley toward the Ibaru Ridge. Wallace and the others were more securely positioned behind the boulders.[7]

After Buckner had been watching events for some time, Wallace suggested that it might be prudent to replace his distinctive general's helmet with one a little less conspicuous. Buckner refused. "I haven't come up to the front," he said softly, "to hide." He added: "I want the Japanese to realize that further resistance is futile, and perhaps such a realization will persuade them to encourage the Okinawan civilians who are with them to surrender."

Not long after this comment, Wallace's radio operator told his boss that he had just intercepted a message from Captain Pickett, the 1/8th Marines' operations officer, who, when looking back at the OP, could see the three stars on Buckner's helmet "plainly visible." Overhearing this exchange, a smiling Buckner took off the offending item and placed it on the coral rock beside him. He then replaced it with a helmet provided by Chamberlin with no badge of rank. "Those people down there have enough to worry about," he commented good-humoredly, "without me adding to their problems."

A few minutes later—by which time it was 1:15 p.m., and Buckner had been enjoying the spectacle from the OP for about an hour—a Japanese shell of unknown caliber (possibly from a 47 mm anti-tank gun) exploded without warning at the foot of the gap between the two boulders, hurling shrapnel and pieces of coral rock into Buckner's right breast.* Wallace and Chamberlin were standing on either side

* "It was the opinion of most of the observers present," recorded Captain Haley, "that the Japanese, with their excellent sighting instruments, had picked up the three stars on the helmet and dropped an artillery shell or mortar shell in the Observation Post." (Haley, "The General Dies at Noon," p. 31.)

of Buckner, but neither was wounded. The only other minor casualty was Hubbard who suffered a perforated eardrum. Though badly hurt, Buckner's first thought was for the men with him. Has anyone else been hit? he asked. Told they had not been, he seemed relieved.

He was carried in a poncho back over the crest to the relative safety of the reverse slope where he was put on a field stretcher. By the time Captain Haley arrived on the scene—informed by radio message—Buckner was being treated by the battalion surgeon, Lieutenant Tom Sullivan, USN, who, assisted by a corpsman, was trying to infuse plasma. But it was clear to Haley that the general "was beyond medical help." As his life ebbed out of him, Buckner tried to get to his feet but was unable to do so. "His piercing eyes remained fierce and commanding," noted Haley, "his dungaree jacket was shredded and bloody, his silvery hair was mud-splattered."

Some members of Buckner's party were trying to transmit by radio the seriousness of Buckner's wounds to army headquarters, while others tried to persuade an artillery spotter plane to land nearby so that the general could be flown to a field hospital. But there was nowhere for the plane to land and, in any case, it was too late to save him. Close to death, Buckner reached out his right hand as if he wanted to be helped to his feet. For a moment, no one responded. Then one of Haley's runners, "a very intellectual, courageous Marine," grasped the outstretched hand with both of his and held it tightly until Buckner died.

"You are going home, General," said the soldier, folding Buckner's hand on his chest, "you are homeward bound."

Those present were stunned. Wallace, unsure what to do, was pacing back and forth like a caged lion, shouting at anyone who approached to "Stand back!"

Finally, a member of Buckner's party began reciting the words of the 23rd Psalm:

> Yea, though I walk through the valley of the Shadow of Death,
> I will fear no evil, for Thou art with me.
> Thy rod and Thy Staff they comfort me.
> Thou preparest a table before me in the presence of mine
>   enemies,
> Thou anointest my head with oil,

My cup runneth over.
Surely goodness and mercy shall follow me all the days of my life,
And I will dwell in the House of the Lord forever.[8]

Informed that Buckner had been badly wounded at 1:30 p.m., Brigadier General Post had set out at once to see if he could help. He arrived at 2:45 p.m. to be told the grim news. "[I] had his magnificent body moved from the ambulance to a tent," he informed Buckner's wife Adele, "where I had him uncovered so I could see for the last time the man whom I had worshipped for so many years. You may be pleased to know that he looked marvelous. He had been hit by only one fragment—in the chest. His face looked completely natural as though in peaceful sleep with the suggestion of a smile on his face."

At 9:00 a.m. the following day, Buckner was buried "with the simple rites of a soldier fallen in battle" in the 7th Division cemetery, near the Hagushi beaches. It was a brief ceremony, at which all Buckner's "many friends and admirers were present." Post represented the family, and in that capacity received the flag covering the casket which he later sent to Adele Buckner. "The country has lost a great man," Post assured Adele, "the Army a superb leader, and I, the friendship of a man who I regarded as perfect in every respect. My deepest sympathy to you for I know of the great loss you have suffered."[9]

Promoted posthumously to the rank of full general, Buckner was the most senior American soldier to be killed in action during the Second World War. His death sparked a race to replace him that was won, temporarily, by Lieutenant General Geiger. Informed by Brigadier General Post that Geiger was Buckner's preferred successor as Tenth Army commander, Nimitz confirmed his appointment on June 19, much to the fury of Major General Wallace, the garrison commander, who felt that as the senior army officer he should take precedence. Geiger became the first Marine general to command an army. But this accolade was short-lived because, on being consulted by General Marshall, MacArthur said he preferred Lieutenant General Oscar W. Griswold, the XIV Corps commander, and, if he was not acceptable, General Stilwell. Marshall chose Stilwell, and MacArthur passed on the good news. "Radio from Doug," wrote a delighted Stilwell in his diary. "'Command 10th Army. Return to Guam at once.'"[10]

39

"Every man will...fight to the end"

On the day Lieutenant General Buckner was killed, effective Japanese resistance on Okinawa came to an end. Colonel Yahara realized as much when he received word in the Thirty-Second Army headquarters cave at Mabuni Hill that both flanks of the defensive line had "collapsed simultaneously": on the right, tanks and troops of the U.S. 7th Infantry Division overran the 44th Mixed Brigade's command post on Hill 89 and then captured "a low-lying hill some 1,500 meters east of Mabuni"; and on the left, "enemy marines" broke through the lines of the 89th Regiment, and appeared at Makabe village, north-east of the 24th Division command post. With American tanks having penetrated "deep" into the Japanese defense zone, not far from Komesu village, just two miles west of the headquarters cave, Yahara knew the collapse of the "entire army was imminent."[1]

From outside the cave could be heard the sound of machine-gun fire, reminding Yahara of the last few days at Shuri. All telephone lines to front-line units had been cut and even radio messages arrived intermittently. Orders had to be sent out by messenger, and by return came the news of "commanders killed and battalions annihilated." It was, recalled Yahara, "grim and disheartening," and his "blood curdled at each such message."

Aware that the end was near, Major General Chō muttered: "So much for that. I should be satisfied." It was almost as if, his mission accomplished, he could finally relax.

Lieutenant General Ushijima, meanwhile, was still issuing orders. One—a handwritten and sealed directive—he handed to Captain Tadashi Masunaga, a Thirty-Second Army intelligence officer, assigning him the mission of leading guerilla warfare on Okinawa "after the cessation of organized combat by the army." The mission included assassinating American leaders, destroying army barracks and creating general confusion. He was to head for Kunigami in the north, and be followed by the surviving members of the Blood and Iron Student Corps' Chihaya Unit, including 19-year-old Private Second Class Masahide Ōta. "We were," recalled Ōta, "to gather in the north to fight an 'intelligence war.' A guerilla war, we'd call it now. We were ordered to allow ourselves to be captured by the Americans. Our mission, then, was to move around behind their lines gathering intelligence." But Ōta was wounded soon after leaving the cave, and went into hiding near Mabuni with other stragglers.*[2]

Other members of the Blood and Iron Corps, including 16-year-old Shigetomo Higa, were divided into squads and sent on suicide missions with makeshift explosives. Shigetomo, like most of the others, failed in his hopeless mission and threw the explosive away before returning to a cave near Makabe.[3]

Ushijima, meanwhile, was dictating a final order to be sent to all units. It read:

> My Beloved Soldiers,
>
> You have all fought courageously for nearly three months. You have discharged your duty. Your bravery and loyalty brighten the future.
>
> The battlefield is now in such chaos that all communications have ceased. It is impossible for me to command you. Every man in these fortifications will follow his superior's order and fight to the end for the sake of the motherland.
>
> This is my final order.
>
> Farewell.

Chō, after reading the draft, added in red ink: "Do not suffer the shame of being taken prisoner. You will live for eternity."

Once Ushijima had added his signature, the final order was ready to be sent out. For Yahara, whose official duties had now come to a

* Ōta and some other fugitives finally surrendered to the Americans in late October 1945, long after the war had ended.

close, there was a feeling of "sudden bliss at being free of all worldly burdens."[4]

As dusk fell in the cluster of hospital caves at Ihara, two miles to the west of the Thirty-Second Army headquarters at Mabuni Hill, the order was given to deactivate the Himeyuri Student Corps. Kikuko Miyagi was among a large group of students and teachers at the 1st Surgical Unit cave who were told to escape as individuals because enemy soldiers were "quite close" and a large group would be easier to spot. "Everyone shed tears," she recalled, "but what could we say? We didn't know what to do. And our friends, lying there injured, were listening to the order, too. They knew they would be left behind. There was no way to take them with us. None."[5]

Tomi Shimabukuro, 18, had only just arrived at the 1st Surgical Unit cave when she heard a doctor shouting that the nurses were to leave as soon as possible. Spotting a pile of rice sacks, she scooped up some for herself and distributed the rest among the other students. They were about to leave when two teachers arrived from the 2nd Surgical Unit saying their cave had been "straddled" and attacked by enemy soldiers, and many of their fellow students had been killed and wounded.

One of the student nurses replied: "*Sensei!* [Teacher!] They've disbanded us. Teachers and students have to leave the cave. Only the seriously wounded students are remaining here."

"Is that right?" said a teacher, obviously shocked, before going into the cave to comfort the students who had to be left behind.

One of them, a friend of Tomi's, grabbed at her trousers and said, "Don't go away! Don't leave us here alone."

Unsure what to do, Tomi gathered water trickling from the cave wall into a bowl and gave it to her friend. Just then a surgeon appeared, brandishing his samurai sword, shouting, "Get out! Or I'll cut your heads off! I'll take care of the patients. You will all be killed if you stay here."[6]

They left. Ignoring the warning to travel as individuals, Kikuko Miyagi was part of a group of sixteen students and three teachers that departed together. They had not gone far when a large bomb exploded nearby, wounding four of them. The rest continued on their hands and knees as bombs continued to fall. By morning they were still in sight of the cave they had left, and American tanks and troops were all around. "I heard a great booming sound," recalled Kikuko, "and passed out. Eventually, I came to my senses. I was covered in blood and couldn't hear a thing. In front of me, two classmates were soaked in their own blood. Then they were screaming in pain. Third-year student Akiko wasn't moving. She'd died there. Two teachers in their twenties had disappeared. We never saw them again."

Nearby, Japanese soldiers were yelling, "Armor! Armor!"

Kikuko could see the flamethrowing tanks moving forward, "spewing out a stream of fire." She was shaking with fear.

"Follow me!" shouted the vice principal, the only teacher left. They did so, encouraging their wounded friends to keep up. "I can't," one responded. "I can't go on. It hurts."[7]

In the 3rd Surgical Unit cave, meanwhile, some of the students hesitated and never got out. "We were waiting for a lull," recalled 18-year-old Ruri Morishita, "but the gunfire wouldn't stop."

Eventually they heard footsteps approaching the cave entrance and a soldier from the Japanese signal corps went to check. "Enemy!" he whispered. "It's the enemy! They're here. I heard them talking."

The students tried to remain as silent as possible, but in the damp conditions many of them had contracted coughs. "Don't cough! The enemy will hear it," they were warned.

So when someone could not stop themselves, they gathered round her to muffle the sound.

The silence was broken by a voice in Japanese. "Are there any civilians in this cave? Any soldiers? If you are in the cave, come out! Otherwise we'll blast the cave. Do you hear?"

The warning was repeated, but when there was no response the footsteps fell away. Fearful of what might happen next, Ruri advised some friends to come deeper into the cave. Only one agreed to go with her. "It's dark inside," said the another, "and it's too narrow. As things stand now, I don't care what happens to me."

Ruri and her friend were picking their way toward the inner part of the cave when they heard an explosion and "the cave was instantly filled with white smoke." They feared a gas attack, but it was smoke from a phosphorus grenade.

"I felt," remembered Ruri, "as if I were being strangled, and I could hardly breathe. Calling for help, I crept around on the floor, looking for a rock crack or a hollow spot among rocks to put my face in."

People around her were calling out, "Can't breathe! I can't breathe!," "Help me, Mother!"

Rolling down to a ledge in the inner part of the cave, Ruri told herself, "You can't possibly die in a place like this! Who will tell your parents?" As she struggled for breath, she heard one of her teachers singing the "Umiyukaba," which eulogized an honorable death for the emperor. Then there was the sound of a loud bang as he committed suicide by detonating a grenade. It was the last thing Ruri heard before she lost consciousness.[8]

Incredibly Ruri survived. But most of the others in the cave—a total of eighty people, including thirty-nine students and four teachers—were either choked to death or took their own lives. They and other Okinawan civilians who preferred death to capture were victims not only of their patriotic education, which had taught them that they should "sacrifice their lives for their country," but also of their willingness to believe Japanese soldiers who told them that American soldiers would "split men in half" and rape and torture women to death.[9]

Kikuko Miyagi was among the many students who headed south to the coast, and took refuge in caves. At one point they saw an American boat approach and heard a voice say in Japanese: "Those who can swim, swim out! We'll save you. Those who can't swim, walk toward Minatogawa! Walk by day. Don't travel by night. We have food! We will rescue you!"

But Kikuko and her friends did not believe this. From childhood they had been taught to hate the Americans. They would, Kikuko believed, "strip the girls naked and do with them whatever they wanted, then run them over with tanks." Only later did she realize that the lies they had been told would cost many students their lives. The end came on June 21 when a voice in "strangely accented Japanese" shouted, "Come out! Come out!"

When they refused, the Americans opened fire, killing a Japanese soldier and three students. In desperation, a teacher detonated a hand grenade, killing himself and nine students. To Kikuko, the sight was "hell itself." The teacher was lying in the center of the group, "his intestines blown out." Others were "mangled almost beyond recognition." Kikuko recalled:

> I simply sat there where I'd slumped down. An American soldier poked me with the barrel of his gun, signaling me to move in the direction he indicated. I didn't speak English. I couldn't do anything but move as he ordered. To my surprise, three senior students had been carried out. Their wounds had been dressed and bandaged and they were being given saline injections. Until that moment I could think of the Americans only as devils and demons. I was simply frozen. I couldn't believe what I saw.[10]

Of the original 222-strong Himeyuri Student Corps and eighteen teachers who were mobilized to the army field hospital, only 104 survived the battle. Kikuko was among the lucky ones.[11]

40

"Suppose it doesn't go off?"

At 3:30 p.m. on June 18,* President Harry Truman met with his senior military advisers in the White House to discuss how to force Japan to surrender unconditionally and so end the Pacific War. In attendance were his Joint Chiefs of Staff: General George C. Marshall, Fleet Admiral Ernest King, and Lieutenant General Ira Eaker (representing General of the Army Henry H. "Hap" Arnold, USAAF, who was recovering from a heart attack). Also present were Fleet Admiral Bill Leahy, Truman's military chief of staff, Secretary of the Navy James Forrestal, Secretary of War Henry Stimson, and Assistant Secretary of War John J. McCloy.

"I've called this meeting," explained Truman, "for the purpose of hearing more details about the proposed campaign against Japan set out in Admiral Leahy's memorandum to the Joint Chiefs of Staff four days ago. General Marshall, what are your thoughts?"

The U.S. Army chief of staff began by saying the situation in Japan was "practically identical" to that in Europe prior to D-Day: to bring Japan to its knees—as Germany had been—a ground invasion was necessary. The location and date, said Marshall, had been agreed by the Joint Chiefs and the senior military commanders in the Pacific, General MacArthur and Admiral Nimitz, as Kyushu Island, the most southerly of the Japanese home islands, on November 1, 1945. That would give enough time to "smash practically every industrial target worth hitting in Japan as well as destroying huge areas in the Jap cities"; the Japanese navy, "if any still exists," would by that point be "completely powerless"; and American air and sea power would have

* Or 4:30 a.m. on Tuesday June 19 in Okinawa, given the eleven-hour time difference between Washington, DC, and Naha.

"cut Jap reinforcement capabilities from the mainland to negligible proportions." To wait any longer than November 1, however, would risk a delay of "up to six months" because of winter weather.

The Kyushu option was, said Marshall, "essential to a strategy of strangulation" and appeared to be "the least costly worthwhile operation following Okinawa." It would act as a stepping stone to an invasion of the Tokyo Plain on the neighboring Honshu Island.

As for likely casualties, Marshall gave a number of comparative examples. At Luzon, there had been 31,000 American casualties to 156,000 Japanese (mostly killed), a ratio of 1:5. Yet the more recent battles in the Pacific were costlier. At Iwo Jima, there were 20,000 American casualties to 25,000 Japanese, and at Okinawa—the bloodiest American campaign of the Pacific, but one in which U.S. forces were still fighting—the running totals were 41,700 American casualties (U.S. Army and Navy combined) to 81,000 Japanese. With casualty ratios of 1:1.25 and 1:2 respectively, it was clear to the U.S. military that the closer they got to Japan proper, the harder the defenders fought. Marshall did not think U.S. casualties for the first thirty days of fighting on Kyushu would exceed the price "paid for Luzon"—31,000 men—but added: "It is a grim fact that there is not an easy, bloodless way to victory in war and it is the thankless task of the leaders to maintain their firm outward front which holds the resolution of their subordinates."

After reading out a supportive telegram from Douglas MacArthur—stating that the proposed operation "presents less hazards of excessive loss than any other that has been suggested"—Marshall said it was his personal view that "the operation against Kyushu was the only course to pursue." Air power alone was "not sufficient to put the Japanese out of the war," any more than it had been to defeat the Germans. The invasion of Kyushu would be no more difficult "than the assault in Normandy" and he was convinced that all U.S. servicemen in the Pacific needed to be "indoctrinated with a firm determination to see it through."

Admiral King backed up Marshall by saying that "Kyushu followed logically after Okinawa" and was a "natural set-up." When Admiral Leahy was asked for his views, he said that the troops on Okinawa had suffered about thirty-five percent casualties of the total number of troops involved, and that he expected a similar proportion to be lost on Kyushu. He therefore wanted to know how many would be involved.

King interjected, by saying that the two campaigns were not comparable: whereas there had only been "one way to go on Okinawa"—a "straight frontal attack against a highly fortified position"—on Kyushu there would be three simultaneous landings on separate fronts and therefore "much more room for maneuver." His estimate of casualties, therefore, was "somewhere between" the Luzon and Okinawa figures, by which he probably meant a loss-to-kill ratio of around one American to every three Japanese.

To help with the grim calculations, Marshall explained that 766,700 American troops would assault Kyushu. They would be opposed by an estimated eight Japanese divisions, or 350,000 men. Further reinforcement of those defenders was possible, but "becoming increasingly unlikely." Though no one said as much, it was implied by the figures and statistics given that American casualties for the Kyushu operation alone would be at least 120,000 men (a third of the Japanese defenders) and possibly double that. But that was just the start, because Truman knew from the Joint Chiefs of Staff memorandum that a second, far bigger invasion of Honshu, in the vicinity of the Tokyo Plains, was scheduled for the spring of 1946, and it might be the autumn of that year before Japan finally surrendered. Total casualties for both invasions, therefore, could be as high as 750,000 to a million men.*

Fully aware that the capture of Kyushu would not necessarily end the war, Truman suggested that the operation would simply create "another Okinawa closer to Japan." The Joint Chiefs agreed that this was so.

The president now turned to Eaker, the airman, who confirmed that he and General Arnold were in complete agreement with the other Joint Chiefs. "Any blockade of Honshu," he added, "is dependent upon aerodromes on Kyushu."

On being asked his opinion, Henry Stimson said he was supportive of the plan. Yet he also felt, as a politician, that there was a "large

* Secretary of War Stimson later wrote that the combined invasion plans would have involved 5 million U.S. servicemen, with expected casualties of "over a million." (Stimson, *On Active Service*, pp. 618–19.)

submerged class in Japan who do not favor the present war and whose full opinion and influence had never yet been felt." Yet even they would "fight tenaciously" against American troops "if attacked on their home ground." The trick, therefore, was to find a way "to arouse them and to develop any possible influence they might have before it became necessary to come to grips with them."

Truman agreed, saying the possibility was being worked on all the time. "I wonder," he mused aloud, "if the invasion of Japan by white men would not have the effect of more closely uniting the Japanese?"

Stimson said there was "every prospect of this" and, while he agreed that the plan proposed by the Joint Chiefs was the "best thing to do," he still hoped for "some fruitful accomplishment through other means."

Asked for his view, James Forrestal argued that even a siege of Japan for a year, or a year and a half, would require Kyushu's capture, and that it was the "sound decision" to go ahead. But James McCloy, Assistant Secretary of War, backed his boss. "The time is propitious now," he said, "to study closely all possible means of bringing out the influence of the submerged group in Japan" that Stimson had been referring to.

Leahy's suggestion was to do away with the demand for "unconditional surrender," an article of faith almost since Pearl Harbor. "What I fear," he said, "is that our insistence on unconditional surrender will result only in making the Japanese desperate and thereby increase our casualty lists. I do not think that this is at all necessary."

Truman's response was cautious. He knew that a conditional—or negotiated—surrender might be seen by American public opinion as both a failure and a betrayal of FDR, who had always insisted on complete surrender. Yet he was also sympathetic to Leahy's argument, which is why he had "left the door open for Congress to take appropriate action." He did not feel, he added, that he could "take any action at this time to change public opinion on the matter."

Summing up, Truman said that he had called this meeting with the Joint Chiefs because he wanted to know "how far we could afford to go in the Japanese campaign." He had hoped there might be a "possibility of preventing an Okinawa from one end of Japan to the other." But they had told him otherwise and he was now "quite sure that the Joint Chiefs should proceed with the Kyushu operation."[1]

As they were about to move on to other matters, Truman asked John McCloy—who had contributed the least of anyone to the discussion—if he thought there was any real alternative to a ground invasion. McCloy turned to Stimson, as if seeking permission to speak. "Say what you feel about it," said his boss.

"Well," said McCloy, "I do think you've got an alternative. And I think it's an alternative that ought to be explored and that, really, we ought to have our heads examined if we don't explore some other method by which we can terminate this war than just by another conventional attack and landing."

McCloy's first suggestion was that the Japanese might surrender if they were allowed to keep Emperor Hirohito as head of state. Acting Secretary of State Joseph C. Grew had said the same thing to Truman, at a separate meeting, and it was certainly an option the president was prepared to consider. But it was McCloy's mention of the atomic bomb that got everyone's attention. As soon as he did, "even in that select circle, it was a bit of a shock," remembered McCloy. "You didn't mention the bomb out loud; it was like mentioning Skull and Bones* in polite society at Yale. It just wasn't done."

Ignoring the disapproving glances, McCloy said they should warn the Japanese about the bomb, and, if they still refused to surrender, detonate it. "I think our moral position would be better," he added, "if we gave them a specific warning of the bomb."

The response, from one of those present, was that they didn't yet know if the bomb would work. "Suppose it doesn't go off? Our prestige will be greatly marred."

McCloy responded: "All the scientists have told us that the thing will go. It's just a matter of testing it out now, but they're quite certain from reports I've seen that this bomb is a success."

Truman, of course, had already received advice from Stimson and the Interim Committee that the bomb "should be used against Japan as soon as possible" and "without prior warning." McCloy's advice differed in that he felt a warning should be used, and this chimed with Truman's own feelings. Advised that the test explosion would take place within thirty days—around the middle of July—Truman

* Skull and Bones is a secret student society at Yale University that was founded in the nineteenth century.

told the meeting that if it was successful, they should "give Japan a chance to stop the war by a surrender." In other words, issue an ultimatum that hinted at what might come: and if the Japanese ignored it, drop the bomb.

In the meantime, the Joint Chiefs should move ahead with their plans to invade Kyushu on November 1.[2]

41
"What a splendid last moment!"

At dawn on June 20, watching from the mouth of the Thirty-Second Army headquarters cave, Colonel Yahara could see hundreds of civilians in small groups heading away from Mabuni. "Everything looked so tranquil," he recalled, "that it did not seem like a battlefield, but this peaceful scene would not last."

Later that day, twenty American tanks lumbered up Mabuni Hill and fired shells into the remaining Japanese positions. They also swarmed into the nearby villages of Komesu, Odo and Maedera, the latter the location of the 24th Division's command post where General Amamiya was making his last stand. Amidst the smoke, noise and confusion, Yahara could no longer distinguish friendly forces from foe. By nightfall the enemy tanks had withdrawn, but the respite, Yahara knew, would be only temporary.

That evening, he had just dozed off when the chief code clerk ran into his room, shouting: "A telegram of commendation has come from Imperial Headquarters."

Scanning the characters, Yahara was elated. The Okinawa operation had been, he knew, doomed from the start. But this was proof that their efforts had "far surpassed Imperial Headquarters' expectations."

He took it at once to generals Chō and Ushijima and, with "adjutants, guards, young women, and everyone else in the vicinity, listening closely," read it out aloud:

> Under command of Lieutenant General Mitsuru Ushijima, you have fought courageously for three months against a formidable enemy, ever since his landing on Okinawa. You have destroyed the enemy in every battlefield, causing great damage. You have

> truly displayed the greatness of the Imperial Army. In addition you have restrained the enemy's overwhelming naval power. You have also contributed greatly to our air raids against enemy fleets.

As Yahara finished reading, both generals closed their eyes, as if content. Then Chō dictated a reply which Yahara wrote out in pencil:

> Against the overwhelmingly powerful enemy, with our survivors at hand, as we were about to make an all-out suicide attack, we received the commendation letter bestowed by Your Excellency. Nothing can surpass this glory. We are supremely moved. The soldiers who have died shedding their blood on these islands of Okinawa can now rest in peace forever. The remaining soldiers at this final stand are encouraged to fight to the death. With all our strength we will fight bravely so that we will come up to your expectations. We are very grateful.

Once Chō had made a couple of minor corrections—including a sentence saying they would always be "loyal subjects of the emperor"—he asked Yahara to send the reply, and to make copies for all units.

The following day, June 21, American troops of the 7th Infantry Division fought their way to the top of Mabuni Hill, located the vertical entrance shaft to the headquarters cave and dropped explosives in it, killing several staff officers. Yahara had earlier ordered the sealing of the cave entrance facing Mabuni village. Now the only exit opened onto a ledge in the 290-foot cliff facing the sea. That evening another cable arrived from Tokyo, this time from General Korechika Anami, the war minister, and General Yoshijiro Umezu, the IJA's chief of staff. It not only congratulated Ushijima and the Thirty-Second Army for their superb defense against a far superior force, but also mentioned that they had "killed the enemy commander, [Lieutenant] General Simon Buckner, and delivered deadly blows against his eight divisions of troops."

Tokyo had heard reports of Buckner's death on American radio broadcasts, but this was the first time the Thirty-Second Army learned the truth. It was, wrote Yahara, "the greatest news of the entire operation. We had managed to kill the enemy leader before our own commanding general committed ceremonial suicide. It seemed as if our forces had actually won a victory."

Chō, like Yahara, was elated. But not Ushijima. "He looked grim," remembered Yahara, "as if mourning Buckner's death. Ushijima never spoke ill of others. I had always felt he was a great man, and now I admired him more than ever."[1]

With time running out, the generals prepared for their ritual suicide. At 10:00 p.m., they and their remaining staff officers, enjoyed a final banquet of "rice, canned meats, potatoes, fried fish cakes, salmon, bean-curd soup, fresh cabbage, pineapples, tea and sake."[2] During the meal, Chō and Yahara reminisced. "We drank in Saigon before the war started," said Chō. "Do you remember the beautiful movie we saw at the theater across from the Majestic Hotel? It was *Daniuvu no kazanami* [Waves of the Danube]. You and I always behaved properly. We shared much pain together, and now we face our final day."

On choosing their own honorable death, Ushijima and Chō had exempted the young staff officers from following their lead. Chō, in particular, had long felt the IJA was unnecessarily handicapped by the "self-destruction of staffs in the Pacific." He had therefore ordered all the Thirty-Second Army staff officers to escape: some to fight as guerillas on Okinawa, others, like Yahara, to try to return to Tokyo and report to the Imperial GHQ. He now reminded Yahara of this. "Ever since my arrival on Okinawa," Chō continued, "I said you would not die here. I am happy to have kept this promise. You must break through the enemy lines and succeed. Be cautious, and do not make rash decisions if you can help it. I will give you this pill in case you become ill. Take it and you will recover."

Chō handed over the pill—which looked to Yahara like Chinese medicine—and also a 500-yen note. They had rarely seen eye to eye with regard to strategy, and their ideologies were "poles apart." Yet overcome by Chō's generosity, Yahara wept.

Returning to his room to rest, Yahara was summoned at 3:00 a.m. He found both generals in full field uniform with their medals. Ushijima was sitting cross-legged; Chō drinking his favorite King of Kings whisky. He seemed to be very drunk. Offering Yahara a whisky and some pineapple, he extended a piece of the fruit on the tip of his sword. A bemused Yahara took and ate it.

"General," said Chō to Ushijima, "you took a good rest. I waited patiently for you to waken, for time is running out."

Ushijima smiled. "I could not sleep because you snored so loudly. It was like thunder."

Chō ignored the jibe. "Who will go first, you or me?" he asked. "Shall I die first and lead you to another world?"

"I will take the lead," said Ushijima.

"Excellency, you will go to paradise. I to hell. I cannot accompany you to that other world. Our hero, Saigō Takamori,* before committing hara-kiri, played chess with his orderly, and said, 'I will die whenever you are ready.' As for me, I will drink King of Kings while awaiting death."

Having exchanged poems, the two generals said their final goodbyes to the remaining officers and men who had "shared the hardships of war." Then Chō took off his tunic and, candle in hand, led Ushijima and the others down the dark tunnel to the cave entrance. When they reached it, recalled Yahara, "the moon shone on the South Seas. Clouds moved swiftly. The skies were quiet. The morning mist crept slowly up the deep valley. It was as if everything on earth trembled, waiting with deep emotion."

It was 4:10 a.m., and just before dawn. Moving out onto the narrow ledge, Ushijima and Chō knelt on a quilt covered with a white sheet to signify death. With no room to perform the ceremony properly by facing the Imperial Palace to the north, they looked south over the ocean. On the back of Chō's white shirt, written in immaculate brushstrokes, were the words:

With bravery I served my nation,
With loyalty I dedicate my life.

Silently the two men unbuttoned their shirts to bare their abdomens. Then an aide, Lieutenant Yoshino, handed Ushijima a knife with half its blade wrapped in white cloth. As the general plunged it with both

* One of the three great samurai nobles of the Meiji Restoration, Saigō Takamori reluctantly agreed to lead the Satsuma Rebellion in 1877. Wounded in battle, he committed ritual suicide by thrusting a short sword into his stomach before his head was severed by a colleague.

hands into his stomach, Adjutant Sakaguchi, standing to his right rear, brought his samurai sword down on Ushijima's neck, "severing his spinal column." He fell forward on the sheet, lifeless. Then it was Chō's turn and the ritual was repeated.

Once their generals were dead, remembered Yahara, "the remaining soldiers broke ranks and ran down the cliff." While three orderlies buried the generals nearby, Yahara sat down outside the cave with a white-faced but exultant Sakaguchi who declared: "I did it!"

Utterly exhausted, they watched the sky slowly brighten. "What a splendid last moment!" recalled Yahara. "It marked the glorious end to our three months of hard battle, our proud Thirty-Second Army, and the lives of our generals."[3]

At 1:05 p.m. that day, June 22, temporary Tenth Army commander General Geiger announced at army headquarters that all organized resistance on Okinawa had ceased. As representatives of the Tenth Army, the two corps and the divisions stood in formation, the band of the 2nd Marine Aircraft Wing played "The Star-Spangled Banner," and the color guard of military policemen raised the American flag over Okinawa. As the flag neared the top of the pole, a sudden breeze swept it out "full against a blue and quiet sky."[4]

There was, of course, still a fair amount of mopping up required before the island was secure. One intelligence summary, dated June 23, estimated that 4,000 Japanese soldiers were still at large on the island: with many hiding in "the hills and crags along the coast south and north-east of Mabuni," while others were "attempting to escape to the northern part of the island" where food was reported to be "plentiful" and "better hiding places" were "available." According to debriefed prisoners of war, Japanese soldiers had been "ordered to dress as civilians, and attempt to move individually or in groups of two to five, to the vicinity of Nago for [the] purpose of conducting guerilla warfare."[5]

The mopping-up operation began on June 23, the day General Stilwell landed on the island to take command, with the two corps assigned respective zones of action and three phase lines they needed to reach. The first sweep to the south produced the greatest results, with cave positions "systematically sealed up by flamethrowers and demolitions," and "several bloody skirmishes" as well-armed groups tried to break through the American lines and head north. Extensive patrolling found a number of soldiers hiding in cane fields and rice paddies. When the American soldiers turned north, however, fewer and fewer of the enemy were discovered and the third and final phase line between Naha and Yonabaru was reached with "comparative ease" on the 30th, three days ahead of schedule. The mop-up had killed an estimated 8,975 Japanese soldiers, and captured a further 2,902, while 906 non-military labor personnel were also taken. American casualties were 783.[6]

There were, for the American troops, some grim discoveries. After only four days on the island, Stilwell "scrambled down" the cliff at Mabuni to get a look inside "Ushijima's cave." He wrote in his diary: "Narrow entrance. Stinking Japs. Back up. All commanders there. Ushijima and [Chō] buried on top. Bugler blew 'To the Colors,' and the flag was raised. Then I made a speech to about 1,000 of the 7th Division massed for the ceremony. Back to [air]strip and home."[7]

A day or two later, Lieutenant Frank Gibney, USN, an intelligence officer with Tenth Army HQ, was led by an engineer captain into a cave near Maedera village. "After a walk through a long tunnel," he recalled, "we came on a huge underground cavern and one of the ghastliest sights I ever saw. Here lay General Amamiya [former commander of the 24th Division], surrounded by his staff and some 200 officers and men. They had all killed themselves with grenades, although Amamiya had thoughtfully given himself a lethal injection to avoid the rigors of ritual suicide. The cave floor was literally carpeted with corpses." They found one survivor: the general's orderly, who had been told "to stay alive and report how they died—to the emperor, presumably."

According to Gibney, the engineer captain who had taken him into the cave was "unhinged by the experience" and "took a long time to recover." The Japanese orderly, on the other hand, "once released from the cave, seemed to shrug off the ordeal," and was seen by Gibney in one of the prison camps later that afternoon "playing volleyball with his fellow captives."[8]

On hearing the battle for Okinawa was over, Winston Churchill sent Truman a congratulatory cable. "The strength of willpower, devotion, and technical resources applied by the United States to this task," wrote the British prime minister, "joined with the death-struggle of the enemy, of whom 90,000 are reported to be killed, places this battle among the most intense and famous in military history."[9]

Hanson W. Baldwin, the Pulitzer Prize-winning military editor of the *New York Times*, agreed. "Never before had there been," he wrote, "probably never again will there be, such a vicious sprawling struggle of planes against planes, of ships against planes. Never before, in so short a space, had the Navy lost so many ships; never before in land fighting had so much American blood been shed in so short a time in so small an area: probably never before in any three months of the war had the enemy suffered so hugely, and the final toll of American casualties was the highest experienced in any campaign against the Japanese. There have been larger land battles, more protracted air campaigns, but Okinawa was the largest combined operation in a 'no quarter' struggle fought on, under and over the sea and land."[10]

Baldwin was correct. Okinawa was by far the bloodiest battle of the Pacific War, and one of the costliest in America's history. The Americans lost thirty-six ships (and a further 368 damaged), 763 planes and just under 50,000 men,* a quarter of whom were killed and missing, and the rest wounded. There were also more than 26,000 non-battle casualties, many suffering from combat fatigue or what today we would diagnose as PTSD.[11] Brigadier General Oliver Smith, who visited a psychiatric hospital near Chatan in late May, wrote of one case: "He had been engaged in the bitter fighting on the southern front. Probably he had lost a lot of sleep and had not gotten much to eat. One night he and his buddy were in a foxhole when a Japanese mortar shell burst on [its] edge . . . [He] was so keyed up emotionally that he lost consciousness when the mortar shell exploded. When he came to he was completely out of his head and had to be taken to the rear." While Smith sympathized with this case, he also felt there were many others of "so-called combat fatigue where

* American battle casualties were 49,151: 12,520 killed and missing, and 36,631 wounded. Army losses were 4,582 killed, 93 missing and 18,099 wounded. Marine losses were 2,938 killed and missing, and 13,708 wounded. Navy losses were 4,907 killed and 4,824 wounded. Non-battle casualties were 26,211: 15,613 for the army and 10,598 for the Marines.

the men should not have gotten back to the hospitals but should have been kept with their units until they had gotten over their fatigue or it was determined that they were shamming."[12]

The scale of Japanese and Okinawan losses was even more horrific. When the fighting ended on June 30, 100,000 soldiers and home guard (including 15,000 Okinawans) and 125,000 Okinawan civilians—totalling a third of the pre-war island population—had lost their lives. A further 7,400 soldiers were taken prisoner, many of them impressed Okinawans. Local survivor Masahide Ōta, who fought against the Americans and later became governor of the island, put the blame for so many civilian deaths squarely on the Japanese military. He wrote:

> The Japanese Imperial Army's objective was not to protect the local Okinawans, but instead to engage the Americans in combat for the longest time possible in order to earn time for further defensive preparations on the home islands. Rather than putting efforts into evacuation or the creation of a safe zone for civilians, the Okinawan people were used as a source of labor to build shelters, tunnels and other emplacements, to supplement combat units and to tend to wounded soldiers...
>
> The Japanese army's heartless approach to ejecting local civilians from caves was matched by their killing hundreds, maybe even thousands, of their own soldiers who were too badly wounded to retreat southward from hospital shelters.[13]

As the battle neared its end, atrocities by individual soldiers were commonplace. "Knowing that death was imminent," writes Thomas Huber, author of an account of the battle from the Japanese perspective, "the soldiers freely committed rape. In some cases, fearing discovery, [they] forced parents to kill their crying babies, or the soldiers killed the infants themselves. Sometimes, they killed Okinawans seeking to share a cave, fearing they were spies. This widespread abusiveness left deep scars and, to this day is a divisive influence between the people of Japan and of Japan's Okinawa...The no-surrender policy for the mass of soldiers was dehumanizing and had the unintended consequence of victimizing large numbers of Japanese civilians."[14]

Evidence supporting Huber's argument is contained in multiple eyewitness accounts by civilian survivors that are housed in the archives of the Okinawa Prefectural Peace Memorial Museum at Mabuni. The following three examples are typical. Nineteen-year-old Haru Maeda from Itoman had left a cave to find water when she came upon her mortally wounded younger brother and sister. They told her that Japanese soldiers had decapitated their mother, before stabbing both of them. "I gave them some water," she recalled, "and I held their hands. Before they died, they trembled all over, their teeth chattering. They said they were going to die and asked me what I would do after they died. I told them not to worry because I was going to join them soon anyway, and tried to make them feel comfortable. One of them was really in pain, trembling and crying [out] loud till the last moment."

Maeda then tried to commit suicide by strangling herself, but could not go through with it. Instead she found and confronted the guilty soldiers nearby, asking why they had done it. They just "couldn't help it," they replied, because they "were fighting a battle."

Another young Okinawan woman, Toyo Gima, was hiding in a cave near Makabe village, when a young boy started to cry. Worried the boy might betray them to the Americans, a Japanese soldier asked if his parents were present. When no one responded, recalled Gima, "they took him deeper into the cave and killed him." At first they "tried to strangle him with a triangular bandage for dressing a wound." When this did not work, they tore the cloth into thinner strips and used them. "All the civilians who saw it were crying," said Gima. "I actually saw them put the string round the boy's neck. But it was so horrible I couldn't watch it to the end."

The third testimony was provided by Mitsutoshi Nakajo, 16, from Yamagusuki village in the Kiyan Peninsula. He was also hiding in a cave with Japanese soldiers who suddenly announced they were going to kill the five children under three because they "might attract the enemy's attention." When Mitsutoshi and others offered to leave the cave with the children, the Japanese officer refused. "He said we would become spies," said Mitsutoshi. "He posted guards at the entrance of the cave and would not let us out. Then four or five soldiers came to us and took away the children from us one by one, including my brother, and gave them…injections [of poison]."

The following morning, the soldiers told Mitsutoshi and the remaining civilians in the cave that they were going to "dispose" of them "before the Americans captured us and crushed us under their tanks." It was a ruse to steal their food. Fortunately American soldiers attacked the cave before this could happen, throwing charges inside that killed most of the soldiers. Mitsutoshi survived.[15]

The behavior of the Japanese was, for Masahide Ōta, in marked contrast to that of the American military who had from the start of the campaign provided "food, clothing, and shelter to displaced residents in areas that it had already secured." They had "planned ahead and prepared for this contingency and their kindness in this respect no doubt saved tens of thousands of Okinawans from death by starvation." Writing in 2013, four years before his death, Ōta acknowledged the recent ill feeling by Okinawans toward the large U.S. military presence on the island, but said it could never erase the fact that the immediate post-war years "were marked by strong feelings of gratitude among Okinawans toward the United States for its efforts to avoid a humanitarian disaster."[16]

42

"All he talked about was you"

After they were pulled off Kunishi Ridge on June 15, Lieutenant Bruce Watkins and the other fifty-four survivors of Easy Company, 2/1st Marines, saw no more serious fighting on Okinawa. Instead, after a few days' rest, they were put into a defense line "strung across the island to pick up any enemy stragglers." From a Seabee camp next door they got some "great food." In return, they let the Seabees man their machine guns and rifle pits at night. The construction men "thought it was great," noted Watkins, "as they fired at shadows all night."

As the days passed, Easy was sent two replacement officers, and a handful of lightly wounded enlisted men returned from hospital. Watkins used the time to write to the relatives of all forty-five Easy men killed in battle. It was a sad, difficult task, and he tried to give the families "all the facts at hand, asking all remaining men to contribute." It became, however, a "healing process" for Watkins and, once done, his "mood was greatly improved."[1]

In early July, with the island secure, Easy Company moved with the rest of the 1st Marine Division to a camp on the northwestern shore of the Motobu Peninsula. "The countryside," remembered one officer, "was clean, open, pine-wooded, and really attractive, though too hot for comfort at this season. The land rose steeply in coral cliffs to a ridge, then sloped gradually through a broad, fertile plain to rather steep mountains."[2]

It was a training camp for the division's next stop, Japan, and the men were housed in large pyramidal tents with, "wonder of wonders," cots and blankets. "We even erected mess halls," wrote Watkins, "with canvas sides and tin roofs; quite luxurious. Food got better and morale went up." Less welcome was the rumor that all six Marine Divisions would take part in the assault on Kyushu, scheduled for November 1. Watkins heard that casualties among the assault troops were expected to be eighty percent. "I know," he wrote, "that it affected me deeply and it was hard to be cheerful. The odds were getting very bad."[3] When "Jep" Carrell of King Company, 3/7th Marines, was told that the 1st Marine Division would be in the "first wave" to land on Honshu, and that losses would top half a million men, he and others "who had survived Okinawa" felt "thoroughly depressed."*[4]

The lucky ones—those who had been overseas for thirty months, and had the requisite points score—were rotated home. They included Lieutenant Chris Donner, the forward artillery observer, who kept repeating to himself: "Going home; going back safe and sound after almost two and a half years." He prayed he would not be needed for the "big push to finish Japan."[5]

To pay his last respects to his fallen comrades, Watkins visited the divisional cemetery near Yontan airfield. Containing row upon row of identical white crosses, it reminded him of the poem "In Flanders Fields" by the Canadian artillery officer John McCrae.† Looking first for the grave of his close friend Lee Height, he found "a simple cross bearing the legend '1st Lt Leon Hartson Height, USMCR.'" He stood for a long time in quiet contemplation, then moved on to the graves of "PFC Castro, whose last act was to fire into a cave; Capt. Ray Tiscornia, who had caught my touchdown pass last Christmas; PFC Dale Hansen, who was to receive the Congressional Medal of Honor; Frank Carey and his gesture of defiance; and some forty other men of E Company." It seemed so sad to him that these men, his brothers, had been "cut off in the very prime of life." How could it be, he wondered, that he "who had been everywhere with them was

* Watkins and Carrell were misinformed. Only the V Amphibious Corps (comprising the 3rd, 4th and 5th Marine Divisions) was slated for Operation Olympic, the invasion of Kyushu, on November 1, 1945, as part of General Krueger's 6th U.S. Army. The Tenth Army (including the III Amphibious Corps) would not be used until Operation Coronet, the much larger invasion of Honshu, in the spring of 1946. It would fight alongside the 8th and 1st Armies (the latter brought over from Europe), and a large force of British and Commonwealth troops. Both invasions were known collectively as Operation Downfall.

† Written in 1915, the first two lines read: "In Flanders fields the poppies blow/ Between the crosses, row on row."

spared? There were no answers as I silently said goodbye to them all and quietly left."[6]

Back in the United States, the families of those recently laid to rest in cemeteries on Okinawa were receiving the news they had long been dreading. In one such household, 1214 New York Avenue—a small detached timber-frame home a couple of blocks from the ocean in Cape May, New Jersey—lived Mrs. June Mackin, wife of Second Lieutenant Harold J. Mackin who had joined the 2/5th Marines as a replacement officer in late May 1945. Given command of the machine-gun section, Mackin was all for charging the nearest Japanese mortar positions on his first day in action until he was persuaded by his veteran squad leader, Corporal Jim Johnston, that it "wasn't a prudent thing to do at night." Mackin was, noted Johnston, "a big, brave, pleasant Irishman, a ninety-day wonder, and this was his first dose of combat." He added: "He was a great fellow. If we could have kept him alive long enough for him to get some idea about the war to go along with his book learning, I know he would have made a good officer."[7]

Unfortunately, Johnston was wounded a few days after Mackin's arrival and so not able to help the rookie officer bed in. The almost inevitable outcome was the delivery of a Western Union telegram to Mrs. Mackin on July 7:

> Deeply regret to inform you that your husband Second Lieutenant Harold J. Mackin Jr., USMCR, died June 21, 1945, of wounds received in action at Okinawa Island, Ryukyu Islands, in the performance of his duty and service of his country. When information is received regarding burial you will be notified. To prevent possible aid to our enemies do not divulge the name of his ship or station. Please accept my heartfelt sympathy.
>
> A. A. Vandegrift, General, USMC, Commandant of the Marine Corps.[8]

Such news at any time would have been bad enough. But for June Mackin it was especially heartbreaking because she was pregnant with the couple's first child. Once over the initial shock, she was desperate to know the circumstances of her husband's death: what were his last words, if any? And had he mentioned her and their unborn child?

The first proper details did not reach her until early October in the form of a letter from one of her husband's soldiers, Corporal Bob Miles, who was serving with the 5th Marines in China. "I would have written some time ago," noted Miles, but "I have just returned from the hospital myself."

> It was my privilege and pleasure to have served under your husband, Lt Harold Mackin, affectionately known to me as "Mack." Mack & I were both wounded by the same bullet. We were evacuated to the same hospital, at the same time. It was there that Mack ask[ed] me to write you.
>
> I would like for you to know Mrs. Mackin, Mack was loved and admired by all who knew him, and although an officer, Mack was considered just one of the boys. Mack lived and fought & died just like the man which he was.
>
> I, as one of Mack's best friends, wish to offer you my condolence, and if it is in my power ever to be of any assistance, please don't hesitate to let me know.

Unsatisfied by this bald account of her husband's death, and taking Corporal Miles at his word, June Mackin did what thousands of widows processing similar tragedies might have lacked the audacity to do, and wrote back asking for the "full details," however distressing. They were given in a second letter from China:

> Mrs. Mackin, your husband was wounded late on the afternoon of June 20, during the assault and taking of Hill 81...The Japs let the first [squad] pass, then started shooting, cutting us off... We were out in front of the lines about 700 yards. Mack & I jumped into a shell hole. It was very shallow. A sniper was shooting from our rear, a sniper from the right, and a machine gun from the front. The sniper on the right could see us enough to shoot. His first two shots hit between Mack & I. So we jumped up and ran for a large mound of dirt. Just then the machine gun started firing.
>
> The first bullet hit both Mack & I. We were running toward

> our front lines. The bullet passed through my right chest, struck Mack in the left buttocks. We both fell behind the mound of dirt.

Stretchered out under the cover of smoke, explained Corporal Miles, they were taken to the battalion aid station where they were both "laughing and joking about going home." Noticing Mack frown, Miles asked if he was badly hurt. "He did not say anything," recalled Miles, "just smiled. That is when I found out the bullet had entered his buttocks, turned up, passed through his stomach. I never knew he was hit that bad. He never complained about pain." That night they operated on Mack in a field hospital in a desperate attempt to save him. When he was returned to the ward, noted Miles, "they couldn't keep him still." Fortunately he recognized his corporal's voice and "did what I told him to." Miles added: "All he talked about was you and the prospect of being a father. He was always telling me about the hamburgers you and he used to eat at the boardwalk. I told him it would be no time at all, until you & j[unio]r and himself would be there together."

But Mack knew that he was "going fast," and that there was no use "kidding himself." It was then that he asked Miles to write to his wife and tell her "all I could think of, if I pulled through." A few minutes later, Miles was evacuated out of Okinawa by air. Before leaving, the doctor assured him that he would "do everything in his power to save Mack, but his chances were very slim." So it proved, and Mack died the following day.

Having apologized for writing in such a blunt manner, Miles had a final request of his own: "When & if the new arrival comes, I would like to know if it is a boy or a girl? Mack wanted a boy. Please don't think of me as forward in asking about the baby."[9]

In mid-July, Watkins left his camp in the north of Okinawa to visit a navy friend whose ship was anchored in Buckner Bay, the former Nakagusuku Bay renamed by American troops in honor of their late commander. He soon "got a ride in a jeep with a driver, interpreter, and a captured Jap colonel." They drove most of the way on a "one-lane dirt road," but by Shuri it had expanded into a "four-lane crushed coral highway." The sight of a "a huge rotary [i.e. roundabout] with all kinds of military trucks in motion" caused the colonel to say in Japanese: "Now I know why we lost the war."[10]

Only later did Watkins learn that the colonel was Hiromichi Yahara, the architect of Japan's ferocious defense of the island. Dressed in civilian clothes, he had left the headquarters cave at Mabuni on June 23 and was captured by American soldiers a couple of days later. At first he managed to convince them he was a civilian refugee, and it was only in mid-July that he was denounced as an IJA colonel by a former member of his staff who was working for the Americans. He was being driven to the new Tenth Army headquarters, near Goeku village in central Okinawa, when he briefly crossed paths with Bruce Watkins.

Taken to a special stockade, Yahara was interrogated by intelligence officer Lieutenant Ken Lamott, who was fluent in Japanese, with Lieutenant Frank Gibney assisting. Well aware that the Tenth Army would soon take part in the invasion of Japan, Lamott and Gibney were anxious to get as much useful information out of Yahara as possible. "Our experience with the diehard resistance on Okinawa," noted Gibney, "seemed to presage an even bloodier struggle for the Japanese homeland."

But while Yahara was "quite ready to review and explain the Japanese side of the Okinawa operation," remembered Gibney, he was "reluctant to discuss anything bearing on the future." They pressed him only once. Having just attended a long staff conference on possible landing sites in Honshu, they asked him rather casually where *he* would choose if he had to invade the island. "Why, Kujikuri-hama, I suppose," he replied. "It's the obvious place." They kept it from him, of course, but the staff conference, after much arguing, had come to the same conclusion.[11]

As Colonel Yahara was being interrogated on Okinawa, a conference was taking place in the Berlin suburb of Potsdam that would have momentous consequences for the millions of American servicemen due to invade Japan proper. Hosted by the Soviets, it was a meeting of the "Big Three"—Harry Truman, Winston Churchill and Soviet dictator Joseph Stalin—to discuss a host of global issues, including the post-war political and territorial settlement of Europe, and the possibility that the Soviet Union might enter the war in the Pacific on the Allied side. Before leaving for Europe on July 6, Truman had spoken in the White House with Secretary of War Henry Stimson on the options for ending the war with Japan. The purpose of this meeting was for Truman to read a memorandum that Stimson had drawn up, in consultation with the Secretary of the Navy, the acting Secretary of State and the Joint Chiefs of Staff, entitled "Proposed Program for Japan."

The memo began by stating that, in line with the decision taken at the June 18 meeting, preparations for the invasion of Japan "are now actually going on." Yet, it continued, there was "reason to believe that the operation for the occupation of Japan following the landing may be a very long, costly and arduous struggle on our part." This was partly because of the rugged terrain—which, in Stimson's opinion, "would be susceptible to a last-ditch defense such as has been made on Iwo Jima and Okinawa and which of course is very much larger than either of those two areas"—and partly because the "highly patriotic" Japanese were likely to put up a "fanatical resistance." It would be, for the United States, "an even more bitter finish fight than in Germany," with enormous losses and the virtual destruction of Japanese infrastructure.

So was there, Stimson asked, a viable alternative to a forceful occupation that would secure for the United States "the equivalent of an unconditional surrender of her forces and a permanent destruction of her power again to strike an aggressive blow at the 'peace of the Pacific'"? Stimson thought that there was, in the form of a "warning of what is to come and a definite opportunity to capitulate." There were, after all, a number of factors in America's favor: Japan had "no allies"; her navy was "nearly destroyed" and she was vulnerable to a sea blockade that would deprive her of "food and supplies"; she was open to concentrated air attack; she was facing not only Anglo-American forces but also "the rising forces of China and the ominous threat from Russia"; America had "inexhaustible and untouched industrial resources," and the "great moral superiority" of being the "victim" of Japan's "first sneak attack."

The memo made no mention of the atomic bomb, mainly because, on grounds of secrecy, it was never referred to unless it was absolutely necessary. But it was discussed at the meeting by Truman and Stimson. The latter wanted the warning to Japan to refer to the "varied and overwhelming character of the force" they were about to "bring to bear on the islands," and the "inevitability and completeness of the destruction which the full application of this force will entail." This was, of course, code for the bomb and a decision on whether or not to mention it specifically in the warning was still to be decided. But Stimson was convinced that such a warning might work, not least because Japan was "susceptible to reason in such a crisis to a greater extent than is indicated by our current press." He wrote: "Japan is not a nation composed wholly of mad fanatics of an entirely different mentality from ours."

If, however, the warning was ignored, and Japan refused to capitulate, he reasoned that the use of the bomb would be entirely justified. It all now depended on the test explosion which was scheduled for the morning of July 16. Truman gave his approval in principle for what would become the Potsdam Declaration. The only element of the memorandum he was still unsure about was Stimson's suggestion that, as a sop to the conservatives, Japan should be allowed to keep its emperor. But he did agree that, if the test was successful, Stalin should be told of the bomb's existence and that America "intended to use it against the enemy, Japan."[12]

Everything now hinged on the test in the New Mexico desert.

43

“The most terrible thing ever discovered”

As the clock approached 5:29 a.m. on July 16, the watching scientists grew increasingly nervous. All eyes were fixed on the top of a hundred-foot-high steel tower in a remote section of the Alamogordo Air Base in New Mexico. There, 10,000 yards north of the control shelter, the first detonation of an atomic bomb in history was due to take place. The size of a Volkswagen car, the bomb looked like a ball with wires poking out in all directions. It was a “Fat Man” implosion-type device, using plutonium enriched at the reactor in Hanford.

Thunder and lightning had already delayed the detonation from its original time of 4:00 a.m., and some scientists thought a longer postponement was necessary. But Dr. Robert Oppenheimer, director of the Manhattan Project, held his nerve and the weather had cleared.

As the last seconds ticked off, Oppenheimer “grew tenser” and “scarcely breathed.” He was holding on to a post to steady himself, staring straight ahead, when the announcer shouted, “Now!”

A tremendous burst of light—“equal to several suns in midday,” a “huge ball of fire” which “mushroomed and rose to a height of over 10,000 feet before it dimmed”—was followed by the “deep growling roar of the explosion.” The fireball was seen clearly at Albuquerque, Santa Fe, El Paso and other points up to 180 miles away. The sound traveled more than a hundred miles. In its wake it left a massive cloud which “surged and billowed upward with tremendous power, reaching the substratosphere at an elevation of 41,000 feet, in just a few minutes.” Where the tower had stood was left a crater, from which “all vegetation had vanished,” with a diameter of 1,200 feet and a slight slope toward the center. The steel tower had “evaporated.”

One witness described the effects of the explosion as "unprecedented, magnificent, stupendous and terrifying." The whole terrain was lit by a "golden, purple, violet, gray and blue" color and a clarity and beauty that could not be described. Then, thirty seconds later, came an "air blast pressing hard against the people and things, to be followed almost immediately by the strong, sustained, awesome roar which warned of doomsday and made us feel puny."

Watching the bomb ignite, Oppenheimer's face "relaxed into an expression of tremendous relief," though many of the observers standing at the back of the shelter were "knocked flat by the blast." The tension in the room dissipated as the scientists started to congratulate each other. "Everyone sensed, 'This is it!'" wrote a brigadier general who was present. "No matter what might happen now all knew that the impossible scientific job had been done. Atomic fission would no longer be hidden in the cloisters of the theoretical physicists' dreams. It was almost full grown at birth. It was a great new force to be used for good or for evil. There was a feeling in that shelter that those concerned with its nativity should dedicate their lives to the mission that it would always be used for good."

Dr. Kistiakowsky, the "impulsive Russian" who had developed the "highly special explosive," threw his arms around Oppenheimer with shouts of glee. "All the pent-up emotions were released in those few minutes," wrote the brigadier general, "and all seemed to sense immediately that the explosion had far exceeded the most optimistic expectations and wildest hopes of scientists. All seemed to feel that they had been present at the birth of a new age—The Age of Atomic Energy." They also felt that, "no matter what else may happen," America now had the means to bring the Pacific War to a "speedy conclusion and save thousands of American lives."[1]

After a "wonderful" nine-day crossing of the Atlantic on the heavy cruiser USS *Augusta*, President Truman and his party disembarked at Antwerp in Belgium on July 15 before flying on to Berlin's Gatow airfield. Met by Henry Stimson, Admiral King and a Soviet delegation, Truman inspected an honor guard from the U.S. 2nd Armored "Hell on Wheels" Division before he was driven to his quarters—a comfortable "three-story stucco residence," the former home of the head of the German film colony, and henceforth known as "the Little

White House" (though it was painted yellow)—in the nearby town of Babelsberg.

Next morning, July 16, the British prime minister came to call. It was their first face-to-face meeting, and Truman was impressed. "I had an instant liking for this man," he wrote later, "who had done so much for his own country and for the Allied cause. There was something very open and genuine about the way he greeted me." Though they did not discuss the conference in any detail, Truman told Churchill that he had an agenda and asked him if he had one too.

"No," replied Churchill, "I don't need one."

His scheduled meeting with Stalin delayed until the following day—the Soviet premier, it later transpired, had had a minor heart attack—Truman spent the afternoon sightseeing in Berlin. Driving past the destroyed Reich Chancellery, on Wilhelmstrasse, where Hitler had often harangued his Nazi followers, Truman commented: "That's what happens when a man overreaches himself."[2]

That evening, as coffee was being served after dinner, Truman was informed that Stimson and General Marshall were on their way to discuss an important matter. He received them in his second-floor office. Jimmy Byrnes, recently appointed Secretary of State, was also present. Stimson gave the president a cable just in from George L. Harrison, his special assistant and a member of the Interim Committee, in Washington, DC. It read:

> Operated on this morning. Diagnosis not yet complete but results seem satisfactory and already exceed expectations. Local press release necessary as interest extends great distance. Dr. Groves pleased. He returns tomorrow. I will keep you posted.

Truman and Byrnes were overjoyed. This was the news they had all been waiting for: the test explosion had been a success. The other piece of good news, said Stimson, was that Japan had apparently put out a peace-feeler to Russia, though this needed to be verified. Either way, it was a good time to deliver the ultimatum to Japan that they had discussed before Truman's departure. If Japan ignored it, they could bring to bear the "full force" of their new weapons.[3]

The following day, Truman met Stalin for the first time. He was surprised by the Soviet dictator's short stature—"he was not over five feet five or six inches tall"—but was mostly "pleased" with how the meeting went. "He seemed to be in good humor," noted Truman. "He was extremely polite, and when he was ready to leave, he told me that he had enjoyed the visit." They met again, later that day, during the first session of the Potsdam Conference at the Cecilienhof Palace, a "two-story brownstone house of four wings with a courtyard in the center." But it was not until July 24 that he "casually" mentioned to Stalin that the United States had a "new weapon of unusual destructive force." Stalin did not seem particularly interested. His only comment was that he was glad to hear about the weapon and hoped the Americans would make "good use of it against the Japanese."[4]

Churchill, who had known of the project from the beginning, was told about the successful test by Stimson on July 17. He had no doubt that it needed to be used if it could end the war. He wrote later:

> Up to this moment we had shaped our ideas toward an assault upon the homeland of Japan by terrific air bombing and by the invasion of very large armies. We had contemplated the desperate resistance of the Japanese fighting to the death with samurai devotion, not only in pitched battles, but in every cave and dugout. I had in my mind the spectacle of Okinawa island, where many thousands of Japanese, rather than surrender, had drawn up in line and destroyed themselves with hand-grenades after their leaders had solemnly performed the rite of hara-kiri. To quell the Japanese resistance might well require the loss of a million American lives and half that number of British—or more if we could get them there: for we were resolved to share the agony. Now all this nightmare picture had vanished. In its place was the vision—fair and bright it seemed—of the end of the whole war in one or two violent shocks.[5]

There were only two questions now for Truman and his advisers. What should the warning to Japan say? And, if it was ignored, which cities should be targeted? On the latter question, Truman agreed with the Interim Committee's advice that a war plant surrounded by workers' homes was the ideal target, telling Stimson that, in line with the "laws of war," the bomb should be dropped on a "war-production center of prime military importance." Various cities were considered, including Kyoto, the old imperial capital. But it was removed from the list when Stimson pointed out its importance to the Japanese as a "cultural and religious shrine." The final shortlist, agreed by Truman after consultation with Stimson, George Marshall and "Hap" Arnold, was: Hiroshima, Kokura, Niigata and Nagasaki. "The order of selection," wrote Truman, "was in accordance with the military importance of these cities, but allowance would be given for weather conditions at the time of the bombing."[6] He noted in his diary: "I have told... Stimson to use it so that military objectives and soldiers and sailors are the target and not women and children. Even if the Japs are savages, ruthless, merciless and fanatic, we, as the leader of the world for the common welfare, cannot drop this terrible bomb on the old Capitol or the new [Tokyo]."[7]

On July 24, General Carl Spaatz, commanding the U.S. Army's Strategic Air Forces, was ordered to drop the first bomb "as soon after August 3 as weather would permit." The order would stand, Truman told Stimson, unless he notified him that the Japanese reply to the ultimatum was "acceptable."[8] He had chosen early August because, according to Commander George Elsey, a duty officer in the White House Map Room* who was in Potsdam, by then Truman would have left Germany. "He wanted to be away from the Russians," recalled Elsey, "and on his way home before the actual dropping of the first bomb."[9]

After consulting with his co-signatories Churchill and Chiang Kai-shek, the Chinese nationalist leader, Truman issued the ultimatum to Japan—known as the Potsdam Declaration—in the evening of July 26. "We," it began, "the President of the United States, the President of the National Government of the Republic of China, and the Prime Minister of Great Britain, representing the hundreds of millions of our countrymen, have conferred and agree that Japan shall be given an opportunity to end this war." Prodigious forces—many times greater than those used against Germany—were "poised to

* The president's intelligence and communications center which received a constant flow of secret information from the War, Navy and State departments, as well as foreign militaries and governments.

strike the final blows." The time had therefore come "for Japan to decide whether she will continue to be controlled by those self-willed militaristic advisers whose unintelligent calculations have brought the Empire of Japan to the threshold of annihilation, or whether she will follow the path of reason."

In spite of Stimson's reservations, the document demanded the "unconditional surrender of all Japan's armed forces" or the country would face "prompt and utter destruction." It included no specific mention of the bomb, though the threat was implicit. Nor was there an offer for the Japanese to keep their emperor. Instead, the declaration warned that the authority and influence of those who had "deceived and misled the people of Japan into embarking on world conquest" would be "eliminated for all time." Japanese sovereignty, moreover, would be limited to the home islands, "and such minor islands as we determine." In return, the Japanese military forces, after they had been disarmed, would be allowed "to return to their homes with the opportunity to lead peaceful and productive lives." It continued:

> We do not intend that the Japanese shall be enslaved as a race or destroyed as a nation, but stern justice shall be meted out to all war criminals, including those who have visited cruelties upon our prisoners. The Japanese Government shall remove all obstacles to the revival and strengthening of democratic tendencies among the Japanese people. Freedom of speech, of religion, and of thought, as well as respect for the fundamental human rights shall be established.
>
> Japan shall be permitted to maintain such industries as will sustain her economy... Eventual Japanese participation in world trade relations shall be permitted.[10]

Not that Truman expected the Japanese to comply. "We will issue a warning statement," he wrote in his diary on July 25, "asking the Japs to surrender and save lives. I'm sure they will not do that, but we have given them the chance. It is certainly a good thing for the world that Hitler's crowd or Stalin's did not discover this atomic bomb. It seems to be the most terrible thing ever discovered, but it can be made the most useful."[11]

As Truman had anticipated, there was no formal response from the Japanese government to the ultimatum. Instead, on July 28, Radio Tokyo announced that Japan would continue to fight.[12]

44

"My God, what have we done?"

At 2:45 a.m. on August 6, 1945, the *Enola Gay*—a modified B-29 Superfortress bomber—took off from the Northern Mariana island of Tinian bound for Hiroshima, a city of 245,000 inhabitants, in Honshu, Japan. It was piloted by thirty-year-old Colonel Paul Tibbets, commanding the 509th Composite Group, who had named the bomber after his mother. Also on board was a crew of seven and an atomic bomb—code-named "Little Boy,"* a uranium-235 gun-type mechanism—that was ten feet long, twenty-eight inches across, and weighed close to four and a half tons.

Worried the bomber might crash on take-off and destroy half the island, the weaponeer, Captain William S. "Deak" Parsons, waited until they were airborne before he armed "Little Boy." Four hours into the flight, with Parsons' work complete, Tibbets announced over the intercom: "This is it, we are dropping the first atomic bomb."[1]

At around 7:00 a.m., Japanese radar detected the *Enola Gay* and two observation planes, loaded with cameras and scientific equipment, heading toward Honshu. An alert was broadcast throughout

* The enriched uranium and other parts needed for the assembly of "Little Boy" had been transported from the United States by the heavy cruiser USS *Indianapolis* which averaged twenty-nine knots—a record that still stands today—on its 74.5-hour voyage from San Francisco to Pearl Harbor. Continuing on to Tinian, the *Indianapolis* delivered its top-secret cargo on July 26. Four days later, sailing between Guam and Leyte in the Philippines, the cruiser was hit by two torpedoes from the Japanese submarine *I-58* and sunk. Three hundred crew members went down with the ship, leaving almost 900 adrift in the water, many without life jackets. By the time the survivors were spotted by an American plane on August 2, only 316 were still alive. The rest had died from exposure, salt poisoning, dehydration and shark attack. It was the worst maritime disaster in the history of the U.S. Navy.

the Hiroshima area. But when the only plane in sight was an American weather aircraft, the citizens of Hiroshima thought the danger had passed and went about their business.

Another warning for people to take shelter was broadcast on Japanese radio as the B-29s approached the city. Many people ignored it. At 8:09 a.m., with visibility perfect, the crew of the *Enola Gay* could see the city 31,000 feet beneath them. They headed for their target—a T-shaped bridge at the junction of the Honkawa and Motoyasu rivers in downtown Hiroshima—and, at 8:15 a.m., the bombardier Major Thomas Ferebee released "Little Boy."

The sudden loss of weight caused *Enola Gay*'s nose to lurch up dramatically as Tibbets executed a "very steep turn" so that they could make their escape. It took the bomb forty-three seconds to fall to its predetermined detonation height of 1,900 feet. Tibbets had asked the tail gunner, Technical Sergeant Bob Caron, to describe to the rest of the crew what he could see when the bomb exploded. "It was," Caron recalled, "an awesome sight." A vast mushroom cloud, white on the outside, purplish black toward the interior, with a fiery red core, was boiling up from the city. As they got further away, Caron could see the city, not just the mushroom, and it was covered with a "low, bubbling mass," like molasses, "spreading out and running up into the foothills." Flames were springing up through this mass "in different spots." It was now, Caron recalled, that "Tibbets turned the airplane around so that everybody could get a look at it."

Tibbets remembered an "awful cloud...mushrooming, terrible and incredibly tall." For a moment, no one spoke; "then everyone was talking." The co-pilot, Captain Robert Lewis, pounded Tibbets on the shoulder and said: "Look at that! Look at that! Look at that!"

Ferebee wondered if the radioactivity would make them all "sterile," and Lewis said he could "taste the atomic fission" and it was like "lead."

Keeping a log of the flight, Lewis scribbled: "If I live a hundred years, I'll never quite get these few minutes out of my mind. Everyone on the ship is actually dumbstruck even though we had expected something fierce. I honestly have the feeling of groping for words to explain this or I might say, my God, what have we done?"

The navigator Captain Theodore "Dutch" Van Kirk, on the other hand, was thinking the same thought that would occur to thousands of American soldiers when they heard the news: "Thank God the war is over and I don't have to get shot at anymore. I can go home."[2]

Mrs. Hatsuyo Nakamura, a tailor's widow, was standing by her kitchen window, watching a neighbor tear down his house to create an air-raid defense fire lane, when she was blinded by a white flash.* She thought at once of her children, but had taken only a single step when she was lifted off her feet and thrown into the next room, over the raised sleeping platform, followed by bits of her house. Timbers and house tiles fell around and on her. Shaking off the debris, she heard her youngest, 5-year-old Myeko, cry: "Mother, help me!"

While she struggled to free Myeko, buried up to her chest, she heard more voices shouting from below: "*Tasukete! Tasukete!* [Help! Help!]"

"Toshio! Yaeko!" she yelled, calling the names of her son and elder daughter, 10 and 8 years old respectively. Their answers were barely audible.

Leaving Myeko, still partly trapped but able to breathe, she tore desperately at the wreckage covering her other children. At last she spotted Toshio's head and, by gripping it, was able to pull him out. He told her he had been blown ten feet across the room, and landed on his elder sister. The mother kept digging until she found Yaeko and yanked on her arm.

"*Itai!* [It hurts!]" cried the child.

"There's no time to say whether it hurts or not," replied the mother, hauling with all her strength until her daughter broke free. The last to be released was young Myeko. All three were dirty and bruised, but otherwise uninjured.

She took them out into the street and, though it was a hot day, returned to the wrecked house to find clothes for them, including padded-cotton air-raid helmets known as *bokuzuki*. Myeko kept asking: "Why is it night already? Why did our house fall down? What happened?"

Her mother looked around and saw through the gloom that every house in the neighborhood had collapsed. The neighbor, who had

* Mrs. Nakamura's house was three-quarters of a mile from the center of the explosion.

been tearing down his house for the good of the community, lay dead.[3]

At the city's Red Cross Hospital, 25-year-old surgeon Dr. Terufumi Sasaki was walking along the main corridor with a blood specimen in his hand when a blinding flash of light forced him to his knees. "Sasaki, *gambare!* [Be brave!]" he said to himself.

Moments later, the bomb blast tore through the hospital, knocking off Sasaki's glasses and shattering the bottle of blood he was carrying. He ran to the chief surgeon's office and found him badly cut by flying glass. "The hospital," read one account, "was in horrible confusion: heavy partitions and ceilings had fallen on patients, beds had overturned, windows had blown in and cut people, blood was spattered on the walls and floors, instruments were everywhere, many of the patients were running about screaming, many more lay dead."

The only doctor to escape injury, Sasaki collected bandages to bind the wounds of those less fortunate. Meanwhile, outside, "maimed and dying citizens turned their unsteady steps toward the Red Cross Hospital," a trickle that by nightfall had became a torrent of 10,000 people.[4]

Hearing an aircraft, a young woman looked up and saw a "big flash." She immediately fell forward to protect her face and was knocked unconscious. When she came to, there was no sign of any of her friends. They had been "either blown to bits or burned." She recalled: "All my clothes were torn away, except my undergarment. My skin just peeled off and was hanging from my body...The heat was so intense that I jumped into the nearby river, the small river that was running through the city. All my friends were in the river."[5]

Hajimi Kito, a 19-year-old soldier, could hear lots of voices and young children running toward him. "What I remember most," he said later, "are the screams for water. There were so many people, you couldn't possibly provide water for a fraction of them. It was just an impossibility. And they did die. We had to carry these bodies and burn, cremate them in some way. Because they were corpses now."[6]

* * *

In the suburbs, Kiyoshi Tanimoto, the pastor of the Hiroshima Methodist Church, was unloading a handcart of belongings at the house of a well-wisher when the bomb exploded two miles away. He saw a tremendous flash of light traveling from east to west, from the city toward the hills. Throwing himself between two big rocks in the garden, he felt a blast wave wash over him, followed by wooden fragments and pieces of tile from the house. Barely able to see from the dust cloud in the air, he ran out into the street and saw a squad of soldiers emerge from a dugout, "one of thousands of dugouts in which the Japanese apparently intended to resist invasion, hill by hill, life for life." It should have protected them. But blood was pouring from their heads, chests and backs. They were stupefied.

That evening, as he gave water to survivors, one told him: "I couldn't help my sister who was buried under the house, because I had to take care of my mother who got a deep wound in her eye and our house soon set fire, and we hardly escaped. Look, I lost my home, my family." But he was still determined, he told Tanimoto, to dedicate what he had to win the war "for our country's sake."

Next morning, many of those the pastor had helped were dead. Not one of them had cried out, though their wounds were excruciatingly painful. "They died in silence," noted Tanimoto, "with no grudge, setting their teeth to bear it. All for the country!"[7]

Perhaps the most unlikely survivor was Akiko Takakura, 20, who was in the Bank of Hiroshima when the bomb exploded at a distance of just 300 meters. With terrible lacerations to her back, she stumbled outside to find a wasteland of rubble and corpses. "The fingertips of those dead bodies caught fire," she remembered, "and the fire gradually spread over their entire bodies from their fingers...I was shocked to know that fingers and bodies could be burned and deformed like that." The heat was so intense that she was finding it hard to breathe. "Maybe because the fire burned all the oxygen," she speculated. "I don't know. I could not open my eyes because of the smoke, which was everywhere."[8]

The bomb had detonated with the equivalent force of 20,000 tons of TNT, totally destroying over four square miles of city, including seventy percent of Hiroshima's buildings. Around 80,000 people were killed by the blast and the subsequent firestorm, a quarter of them soldiers. The dead included six American crew members of the B-24 bomber *Lonesome Lady* which had been shot down by flak during a mission to bomb the Japanese battleship *Haruna* in nearby Kure Harbour on July 28. Captured and taken to Chugoku Military Police headquarters in Hiroshima, most of the crew were still there when the bomb fell, and died in the conflagration. The exception was the 21-year-old pilot, who, a couple of days earlier, had been transferred to an interrogation center in Tokyo. It saved his life.[9]

President Harry Truman was eating lunch aboard the *Augusta*, four days into his journey back across the Atlantic, when he was handed a message:

> Big bomb dropped on Hiroshima August 5 at 7:15 p.m. Washington time. First reports indicate complete success which was even more conspicuous than earlier test.

He jumped to his feet and shouted: "This is the greatest thing in history. It's time for us to get home."

Within minutes, the ship's radio receivers began to carry news bulletins from Washington about the atomic bomb, as well as a press statement that Truman had authorized before he left Berlin. "Sixteen hours ago," began the president's statement, "an American airplane dropped one bomb on Hiroshima and destroyed its usefulness to the enemy. That bomb had more power than 20,000 tons of TNT. It had more than 2,000 times the blast power of the British 'Grand Slam' which is the largest bomb ever used in the history of warfare. The Japanese began the war from the air at Pearl Harbor. They have been repaid manyfold." The statement continued:

> What has been done is the greatest achievement of organized science in history. It was done under high pressure and without failure.
>
> We are now prepared to obliterate more rapidly and completely every productive enterprise the Japanese have above ground in any city. We shall destroy their docks, their factories,

> and their communications. Let there be no mistake; we shall completely destroy Japan's power to make war.
>
> It was to spare the Japanese people from utter destruction that the ultimatum of July 26 was issued at Potsdam. Their leaders promptly rejected that ultimatum. If they do not now accept our terms, they may expect a rain of ruin from the air, the like of which has never been seen on this earth. Behind this air attack will follow sea and land forces in such numbers and power as they have not yet seen and with the fighting skill of which they are already aware.[10]

When, in the aftermath of the Hiroshima bomb, no surrender offer came from Tokyo, General Spaatz was ordered to continue operations as planned. This meant dropping a second bomb as soon as preparations were complete, and the fact that Russia declared war on Japan on August 8 made no difference. A day later, the B-29 Superfortress *Bockscar*, piloted by Major Charles W. Sweeney, dropped the more complex plutonium bomb "Fat Man," weighing a little under five tons, on the Kyushu city of Nagasaki. The primary target that day, Kokura, was obscured by cloud, so after three passes Sweeney moved on to Nagasaki. The bomb was exploded at 1,800 feet, just north of the Mitsubishi Steel and Armament Works, with an estimated force of 22,000 tons of TNT.

Unlike Hiroshima, there was no firestorm and, thanks to the hilly topography, the total area of destruction was smaller than that caused by the earlier blast. Yet it still killed 40,000 people outright and wounded about the same number. Many more would die in the months ahead from the effects of burns, radiation sickness and other injuries. Among the fortunate survivors was Private Bill Franklin of 242 Squadron, Royal Air Force, who had been taken prisoner by the Japanese in 1942 and was working in a dockyard, three or four miles south of Nagasaki, when the bomb went off. He recalled:

> At approximately 10:50 a.m. by the foreman's watch, the students drew our attention to a distant object visible within the limits of our patch of blue sky. It appeared to be suspended on parachutes. Moments later a blinding white flash, brighter than a thousand rising suns, engulfed us.

> Following the flash, I did not hear any loud bang. In fact, there was a period of total silence, broken only by the clanging of the gong. Between the steps and me was 900 feet, with several obstacles: piles of debris, poles, keel blocks, and scrap metal strewn everywhere. Our group started to move out, every man for himself, in fear that the caisson would collapse and the sea rush in and swallow us up. I looked upward and saw the five stories of flimsy walls, which were built between the concrete, gradually bulge and burst open. The whole side of the installation appeared like a vast honeycomb.

Directed by guards back to the POW camp, they passed through crowds of panicked civilians, "crushing and trampling" as they tried to get away. By now a "mushroom-shaped formation of dirt and gasses" had gathered over Nagasaki "like an opened umbrella." Assuming, correctly, that it was a new type of bomb, Franklin felt a sense of satisfaction and relief. "We had finally witnessed retaliation," he wrote, "after being on the receiving end for three and a half years. It was some measure of reprisal for the vast number of our friends who had died from starvation and physical abuse. Now, there was no doubt in our minds that the end of the war was close."[11]

Exactly how close became clear at 7:33 a.m. on August 10 when Radio Tokyo stated that the Japanese government, "in conformity with the august wish of His Majesty [Emperor Hirohito] to restore the general peace," was "ready to accept the terms enumerated in the joint declaration which was issued at Potsdam, July 26, 1945 ... with the understanding that said declaration does not comprise any demand which prejudices the prerogatives of His Majesty as a sovereign ruler." In other words, they were prepared to surrender as long as Hirohito kept his throne.

Summoning Admiral Leahy and his chief political advisers, Truman asked their opinion. Leahy and Secretary of War Henry Stimson thought Hirohito should be allowed to remain, and that his presence would discourage renegades from fighting on regardless. Secretary of State Jimmy Byrnes was "less certain" that anything short of unconditional surrender was acceptable, and argued that only the United States should dictate terms. A compromise position was suggested by James Forrestal, Secretary of the Navy: to accept Japan's offer in principle, but only if the terms of surrender were spelled out so that they were clearly in line with the Potsdam Declaration. In effect, the emperor could stay if he signed the unconditional surrender document.

Truman backed Forrestal's response and—apart from a minor change suggested by the new British prime minister, Clement Attlee,* and his foreign secretary, Aneurin Bevan, that the emperor "should authorize and ensure the signature by the Government of Japan and the Japanese General Headquarters of the surrender terms necessary to carry out the provisions of the Potsdam Declaration"—it was duly dispatched to Tokyo, via Switzerland, on August 11.

For two days, there was no response. Finally, on August 14, Tokyo replied via the Swiss chargé d'affaires in Washington. The emperor had "issued an Imperial rescript regarding Japanese acceptance of the provisions of the Potsdam declaration." He was, moreover, "prepared to authorize and ensure the signature" by his government and military chiefs to conform with the terms of the Potsdam Declaration, and to order all military forces to "cease active operations" and "to surrender arms."

Japan had surrendered and the war was over. In his moment of triumph, Truman thought of Roosevelt, "who had not lived to see this day." He wrote: "He would have rejoiced in the fulfillment of the pledge he had given the nation when war was forced upon us in December 1941. I reached for the telephone and called Mrs. Roosevelt. I told her that in this hour of triumph I wished that it had been President Roosevelt, and not I, who had given the message to our people."[12]

* Clement Attlee had replaced Sir Winston Churchill as prime minister on July 26 after his Labor Party won a landslide at the first post-war general election.

45

"We were going to live!"

Harry Truman's decision to drop two atomic bombs on Japan still divides opinion today. It is one of the most debated ethical questions in the history of the American presidency. Was it necessary to kill so many non-combatants,* some people ask, when Japan was going to surrender anyway? Was it done as a warning to Stalin, the first blow struck in the Cold War? Would the bombs have been dropped on a European foe like Germany, or did a racist attitude toward the Japanese play into the decision?

Admiral Leahy, who voiced no opposition prior to Hiroshima, wrote later that the "use of this barbarous weapon" made no difference because the Japanese were "already defeated and ready to surrender because of the effective blockade and the successful bombing with conventional weapons." Being the first to use atomic bombs, wrote Leahy, "we had adopted an ethical standard common to the barbarians of the Dark Ages."[1] This is nonsense. The U.S. Army Air Forces had already inflicted far greater civilian casualties by firebombing Japanese cities, a strategy that Leahy raised no objection to. Nor was there any guarantee that, prior to the dropping of the bombs, Japan was ready to make peace on Allied terms. Even Shigenori Tōgō, Japan's foreign minister and a man keen to end the war, acknowledged later that there was no appetite for "unconditional surrender" in the summer of 1945. "We were concerned," he said, "with the steps to be taken to obtain suitable conditions; in other words, with how we could obtain a negotiated peace."[2] As that was unacceptable to the Allies, the war was bound to continue if the bombs had not been

* Sources vary, but at least 200,000 Japanese, and possibly many more, were killed by the two atomic bombs.

used. Even when they were, the senior military men—War Minister Anami, Army Chief of Staff Umezu, and Chief of Naval Staff Toyoda*—argued against peace. "I was," recalled Tōgō,

> unable to keep the military men from insisting to the very end that they were not beaten, that they could fight another battle, and that they did not want to end the war until they had staged one last campaign. I could understand how they felt, they were sure they could deal a punishing blow to the American invaders in one last battle, and they were reluctant to drop all their preparations and sue for peace when they knew they could do so—or perhaps even repulse them completely.

The peace party won out because Tōgō had the support of a majority of the Cabinet and, crucially, the emperor who realized, after the dropping of the bombs, that further resistance was hopeless. But even then it was a close-run thing. "From the 12th [of August] on," noted Tōgō, "the young officers in the army grew increasingly restive, and there was talk of a *coup d'état* to protect the emperor...There were signs of activity among the military from the 12th until the evening of the 13th—the situation was threatening until around the 14th—but fortunately nothing serious happened...If there had actually been a *coup d'état*, the peace negotiations would have been blown sky-high."[3]

Tōgō's testimony, given in 1949, leaves little doubt that, but for the use of atomic weapons, Japan would have fought on.

Truman himself never worried he had made the wrong decision. "I knew what I was doing," he wrote in 1963, "when I stopped the war that would have killed a half-million youngsters on both sides if those bombs had not been dropped. I have had no regrets and, under the same circumstances, I would do it again."[4]

In truth, by authorizing the use of the atomic bomb, he was acting on the advice of *all* his senior political, military and scientific advisers. The most compelling justification was provided by Secretary of War Stimson, who wrote in 1947:

* Toyoda had replaced the previous chief, Admiral Koshirō Oikawa, after the latter resigned in protest at the emperor's refusal to consider peace proposals in late May 1945.

> On July 28 the premier of Japan, Suzuki, rejected the Potsdam ultimatum by announcing that it was "unworthy of public notice." In the face of this rejection we could only proceed to demonstrate that the ultimatum had meant exactly what it said...
>
> Hiroshima was bombed on August 6, and Nagasaki on August 9. These two cities were active working parts of the Japanese war effort. One was an army center; the other was naval and industrial. Hiroshima was the headquarters of the Japanese army defending southern Japan and was a major military storage and assembly point. Nagasaki was a major seaport and it contained several large industrial plants of great wartime importance...
>
> Had the war continued until the projected invasion on November 1, additional fire raids of B-29s would have been more destructive of life and property than the very limited number of atomic raids which we could have executed in the same period. But the atomic bomb was more than a weapon of terrible destruction; it was a psychological weapon. In March 1945, our Air Forces had launched the first great incendiary raid on the Tokyo area. In this raid more damage was done and more casualties were inflicted than was the case at Hiroshima... Similar successive raids burned out a great part of the urban area of Japan, but the Japanese fought on. On August 6 one B-29 dropped a single atomic bomb on Hiroshima. Three days later a second bomb was dropped on Nagasaki and the war was over... As Dr. Karl Compton has said, "it was not one atomic bomb, or two, which brought surrender; it was the experience of what an atomic bomb will actually do to a community, *plus the dread of many more*, that was effective."

Stimson was convinced that the bomb served its purpose. "The peace party," he wrote, "was able to take the path of surrender, and the whole weight of the emperor's prestige was exerted in favor of peace. When the emperor ordered surrender, and the small but dangerous group of fanatics who opposed him were brought under control, the Japanese became so subdued that the great undertaking of occupation and disarmament was completed with unprecedented ease." Stimson's chief purpose "was to end the war in victory with the least possible cost in lives of the men in the armies." In the light of the alternatives then open to him and his colleagues, he was convinced that "no man, in our position and subject to our responsibilities, holding in his hands a weapon of such possibilities for accomplishing this purpose and saving lives, could have failed to use it and afterward looked his countrymen in the face."[5]

Winston Churchill agreed. "The final decision...lay in the main with President Truman," he wrote later, "who had the weapon; but I never doubted what it would be, nor have I ever doubted since that he was right. The historic fact remains, and must be judged in the after-time, that the decision whether or not to use the atomic bomb to compel the surrender of Japan was never an issue. There was unanimous, automatic, unquestioned agreement around our table; nor did I ever hear the slightest suggestion that we should do otherwise."[6]

A key, and often overlooked, factor in Truman's decision—though one acknowledged by Churchill—was the effect the fanatical Japanese resistance on Iwo Jima and, in particular, Okinawa, not to mention the crippling civilian casualties, had on him and his advisers. His predicament was ably summed up by Commander George Elsey, a duty officer in the White House Map Room:

> We were losing tragically large numbers of soldiers, sailors, marines and airmen in the Pacific. We had been through those bitter struggles of Iwo Jima and Okinawa. We knew the ferocity with which the Japanese would defend every square yard of territory that they held. We had seen the effects of the kamikaze raids. We were proceeding with plans for the invasion of Japan in the Fall, and the casualty estimates which the army and navy were making were heart-sickening. Not only would *Americans* have lost their lives in great numbers, so would the Japanese... And while the bomb was a horrible thing, the numbers of lives lost by the dropping of those two bombs, was a fraction of the number of lives that would have been lost had the war proceeded to go on to the mainland of Japan.[7]

If Truman's advisers and allies were united in their belief that dropping the atomic bombs was the correct thing to do, so too were the men who dropped them and the many soldiers whose lives might have been lost if the invasion of Japan had gone ahead. The *Enola Gay*'s pilot Colonel Tibbets, who died aged 92 in 2007, always insisted that he had no regrets. In a radio interview in 2000, he said: "I thought to myself, 'Gee, if we can be successful, we're going to prove to the Japanese the futility in continuing to fight because we can use the weapons on them. They're not going to stand up to this thing.' After I saw what I saw I was more convinced that they're gonna quit."

His crew felt the same. Asked in 1985 if he would do it again, Lieutenant Jacob Beser, a radar specialist and the only man to serve on both missions (in the *Enola Gay* and *Bockscar*), replied: "Given the same circumstances in the same kind of context, the answer is yes... Three million men were gonna be thrown against Japan. There were about 3 million Japanese digging in for the defense of their homeland, and there was a casualty potential of over a million people. That's what was avoided. If you take the highest figures of casualties of both cities, say, 300,000 combined casualties...versus a million, I'm sorry to say, it's a good trade-off."

While Captain "Dutch" Van Kirk, the *Enola Gay*'s navigator, also felt the bombs "saved lives in the long run," and that most of them "were Japanese," he came as close as any to expressing some form of regret. "Such a terrible waste," he said in 2005, "such a loss of life. We unleashed the first atomic bomb, and I hope there will never be another. I pray that we have learned a lesson for all time. But I'm not sure that we have."[8]

Such moral qualms were felt by few of the veterans who had survived the horrors of the Okinawa campaign and were dreading a repeat. "In my judgment," wrote Corporal Jim Johnston of Easy Company, 2/5th Marines, "if you must go to war and send your young men to some far off hellhole to be slaughtered, then *anything* goes." He added:

> The bomb put an end to the Japanese thinking that they could barter better peace terms by killing as many of us as possible wherever we attacked them...I would have blown Okinawa and

all the sons of bitches on it into the sea. I wouldn't have hesitated to do the same thing to Japan.

Thousands of good young American servicemen died in the last days of the war, on the threshold of the atomic age. Had it been handled differently, those faithful, sacrificing young American men might have come home to their families instead of making so many corners of Oriental fields forever American.[9]

Lieutenant Bruce Watkins was "standing in a chow line" on Okinawa when he was told an atomic bomb had destroyed the city of Hiroshima. "We scoffed at this news," he recalled, "as we had no conception of such a bomb. But gradually, as more news kept coming in, we began hoping." When word arrived of the Japanese surrender, it was joyfully received but hard to process.

For someone who had fought through a three-month-long battle, losing countless friends along the way, it must have seemed hardly real. "Our hopes had been dashed so often," wrote Watkins, "that it took several days to absorb the impact of this event. Relief flooded slowly into our veins and we began to dare to think of going home. The fear engendered by plans for invading Japan, was slow to seep away."[10]

PFC Eugene Sledge also felt "an indescribable sense of relief," but tinged with sadness. "We thought," he noted, "the Japanese would never surrender. Many refused to believe it. Sitting in stunned silence, we remembered our dead. So many dead. So many maimed. So many bright futures consigned to the ashes of the past. So many dreams lost in the madness that had engulfed us. Except for a few widely scattered shouts of joy, the survivors of the abyss sat hollow-eyed and silent, trying to comprehend a world without war."[11]

Mortarman Don Dencker was en route with his battalion to Mindoro Island in the Philippines when he heard about the Hiroshima bomb. "Predictably," he recalled, "the attitude among Company L battle veterans was not charitable, being that they should 'atom-bomb' the Japs until they surrendered or were obliterated." They regarded the second Nagasaki bomb as a "lifesaver, for who knows how many of us would have been lost in an invasion of the main islands of Japan?" But, as on Okinawa, the news of the surrender produced mixed feelings. "It was a day long sought," remembered

Dencker, "but surprisingly tame in celebration. There was no wild firing of weapons; this was left to the rear-echelon troops. We who had borne the brunt of the war realized how lucky we had been, and my thoughts and the thoughts of others turned to our buddies who had been killed or seriously wounded."[12]

For Lieutenant "Jep" Carrell, however, one thought was paramount: "We were going to live!"[13]

Epilogue: "Those dark corners are still there"

In midafternoon on August 15, 1945, Vice Admiral Matome Ugaki made a final entry in his diary at the 5th Air Fleet headquarters at Ōita, Kyushu:

> Broadcasts from abroad said that Japan had surrendered unconditionally, and that the emperor himself would broadcast at noon today. So I made up my mind to ram enemy vessels at Okinawa, directly leading special-attack aircraft, and gave an order to prepare "Suisei" planes at this base immediately.
>
> At noon, following the national anthem, His Majesty himself made a broadcast. What he said wasn't very clear because of the poor radio conditions, but I could guess most of it. I've never been filled with so much trepidation…I'm going to follow in the footsteps of those many loyal officers and men who devoted themselves to the country, and I want to live in the noble spirit of the special attack.

Shortly after 4:00 p.m., having drunk a farewell toast of sake with his staff, he was driven to Ōita airfield where he was met by Lieutenant Tatsuo Nakatsuru, commanding the 701st Air Group Detachment, and twenty-one flying crewmen. On each man's forehead was a white headband with a red disc, signifying the rising sun of Japan. Nearby eleven "Suisei" dive-bombers were warming up, "their roaring engines blowing the summer grass."

Seeing the number of planes and their pilots, Ugaki asked Nakatsuru why there were so many. "Commander," Ugaki said, "the order must be given for five planes."

Nakatsuru responded: "Although our commander-in-chief is going to launch a special attack by himself, we can't stand by and see only five planes dispatched. My unit is going to accompany him with full strength!"

Hearing this, Ugaki climbed onto a dais and asked the pilots: "Will all of you go with me?"

"Yes, sir!" they shouted back, raising their right hands in the air.

"Many thanks to all of you," replied Ugaki, before climbing down to say his last goodbyes to his personal staff.

Minutes later he and the other pilots boarded the planes, taxied and took off. Flying south, he sent a final message at 7:24 p.m.:

> Despite brave fighting by each unit under my command for the past six months, we have failed to destroy the arrogant enemy in order to protect our divine empire, a failure which should be attributed to my lack of capabilities. And yet, believing that our empire will last forever and the special-attack spirit of the Ten [i.e. Ten-Go kamikaze campaign] Air Force will never perish, I am going to proceed to Okinawa where our men lost their lives like cherry blossoms, and ram into the arrogant American ships, displaying the real spirit of a Japanese warrior. All units under my command shall keep my will in mind, overcome every conceivable difficulty, rebuild a strong armed force, and make our empire last forever. The emperor banzai!

There is no record of Ugaki or any of the other planes making a successful attack on a U.S. ship. They were either shot down or lost at sea.[1]

Ugaki was typical of the diehard Japanese militarists who could not come to terms with military defeat, some of whom, like him, preferred suicide to dishonor. They included the war minister, General Korechika Anami, who committed *seppuku* on the morning of the 15th.

Released from captivity in January 1946, Colonel Hiromichi Yahara returned to the old Imperial Army headquarters—renamed the First Demobilization Ministry—in Tokyo to make his report on the battle (in line with Chō's final instructions). He was coolly received by the lieutenant general in charge who "heard him out, with formal sympathy, then excused himself for lunch." During the meal, to which he was not invited, Yahara overheard the general mention his name and the word "prisoner." Harsh laughter followed.

Asked years later to help train Japan's new Self-Defense Forces, Yahara declined. He had had enough of military service. He did, however, write a firsthand account of the campaign, *Okinawa Kessen* (Battle for Okinawa), that was published in 1972 and later translated into English. As Yahara was at the center of all the key decisions taken at the Thirty-Second Army headquarters, his book remains the most authoritative Japanese source for the battle. He wrote it chiefly to set the record straight, "particularly since he had been so heavily criticized by other surviving military men for making his escape." He died, at the age of 78, in 1981.[2]

Shigeko Araki gave birth to a son on Christmas Day 1945, and named him Yūkyū ("Eternity") after his late father's kamikaze unit. "This is," announced Shigeko's adoptive father, "Haruo's reincarnation!"

She and her parents took "special care" of the boy. But all their hopes were dashed the following November when the tiny infant, not yet a year old, died of a sudden illness. "I was holding him in my arms. Everything was over and I was only 22 years old." Convinced "there was no God, no Buddha in the world," she fainted at her baby's funeral.

Shigeko later remarried and had two children. Often she would ask herself: if Haruo came back, who would I choose? It was a relief when her second husband finally died. "Haruo can come back anytime now," she thought.

As a grandmother she visited Kadena Bay, off Okinawa, where she suspected Haruo had died. "When I was there," she recalled, "I called to him by name, shouting loudly 'Haruo-san!'" Returning home with some sand and pebbles that she placed by Haruo's memorial, she vowed not to return. "Haruo died to protect Okinawa," she told an interviewer. "I get angry when they consider themselves just victims. Did you hear about the incident when they even burned our flag? I'd hate to set foot on the soil of Okinawa again."[3]

* * *

The young Kaiten pilot Yutaka Yokota never did get to die for his emperor. After his third and final launch attempt was aborted because of a crack in his Kaiten's main fuel-line pipe, he "wanted to crawl in a corner" and disappear. "It didn't help," he recalled. "I was really beaten up this time, called a disgrace to the Kaiten Corps for coming back alive! Because of that beating I still have difficulty hearing with my left ear, and I bear scars on my left hand, too."

Hearing the news of Japan's surrender from a maintenance mechanic, he shouted, "What are you saying, you filthy bastard!"

When his commander confirmed the report, Yokota cried bitter tears. Not because Japan had lost the war. "They were shed," he admitted, "for the loss of my fellow pilots. My comrades. I even thought of killing myself…I got some explosives, but I didn't have the guts."[4]

Former student nurse Kikuko Miyagi spent three months in a refugee camp in the north of Okinawa before she was finally reunited with her parents. Spotting Kikuko, her mother ran barefoot out of a tent and cried, "You lived! You lived!"

It took a long time for Kikuko to be able to talk about what she had gone through. In later life she was sometimes asked by younger Okinawans: "Why did you take part in such a stupid war?"

Her response was that, for her and her fellow schoolgirls, the "Emperor and the Nation were supreme," and that they were prepared to sacrifice their lives for the greater good. "We had been trained for the Battle of Okinawa," she confessed, "from the day the war with America began. I hate to admit it, but that spiritual training taught us how to endure."

Kikuko helped to found the Himeyuri Peace Museum at Ihara in southern Okinawa. Dedicated to the memory of the Himeyuri Students Corps and to the ideal of peace, it was opened in 1989 on the site of the 3rd Surgical Cave, and includes pictures of all 227 students and teachers from the Okinawa Female Normal School and First Girls' High School who were killed in the Battle of Okinawa.*[5]

* Of these 227 people who died, 136 (including thirteen teachers) had been mobilized as the Himeyuri Student Corps; ninety-one others who were killed (including three teachers) were not part of the mobilized group.

The relief Lieutenant Bruce Watkins felt at hearing the war was over was quickly tempered by the news that he would not be going home just yet. Instead he and the rest of the 1st Marine Division were sent to China to repatriate the large Japanese garrison. "Our duties," wrote Watkins, "involved disarming remaining Jap soldiers and breaking up Chinese crowds that tried to lynch them. These crowds were monumental in size. Forming in a matter of minutes, the crowds would choke the streets. Trying to disband [them] was a considerable chore."

With enough points accumulated for "time overseas, combat engagements, medals, and wounds," Watkins returned to the United States in early November 1945 for an emotional reunion with his wife June. A few months later, he was awarded a second Silver Star—for gallantry on Okinawa—at a ceremony in his hometown of Manchester, Connecticut. It made him think of "all those who had died, quietly doing their duty." As he had been spared, and had "much to be thankful for," he made a promise to God to make light of future troubles. Bruce and June settled in Manchester where they raised three sons and a daughter. He managed the family furniture business, Watkins Brothers, and repaired antique furniture for fun. He died in 2013.[6]

Like Watkins, Second Lieutenant "Jep" Carrell went with his battalion to China where he remained until the late spring of 1946. Discharged that August, he was recalled from the reserves to fight in Korea and retired with the rank of captain. Awarded an MA and PhD from the University of Pennsylvania, he worked in urban government, writing many books and articles on the subject. He described infantry combat as a "searing experience":

> There are so many tragedies in intensive and prolonged fighting, and it is so often conducted in conditions of weather and filth no human should bear, that one would think there can be no conceivable satisfaction connected with it. There is one.
>
> It was simply an honor and privilege to serve with the men in my platoon. I found them to be frightened but brave, tough in body and sturdy in emotions, loyal to the point of willingness to risk their lives for their buddies, aware of the need for teamwork and determined to do their proper part. And they were, to a man, modest about their own contributions. I loved those men.

He lived much of his later life in Oberlin, Ohio, where he was the director of the Nordson Foundation. The father of three children, and grandfather of seven, he died in 2007 at the age of 84.[7]

Promoted to sergeant, Don Dencker arrived back in Minneapolis in late January 1946 and was met by his parents who "shed tears of joy that their only child was safely home." He completed his education at the University of Minnesota, graduating with a BSc in civil engineering. He also served in Korea—as a second lieutenant with an engineer aviation battalion—and returned in 1952 to join a firm of consultant engineers. Married with four daughters, he worked as a city engineer and later as a manager of a food corporation in Madison, Wisconsin, and in 2002 published *Love Company*, a tribute to the "Citizen Soldiers" he served alongside in Leyte and Okinawa. He wrote in the introduction: "Most of the heroes of World War II were killed or wounded during their courageous endeavors. I certainly was not a hero. I just tried to do my best and stay alive."[8]

Discharged after recovering from the bullet wound to his foot, tank commander Sergeant Robert Dick returned to his parents' home in El Monte, California, in late September 1945. "I took a deep breath," he recalled, "knocked, opened the screen door, and stepped inside. Their faces turned toward me, and surprise was followed by joy. I moved forward, and all of us stood there, not saying a word, arms around each other, tears in our eyes. We stood like that for what seemed a long time." Dick joined the fire department in Arcadia, California, and retired twenty-seven years later as the fire chief. Encouraged by his wife, Linda May, he wrote a graphic and unsparing account of his time as a tank driver in the Pacific. It was published as *Cutthroats*, the name of his Sherman, in 2006.[9]

A fortnight after his heroics at Hacksaw Ridge, combat medic Corporal Desmond Doss was badly wounded in the legs and arm as he tried to assist wounded men. Evacuated back to the United States, he was honorably discharged. He received his Medal of Honor from President Harry Truman at the White House on October 12, 1945. Truman, who had little time for conscientious objectors, wrote of Doss:

> The only one of 'em I ever came in contact with, whom I thought to be on the level, was the little skinny pharmacist's mate to whom I gave the Congressional Medal of Honor…He'd carried wounded man after wounded man to safety from under fire at the front and was finally shot himself and still kept working on the other wounded. He said he thought he could serve the Lord acceptably under fire if he himself didn't try to kill anyone. He did his heroic job on Okinawa.[10]

Diagnosed with tuberculosis in 1946, Doss had extensive hospital treatment that cost him a lung and five ribs. Despite his disability, he and his wife, Dorothy, raised a son on a small farm in Rising Fawn, Georgia. Ten years after his death in 2006, the blockbuster movie *Hacksaw Ridge* made him famous for his struggles as a conscientious objector and his selfless courage on Okinawa.

The men of Able Company, 1/5th Marines, were attacking a feature known as Hill 79, west of Mezado village, on June 18 when their charismatic skipper, Julian Dusenbury, was shot in the back by a sniper, the bullet severing his spinal column and damaging his liver and a kidney. After a long convalescence, he returned home to Florence, South Carolina, in 1946 and spent the rest of his life in a wheelchair. But this did not prevent him from leading an active life as a farmer and state legislator, serving two terms as a Democratic member of the House of Representatives. He also married and fathered three children—two girls and a boy—and was prominent in veteran associations until his early death at the age of 54, from complications linked to his wartime injuries, in 1976. Three years later, Dusenbury's only son, Tim, a Marine aviator, was tragically killed in a helicopter crash in Greece.[11]

Sergeant William Manchester was recovering from his serious shrapnel wounds at a hospital in San Diego when a nurse ran in and cried: "The war's over! The Japs have surrendered!" All he could think to say was, "Thank you." He became a journalist and celebrated author, publishing eighteen works of fiction and non-fiction, including the bestselling *The Death of a President*, an account of JFK's assassination, and *American Caesar*, a biography of General Douglas MacArthur. His most moving book, however, was *Goodbye, Darkness*, a partly fictionalized personal meditation on the Pacific War that was published in 1980. "This, then," he wrote, "was the life I knew, where Death sought me, during which I was transformed from a cheeky youth to a troubled man who, for over thirty years, repressed what he could not bear to remember." One of the finest history/memoirs of the Second World War, *Goodbye, Darkness* was, for Manchester, an act of personal catharsis. George W. Bush presented him with the National Humanities Medal in 2006. Three years later, Manchester died.[12]

Another veteran who found it hard to process what he had gone through was Jim Johnston. Promoted to sergeant while he was recovering from his wounds on Okinawa, he was offered a second jump to gunnery sergeant ("gunny"), the top NCO in the platoon, if he agreed to stay on for the next campaign. He was tempted, but the thought of seeing his "folks" tipped the decision in favor of going home. He recalled:

> I went back to Nebraska, but not back to the life as it had been. I had given the corps the best I had, and it had given me a new set of values. I didn't give a damn about going back to college, or trying to become what our society seems to think is a success. Wealth and influence had lost all significance. In the dark corners of my mind, the only power under God that meant anything to me came out of the bore of a .30-06—or if you were close enough, a .45. Those dark corners are still there.

Johnston worked in retail sales, oil exploration and real estate, and in 1998 published a brutally frank account of his combat experience, *The Long Road of War*. It had, he confessed, left him changed forever. "You walk down the street," he wrote, "looking much the same [as everyone else], but you do not feel or think the same. Most of the traditional, social, moral, and economic considerations are ludicrous to you. You pray that you will be able to maintain a behavior that will keep you out of trouble in a normal, peaceful society without compromising too much of what you believe. You are, inside, much closer to the jungle than to the city street."[13]

Acknowledgments

Okinawa was the last great battle of the Second World War. During its bloody three-month span, legendary U.S. President Franklin D. Roosevelt died, the war in Europe ended and more than 240,000 people lost their lives on or near the largest island in the Japanese-governed Ryukyu chain. The fatalities included the vast majority of the 110,000 Japanese and Okinawan defenders, many of whom refused to surrender; 12,500 American servicemen (out of total casualties of 76,000), making it by far the bloodiest U.S. battle of the Pacific, and one of the costliest in the country's history; and, most tragically, 125,000 Okinawan civilians (a third of the pre-war population) who were either caught in the cross-fire or believed Japanese propaganda that it was better to commit mass suicide than be raped and murdered by the Americans.

It's hard to convey in a book title the unique horror of these events. I chose *Crucible of Hell* because those were the words used by an American naval veteran to describe the ordeal of the ground troops. "While on Okinawa," he said, "the marines and soldiers were going through their crucible of hell brought on by rain, heat, poison, snakes, mosquitoes...the stench of human feces and rotting human flesh filled with maggots."[1]

The research for this project was completed in three continents: Europe, North America and Asia. I'm particularly grateful for the assistance provided by John Lyles of the U.S. Marine Corps Archive in Quantico, VA; David Holbrook of the Dwight D. Eisenhower Presidential Library and Museum in Abilene, KS; David Clark of the Harry S. Truman Presidential Library & Museum in Independence, MO; Tsugiko Taira of the Haeburu Town Museum in Okinawa; and the staffs of the Prefectural Peace Museum and the Himeyuri Peace

Museum in Okinawa, the UK National Archives and the Imperial War Museum in London, and the U.S. National Archives and Records Administration in College Park, MD.

Others who assisted in various ways include Ann Dencker (daughter of the late Don Dencker whose story appears in the book), Dr. Andy Boyd, Cherry David, Aminatta Forna, Simon Fowler, Sydney Soderberg and Chris Majeski, the director of the Battle of Okinawa Museum at Camp Kinser, who showed me round the battlefield. Thank you.

Lastly I'm indebted to my agent Caroline Michel; to Arabella Pike, Katherine Patrick, Iain Hunt and Julian Humphries at HarperCollins in London; to David Lamb, Michael Barrs, Mike Giarratano, Melissa Mathlin and Amanda Kain at Hachette Books in New York; and to my wife Louise, and daughters Nell, Tamar and Tashie, who are never entirely convinced that research trips to far flung places count as "work."

Notes

Prologue: Love Day

1. Abilene, KS, Dwight D. Eisenhower Presidential Library and Archive (DDE), Vernon E. Megee Papers, 1919–92, Box 7, A94-17, "Memoirs," p. 166.
2. DDE, Simon Bolivar Buckner Papers, 1908–17 and 1941–5, Box 1, A92-16, Buckner Diary, March 31, 1945.
3. Ibid., April 1, 1945; Roy E. Appleman, James M. Burns, Russell A. Gugeler and John Stevens, *Okinawa: The Last Battle* (Washington, DC: Center of Military History, U.S. Army, 1948), p. 69.
4. Megee, "Memoirs," p. 167; Buckner Diary, April 1, 1945.
5. Ernie Pyle, *Last Chapter* (New York: Henry Holt & Co., 1946), p. 99.
6. Buckner Diary, April 1, 1945.
7. Pyle, *Last Chapter*, pp. 99, 101.
8. James R. Stockman, *The First Marine Division on Okinawa: 1 April–30 June 1945* (Quantico, VA: History Division U.S. Marine Corps, 1946), p. 1.
9. Quantico, VA, U.S. Marine Corps Archives (USMCA), William A. Looney Memoir, 1942–5 COLL/5276, A/5/J/6/4, "Okinawa," pp. 1–3.
10. James W. Johnston, *The Long Road of War: A Marine's Story of Pacific Combat* (Lincoln, NB: University of Nebraska Press, 1998), pp. 120–5.
11. Ibid., p. 127.
12. Looney, "Okinawa," p. 3.
13. Johnston, *The Long Road of War*, p. 128.
14. Pyle, *Last Chapter*, p. 100.
15. Megee, "Memoirs," p. 167.
16. USMCA, Oliver P. Smith Papers, COLL/213, A/30/D/3/1, Box 54, Folder 1, "Personal Narrative: 10th Army and Okinawa," p. 78.
17. Buckner Diary, January 30, 1945.
18. Buckner to his wife Adele, April 1, 1945, in Nicholas Evan Sarantakes (ed.), *Seven Stars: The Okinawa Battle Diaries of Simon Bolivar Buckner, Jr., and Joseph Stilwell* (College Station, TX: Texas A&M University Press, 2004), p. 29.
19. Colonel Hiromichi Yahara, *The Battle for Okinawa: A Japanese Officer's Eyewitness Account of the Last Great Campaign of World War II* (New York: John Wiley & Sons, Inc., 1995), pp. xi, 18.

20. Ibid., pp. 16–18.
21. Frank B. Gibney, "Two Views of Battle" in Yahara, *The Battle for Okinawa*, pp. xv–xvii, 24.
22. Yahara, *The Battle for Okinawa*, pp. 5–16.
23. Ibid., pp. 20–4.
24. Thomas M. Huber, "Japan's Battle of Okinawa, April–June 1945," *Leavenworth Papers*, Number 18 (199), p. 7; Yahara, *The Battle for Okinawa*, p. 35.
25. Yahara, *The Battle for Okinawa*, pp. xii–xiii.
26. Donald M. Goldstein and Katherine V. Dillon (eds), *Fading Victory: The Diary of Admiral Matome Ugaki 1941–1945*, trans. by Masataka Chihaya (Pittsburgh, PA: University of Pittsburgh Press, 1991), pp. 566–9.
27. USMCA, COLL/2925, A/30/A/2/2, Otha L. Grisham Papers, "A Young Man from Texas Goes to War: The Making of an Alligator Marine," p. 24.
28. Samuel W. Mitcham Jr. and Friedrich von Stauffenberg, *The Battle of Sicily: How the Allies Lost their Chance for Total Victory* (New York: Orion Books, 1991), p. 63; Antony Beevor, *D-Day* (London: Penguin, 2006), pp. 151n.
29. Looney, "Okinawa," pp. 1–2.
30. Appleman et al., *Okinawa*, p. 36.
31. David Hobbs, *The British Pacific Fleet: The Royal Navy's Most Powerful Strike Force* (Barnsley, UK: Seaforth Publishing, 2011; repr. 2017), pp. 126–8.

1: "Where's Douglas?"

1. Jean Edward Smith, *FDR* (New York: Random House Inc., 2007; repr. 2008), p. 620.
2. Edwin P. Hoyt, *How They Won the War in the Pacific: Nimitz and his Admirals* (New York: Weybright and Talley, 1970), p. 411; Edward Smith, *FDR*, p. 620.
3. Edward Smith, *FDR*, pp. 621–2; Hoyt, *How They Won the War in the Pacific*, p. 412.
4. Hoyt, *How They Won the War in the Pacific*, p. 412.
5. Buckner Diary, 29 July 1944.
6. Edward Smith, *FDR*.
7. Andrew Roberts, *Masters and Commanders: How Roosevelt, Churchill, Marshall and Alanbrooke Won the War in the West* (London: Allen Lane, 2008), pp. 518–20.
8. Appleman et al., *Okinawa*, pp. 1–4.
9. Hoyt, *How They Won the War in the Pacific*, pp. 425–7.
10. Appleman et al., *Okinawa*, p. 4; London, UK, The National Archives (TNA), ADM/234, Piece 368, Naval Staff History, Battle Summary No. 47, "Naval Operations Okinawa," 1950, pp. 1–2.

2: Operation Iceberg

1. Buckner Diary, October 4, 1944.
2. "Buck's Battle," *Time* magazine, April 16, 1945.
3. Sarantakes (ed.), *Seven Stars*, pp. 10–11.
4. Smith, "Personal Narrative," p. 3.
5. Ibid., p. 1.
6. Ibid., p. 2.
7. Buckner Diary, August 22, 1944.
8. Ibid., October 7, 1944.
9. Smith, "Personal Narrative," pp. 2–8.
10. Buckner Diary, February 24, 1945.
11. Appleman et al., *Okinawa*, pp. 7–10, 14, 17.
12. Smith, "Personal Narrative," pp. 11–13.
13. Hoyt, *How They Won the War in the Pacific*, pp. 136–7; Gordon W. Prange, Donald M. Goldstein and Katherine V. Dillon, *Pearl Harbor: The Verdict of History* (New York: McGraw-Hill, 1985), pp. 292–5.
14. Smith, "Personal Narrative," pp. 12–13.
15. Ibid., p. 13.
16. Buckner Diary, November 11, 1944.
17. Michael D. Hull, "Modest Victor of Midway," *World War II* magazine, 13/1 (May 1998), 36–43.
18. Buckner Diary, December 31, 1944.
19. Smith, "Personal Narrative," p. 33.
20. Ibid., p. 32; USMCA, COLL/185, A/14/F/3/3, Lt Col. J. Frederick Haley Papers, "The General Dies at Noon," pp. 5, 24.

3: "Everybody go home!"

1. Yoshiko Sakumoto Crandell, "Surviving the Battle of Okinawa: Memories of a Schoolgirl," *Asia-Pacific Journal*, 12/14 (2014), 1–31 (pp. 1–15).
2. Carl Nolte, "Teen survivor of WWII torpedoed ship a pacifist at 85," *San Francisco Chronicle*, February 20, 2016.
3. Crandell, "Surviving the Battle of Okinawa," p. 15.
4. Appleman et al., *Okinawa*, p. 45.
5. Huber, "Japan's Battle," pp. 6–9; Appleman et al., *Okinawa*, pp. 92–4.
6. Interrogation Report of POW Akira Shimada, July 24, 1945, in Yahara, *The Battle for Okinawa*, pp. 222–3.
7. Huber, "Japan's Battle," p. 9.
8. Ibid., p. 11.
9. Ibid., pp. 12–13.
10. Interrogation Report of POW Akira Shimada, July 24, 1945, in Yahara, *The Battle for Okinawa*, p. 223.
11. *Descent into Hell: Civilian Memories of the Battle of Okinawa*, trans. by Mark Ealey & Alastair McLauchlan (Portland, ME: MerwinAsia, 2014), pp. 44–53.

4: The Divine Wind

1. Captain Rikihei Inoguchi and Commander Tadashi Nakajima, *The Divine Wind: Japan's Kamikaze Force in World War II* (Annapolis, MD: United States Naval Institute, 1958; repr. 1994), pp. 3–16; Albert Axell and Hideaki Kase, *Kamikaze: Japan's Suicide Gods* (London: Pearson Education, 2002), p. 48.
2. Axell and Kase, *Kamikaze*, pp. 50–1, p. 16.
3. Ibid., pp. 4–12.
4. Ibid., p. 52.
5. Naoji Kōzu, "Human Torpedo," in Haruko Taya Cook and Theodore F. Cook, *Japan at War: An Oral History* (New York: W. W. Norton & Co., 1992), pp. 313–16.
6. Rear Admiral Sadatoshi Tamioka, Doc. No. 5072, in General Headquarters, Far East Command, Military Intelligence Section, General Staff, *Statements of Japanese Officials on World War II (English Translations): Vol. 4*, 1949–50, pp. 316–22.
7. Commander Yoshimori Terai, *Statements of Japanese Officials: Vol. 4*, pp. 316–22.
8. Ibid.

5: "More concerned with furlough than fighting"

1. Buckner Diary, January 18, 1945; Smith, "Personal Narrative," p. 36.
2. Smith, "Personal Narrative," p. 37.
3. Ibid., pp. 37–8.
4. Buckner Diary, January 20, 1945; Smith, "Personal Narrative," p. 38.
5. Smith, "Personal Narrative," p. 39.
6. Ibid., pp. 34–5.
7. Ibid., p. 40.
8. Buckner Diary, January 24, 1945; Smith, "Personal Narrative," p. 41.
9. Buckner Diary, January 24, 1945.
10. Ibid., January 25, 1945.
11. Smith, "Personal Narrative," p. 47.
12. Buckner Diary, January 27 and 29, 1945.
13. Ibid., January 30, 1945.
14. Ibid., February 1–2, 1945.
15. Smith, "Personal Narrative," p. 51; Buckner Diary, February 2, 1945.
16. Haley, "The General Dies at Noon," pp. 3–5.
17. Buckner Diary, February 3, 1945; Smith, "Personal Narrative," p. 52.
18. Smith, "Personal Narrative," p. 53.

6: "I'm going simply because I've got to—and I hate it"

1. Pyle, *Last Chapter*, pp. 8–11.
2. William F. Nelson, *Appointment at Ie Shima* (privately published, 2014), pp. 26–7.

3. Ernie Pyle, "The Death of Captain Waskow," January 10, 1944, in https://sites.mediaschool.indiana.edu/erniepyle/1944/01/10/the-death-of-captain-waskow/ (accessed April 1, 2019).
4. David Nichols (ed.), *Ernie's War: The Best of Ernie Pyle's World War II Dispatches* (New York: Simon & Schuster, 1987), pp. 335–7.
5. Ernie Pyle, "Farewell to Europe," September 5, 1945, in https://sites.mediaschool.indiana.edu/erniepyle/1944/09/05/farewell-to-europe/ (accessed 1 April 2019).
6. Arthur Miller, *Timebends: A Life* (New York: Grove Press, 1987), p. 282.
7. Ernie Pyle, "In the Movies," February 14, 1945, in https://sites.mediaschool.indiana.edu/erniepyle/1945/02/14/in-the-movies/ (accessed April 1, 2019).
8. Ernie Pyle, "Back Again," February 6, 1945, in https://sites.mediaschool.indiana.edu/erniepyle/1945/02/06/back-again/ (accessed April 1, 2019).
9. Pyle, *Last Chapter*, pp. 13–14.
10. Ibid., pp. 3–5.
11. Ibid., p. 27.
12. Ernie Pyle, "Back Again."
13. Pyle, *Last Chapter*, pp. 35–41.
14. Ibid., pp. 55–82.
15. Ugaki, *Fading Victory*, pp. 552–6.
16. Pyle, *Last Chapter*, pp. 83–6.

7: "I was crying as I did it and she was crying too"

1. Robert C. Dick, *Cutthroats: The Adventures of a Sherman Tank Driver in the Pacific* (New York: Presidio Press, 2006), p. 139.
2. Smith, "Personal Narrative," pp. 72–3; Appleman et al., *Okinawa*, p. 41.
3. Dick, *Cutthroats*, pp. 1–25, 30–1, 40–1, 93–5, 125, 139.
4. Appleman et al., *Okinawa*, pp. 53–6.
5. DDE, Simon Bolivar Buckner Papers, 1908–17 and 1941–5, Box 1, A92-16, "Lt Gen. Simon Bolivar Buckner: Private Letters relating to the Battle of Okinawa," ed. A. P. Jenkins, in *Ryudai Review of Euro-American Studies*, 42 (1997), 63–113 (p. 77).
6. Shigeaki Kinjo interviewed by Michael Bradley, in "'Banzai!' The Compulsory Mass Suicide of Kerama Islanders in the Battle of Okinawa," *Asia-Pacific Journal*, 11/22 (2014).
7. Appleman et al., *Okinawa*, p. 58.
8. Ibid., pp. 64–5.
9. Kikuko Miyagi, "Student Nurses of the 'Lily Corps,'" in Cook and Cook, *Japan at War*, pp. 354–5.
10. *Himeyuri Peace Museum: The Guidebook* (Itoman, Okinawa: 2016), pp. 6–14; Itoman, Okinawa, Himeyuri Peace Museum Archives (HPMA), "Historical Chart."
11. Miyagi, "Student Nurses of the 'Lily Corps,'" in Cook and Cook, *Japan at War*, p. 355.
12. Ibid.
13. Sakumoto Crandell, "Surviving the Battle of Okinawa," pp. 18–25.

8: "Tomorrow is our big day"

1. Buckner Diary, March 26 and 27, 1945.
2. Smith, "Personal Narrative," p. 71.
3. Megee, "Memoirs," pp. 165–6.
4. Smith, "Personal Narrative," p. 74.
5. Buckner Diary, March 28, 1945.
6. Smith, "Personal Narrative," p. 75.
7. Ibid., p. 75.
8. Buckner Diary, March 31, 1945.
9. Smith, "Personal Narrative," p. 76.
10. Buckner to his wife Adele, March 31, 1945, in "Private Letters," p. 78.
11. Donald O. Dencker, *Love Company: Infantry Combat Against the Japanese World War II—Leyte and Okinawa* (Manhattan, KS: Sunflower University Press, 2002), pp. 2–163.
12. Donald M. Carlton, "Do you want to live forever? A true story of an Infantryman's experiences during the battle for the island of Okinawa," pp. 1–6; Donald M. Carlton, "Memoir"; and Interview with Don Carlton, 18 November 2010, Veterans History Project, all in https://memory.loc.gov/diglib/vhp/story/loc.natlib.afc2001001.00033/ (accessed April 16, 2019).
13. William Manchester, *Goodbye, Darkness: A Memoir of the Pacific War* (New York: Little, Brown & Co., 1980; repr. 2002), p. 352.
14. Ibid., pp. 15–29.
15. Ibid., pp. 15–29, 128–34, 350–3.

9: "It was quite a show"

1. Dencker, *Love Company*, pp. 153, 163–4.
2. After Action Report of 763rd Tank Battalion, April 22, 1942–June 30, 1945, in http://cgsc.cdmhost.com/cdm/ref/collection/p4013coll8/id/3462 (accessed April 16, 2019); Dick, *Cutthroats*, pp. 141–2.
3. Dick, *Cutthroats*, pp. 142–3.
4. Dencker, *Love Company*, pp. 151–5, 163–7.
5. Carlton, "Do you want to live forever?," pp. 7–9.
6. Pyle, *Last Chapter*, pp. 100–13.

10: "There's always some poor bastard who doesn't get word"

1. USMCA, COLL/92, A/11/J/6/3, Christopher S. Donner, "Memoir," dated January 1946, pp. 1–55.
2. USMCA, COLL/1605, A/5/L/3/1, Jeptha J. Carrell, "King One: Service in the United States Marine Corps in World War II," p. 20.
3. George Feifer, *Tennozan: The Battle of Okinawa and the Atomic Bomb* (New York: Houghton Mifflin, 1992), p. 145.
4. Manchester, *Goodbye, Darkness*, p. 354.
5. USMCA, COLL/5674, A/31/J/5/4, Salvatore Giammanco, "The First Okinawa Wounded Marine," pp. 1–6; Milt Thomas, "World War II veterans

unknowingly cross paths," *Vero Beach Newsweekly*, November 10, 2011, pp. 10–11.
6. Smith, "Personal Narrative," p. 77.
7. Appleman et al., *Okinawa*, p. 75.
8. Buckner Diary, April 1, 1945.
9. Quoted in Laura Homan Lacey, *Stay Off the Skyline: The Sixth Marine Division on Okinawa* (Dulles, VA: Potomac Books, Inc., 2005; repr. 2007), p. 45.

11: "The smell of burnt flesh hung about for days"

1. Feifer, *Tennozan*, pp. 148–9; Miyagi, "Student Nurses of the 'Lily Corps,'" in Cook and Cook, *Japan at War*, p. 367.
2. Huber, "Japan's Battle," pp. 27–8.
3. Quoted in Feifer, *Tennozan*, p. 141.
4. Quoted in ibid., pp. 143–4.
5. Yutaka Yokota, "Volunteer," in Cook and Cook, *Japan at War*, pp. 306–9.
6. Feifer, *Tennozan*, pp. 3–14; Morison, Samuel Eliot, *History of the United States Naval Operations in the Pacific: Volume 14—Victory in the Pacific, 1945* (New York: Little, Brown, 1975; repr. 2012), pp. 200–2.
7. London, Imperial War Museum Archives (IWM), 14048, Private Papers of N. B. Gray, "Memoirs" and "Diary," April 1, 1945.
8. Hobbs, *The British Pacific Fleet*, p. 138.
9. N. B. Gray, "Memoirs" and "Diary," April 1, 1945; Hobbs, *The British Pacific Fleet*, p. 138.
10. Sir Philip Vian, *Action This Day: A War Memoir* (London: Frederick Muller Ltd, 1960), pp. 178–9.

12: "War is indeed hell"

1. Appleman et al., *Okinawa*, pp. 76–7; "10th Army Action Report: Ryukus, 26 March to 30 June 1945," Volume 1, Part 4, Ike Skelton Combined Arms Research Library (ISCARL), in http://cgsc.cdmhost.com/cdm/compoundobject/collection/p4013coll8/id/599/rec/22 (accessed December 31, 2018).
2. Manchester, *Goodbye, Darkness*, p. 356.
3. Pyle, *Last Chapter*, pp. 114–15; https://soh.alumni.clemson.edu/scroll/julian-delano-dusenbury/
4. Pyle, *Last Chapter*, pp. 115–20.
5. Ibid., pp. 120–4.
6. Megee, "Memoirs," pp. 168–70.
7. Buckner to his wife Adele, April 2 and 3, 1945, in "Private Letters," pp. 78–9.
8. Appleman et al., *Okinawa*, pp. 79–83.
9. *Second to None! The Story of the 305th Infantry in World War II* (Washington, DC: Infantry Journal Press, 1949), p. 159; Major Charles S. Nichols Jr. and Henry I. Shaw, *Marines in World War II—Okinawa: Victory in the Pacific* (1955), p. 111; Buckner Diary, April 3, 1945.

13: "I could see him floating by, face upward"

1. Huber, "Japan's Battle," pp. 29–31.
2. Prisoner of War Interrogation Report of Colonel Hiromichi Yahara, August 6, 1945, in Yahara, *The Battle for Okinawa*, p. 212.
3. Huber, "Japan's Battle," p. 31.
4. Miyagi, "Student Nurses of the 'Lily Corps,'" in Cook and Cook, *Japan at War*, pp. 355–6.
5. Robin L. Reilly, *Kamikaze Attacks of World War II* (Jefferson, NC: McParland & Co., Inc., 2010), p. 211; Robin L. Reilly, *Kamikaze, Corsairs and Picket Ships: Okinawa, 1945* (Havertown, PA: Casemate, 2008), p. 109.
6. Reilly, *Kamikaze, Corsairs and Picket Ships*, pp. 109–21.
7. Megee, "Memoirs," p. 171.
8. Ugaki, *Fading Victory*, pp. 572–3.

14: "Gone? She's gone?"

1. Feifer, *Tennozan*, p. 19.
2. Ugaki, *Fading Victory*, pp. 572–4.
3. Feifer, *Tennozan*, p. 21.
4. Mitsuru Yoshida, *Requiem for Battleship Yamato* (Washington: University of Washington Press, 1985; repr. ebook, 1999), trans. by Richard H. Minear, Translator's Introduction and Chapters 6 and 7.
5. Feifer, *Tenozan*, pp. 19–22; Morison, *Victory in the Pacific*, pp. 202–4.
6. Yoshida, *Requiem for Battleship Yamato*, Chapters 8–13.
7. Morison, *Victory in the Pacific*, p. 206.
8. Yoshida, *Requiem for Battleship Yamato*, Chapters 15–25; Morison, *Victory in the Pacific*, pp. 208–9.
9. Ugaki, *Fading Victory*, p. 575.
10. Feifer, *Tennozan*, p. 33.

15: "They just knocked the heck out of us"

1. Appleman et al., *Okinawa*, p. 110.
2. Buckner Diary, April 7, 1945; Interview with Don Carlton, November 18, 2010, Veterans History Project.
3. Appleman et al., *Okinawa*, pp. 111–12.
4. Buckner Diary, April 7, 1945.
5. Megee, "Memoirs," p. 171.
6. USMC, COLL/921, A/5/L/7/2, Colonel Bruce Porter Papers, Barrett Tillman, "Hunter in the Dark," *Wings Magazine*, 7/4 (August 1977), p. 10.
7. USMCA, COLL/5480, A/13/F/7/1, Box 2, Marine Night Fighter Squadron 542 Association Collection, Donald E. Marpe, "My Service in the United States Marine Corps, 1942–1945 and 1949–1951," pp. 37–41.
8. Appleman et al., *Okinawa*, p. 113.

9. Interview with Richard Johnson, July 19, 2004, Veterans History Project, in https://memory.loc.gov/diglib/vhp-stories/loc.natlib.afc2001001.20719/transcript?ID=sr0001 (accessed May 24, 2019).
10. Appleman et al., *Okinawa*, pp. 115–19.
11. Donner, "Memoir," pp. 63–9.
12. Appleman et al., *Okinawa*, pp. 119–25.
13. Donner, "Memoir," pp. 70–2.
14. Dencker, *Love Company*, pp. 179–81.
15. Appleman et al., *Okinawa*, pp. 125–6.
16. Buckner to his wife Adele, April 8, 1945, in "Private Letters," p. 80; Buckner Diary, April 8, 1945.
17. Buckner Diary, April 8 and 9, 1945.
18. Ibid., April 11, 1945.
19. Ibid., April 2, 1945.
20. Sarantakes (ed.), *Seven Stars*, p. 30.
21. Smith, "Personal Narrative," pp. 82–3.

16: "I want to marry Shigeko"

1. Huber, "Japan's Battle," pp. 31–2.
2. Yahara Interrogation Report, August 6, 1945, in Yahara, *The Battle for Okinawa*, p. 213.
3. Huber, "Japan's Battle," p. 31; Yahara Interrogation Report, August 6, 1945, in Yahara, *The Battle for Okinawa*, p. 213.
4. Appleman et al., *Okinawa*, pp. 130–4; Huber, "Japan's Battle," pp. 32–4; Dencker, *Love Company*, p. 181; Yahara Interrogation Report, August 6, 1945, in Yahara, *The Battle for Okinawa*, p. 213.
5. http://www.cmohs.org/recipient-detail/2616/anderson-beauford-t.php (accessed May 2, 2019).
6. Appleman et al., *Okinawa*, pp. 135–7.
7. Yahara Interrogation Report, August 6, 1945, in Yahara, *The Battle for Okinawa*, pp. 212–13.
8. Shigeko Araki, "Bride of a Kamikaze," in Cook and Cook, *Japan at War*, pp. 319–26.
9. Inoguchi and Nakajima, *The Divine Wind*, pp. 151–2; Morison, *Victory in the Pacific*, p. 222.
10. Inoguchi and Nakajima, *The Divine Wind*, pp. 140–1.
11. Ibid., pp. 153–4.
12. Morison, *Victory in the Pacific*, p. 224.
13. Ibid., p. 225; Reilly, *Kamikazes, Corsairs and Picket Ships*, pp. 141–2.

17: "Harry, the president is dead"

1. Harry S. Truman, *Year of Decisions*, 2 vols (New York: Doubleday & Co., 1955; repr. 1965), I, pp. ix–x, 11–15; A. J. Baime, *The Accidental President: Harry S. Truman, the Bomb and the Four Months That Changed the World* (New York: Houghton Mifflin Harcourt, 2017; repr. 2018), pp. 24–6.

2. Baime, *The Accidental President*, pp. 41–89.
3. Truman, *Year of Decisions*, I, pp. 15–21.
4. Baime, *The Accidental President*, pp. 33–4.
5. Ibid., p. x.
6. Winston Churchill, *The Second World War*, 6 vols (London: Cassell, 1948–54), VI, pp. 412–13.
7. Ugaki, *Fading Victory*, p. 584.
8. Buckner to his wife Adele, April 14, 1945, in "Private Letters," p. 82.
9. https://www.mossletters.com/13-april-1945/ (accessed May 9, 2019).
10. USMCA, COLL/5223, A/26/J/7/2, Richard Bruce Watkins, "Brothers in Battle: One Marine's Account of War in the Pacific," p. 39.
11. Independence, MO, Harry S. Truman Presidential Library & Museum (HST), "Oral History Interview with George M. Elsey," July 7, 1970, www.trumanlibrary.org/oralhist/elsey7.htm (accessed November 12, 2018).
12. Yahara, *The Battle for Okinawa*, p. 45.

18: "His eyes were rolling in panic"

1. Manchester, *Goodbye, Darkness*, p. 356.
2. Appleman et al., *Okinawa*, pp. 138–44.
3. Manchester, *Goodbye, Darkness*, p. 357.
4. Nichols and Shaw, *Marines in World War II—Okinawa*, p. 96; Appleman et al., *Okinawa*, p. 144.
5. Manchester, *Goodbye, Darkness*, pp. 257–8.
6. Nichols and Shaw, *Marines in World War II—Okinawa*, p. 98.
7. USMCA, COLL/4346, A/26/D/2/4, Joseph M. Hiott, "My Marine Corps Experience: How I Became a Man," pp. 25–6.
8. Nichols and Shaw, *Marines in World War II—Okinawa*, p. 99.
9. USMCA, COLL/2525, A/30/A/4/2, Mel Heckt, "Pacific Diary," April 15, 1945.
10. Manchester, *Goodbye, Darkness*, pp. 140–3.
11. Ibid., p. 357.
12. Nichols and Shaw, *Marines in World War II—Okinawa*, p. 99.
13. https://themedalofhonor.com/medal-of-honor-recipients/recipients/bush-richard-world-war-two (accessed May 13, 2019).
14. Appleman et al., *Okinawa*, p. 147; Heckt, "Pacific Diary," April 16, 1945.
15. Citation for the award of the Navy Cross to Colonel Wiliam J. Whaling, January 20, 1948, in https://valor.militarytimes.com/hero/8236 (accessed May 14, 2019).
16. Appleman et al., *Okinawa*, p. 148.
17. Manchester, *Goodbye Darkness*, pp. 3–7.

19: "Three bullets had ripped into his temple"

1. Quoted in Nelson, *Appointment at Ie Shima*, p. 135.
2. Pyle, *Last Chapter*, pp. 138–40.
3. Appleman et al., *Okinawa*, pp. 149–59.

4. Nelson, *Appointment at Ie Shima*, p. 144.
5. Ibid., pp. 146–150; "Ernie Pyle is Killed on Ie Island," *New York Times*, April 19, 1945.
6. "Ernie Pyle is Killed on Ie Island," *New York Times*, April 19, 1945; "My Day" by Eleanor Roosevelt, April 19, 1945, in https://www2.gwu.edu/~erpapers/myday/displaydoc.cfm?_y=1945&_f=md000003 (accessed May 15, 2019).
7. Statement by the President on the Death of Ernie Pyle, April 18, 1945, in https://www.trumanlibrary.org/publicpapers/index.php?pid=14&st=&st1= (accessed May 15, 2019).
8. Sterling Mace, *Battleground Pacific: A Marine Rifleman's Combat Odyssey in K/3/5* (New York: St. Martin's Press, 2012), pp. 261–2.
9. Sakumoto Crandell, "Surviving the Battle of Okinawa," pp. 27–30.
10. Appleman et al., *Okinawa*, pp. 415–17.
11. Sakumoto Crandell, "Surviving the Battle of Okinawa," pp. 30–1.
12. Buckner to his wife Adele, April 8, 1945, in "Private Letters," p. 80.
13. Mace, *Battleground Pacific*, pp. 247–9.
14. Mabuni, Okinawa, Okinawa Prefectural Peace Museum (OPPM), Testimony of Matsu Tamaki, April 7, 1945.

20: "Progress not quite satisfactory"

1. Buckner Diary, April 18, 1945.
2. Appleman et al., *Okinawa*, pp. 184–5.
3. Smith, "Personal Narrative," pp. 85–6.
4. Buckner Diary, April 19, 1945.
5. Smith, "Personal Narrative," p. 87.
6. Dencker, *Love Company*, pp. 193–4.
7. Appleman et al., *Okinawa*, p. 207.
8. Megee, "Memoirs," pp. 175–6.
9. Buckner Diary, April 20, 1945.
10. Appleman et al., *Okinawa*, pp. 208–11.
11. Dencker, *Love Company*, pp. 194–7.
12. Dick, *Cutthroats*, pp. 166–8.

21: "All Kaitens prepare for launch!"

1. Yokota, "Volunteer," pp. 309–11.
2. Huber, "Japan's Battle," pp. 35–9.
3. Appleman et al., *Okinawa*, p. 248.
4. Buckner to his wife Adele, April 22, 1945, in "Private Letters," pp. 85–6.
5. Appleman et al., *Okinawa*, pp. 258–60.
6. Buckner Diary, April 22, 1945.
7. Appleman et al., *Okinawa*, p. 262.
8. Smith, "Personal Narrative," pp. 99–100; Buckner Diary, April 29, 1945.
9. Buckner to his wife Adele, April 27, 1945, in "Private Letters," pp. 90–1.

22: "The most terrible weapon"

1. Truman, *Year of Decisions*, p. 101.
2. Ibid., pp. 21, 104.
3. HST, Eben A. Ayers Papers, "The Atomic Bomb," *c.*1951, pp. 1–2, in https://www.trumanlibrary.org/whistlestop/study_collections/bomb/large/documents/index.php?documentid=26&pagenumber=1 (accessed May 20, 2019).
4. Baime, *The Accidental President*, pp. 168–9.
5. Ibid., p. 169.
6. Henry L. Stimson, *On Active Service in Peace and War* (New York: Harper & Brothers, 1947), pp. 612–13.
7. Baime, *The Accidental President*, pp. 170–1.
8. Stimson, *On Active Service*, p. 613.
9. Baime, *The Accidental President*, p. 173.
10. Stimson, *On Active Service*, pp. 615–16.
11. Truman, *Year of Decisions*, pp. 104–5; Stimson, *On Active Service*, p. 616.

23: "Corpsman!"

1. Johnston, *The Long Road of War*, p. 138.
2. Stockman, *The First Marine Division on Okinawa*, p. 3.
3. Johnston, *The Long Road of War*, pp. 131–2, 136.
4. Watkins, "Brothers in Battle," p. 39.
5. USMCA, COLL/4840, A/5/I/6/1, Robert A. Neal, "When I Was Young: I Served in the United States Fleet Marines," pp. 76–7.
6. Stockman, *The First Marine Division on Okinawa*, p. 4.
7. Johnston, *The Long Road of War*, pp. 138–41.
8. Mace, *Battleground Pacific*, pp. 4–5, 227–8, 269–71.
9. Buckner Diary, May 2 and 3, 1945.
10. Appleman et al., *Okinawa*, p. 274; Buckner Diary, May 2 and 3, 1945.
11. Stockman, *The First Marine Division on Okinawa*, p. 5.
12. https://themedalofhonor.com/medal-of-honor-recipients/recipients/bush-robert-world-war-two (accessed May 23, 2019).
13. Looney, "Okinawa," p. 5.
14. Johnston, *The Long Road of War*, pp. 141–2.
15. USMCA, COLL/3092, A/10/L/4/2, Paul E. Ison, "How the Combat Picture was Taken," pp. 1–5.

24: Hacksaw Ridge

1. Appleman et al., *Okinawa*, pp. 274–80.
2. Dick, *Cutthroats*, pp. 175–81; After Action Report, 763rd Tank Battalion, April 22, 1942–June 30, 1945, in ISCARL, http://cgsc.cdmhost.com/cdm/ref/collection/p4013coll8/id/3462 (accessed May 24, 2019).
3. Appleman et al., *Okinawa*, pp. 280–1.

4. Frances M. Doss, *Desmond Doss: Conscientious Objector* (Nampa, ID: Pacific Press, 2005), p. 99.
5. Personal Narrative of Desmond T. Doss, Veterans History Project, at http://memory.loc.gov/diglib/vhp/story/loc.natlib.afc2001001.32978/narrative?ID=pn0001 (accessed May 24, 2019).
6. Booton Herndon, *The Hero of Hacksaw Ridge* (Coldwater, MI: Remnant Publications, Inc., 2016), pp. 8–18.
7. "Conscientious Objector, Medical-Aid Man, Awarded Medal of Honor," *Advent Review and Sabbath Herald*, 1 November, 1945, at http://documents.adventistarchives.org/Periodicals/RH/RH19451101-V122-44.pdf (accessed May 24, 2019).
8. Doss, *Desmond Doss*, pp. 99–100.
9. Personal Narrative of Desmond T. Doss; Appleman et al., *Okinawa*, p. 281.
10. Interview with Staff Sergeant Elwyn Gaines, B/1/307th Infantry, Veterans History Project, at http://www.memory.loc.gov/diglib/vhp/story/loc.natlib.afc2001001.00169/transcript?ID=sr0001 (accessed May 27, 2019).
11. Doss, *Desmond Doss*, pp. 101–3; Interview of Corporal Desmond Doss, B/1/307th Infantry, Veterans History Project, at http://memory.loc.gov/diglib/vhp/story/loc.natlib.afc2001001.32978/ (accessed May 24, 2019).
12. Appleman et al., *Okinawa*, pp. 281–2.

25: "We will fight to the last man"

1. Appleman et al., *Okinawa*, p. 283; Huber, "Japan's Battle," p. 41.
2. Yahara Interrogation Report, August 6, 1945, in Yahara, *The Battle for Okinawa*, p. 214.
3. Huber, "Japan's Battle," pp. 81–3; Yahara Interrogation Report, August 6, 1945, in Yahara, *The Battle for Okinawa*, p. 214; Appleman et al., *Okinawa*, p. 283.
4. Appleman et al., *Okinawa*, pp. 286–7; Huber, "Japan's Battle," pp. 84–6.
5. Morison, *Victory in the Pacific*, pp. 251–2.
6. Appleman et al., *Okinawa*, pp. 287–9; Stockman, *The First Marine Division on Okinawa*, p. 11; Watkins, "Brothers in Battle," p. 39.
7. Appleman et al., *Okinawa*, pp. 287–9.
8. Ibid., p. 296; Huber, "Japan's Battle," pp. 87–8; Morison, *Victory in the Pacific*, pp. 266–7.
9. Morison, *Victory in the Pacific*, pp. 264–5, 391–2; IWM, 15723, Box No: 08/59/1, Private Papers of D. Hulme, War Diary, May 4, 1945.
10. Huber, "Japan's Battle," pp. 88–90.
11. Yahara, *The Battle for Okinawa*, pp. 41–4.
12. Ibid., p. 44; Appleman et al., *Okinawa*, p. 303.
13. Quoted in Appleman et al., *Okinawa*, p. 302.
14. Miyagi, "Student Nurses of the 'Lily Corps,'" in Cook and Cook, *Japan at War*, p. 356.
15. HPMA, English Translation of Testimonies 1, No. 6: Yoshiko Yabiku, "Itokazu Detachment," p. 12; *Himeyuri Peace Museum*, p. 20.

16. HPMA, English Translation of Testimonies 1, No. 2: Hisa Kishimoto, "Limb amputated without anesthetic," p. 6.
17. Masako Shinjo Summers Robbins, "My Story: A Daughter Recalls the Battle of Okinawa," *Asia-Pacific Journal*, 13/8 (23 February 2015), pp. 1–22, at https://apjjf.org/2015/13/7/Masako-Shinjo-Summers-Robbins/4286.html (accessed June 4, 2019).

26: "Doc, this one is worth saving"

1. Appleman et al., *Okinawa*, p. 304; Stockman, *The First Marine Division on Okinawa*, pp. 12–14.
2. https://themedalofhonor.com/medal-of-honor-recipients/recipients/hansen-dale-world-war-two (accessed May 30, 2019).
3. Watkins, "Brothers in Battle," pp. 12–13, 35–6, 40–3.
4. Stockman, *The First Marine Division on Okinawa*, p. 15; Donner, "Memoir," pp. 87–8.
5. Stockman, *The First Marine Division on Okinawa*, p. 15; Watkins, "Brothers in Battle," pp. 41–2.
6. https://valor.militarytimes.com/hero/7742 (accessed May 31, 2019).
7. Ison, "How the Combat Picture was Taken," pp. 11–13.
8. Johnston, *The Long Road of War*, p. 146.
9. E. B. Sledge, *With the Old Breed* (New York: Presidio Press, 1981; repr. 2007), p. 251.
10. Johnston, *The Long Road of War*, p. 147.
11. Buckner Diary, May 8, 1945.
12. Moss to his parents, May 9, 1945, in https://www.mossletters.com/9-may-1945/ (accessed May 31, 2019).
13. USMCA, COLL/3286, A/24/L/5/3, Box 3, Joseph Kohn Letters, Kohn to his family, May 8, 1945.
14. Mace, *Battleground Pacific*, pp. 293–4.

27: "The happy dream is over"

1. Araki, "Bride of a Kamikaze," in Cook and Cook, *Japan at War*, pp. 322–3, 325.
2. Morison, *Victory in the Pacific*, pp. 262–3, 392.
3. Alexander Burnham, "Okinawa, Harry Truman, and the Atomic Bomb," *VQR*, 71/3 (Summer 1995), in https://www.vqronline.org/essay/okinawa-harry-truman-and-atomic-bomb (accessed June 2, 2019), pp. 1–14.
4. Yahara, *The Battle for Okinawa*, pp. 49–51; Huber, "Japan's Battle," p. 92.
5. Robbins, "My Story," p. 11.
6. *Descent into Hell*, pp. 53–7.

28: Sugar Loaf Hill

1. Buckner Diary, May 11, 1945.
2. Appleman et al., *Okinawa*, pp. 311–12.
3. Manchester, *Goodbye, Darkness*, pp. 358–60.
4. Appleman et al., *Okinawa*, p. 313.
5. Ibid., p. 314.
6. USMCA, COLL/1908, A/14/C/3/1, Howard W. Arendt, "Memoirs, 1943–1945," pp. 1–25.
7. Nichols and Shaw, *Marines in World War II—Okinawa*, pp. 159–60.
8. Dick Camp, "Assault on Sugar Loaf Hill," *Leatherneck*, 100/9 (September 2017), p. 1.
9. Appleman et al., *Okinawa*, pp. 317–18.
10. Manchester, *Goodbye, Darkness*, p. 363.
11. Camp, "Assault on Sugar Loaf Hill," pp. 1–4.
12. Ed Pesely, F/2/22, in Lacey, *Stay Off the Skyline*, p. 90.
13. "Twenty Second Marines Special Action Report," May 7–20, 1945, in USMCA, COLL/3658, A/30/J/6/1, PFC John S. Kovaleski Papers.
14. Manchester, *Goodbye, Darkness*, p. 379.
15. Pesely, in Lacey, *Stay Off the Skyline*, pp. 91–4.
16. USMCA, COLL/3286, A/24/L/5/3, Box 3, Joseph Kohn, "Memoir," p. 3.
17. Pesely, in Lacey, *Stay Off the Skyline*, pp. 91–4, 155; Bill Sloan, *The Ultimate Battle: Okinawa 1945—The Last Epic Struggle of World War II* (New York: Simon & Schuster, 2007), pp. 187–9.
18. Kohn, "Memoir," p. 3.
19. Pesely, in Lacey, *Stay Off the Skyline*, p. 94; "Twenty Second Marines Special Action Report," May 7–20, 1945; Appleman et al., *Okinawa*, pp. 319–20.

29: "Hell's own cesspool"

1. Buckner to his wife Adele, May 13, 1945, in "Private Letters," p. 97.
2. Appleman et al., *Okinawa*, pp. 351–7.
3. Buckner Diary, May 13, 1945.
4. Buckner to his wife Adele, May 13, 1945, in "Private Letters," pp. 97–8.
5. Sarantakes (ed.), *Seven Stars*, p. 57.
6. Appleman et al., *Okinawa*, pp. 322–3.
7. Manchester, *Goodbye, Darkness*, pp. 365–82.
8. Heckt, "Pacific Diary," May 21–29, 1945.
9. Nils Andersen, in Lacey, *Stay Off the Skyline*, pp. 119–24.
10. https://history.army.mil/moh/wwII-a-f.html#COURTNEY (accessed June 10, 2019)
11. Manchester, *Goodbye, Darkness*, p. 379.
12. Appleman et al., *Okinawa*, p. 330; Stockman, *The First Marine Division on Okinawa*, pp. 26–7.
13. Carrell, "King One," pp. 35–7.
14. Appleman et al., *Okinawa*, p. 330.
15. Stockman, *The First Marine Division on Okinawa*, p. 32.

16. Johnston, *The Long Road of War*, pp. 114, 149.
17. Watkins, "Brothers in Battle," pp. 44–5.
18. Appleman et al., *Okinawa*, pp. 365–6.
19. Sledge, *With the Old Breed*, pp. 268–73.

30: "I still hear those cries today"

1. Marpe, "My Service in the United States Marine Corps," p. 43.
2. Ibid.; Tillman, "Hunter in the Dark," pp. 13–16.
3. Marpe, "My Service in the United States Marine Corps," p. 43.
4. USMCA, Marine Night Fighter Squadron 542 (VMF(N) 542) Association Collection, 1984–97 COLL/5480, A/13/F/7/1, "War Diary of Joseph S. Sama," May 25, 1945.
5. Appleman et al., *Okinawa*, pp. 361–2.
6. Buckner Diary, May 24, 1945.
7. Yahara, *The Battle for Okinawa*, p. 62.
8. Ibid., pp. 62, 68–73, 80–2.
9. *Himeyuri Peace Museum*, p. 30.
10. Miyagi, "Student Nurses of the 'Lily Corps,'" in Cook and Cook, *Japan at War*, p. 357.
11. HPMA, English Translation of Testimonies 1, No. 7: Shizuko Oshiro, "A patient with no legs crawling in the mud," p. 13.
12. HPMA, English Translation of Testimonies 2, No. 15: Nobuko Kinjo, "Water! Water!," p. 6.

31: "The entire enemy line appears to be crumbling"

1. Yahara, *The Battle for Okinawa*, pp. 87–92.
2. Ibid., p. 94.
3. Appleman et al., *Okinawa*, p. 428.
4. Yahara, *The Battle for Okinawa*, pp. 94–103.
5. Appleman et al., *Okinawa*, pp. 389–92.
6. Smith, "Personal Narrative," p. 123.
7. Buckner Diary, May 26–28, 1945.
8. Buckner to his wife Adele, May 28, 1945, in "Private Letters," pp. 102–3.
9. Appleman et al., *Okinawa*, p. 392.
10. Buckner Diary, May 31, 1945.
11. Yahara, *The Battle for Okinawa*, pp. 111–12.

32: "It is terrifying to think about"

1. Notes on the Interim Committee Meeting, May 31, 1945, at https://www.trumanlibrary.org/whistlestop/study_collections/bomb/large/documents/index.php?documentid=39&pagenumber=2 (accessed June 4, 2019).
2. Baime, *The Accidental President*, pp. 234–5.
3. Notes on the Interim Committee Meeting, May 31, 1945.

4. Ibid., June 1, 1945, at https://www.trumanlibrary.org/whistlestop/study_collections/bomb/large/documents/index.php?documentdate=1945-06-01&documentid=40&pagenumber=1 (accessed June 4, 2019).
5. Stimson, *On Active Service*, p. 617; Baime, *The Accidental President*, pp. 253–4.
6. Quoted in Baime, *The Accidental President*, p. 237.

33: "There is NO tactical thinking or push"

1. Sarantakes (ed.), *Seven Stars*, pp. 11–13; Barbara Tuchman, *Stillwell and the American Experience in China, 1911–45* (New York: Macmillan, 1971), Chapter 20; Stanford, CA, Hoover Institution Archives (HIA), "The World War II Diaries of General Joseph W. Stilwell," September 1, 1945, in http://media.hoover.org/sites/default/files/documents/1945Stilwell.pdf
2. Stilwell Diaries, May 10 and 26, and June 3, 1945, in http://media.hoover.org/sites/default/files/documents/1945Stilwell.pdf ; Buckner Diary, June 3, 1945.
3. Appleman et al., *Okinawa*, p. 432.
4. Ibid., pp. 424–5; Buckner Diary, June 3, 1945.
5. Stilwell Diaries, June 4–6, 1945, in http://media.hoover.org/sites/default/files/documents/1945Stilwell.pdf
6. Appleman et al., *Okinawa*, p. 434.
7. Buckner Diary, June 7, 1945.

34: "I lost damn near all of them"

1. Johnston, *The Long Road of War*, pp. 154–8.
2. Manchester, *Goodbye, Darkness*, pp. 11–12, 383–4, 391.
3. Carlton, "Do you want to live forever?," pp. 76–80, 88.
4. https://www.mossletters.com/11-june-1945/ (accessed June 23, 2019).

35: "You're just going to have to hang on"

1. Watkins, "Brothers in Battle," pp. 47–8.
2. USMCA, COLL/2874, A/24/G/6/5, William V. Niader Collection, Niader to his parents, May 28, 1945.
3. "Marine's death still lives in letters," *North Jersey Herald & News*, 7 November, 1994.
4. Carrell, "King One," pp. 39–40.
5. Appleman et al., *Okinawa*, p. 452.
6. Watkins, "Brothers in Battle," pp. 49–52.

36: "We were so gullible, so innocent"

1. Buckner Diary, June 9, 1945.
2. Appleman et al., *Okinawa*, pp. 463–5.
3. Sarantakes (ed.), *Seven Stars*, p. 77.

4. Underground Naval Headquarters Museum, Tomigusuki, Okinawa (UNHQM), Rear Admiral Ōta to the Naval Ministry in Tokyo, 2016 hours, June 6, 1945.
5. Yahara, *The Battle for Okinawa*, pp. 125–6.
6. Thomas McKinney, in Lacey, *Stay Off the Skyline*, pp. 211–12.
7. Appleman et al., *Okinawa*, pp. 433–4; Smith, "Personal Narrative," p. 128.
8. Appleman et al., *Okinawa*, pp. 439–43; Yahara, *The Battle for Okinawa*, pp. 121–4.
9. Appleman et al., *Okinawa*, pp. 446–50.
10. Yahara, *The Battle for Okinawa*, pp. 129–32.
11. Araki, "Bride of a Kamikaze," in Cook and Cook, *Japan at War*, pp. 321–5.

37: "We are down to the final kill"

1. Buckner to his wife Adele, June 14, 1945, in "Private Letters," p. 105.
2. Sarantakes (ed.), *Seven Stars*, p. 78.
3. Buckner to his wife Adele, June 14, 1945, in "Private Letters," pp. 105–6.
4. Sarantakes (ed.), *Seven Stars*, pp. 80–1.
5. Appleman et al., *Okinawa*, p. 455.
6. Buckner to his son William Claiborne, June 16, 1945, in "Private Letters," p. 107.
7. Appleman et al., *Okinawa*, p. 364; Morison, *Victory in the Pacific*, pp. 390–2.
8. Tillman, "Hunter in the Dark," pp. 14–17; USMC, COLL/921, A/5/L/7/2, Colonel Bruce Porter Papers, "Interview: WWII Night Fighter Ace Bruce Porter," pp. 16, 25.
9. Dencker, *Love Company*, pp. 259–61.
10. Carrell, "King One," pp. 40–1.
11. USMCA, COLL/1574, A/13/C/6/2, Marius L. Bressoud Jr, "The way it really was, I think: A personal account of the Okinawan Campaign, April 1 to June 21, 1945," pp. 1–5, 164–71.
12. Carrell, "King One," pp. 42–4.

38: "I haven't come up to the front to hide"

1. Stilwell Diaries, June 18, 1945, in http://media.hoover.org/sites/default/files/documents/1945Stilwell.pdf
2. Brigadier General E. D. Post to Adele Buckner, June 19, 1945, in "Private Letters," p. 108.
3. Buckner Diary, June 17, 1945.
4. Post to Adele Buckner, June 19, 1945, in "Private Letters," p. 108; Smith, "Personal Narrative," p. 135.
5. Smith, "Personal Narrative," p. 135.
6. Haley, "The General Dies at Noon," pp. 18–26.
7. Post to Adele Buckner, June 19, 1945, in "Private Letters," p. 109.
8. Haley, "The General Dies at Noon," pp. 26–34.
9. Post to Adele Buckner, June 19, 1945, in "Private Letters," pp. 109–10.
10. Sarantakes (ed.), *Seven Stars*, pp. 86–7; Smith, "Personal Narrative," pp. 135–6.

39: "Every man will...fight to the end"

1. Yahara, *The Battle for Okinawa*, p. 133; Appleman et al., *Okinawa*, pp. 456–8.
2. DDE, 735035, Box 801, G-2 Periodic Reports, 7th Infantry Division, "Summary of Information," June 23, 1945; Yahara, *The Battle for Okinawa*, p. 134; Masahide Ōta, "Straggler," in Cook and Cook, *Japan at War*, pp. 367–71.
3. *Descent into Hell*, pp. 61–2.
4. Yahara, *The Battle for Okinawa*, p. 134.
5. Miyagi, "Student Nurses of the 'Lily Corps,'" in Cook and Cook, *Japan at War*, p. 359.
6. HPMA, English Translation of Testimonies 1, No. 12: Tomi Shimabukuro, "Don't bother about the patients. Get out!," p. 22.
7. Miyagi, "Student Nurses of the 'Lily Corps,'" in Cook and Cook, *Japan at War*, pp. 359–60.
8. HPMA, English Translation of Testimonies 1, No. 13: Ruri Morishita, "I just can't die in a place like this, I said to myself," p. 24.
9. *Himeyuri Peace Museum*, pp. 33, 35.
10. HPMA, English Translation of Testimonies 2, No. 18: Kikuko Kaneshiro (Miyagi), "Arasaka Beach, the end of the world," pp. 10–12; Miyagi, "Student Nurses of the 'Lily Corps,'" in Cook and Cook, *Japan at War*, pp. 360–3.
11. *Himeyuri Peace Museum*, p. 57.

40: "Suppose it doesn't go off?"

1. HST, Miscellaneous Historical Documents Collection, No. 736, "Minutes of Meeting held at the White House on Monday, June 18, 1945 at 1530," at https://www.trumanlibrary.org/whistlestop/study_collections/bomb/large/documents/index.php?documentdate=1945-06-18&documentid=21&pagenumber=1 (accessed June 28, 2019); Truman, *Year of Decisions*, pp. 458–9.
2. Baime, *The Accidental President*, pp. 248–52; Truman, *Year of Decisions*, pp. 458–9; HST, Truman Papers, President's Secretary's File, "Notes regarding June 18, 1945 meeting," June 7, 1954.

41: "What a splendid last moment!"

1. Yahara, *The Battle for Okinawa*, pp. 143–50; Appleman et al., *Okinawa*, pp. 468–70.
2. "Interrogation of Testuo Nakamuta, General Ushijima's cook," June 26, 1945, G-2 Periodic Report, 77th Infantry Division, in http://cgsc.cdmhost.com/cdm/ref/collection/p4013coll8/id/584 (accessed July 2, 2019)
3. Yahara, *The Battle for Okinawa*, pp. 153–6; "Interrogation of Testuo Nakamuta, General Ushijima's cook," June 26, 1945; Appleman et al., *Okinawa*, pp. 470–1.
4. Appleman et al., *Okinawa*, p. 471.

5. G-2 Periodic Reports, 7th Infantry Division, "Summary of Information," June 23, 1945.
6. Appleman et al., *Okinawa*, p. 473.
7. Stilwell Diary, June 27, 1945, in Sarantakes (ed.), *Seven Stars*, p. 89.
8. Frank B. Gibney, "The Battle Ended," in Yahara, *The Battle for Okinawa*, pp. 200–1.
9. Churchill to Truman, June 22, 1945, in Churchill, *The Second World War*, VI, p. 542.
10. Quoted in Feifer, *Tennozan*, p. vii.
11. Appleman et al., *Okinawa*, p. 473.
12. Smith, "Personal Narrative," pp. 119–21.
13. Masahide Ōta, "Introduction: The Battle of Okinawa," January 7, 2013, in *Descent into Hell*, pp. xvii–xix.
14. Huber, "Japan's Battle," pp. 117–18.
15. OPPM, Testimonies of Haru Maeda, Toyo Gima and Mitsutoshi Nakajo.
16. Ōta, "Introduction: The Battle of Okinawa," pp. xvii–xix.

42: "All he talked about was you"

1. Watkins, "Brothers in Battle," p. 52.
2. Donner, "Memoir," pp. 110–11.
3. Watkins, "Brothers in Battle," p. 53.
4. Carrell, "King One," p. 44.
5. Donner, "Memoir," p. 112.
6. Watkins, "Brothers in Battle," pp. 52–3.
7. Johnston, *The Long Road of War*, pp. 152–4.
8. USMCR, COLL/3838, A/13/A/3/1, Harold J. Mackin Jr. Collection, Telegram from General Vandegrift to Mrs. Harold J. Mackin, July 5, 1945.
9. Harold J. Mackin Jr. Collection, Corporal Bob Miles to Mrs. June Mackin, September 25 and October 25, 1945.
10. Watkins, "Brothers in Battle," pp. 52–3.
11. Gibney, "The Battle Ended," in Yahara, *The Battle for Okinawa*, pp. 201–2.
12. Office of the Historian, Department of State, Potsdam Conference, 1945, Volume I, Document 592, "Proposed Program for Japan," Memoradum by Henry Stimson for President Truman, July 2, 1945, at https://history.state.gov/historicaldocuments/frus1945Berlinv01/d592; Baime, *The Accidental President*, pp. 269–70.

43: "The most terrible thing ever discovered"

1. HST, "Memorandum on Alamogordo Air Base atomic fission bomb test" by Brigadier General Leslie Groves, July 18, 1945; Baime, *The Accidental President*, p. 284.
2. Truman, *Year of Decisions*, pp. 368–78.
3. Baime, *The Accidental President*, pp. 286–7.
4. Truman, *Year of Decisions*, pp. 378–9, 458, 462–3.
5. Churchill, *The Second World War*, VI, p. 552.

6. Truman, *Year of Decisions*, p. 463.
7. HST, Papers of Harry S. Truman, Truman Diary, July 25, 1945.
8. Truman, *Year of Decisions*, p. 464.
9. HST, George M. Elsey Oral History Interview, July 7, 1970, www.trumanlibrary.org/oralhist/elsey7.htm (accessed November 12, 2018).
10. Churchill, *The Second World War*, VI, pp. 556–7.
11. HST, Papers of Harry S. Truman, Truman Diary, July 25, 1945.
12. Truman, *Year of Decisions*, p. 464.

44: "My God, what have we done?"

1. Studs Terkel, *The Good War: An Oral History of World War Two* (New York: The New Press, 1984), p. 532.
2. Baime, *The Accidental President*, pp. 333–7; Richard Sisk, "*Enola Gay* Crew Recalled First Use of Atomic Bomb," at https://www.military.com/daily-news/2015/08/06/enola-gay-crew-recalled-first-use-of-atomic-bomb.html; Lorrie Grant, "*Enola Gay* Pilot Paul Tibbets, 92, Dies," *NPR*, November 1, 2007, at https://choice.npr.org/index.html?origin=https://www.npr.org/templates/story/story.php?storyId=15858203; Miss Cellania, "The Crew of the *Enola Gay* on Dropping the Atomic Bomb," August 6, 2015, at http://mentalfloss.com/article/24269/crew-enola-gay-dropping-atomic-bomb; "Tale of Two Cities: Hiroshima and Nagasaki," at http://www.atomicarchive.com/History/twocities/index.shtml.
3. John Hersey, *Hiroshima* (New York: Penguin Group (USA), Inc., 1973; repr. 1985), pp. 3, 10–13.
4. Ibid., pp. 18–21, 61.
5. Anonymous account, in Terkel, *The Good War*, p. 537.
6. Hajimi Kito, in Terkel, *The Good War*, p. 537.
7. Hersey, *Hiroshima*, pp. 7–10, 114–15.
8. "Tale of Two Cities: Hiroshima and Nagasaki," at http://www.atomicarchive.com/History/twocities/index.shtml.
9. Lt T. C. Cartwright, *A Date with the Lonesome Lady* (Fort Worth, TX: Eakin Press, 1998), pp. 1, 24–33.
10. HST, Ayers Papers, "Press Release by the White House, August 6, 1945."
11. IWM, 12965, Private Papers of W. A. Franklin, Box No. 14/17/1, "Through Adversity to Attainment," pp. 100–4.
12. Truman, *Year of Decisions*, pp. 470–83.

45: "We were going to live!"

1. Baime, *The Accidental President*, p. 358.
2. Tōgō, "Historical Facts Surrounding the End of the Pacific War," and "Recollections of the Events on the Eve of Surrender," *Statements of Japanese Officials: Vol. 4*, pp. 253–4.
3. Ibid., pp. 17–18, 34–7.
4. HST, Papers of Harry S. Truman, Truman to Irv Kupcinet, August 5, 1963.
5. Stimson, *On Active Service*, pp. 630–2.

6. Churchill, *The Second World War*, VI, p. 553.
7. HST, George M. Elsey Oral History Interview, July 7, 1970, www.trumanlibrary.org/oralhist/elsey7.htm (accessed November 12, 2018).
8. Cellania, "The Crew of the *Enola Gay* on Dropping the Atomic Bomb."
9. Johnston, *The Long Road of War*, p. 121.
10. Watkins, "Brothers in Battle," p. 54.
11. Sledge, *With the Old Breed*, p. 343.
12. Dencker, *Love Company*, pp. 291, 296.
13. Carrell, "King One," p. 44.

Epilogue: "Those dark corners are still there"

1. Ugaki, *Fading Victory*, pp. 665–6.
2. Yahara, *The Battle for Okinawa*, p. 203.
3. Araki, "Bride of a Kamikaze," in Cook and Cook, *Japan at War*, pp. 323–6.
4. Yokota, "Volunteer," in Cook and Cook, *Japan at War*, pp. 311–12.
5. Miyagi, "Student Nurses of the 'Lily Corps,'" in Cook and Cook, *Japan at War*, pp. 362–3.
6. Watkins, "Brothers in Battle," pp. 54–7; http://brothersinbattle.net (accessed July 10, 2019).
7. Carrell, "King One," p. 50; http://www.chroniclet.com/obituaries/2008/01/17/Jeptha-J-Carrell.html (accessed July 10, 2019).
8. Dencker, *Love Company*, pp. xv, 314.
9. Dick, *Cutthroats*, pp. 246–7.
10. HST, Family, Business and Personal Affairs Papers, Harry S. Truman to Bess W. Truman, December 22, 1946.
11. https://soh.alumni.clemson.edu/scroll/julian-delano-dusenbury/ (accessed July 16, 2019); http://www.singletonfamily.org/getperson.php?personID=I92482&tree=1 (accessed July 16, 2019).
12. Manchester, *Goodbye, Darkness*, pp. 385, 398.
13. Johnston, *The Long Road of War*, pp. 4, 167.

Acknowledgments

1. Leo Drake USN, quoted in Megan Tzeng, "The Battle of Okinawa, 1945: Final Turning Point in the Pacific" in *The History Teacher*, 34/1 (2000), 95–118 (p. 98).

Bibliography

Primary Sources, Unpublished

Dwight D. Eisenhower Presidential Library and Archive (DDE), Abilene, Kansas

Simon Bolivar Buckner Papers
Vernon E. Megee Papers
Records of the 7th Infantry Division, 1944–48
Records of the 27th Infantry Division, 1942–45
Records of the 77th Infantry Division, 1942–46

Harry S. Truman Presidential Library and Museum (HST), Independence, Missouri

Eben A. Ayers Papers
George M. Elsey Oral History Interview, July 7, 1970
Brigadier General Leslie Groves, "Memorandum on Alamogordo Air Base atomic fission bomb test," July 18, 1945
Miscellaneous Historical Documents Collection
Notes on the Interim Committee Meetings, 1945
Papers of Harry S. Truman
President's Secretary's File, "Notes regarding June 18, 1945 meeting," June 7, 1954
Public Papers: Statement by the President on the Death of Ernie Pyle, April 18, 1945

Himeyuri Peace Museum Archives (HPMA), Itoman, Okinawa

English Translation of Testimonies 1: Hisa Kishimoto, Ruri Morishita, Shizuko Oshiro, Tomi Shimabukuro, Yoshiko Yabiku
English Translation of Testimonies 2: Kikuko Kaneshiro (Miyagi), Nobuko Kinjo
"Historical Chart"

Imperial War Museum Archives (IWM), London

Private Papers of W. A. Franklin
Private Papers of N. B. Gray
Private Papers of D. Hulme

Okinawa Prefectural Peace Museum (OPPM), Mabuni, Okinawa

Testimonies of Toyo Gima, Haru Maeda, Mitsutoshi Nakajo and Matsu Tamaki

The National Archives (TNA), Kew, London

ADM 234/368: Naval Staff History, Battle Summary No. 47, "Naval Operations Okinawa," 1950
ADM 358/4439: HMS *Indefatigable*—April 1, 1945, enemy action during the Allied invasion of Okinawa, Japan
CAB 106/95: Despatch on the contribution of the British Pacific Fleet to the assault on Okinawa by Admiral Sir Bruce A. Fraser, May 26, 1945

The National Archives and Record Administration (NARA), College Park, Maryland

Records of Tenth Army, 1944–45
Records of Marine Units, 1914–49

Underground Naval Headquarters Museum (UNHQM), Tomigusuku, Okinawa

Message from Rear Admiral Ōta to the Naval Ministry in Tokyo, 2016 hours, June 6, 1945

U.S. Marine Corps Archives (USMCA), Quantico, Virginia

Howard W. Arendt Papers
Marius L. Bressoud Jr. Papers
Jeptha J. Carrell Papers
Christopher S. Donner Papers
Salvatore Giammanco Papers
Otha L. Grisham Papers
Lieut. Col. J. Frederick Haley Papers
Mel Heckt Papers
Joseph M. Hiott Papers
Paul E. Ison Papers
Joseph Kohn Papers
John S. Kovaleski Papers
William A. Looney Papers
Harold J. Mackin Jr. Papers
Marine Night Fighter Squadron 542 Association Collection
Robert A. Neal Papers
William V. Niader Papers
Colonel Bruce Porter Papers
Oliver P. Smith Papers
Richard Bruce Watkins Papers

Primary Sources, Published

Published Documents, Diaries, Letters and Memoirs

Cartwright, Lt. T. C., *A Date with the Lonesome Lady: A Hiroshima POW Returns* (Fort Worth, TX: Eakin Press, 2002; repr. 2004)

Churchill, Winston S., *The Second World War*, 6 vols (London: Cassell, 1948–54)

Cook, Haruko Taya, and Theodore F. Cook (eds), *Japan at War: An Oral History* (New York: W. W. Norton & Co., 1992)

Crandell, Yoshiko Sakumoto, "Surviving the Battle of Okinawa: Memories of a Schoolgirl," *Asia-Pacific Journal*, 12/14 (2014), 1–31

Dencker, Donald O., *Love Company: Infantry Combat Against the Japanese World War II—Leyte and Okinawa* (Manhattan, KS: Sunflower University Press, 2002)

Descent into Hell: Civilian Memories of the Battle of Okinawa, trans. by Mark Ealey & Alastair McLauchlan (Portland, ME: MerwinAsia, 2014)

Dick, Robert C., *Cutthroats: The Adventures of a Sherman Tank Driver in the Pacific* (New York: Presidio Press, 2006)

Feifer, George, *Tennozan: The Battle of Okinawa and the Atomic Bomb* (New York: Houghton Mifflin, 1992)

Goldstein, Donald M., and Katherine V. Dillon (eds), *Fading Victory: The Diary of Admiral Matome Ugaki 1941–1945*, trans. by Masataka Chihaya (Pittsburgh, PA: University of Pittsburgh Press, 1991)

Green, Bob, *Okinawa Odyssey: The Battle for Okinawa* (Houston, TX: Bright Sky Press, 2004)

Halsey, William F., and J. Bryan III, *Admiral Halsey's Story* (New York: The Curtis Publishing Co., 1947)

Higa, Tomiko, *The Girl with the White Flag: An Inspiring Story of Love and Courage in War Time*, trans. by Dorothy Britton (Tokyo: Kodansha Int., 1991)

Inoguchi, Captain Rikihei, and Commander Tadashi Nakajima, *The Divine Wind: Japan's Kamikaze Force in World War II* (Annapolis, MD: United States Naval Institute, 1958; repr. 1994)

Jenkins, A. P. (ed.), "Lt Gen. Simon Bolivar Buckner: Private Letters relating to the Battle of Okinawa," in *Ryudai Review of Euro-American Studies*, 42 (1997), 63–113

Johnston, James W., *The Long Road of War: A Marine's Story of Pacific Combat* (Lincoln, NB: University of Nebraska Press, 1998)

Levin, Dan, *From the Battlefield: Dispatches of a World War II Marine* (Annapolis, MD: Naval Institute Presss, 1995)

Mace, Sterling, *Battleground Pacific: A Marine Rifleman's Combat Odyssey in K/3/5* (New York: St. Martin's Press, 2012)

Manchester, William, *Goodbye, Darkness: A Memoir of the Pacific War* (New York: Little, Brown & Co., 1980; repr. 2002)

Miller, Arthur, *Timebends: A Life* (New York: Grove Press, 1987)

Nichols, David (ed.), *Ernie's War: The Best of Ernie Pyle's World War II Dispatches* (New York: Simon & Schuster, 1987)

Pyle, Ernie, *Last Chapter* (New York: Henry Holt & Co., 1946)

Robbins, Masako Shinjo Summers, "My Story: A Daughter Recalls the Battle of Okinawa," *Asia-Pacific Journal*, 13/8 (23 February 2015), pp. 1–22

Sarantakes, Nicholas Evan (ed.), *Seven Stars: The Okinawa Battle Diaries of Simon Bolivar Buckner, Jr., and Joseph Stilwell* (College Station, TX: Texas A&M University Press, 2004)

Simpson, William P., *Island "X"—Okinawa* (W. Hanover, MA: The Christopher Publishing House, 1979)

Sledge, E. B., *With the Old Breed* (New York: Presidio Press, 1981; repr. 2007)

Stimson, Henry L., *On Active Service in Peace and War* (New York: Harper & Brothers, 1947)

Terkel, Studs, *The Good War: An Oral History of World War Two* (New York: The New Press, 1984)

Truman, Harry S., *Year of Decisions*, 2 vols (New York: Doubleday & Co., 1955; repr. 1965)

Vian, Sir Philip, *Action This Day: A War Memoir* (London: Frederick Muller Ltd, 1960)

Yahara, Colonel Hiromichi, *The Battle for Okinawa: A Japanese Officer's Eyewitness Account of the Last Great Campaign of World War II* (New York: John Wiley & Sons, Inc., 1995)

Yoshida, Mitsuru, *Requiem for Battleship Yamato*, trans. by Richard H. Minear (Washington: University of Washington Press, 1985; repr. ebook, 1999).

Newspapers and Journals

Advent Review and Sabbath Herald
New York Times
North Jersey Herald & News
San Francisco Chronicle
Time Magazine
Vero Beach Newsweekly

Secondary Sources

Books and Articles

Appleman, Roy E., James M. Burns, Russell A. Gugeler and John Stevens, *Okinawa: The Last Battle* (Washington, DC: Center of Military History, U.S. Army, 1948)

Astor, Gerald, *Operation Iceberg: The Invasion and Conquest of Okinawa in World War II* (New York: Dell, 1996)

Axell, Albert, and Hideaki Kase, *Kamikaze: Japan's Suicide Gods* (London: Pearson Education, 2002)

Baime, A. J., *The Accidental President: Harry S. Truman, the Bomb and the Four Months That Changed the World* (New York: Houghton Mifflin Harcourt, 2017; repr. 2018)

Beevor, Antony, *D-Day* (London: Penguin, 2006)

Belotte, James, and William Belotte, *Typhoon of Steel: The Battle for Okinawa* (New York: Harper & Row, 1970; repr. 1984)

Bradley, Michael, "'Banzai!' The Compulsory Mass Suicide of Kerama Islanders in the Battle of Okinawa," *Asia-Pacific Journal*, 11/22 (2014)
Camp, Dick, "Assault on Sugar Loaf Hill," *Leatherneck*, 100/9 (September 2017)
Doss, Frances M., *Desmond Doss: Conscientious Objector* (Nampa, ID: Pacific Press, 2005)
Edward Smith, Jean, *FDR* (New York: Random House Inc., 2007; repr. 2008)
Frank, Richard, *Downfall: The End of the Japanese Imperial Empire* (New York: Random House, 1999)
Hallas, James H., *Killing Ground on Okinawa: The Battle for Sugar Loaf Hill* (Lincoln, NB: Potomac Books, 2006)
Hastings, Max, *Nemesis: The Battle for Japan, 1944–45* (London: HarperCollins, 2007)
Herndon, Booton, *The Hero of Hacksaw Ridge* (Coldwater, MI: Remnant Publications, Inc., 2016)
Hersey, John, *Hiroshima* (New York: Penguin Group Inc., 1973; repr. 1985)
Himeyuri Peace Museum: The Guidebook (Itoman, Okinawa: 2016)
Hobbs, David, *The British Pacific Fleet: The Royal Navy's Most Powerful Strike Force* (Barnsley, UK: Seaforth Publishing, 2011; repr. 2017)
Hoyt, Edwin P. *How They Won the War in the Pacific: Nimitz and His Admirals* (New York: Weybright and Talley, 1970)
Huber, Thomas M., "Japan's Battle of Okinawa, April–June 1945," *Leavenworth Papers*, No. 18 (199), 1–141
Hull, Michael D., "Modest Victor of Midway," *World War II* magazine, 13/1 (May 1998), 36–43
Lacey, Laura Homan, *Stay Off the Skyline: The Sixth Marine Division on Okinawa* (Dulles, VA: Potomac Books, Inc., 2005; repr. 2007)
Leckie, Robert, *Okinawa: The Last Battle of World War II* (New York: Penguin, 1996)
Mitcham Jr, Samuel W., and Friedrich von Stauffenberg, *The Battle of Sicily: How the Allies Lost Their Chance for Total Victory* (New York: Orion Books, 1991)
Morison, Samuel E., *History of the United States Naval Operations in the Pacific: Volume 14—Victory in the Pacific, 1945* (New York: Little, Brown, 1975; repr. 2012)
Nelson, William F., *Appointment at Ie Shima* (privately published, 2014)
Nichols Jr, Major Charles S., and Henry I. Shaw, *Marines in World War II—Okinawa: Victory in the Pacific* (Washington, DC: Historical Branch, 1955)
Prange, Gordon W., Donald M. Goldstein and Katherine V. Dillon, *Pearl Harbor: The Verdict of History* (New York: McGraw-Hill, 1985)
Reilly, Robin L., *Kamikaze Attacks of World War II* (Jefferson, NC: McParland & Co., Inc., 2010)
—*Kamikaze, Corsairs and Picket Ships: Okinawa, 1945* (Havertown, PA: Casemate, 2008)
Roberts, Andrew, *Masters and Commanders: How Roosevelt, Churchill, Marshall and Alanbrooke Won the War in the West* (London: Allen Lane, 2008)
Second to None! The Story of the 305th Infantry in World War II (Washington: Infantry Journal Press, 1949)

Sloan, Bill, *The Ultimate Battle: Okinawa 1945—The Last Epic Struggle of World War II* (New York: Simon & Schuster, 2007)
Stockman, James R., *The First Marine Division on Okinawa: 1 April–30 June 1945* (Quantico: History Division U.S. Marine Corps, 1946)
Tuchman, Barbara, *Stilwell and the American Experience in China, 1911–45* (New York: Macmillan, 1971)
Willock, Roger, *Unaccustomed to Fear: A Biography of the Late General Roy S. Geiger* (Princeton, NJ: privately published, 1968)

Websites

https://sites.mediaschool.indiana.edu/erniepyle/
http://www.cmohs.org/
https://www.mossletters.com
https://themedalofhonor.com/medal-of-honor-recipients/
https://valor.militarytimes.com
https://www2.gwu.edu/
https://www.trumanlibrary.gov/library/public-papers/
http://www.loc.gov/vets/
https://www.vqronline.org/
https://history.army.mil/moh/
http://media.hoover.org/sites/default/files/documents/1945Stilwell.pdf
http://cgsc.cdmhost.com/
https://history.state.gov/historicaldocuments/frus1945Berlinv01/d592
https://www.trumanlibrary.gov
https://www.military.com/daily-news/2015/08/06/enola-gay-crew-recalled-first-use-of-atomic-bomb.html
https://choice.npr.org/index.html?origin=https://www.npr.org/templates/story/story.php?storyId=15858203
http://mentalfloss.com/article/24269/crew-enola-gay-dropping-atomic-bomb
http://www.atomicarchive.com/History/twocities/index.shtml
http://brothersinbattle.net
http://www.chroniclet.com/obituaries/2008/01/17/Jeptha-J-Carrell.html
http://www.singletonfamily.org/getperson.php?personID=I92482&tree=1
https://soh.alumni.clemson.edu/scroll/julian-delano-dusenbury/

Index